Laudate

a hymn book for the liturgy

Revised edition in accordance with the
2010 translation of the Roman Missal

GW00602638

Praise God in his holy place,
Sing praise in the mighty heavens.
Sing praise for God's powerful deeds,
praise God's surpassing greatness.

Sing praise with sound of trumpet,
Sing praise with lute and harp.
Sing praise with timbrel and dance,
Sing praise with strings and pipes.

Sing praise with resounding cymbals,
Sing praise with clashing of cymbals.
Let everything that lives and that breathes
give praise to the Lord. Alleluia!

Psalm 150

 Decani Music

Decani Music, 28 bury Road, Brandon, Suffolk IP27 0BU
First published in 1999 by Decani Music. Revised in April 2012. Eighth revised printing: October 2017
Printed in the UK by CPI William Clowes, Beccles NR34 7TL
ISBN 978 1 900 314 06 0
For the liturgical material: Jane Porter, 27 June 2011
Nihil Obstat: David Bulmer STL, Censor Deputatus, 9 February 2012
✠ Imprimatur: David Bagstaff, Apostolic Administrator, East Anglia, 24 February 2012

Edited by Stephen Dean. Editorial Advisers (1999 edition): Jennifer Burridge, Susan Dean, Ellen Flynn,
   Martin Foster, Peter Gallacher, Philip Jakob, Paul Kenny, Julie McCann & Peter McGrail
With thanks to Ed Harris and John Limb

Thanks are given to copyright holders who have granted permission for their work to be used in this book. If there any errors
   or omissions we apologise, and will rectify them in future editions.

Addresses of main copyright holders   See p.419 onwards for full copyright details

Ateliers et Presses de Taizé: administered in UK & Ireland by Calamus

Benedictine Foundation of the State of Vermont, via Calamus

Boosey & Hawkes Ltd. 295 Regent Street, London W1R 8JH

Bishops' Conference of England and Wales: contact The Liturgy Office, 39 Eccleston Square, London SW1V 1PL 020 7901 4850 • Liturgy.Office@cbcew.org.uk

Bloomsbury Publishing (administers former Continuum copyrights) www.bloomsbury.com/uk/company/contact-us/

Christian Conference of Asia, Pak Tin Village, Mei Tin Road, Shatin, N.T., Hong Kong

Church Publishing Inc., 445 Fifth Avenue, New York, NY 10016, USA, • copyrights@cpg.org

G.I.A. Publications Inc. administered in UK and Ireland by Calamus

Grail (England), Permissions Department, HarperCollins Publishers, 77-85 Fulham Palace Road, London, W6 8JB • www.harpercollins. co.uk/business-centre/Permissions/Pages/Permissions.aspx

Hope Publishing Co. via Calamus (non-commercial permssions)

Hymns Ancient & Modern, 13a Hellesdon Park Road, Norwich NR6 5DR • www.canterburypress.co.uk/contact-us/rights-and-permis- sions.aspx

International Committee on English in the Liturgy Corporation (ICEL) 1100 Connecticut Avenue, NW, Suite 710, Washington, D.C., 20036, U.S.A. For non-commercial reprint requests apply to the Liturgy Office (above)

The Jubilate Group, Kitley House, St Katherine's Road, Torquay, TQ1 4DE (01803 200132) • copyrightmanager@jubilate.co.uk

Kingsway's Thankyou Music, 26-28 Lottbridge Drove, Eastbourne, E.Sussex BN23 6NT • office@kingsway.co.uk

Kevin Mayhew Ltd., Buxhall, Stowmarket, Suffolk IP14 3DJ 01449 737 978 • www.kevinmayhew.com

McCrimmon Publishing Co. Ltd, 10-12 High Street, Great Wakering, Essex, SS3 0EQ • www.mccrimmons.com

National Council of Churches of Christ, Division of Christian Education, 475 Riverside Drive, New York NY 10027, USA

Novello & Co, 14-15 Berners Street, London W1T 3LJ 020 7612 7400

OCP Publications: administered in UK and Ireland by Calamus

Oxford University Press, Music Department, Great Clarendon Street, Oxford OX2 6DP • https://global.oup.com/academic/rights/music/ rights/reproduction/

Sisters of St Mary of Namur, 909 West Shaw, Fort Worth, Texas 76110

Stainer & Bell Ltd. PO Box 110 Victoria House, 23 Gruneisen Road, London N3 1DZ • post@stainer.co.uk •www.stainer.co.uk

SongSolutions Copycare, 14 Horsted Square, Uckfield, TN22 1QGF • info@songsolustions.org

Stanbrook Abbey (Liturgical Secretary), Wass, York YO61 4AY • www.stanbrookabbeyfriends.org/

Wild Goose Resource Group, Iona Community, 21 Carlton Court, Glasgow G5 9JP. 44 (0)141 429 7281 • www.wildgoose.scot

Timothy Dudley-Smith, administered by Oxford University Press

A.P.Watt Ltd, 20 John Street, London WC1N 2DR

Josef Weinberger Ltd, 12-14 Mortimer St London W1N 7RD 020 7580 2827 •www.josef-weinberger.com/contacts.html

World Library Publications, Inc., 3708 River Road, Suite 400, Franklin Park, IL. 60131-2158, USA. In UK: via Calamus

Asking permission to reproduce

You must *always* obtain permission to reproduce copyright music or words. It is possible to obtain an annual Copyright Licence which removes the necessity of applying for every item separately. All but a few of the items in this book are covered by one of two schemes, the Christian Copyright Licence (CCLI) and Calamus. The Calamus licence allows reproduc- tion of words and melody line and covers mainly G.I.A., OCP, Taizé, Hope, Mayhew, McCrimmon, Weston Priory, Wild Goose, World Library and many individual composers. CCLI has two licences: one which allows reproduction of words only, and an add-on licence which also allows the limited use of music. It covers Mayhew, OUP, Stainer & Bell, Kingsway's Thankyou, Copycare, Wild Goose, Jubilate and many others not in this book.

CALAMUS, 28 Bury Road, Brandon, Suffolk IP27 0BU. 01842 819830 • www. decanimusic.co.uk

CHRISTIAN COPYRIGHT LICENSING INTERNATIONAL, Chantry House, 22 Upperton Road, Eastbourne BN21 1BF 01323 436103 • www.ccli.co.uk/

Contents

LAUDATE is arranged by category. Some hymns are suitable for use in more than one category, and occasionally a 'See also...' cross-reference line will be found. This should help plan music for any liturgical occasion. There are also some guidelines on pages 415-417.

LITURGY OF THE HOURS

'Public and common prayer by the people of God is rightly considered to be among the primary duties of the Church.' (*General Instruction on the Liturgy of the Hours, §1.*) This prayer, which we learn from Christ's example and bidding, has, since the earliest days of the Church, taken the form of prayer at set times of day. This section provides a means of such prayer. Based on the *Liturgy of the Hours,* it may be used in conjunction with it or on its own. The Liturgy of the Hours is a prayer of praise and petition, with psalmody and intercession as its main elements.

MORNING PRAYER

1 Introduction

All make the sign of the cross on their lips

cf. Ps. 51:17

O Lord, o-pen our lips, and we shall praise your name.

➤ *Alternative introduction:* O God, come to our aid (no 11)

2 Morning Hymn I

1 Now that the daylight fills the sky,
we lift our hearts to God on high,
that God in all we do and say
would keep us free from harm today.

2 O Lord, restrain our tongues from strife,
from wrath and anger shield our life;
and guard with watchful care our eyes
that we will choose from all that's wise.

3 O may our inmost hearts be pure,
from thoughts of folly be secure,
and all our pow'rs devoted be
to deeds of love, that keep us free.

4 So we, when this day's work is o'er,
and shades of night return once more,
our path of trial safely trod,
shall give the glory to our God.

5 All praise to God the Father be,
and praise the Son eternally,
whom with the Spirit we adore,
One God alone, for evermore.
Latin, 8th C; tr. J.M. Neale (1818-66), alt.

3 Morning Hymn II (Psalm 94 (95)

1 To God with gladness sing,
your Rock and Saviour bless;
within your temple bring
your songs of thankfulness!
O God of might, to you we sing,
enthroned as King on heaven's height!

2 He cradles in his hand
the heights and depths of earth;
he made the sea and land
he brought the world to birth!
O God most high, we are your sheep,
on us you keep your Shepherd's eye.

3 Your heav'nly Father praise,
acclaim his only Son,
your voice in homage raise
to him who makes all one!
O Dove of peace, on us descend
that strife may end and joy increase!
Versified by James Quinn SJ (1919-2000)

Another setting of Ps 94 (95), the 'Invitatory Psalm', see no. 52. Other morning hymns: 668-673

Morning Thanksgiving (optional)

The leader may give thanks for the day.

Psalmody

One or more psalms are now sung, or recited. Two traditional morning psalms are found below. Other psalms may be taken from the Office of the Day, or elsewhere in the Psalter. A suggested weekly cycle (many of these are found in this book: see Psalm Index on p. 419) is:

Sunday: Psalm 63, Daniel 3,
Psalm 148
Monday: Psalms 5, 28 or 96
Tuesday: Psalms 24, 65 or 144

Wednesday: Psalms 47, 92 or 97
Thursday: Psalms 57, 147a
Friday: Psalms 51, 100
Saturday: Psalms 8, 150

4 Psalm 62 (63):2-9

Antiphon 1

At dawn I look to you, my God, to be my strength this day.

Psalmtone

omit for last stanza

Antiphon 2

My soul is thir-sting for you, O Lord, thir-sting for you, my God.

Gelineau tone

omit for last stanza

2 O Gód, you are my Gód, for you I lóng;
   for yóu my sóul is thírsting.
   My bódy pínes for yóu
   like a drý, weary lánd without wáter.

3 So I gáze on yóu in the sánctuary
   to sée your stréngth and your glóry.

4 For your lóve is bétter than lífe,
   my líps will spéak your práise.

5 So I will bléss you all my lífe,
   in your náme I will líft up my hánds.

6 My sóul shall be fílled as with a bánquet,
   my móuth shall práise you with jóy.

Concludes overleaf

7 On my béd I remémber yóu.
On yóu I múse through the níght
8 for yóu have béen my hélp;
in the shádow of your wíngs I rejóice.
9 My sóul clíngs to yóu;
your ríght hand hólds me fást.

Give práise to the Fáther Almíghty,
to his Són, Jesus Chríst the Lórd;
to the Spírit who dwélls in our héarts
both nów and for éver, Amén.

➤ *Other settings of Psalm 62 (63): My soul is thirsting (49), Your love is finer than life (213).*

Psalm Prayer

(optional) After each psalm there may be a prayer, read by the leader, to which all answer **Amen.**

5 Psalm 150 *(psalmtone version)*

Antiphon

Let ev' - ry - thing that lives praise——— the Lord.

Psalmtone 1

Gelineau tone

1 Praise Gód in his hóly pláce,
Sing práise in the míghty héavens.
2 Sing práise for God's pówerful déeds,
práise God's surpássing gréatness.

3 Sing práise with sóund of trúmpet,
Sing práise with lúte and hárp.
4 Sing práise with tímbrel and dánce,
Sing práise with stríngs and pípes.

5 Sing práise with resóunding cymbals,
Sing práise with cláshing of cymbals.
6 Let éverything that líves and that bréathes
give práise to the Lórd. Amén.

Give práise to the Fáther Almíghty,
to his Són, Jesus Chríst the Lórd;
to the Spírit who dwélls in our héarts
both nów and for éver. Amén.

Text, Antiphon by A. Gregory Murray OSB and Psalmtone 2: J.Gelineau SJ © The Grail.
Psalmtone 1: Laurence Bévenot OSB © Ampleforth Trustees

6 Psalm 150 *(metrical version)*

1 Blest be the Lord our God!
with joy let heaven ring;
Before his presence let all the earth
its songs of homage bring!
His mighty deeds be told;
his majesty be praised;
to God enthroned in heavenly light
let every voice be raised.

2 All that has life and breath
give thanks with heartfelt songs
to him let all creation sing
to whom all praise belongs!
Acclaim the Father's love,
who gave us Christ his Son;
praise too, the Spirit giv'n by both,
with both forever one.

Versified by James Quinn SJ (1919-2010)

© administered by Bloomsbury Publishing

The Word of God

A short scripture passage is read, taken from the Office of the Day or another source.

7 Gospel Canticle: The Benedictus Luke 1:68-75 *(chant version)*

Blessed be the Lord, the God of Israel!
Omit B & C
He has visited his people and redeemed
them.

He has raised up for us a mighty saviour
in the house of David his servant,
as he promised by the lips of holy men,
those who were his prophets from of old.

A saviour who would free us from our foes,
from the hands of all who hate us.
So his love for our fathers is fulfilled
and his holy covenant remembered.

He swore to Abraham our father to grant us,
that free from fear, and saved from the
    hands of our foes,
we might serve him in holiness and justice
all the days of our life in his presence.

As for you, little child,
you shall be called a prophet of God, the
    Most High.
You shall go ahead of the Lord
to prepare his ways before him.

To make known to his people their salvation
through forgiveness of all their sins,
the loving-kindness of the heart of our God
who visits us like the dawn from on high.

He will give light to those in darkness,
those who dwell in the shadow of death,
    (omit C)
and guide us into the way of peace.

Glory be to the Father, and to the Son,
and to the Holy Spirit,
as it was in the beginning, is now and ever
    shall be,
world without end. Amen.

Text: © The Grail. Music: © 1998 Stephen Dean

8 The Benedictus *(metrical version)*

1 Now bless the God of Israel,
    who comes in love and power,
    who raises from the royal house
    deliv'rance in this hour.
    Through holy prophets God has sworn
    to free us from alarm,
    to save us from the heavy hand
    of all who wish us harm.

2 Remembering the covenant
    God rescues us from fear,
    that we might serve in holiness
    and peace from year to year:
    and you, my child, shall go before
    to preach, to prophesy,
    that all may know the tender love,
    the grace of God most high.

3   In tender mercy, God will send
    the dayspring from on high,
    our rising sun, the light of life
    for those who sit and sigh.

God comes to guide our way to peace,
that death shall reign no more,
sing praises to the Holy One!
O worship and adore.

Versified by Ruth Duck

➤ *Another version: Blest be the Lord, the God of Israel (83)*

Intercessions

    The leader now introduces the Intercessions, and all make the response.

9   **Response to the Intercessions**

Fa - ther,   may your king-dom come!

    Intercessions (and responses) may be taken from the Office for the Day or another source (see 26-29, 73 (Advent), 221, 547-552, 740, 928-9).
    The Leader collects all the petitions in the Our Father which may be said or sung.

10   **The Lord's Prayer**

Lord, remember us in your king-dom.   O Lord, teach us to pray.

Our Fa-ther, who art in heav'n, hal-lowed be thy name; thy king-dom come,

thy will be done on earth as it is in heav'n. Give us this day our dai-ly bread,

and for-give us our tres-pas-ses, as we for - give those who tres-pass a-gainst us;

and lead us not in - to temp-ta-tion, but de - li-ver us from e - vil.

➤ *Other versions: 30, 587-88, 1010*

Concluding Prayer

    The prayer is taken from the Office of the Day or another source. All respond **Amen.**

Blessing

    When a priest or deacon presides at Morning Prayer, a blessing is given. When a lay person presides, the conclusion is as follows:

The Lord bless us, and keep us from all evil, and bring us to everlasting life. **Amen.**

Evening Prayer

Evening Prayer may begin with this Introduction, or with a Service of Light as at no. 13 on.

11 Introduction

O God, come to our aid. O Lord, make haste to— help us. Glo - ry be to the

Fa - ther, the Son and the Ho - ly Spi - rit, as it was in the be - gin ning, is

Omitted during Lent

now and ev - er shall be, world with out end. A - men. [Al - le - lu - ia].

12 Evening Hymn 1

Philip Gaisford OSB

1. In the qui - et of the eve - ning, now the work of day is done,
2. In our wand'ring we have tra - velled far from you through-out the day,
3. When our ig - no - rance is dan - ger, or we cre - dit world - ly lies,

turn our thoughts, most lo - ving Fa - ther to the work of Christ, your Son.
yet for - gi - ving all, you sent us Christ to lead us, Christ the way.
then, with time - ly care, you give us Christ the truth to make us wise.

4 As the light of day is fading,
Father, keep us in your sight;
pierce the dark of sin with splendour
shining out from Christ the light.

5 Glory be to God the Father,
glory be to God the Son,
glory be to God the Spirit,
glory to the Three in One.
Patrick Lee (1930-2004)

12a Evening Hymn 2

1 Joyous light of heav'nly glory,
loving glow of God's own face,
you who sing creation's story,
shine on ev'ry land and race.
Now as evening falls around us,
we shall raise our songs to you,
God of daybreak, God of shadows,
come and light our hearts anew.

2 In the stars that grace the darkness,
in the blazing sun of dawn,
of the light of peace and wisdom,
we can hear your quiet song.
Love that fills the night with wonder,
love that warms the weary soul,
love that bursts all chains asunder,
set us free and make us whole.

11 Text: Bishops' Conference of England & Wales; Music: © 1998 Stephen Dean. 12 Text: © 1987 Patrick Lee; Music: © 1988 Worth Abbey Music, Crawley, W. Sussex RH10 4SB. 12a © 1987 GIA Publications Inc.

3. You who made the heaven's splendour,
ev-'ry dancing star of night,
Make us shine with gentle justice,
let us each reflect your light.

Mighty God of all creation,
gentle Christ who lights our way,
Loving Spirit of salvation,
lead us on to endless day.

Marty Haugen

➢ *Other hymns for evening, 674-682*

Continue with Psalmody (opposite.)

Service of Light (Lucernarium)

13 **Greeting**

Je - sus Christ is   the   light   of   the   world!
A   light   the   dark - ness can - not   o - ver - power!

14

Hymn to Christ the Light (1st version)

1 O gracious Light, Lord Jesus Christ,
in you the Father's glory shone.
Immortal, holy, blest is he,
and blest are you, his only Son.

2 Now sunset comes, but light shines forth,
the lamps are lit to pierce the night.
Praise Father, Son and Spirit: God
who dwells in the eternal light.

3 Worthy are you of endless praise,
O Son of God, Life-giving Lord:
wherefore you are through all the earth
and in the highest heaven adored.

Greek, 3rd C., tr. F. Bland Tucker (1895-1984)

15 **Hymn to Christ the Light** (2nd version)

1. Light of glad - ness,   shi - ning ra - diance   of   the   heav'n–ly   Fa- ther's face:

Je - sus Christ, we   greet you, bless   you,   ho - ly   Lord of   sa - ving grace.

2 As the day draws near its ending
sunlight dims with fading rays;
to the Father, Son and Spirit
now we sing our song of praise.

3 Son of God, the world's redeemer,
endless praises are your due;
Lord of life, may all creation
bring its joyful thanks to you.

Greek, 3rd Century, tr. Paul Inwood

➢ *See also O Gladsome Light (677)*

16

Evening Thanksgiving

Let us give thanks to God the Father always and for everything.
In the name of our Lord   Je - sus Christ.

The leader makes the thanksgiving to which all respond: **Amen.** *Continue with Psalmody (opposite.)*

Psalmody

Psalms are found in the Psalter (39-63). The Psalm and Canticle given here may be sung as a simple Evening Prayer on any day.

17   **Psalm 140 (141)** 1st Setting   *Incense may be burnt during the singing of this psalm.*

Music: Stephen Dean

¹ I have called to you, Lord; hasten to help me.
Hear my voice when I cry to you.
² Let my prayer arise before you like incense,
the raising of my hands like an evening
oblation.

³ Set, O Lord, a guard over my mouth;
keep watch, O Lord, at the door of my lips.
⁴ Do not turn my heart to things that are
wrong,
to evil deeds with those who are sinners.

Never allow me to share in their feasting.
⁵ If the upright strike or reprove me it is
kindness;
but let the oil of the wicked not anoint
my head.
Let my prayer be ever against their malice.

⁸ To you, Lord God, my eyes are turned;
in you I take refuge; spare my soul!
⁹ From the trap they have laid for me
keep me safe;
keep me from the snares of those who
do evil.

Give praise to the Father Almighty,
to his Son, Jesus Christ, the Lord.
To the Spirit who dwells in our hearts
both now and for ever. Amen.

18   **Psalm 140 (141)** 2nd Setting

Michael Joncas

Hurry, Lord! I call <u>and</u> call!
Listen! I plead <u>with</u> you.
Let my prayer rise <u>like</u> incense,
my upraised hands, like an eve<u>ning</u> sacrifice.

Lord, guard <u>my</u> lips,
watch my eve<u>ry</u> word.
Let me never speak evil
    or consider hate<u>ful</u> deeds,
let me never join the wicked
    to eat their la<u>vish</u> meals.

If the just cor<u>rect</u> me,
I take their rebuke <u>as</u> kindness,
but the unction of the wicked
    will never touch <u>my</u> head.
I pray and pray against their hate<u>ful</u> ways.

Let them be thrown
    against a rock <u>of</u> judgment,
then they will know I spoke <u>the</u> truth.
Then they will say,
'Our bones lie broken upon <u>the</u> ground,
scattered at <u>the</u> grave's edge.'

Lord my God, I turn to you,
    in you I <u>find</u> safety.
Do not strip me <u>of</u> life.
Do not spring on me the traps of <u>the</u> wicked.
Let evildoers get tangled in their own nets,
    but let me <u>escape</u>.

Glory to the Father, and to <u>the</u> Son,
and to the Ho<u>ly</u> Spirit:
as it was in the beginning, <u>is</u> now,
and will be forever. <u>A</u>men.

Psalm Prayer (optional)   *The leader reads the prayer and all answer* **Amen.**

19 **Canticle of the Lamb (Rev. 19: 1,2,5-7)**   *outside Lent*   *Stephen Dean*

Antiphon *Sundays 1 & 3*

The Lord is King, our God, the Al-migh-ty, al - le - lu - ia!_____

Sundays 2 & 4

Praise God, all you his ser-vants, both__ small and great, al-le-lu - ia, al-le-lu - ia!

Verses

Cantor / *All*

1. Salvation and glory and power be - long to our God. **Al-le-lu - ia!**
2. Praise our God, all you his servants.
3. The Lord our God, the al - mighty reigns.
4. The mar - riage feast of the Lamb has come.

Cantor / *All*

1. His judgements are true and just. **Al-le-lu - ia, al-le-lu - ia!**
2. You who fear him, small and great.
3. Let us rejoice, and exult, and give him the glory.
4. And his bride has made herself ready.

Repeat Antiphon after verses 2 & 4

20 Revelation 15: 3-4

Antiphon

Great and wonder-ful are your deeds, O Lord God the al-migh-ty.

Verses

1. Just and true are your ways, O King of the a-ges. ℟.

2. Who shall not fear and glo - ri-fy your name, O Lord, for you a-lone are ho - ly. ℟.

3. All na - tions shall come and wor-ship you, for your judge-ments have been re - vealed. ℟.

4. Praise the Fa - ther the Son and the Ho - ly Spi - rit, both now and for - e - ver, A - men. ℟.

Music: Margaret Daly-Denton

➤ *Alternative Canticle: Phil. 2.6-11. Before the heaven and earth (754), Every knee shall bow (755)*

21 Lent Canticle (I Peter 2:21-24) 1st Setting

Martin Foster

Antiphon

By his wounds we have been healed.

Psalmtone

Laurence Bévenot OSB

Christ suffered for you, leaving you <u>an</u> example,
that you should follow <u>in</u> his steps.
He committed no sin; no guile was found <u>on</u> his lips.
When he was reviled, he did not revile <u>in</u> return.

When he suffered, he <u>did</u> not threaten;
but trusted to him who <u>judges</u> justly.
He himself bore our sins in his body <u>on</u> the tree,
that we might die to sin and <u>live</u> to righteousness.

I Peter 2:21-24

22 Lent Canticle (I Pet 2:21-24) 2nd Setting

Stephen Dean

Antiphon

Ours were the griefs he bore, ours were the pains he car-ried,
ours were the sins he took on him: and by—— his wounds we are healed.

The verses may be read or sung.

1. Christ suffered for you,
   leaving you an example
   that you should follow in his steps.
   He committed no sin,
   no guile was found on his lips.
   When he was reviled,
   he did not revile in return.

2. When he suffered, He did not threaten;
   but he trusted to him who judges justly.
   He himself bore our sins
   in his body on the tree,
   that we might die to sin
   and live to righteousness.
   I Pet 2:21-24

➤ *Another setting: As prophets foretold (235)*

The Word of God

A short scripture passage is read, taken from the Office of the Day or another source.

23 Gospel Canticle: The Magnificat (Luke 1:46-55) Grail version 1st setting

Joseph Gelineau SJ (1920-2008)

The Lord has done mar-vels for me: ho-ly— is his name.

1	My soul		glorifies	the	Lord,
2	He looks	on his	servant	in her	lowliness;
9	the mercy		promised	to our	fathers,
10	Praise the Father,	the	Son and	Holy	Spirit,

my spirit re-joices in God my Saviour.
hence-forth all ages will call me blessed.
to Abra - ham and his sons for ever.
both now and for ever, world without end.

3	The Al-mighty works marvels	for me.	Holy	his name!
5	He puts forth his arm	in strength,	and scatters the proud-hearted.	
7	He fills the starving with good things,	sends the rich	away empty.	

4	His mercy is from age	to age,	on those who fear him.
6	He casts the mighty from their thrones		and raises the lowly.
8	He pro-tects Israel	his servant,	re-membering his mercy.

24 2nd Setting

Laurence Bévenot OSB (1901-91)

A   B   C   D

My soul glorifies the Lord,
my spirit rejoices in God my Saviour.
He looks on his servant in her lowliness;
henceforth all ages will call me blessed.

The Almighty works marvels for me.
Holy his name!
His mercy is from age to age,
on those who fear him.

He puts forth his arm in strength,
and scatters the proudhearted.
He casts the mighty from their thrones
and raises the lowly.

He fills the starving with good things,
sends the rich away empty. *[Omit B + C]*

He protects Israel his servant,
remembering his mercy,
the mercy promised to our fathers,
to Abraham and his sons for ever.

Give praise to the Father Almighty,
to his Son Jesus Christ, the Lord,
to the Spirit who dwells in our hearts,
both now and for ever. Amen.

25a Hymn Setting 1

1 Sing, my soul, and magnify the Lord my God.
Sing, rejoice, my spirit, God has come to save.
He looks down on me, his servant, humble of
heart;
from this moment all to come will call me
blest.

2 God the mighty, God the holy cares for me;
cares for all who fear and bless his holy name;
God the strong will rout the proud in their
conceit.
thrones are toppled, yet the poor are lifted up.

3 All who hunger will be fed by God's
own hand.
All the rich are empty-handed in God's
plan.
He protects with love and mercy Israel:
mercy promised; love remembered for
all time.

4 Glory sing to God the Father, mighty
Lord,
Glory sing to God the Son, the Word
made flesh;
Glory sing to God the Spirit, gift of grace.
All God's people, through all ages praise
your God.

Martin Foster (from Luke 1:46-55)

25b Hymn Setting 2

1 Great is the Lord my soul proclaims,
in him my spirit sings for joy;
for he who saves has looked on me
with boundless love to raise me high.

2 Ages to come shall know that I
am blessed and favoured by the Lord:
his name is holy, mighty God;
his wondrous power on me is poured.

3 All those who fear him find his love,
in every age, in every land.
His strong right arm puts down the proud,
disperses them like grains of sand.

4 Down from their thrones he casts the
strong,
and raises up the meek of heart.
He gives the hungry choicest food;
in emptiness the rich depart.

5 Israel his servant knows his help,
in keeping with the promise sworn
to Abraham and all his race:
God's love will never be withdrawn.

6 Glory to God: the Father, Son,
and Spirit – Trinity sublime.
All honour, thanks and praise be theirs
across the spans of endless time.

Paul Inwood (from Luke 1:46-55)

➤ *Other settings of the Magnificat: nos. 335-340, 880*

Intercessions

*The leader now introduces the Intercessions, and all make the response. Intercessions may be taken
from the Office for the Day or another source. Suggested responses are given below.*

Prayers should be made for:
*The church throughout the world; our own community; governments and others in authority
(in Lent) those preparing for baptism; (In Eastertide) the newly baptized;
Justice and peace; the harvest; the sick and dying; the faithful departed.*

26 Response to the Intercessions: Advent & Christmastide
➤ *See also no. 73*

Come and re-main with us, come and re-main with us, come and re-main with us, Lord.

27 **Response to the Intercessions: Lent**

Lord, have mer - cy, Lord, have mer - cy, Lord, have mer - cy on your peo - ple.

28 **Response to the Intercessions: Eastertide**

O Christ, Vic - tor o - ver death, have mer - cy on us and hear our prayer.

29 **Response to the Intercessions: Ordinary Time**

Lord, in your mer - cy hear our prayer.

➤ *See also nos. 9, 73 (Advent), 547-552, 740, 928-9*

The Leader collects all the petitions in the Our Father *which may be said or sung:*

30 **Lord's Prayer** *Philip Duffy*

Our Fa - ther, who art in heav'n, hal-lowed be thy name; thy king-dom come,

thy will be done on earth as it is in heav'n. Give us this day our dai - ly bread,

and for-give us our tres-pas-ses, as we for-give those who tres-pass ag-ainst us.

And lead us not in - to temp - ta-tion, but de - li - ver us from e - vil.

➤ *Other versions: 10, 587-88, 1010*

Concluding Prayer
The prayer is taken from the Office of the Day or another source. All respond **Amen.**

Blessing
When a priest or deacon presides at Evening Prayer, a blessing is given. When a lay person presides, the conclusion is as follows:

The Lord bless us, and keep us from all evil, and bring us to everlasting life. **Amen.**

27- 29 © 1989, 1990, 1991 Stephen Dean. 30 Music © Philip Duffy

Night Prayer

31 Introduction

Leader:
O God, come to our aid.

All:
O Lord, make haste to— help us. Glo - ry be to the Fa ther, the Son and the Ho - ly Spi - rit, as it was in the be - gin-ning, is now and ev - er shall be, world with-out end. A - men. [Al-le - lu - ia].

(⌢) Omitted during Lent

Examination of Conscience

An examination of conscience is recommended. This may be included in a penitential act using the formulas given in the Missal.

32 Hymn

1 We praise you, Father, for your gift
  of dusk and nightfall over earth,
  foreshadowing the mystery
  of death that leads to endless birth.

2 Within your hands we rest secure;
  in quiet sleep our strength renew
  yet give your people hearts that wake
  in love to you, unsleeping Lord.

3 Your glory may we ever seek
  in rest as in activity,
  until its fullness is revealed,
  O source of life, O Trinity. (Amen).
      The Benedictine Nuns of West Malling

1. We praise you, Fa - ther, for your gift of dusk and night - fall o - ver earth,
fore-sha-dow-ing the mys-te-ry— of death that leads to end-less birth. A - men.

> *This hymn may be sung to other tunes, e.g. no 199. Other suitable hymns: nos. 674-682*

31 Text: Bishops' Conference of England & Wales; Music: © 1998 Stephen Dean. 32 Text © 1995 Saint Mary's Abbey, West Malling, Kent, ME19 6JX

Psalmody

Other psalms may be chosen from the Psalm section (39-63)

33 Psalm 90 (91)

Antiphon

He will con - ceal you with his wings; you will not fear the ter - ror of the night.

Psalmtone

1 Those who dwell in the shelter of the
  Most High
  and abide in the shade of the Almighty

2 say to the Lord: 'My refuge,
  my stronghold, my God in whom I trust!'

3 It is God who will free you from the snare
  of the fowler who seeks to destroy you;

4 God will conceal you with his pinions,
  and under his wings you will find refuge.

5 You will not fear the terror of the night
  nor the arrow that flies by day,

6 nor the plague that prowls in the darkness
  nor the scourge that lays waste at noon.

7 A thousand may fall at your side,
  ten thousand fall at your right,
  you, it will never approach;

4c God's faithfulness is buckler and shield.

8 Your eyes have only to look
  to see how the wicked are repaid,

9 you who have said: 'Lord, my refuge!'
  and have made the Most High your
  dwelling.

10 Upon you no evil shall fall,
   no plague approach where you dwell.

11 For you God has commanded the angels,
   to keep you in all your ways.

12 They shall bear you upon their hands
   lest you strike your foot against a stone.

13 On the lion and the viper you will tread
   and trample the young lion and the
   dragon.

14 You set your love on me so I will save you,
   protect you for you know my name.

15 When you call I shall answer: 'I am
     with you,'
   I will save you in distress and give you
     glory.

16 With length of days I will content you;
   I shall let you see my saving power.

Give praise to the Father Almighty,
to his Son, Jesus Christ, the Lord,
to the Spirit who dwells in our hearts,
both now and for ever. Amen.

Music: Margaret Daly-Denton. Text: The Grail

34
Psalm 4

Antiphon

Lord,—— have mer - cy and hear me.

Psalmtone

2 When I call, answer me, O God of
   justice;
   from anguish you released me, have
   mercy and hear me!

3 You rebels, how long will your hearts
   be closed,
   will you love what is futile and seek
   what is false?

4 It is the Lord who grants favours to
   those who are merciful;
   the Lord hears me whenever I call.

5 Tremble; do not sin: ponder on your
   bed and be still.

6 Make justice your sacrifice and trust in
   the Lord.

7 'What can bring us happiness?' many say.
   Lift up the light of your face on us, O
   Lord.

8 You have put into my heart a greater joy
   than they have from abundance of corn
   and new wine.

9 I will lie down in peace and sleep
   comes at once
   for you alone, Lord, make me dwell in
   safety.

Give praise to the Father, the Son and
   Holy Spirit
both now and for ages unending. Amen.

Music: Margaret Daly-Denton. Text: The Grail

35a Psalm 133 (134) *Simple setting*

Antiphon

Bless—— the Lord, bless— the Lord through—— the night.

Psalmtone

1 O come, bless the Lord,
   all you who serve the Lord,
   who stand in the house of the Lord,
   in the courts of the house of our God.

2 Lift up your hands to the holy place
   and bless the Lord through the night.

3 May the Lord bless you from Zion,
   God who made both heaven and earth.

Give glory to the Father Almighty
   to his Son, Jesus Christ our Lord;
to the Spirit who dwells in our hearts
   both now and for ever. Amen.

35b Psalm 133 (134) *melodic setting*

Antiphon

mp O come, bless— the Lord, all you who serve the Lord,——— who stand in the house of the Lord, in the courts of the house of our God.——

Verses

1. Lift up your hands to the ho - ly place,— and bless the Lord through the night.— May the Lord bless you from Zi - on, he who made both hea - ven and earth. *Ant.*

2. Glo - ry be to the Fa - ther, the Son and the Spi - rit, as it was, is now,— and for e - ver shall be. A - men. *Ant.*

Music: Stephen Dean.

The Word of God

Hear, O Israel: the Lord our God is one Lord; and you shall love the Lord your God with all your heart, and with all your soul, and with all your might. And these words which I command you this day shall be upon your heart; and you shall teach them diligently to your children, and shall talk of them when you sit in your house, and when you walk by the way, and when you lie down, and when you rise. *(Deuteronomy 6:4-7: Reading for Sunday)*

36 Response to the Word

Response *Omit in Lent*

In - to your hands, O Lord, I com-mend my Spi-rit. [Al-le-lu-ia, al-le-lu - ia.]

Verses *All: Into your hands..*

v.1 You have re - deemed us, Lord God of truth. *All: Into your hands..*

v.2 Glo - ry be to the Fa - ther, and to the Son, and— to the Ho - ly Spi - rit.
All: Into your hands..

37 Gospel Canticle: The Nunc Dimittis (Luke 2:22-24)

Antiphon

Save us, O Lord, while we are a-wake, pro-tect us while___ we sleep,___ that we may keep watch with Christ, and rest here in peace.

Verses

1. At last, all-powerful Master, you give leave to your servant to go in peace, ac-cor-ding to your pro-mise.

2. For my eyes have seen your sal-
3. The light to en-ligh-ten the
4. Give praise to the Father al-
5. To the Spirit who dwells in our

vation which you have pre-pared for all___ na - tions,
Gentiles, and give glo - ry to Is - ra - el your peo - ple.
mighty, to his Son, Je - sus Christ,___ the___ Lord,___
hearts both now and for e - ver. A - men.___

Text © The Grail; Music © 1988 Stephen Dean

➤ *Other settings of the Nunc Dimittis: nos. 174, 176-7*

Concluding Prayer*

Visit this house, we pray you, Lord:
drive far away from it all the snares of the enemy.
May your holy angels stay here and guard us in peace,
and let your blessing be always upon us.
Through Christ our Lord.
Amen.

Blessing

The Lord grant us a quiet night and a perfect end. **Amen.**

Prayer for Sunday; for other days, see the Divine Office

Anthem to Our Lady

Throughout the year: Salve Regina, no 367. During Eastertide: *Regina Caeli, no. 368*

38a Alma Redemptoris Mater

from the first Sunday in Advent until the Feast of the Presentation (February 2)

Al - ma Re-demp-to-ris Ma-ter, quae per-vi-a cae-li Por-ta ma-nes,

et stel-la ma-ris, suc-cur-re caden-ti, Sur-ge-re qui cu-rat, po-pu-lo; tu quae ge-nu-is-ti,

Na-tu-ra mi-ran-te, tu-um sanctum Ge-ni-to - rem,— Vir-go pri-us ac po-ste-ri-us,

Ga-bri-e-lis ab o-re Su-mens il-lud A-ve, pec-ca-to-rum— mi-se-re - re.

38b Ave Regina Caelorum

From the Feast of the Presentation (February 2) through Wednesday of Holy Week

A-ve Re-gi-na cae-lo-rum, A-ve Do-mi-na an-ge-lo-rum, Sal-ve ra-dix, sal-ve por-ta,

Ex qua mun-do lux est or-ta: Gau-de Vir-go glo-ri-o-sa, Su-per om-nes spe-ci-o-sa:

Va-le o val-de de-co - ra, Et pro no - bis Chris-tum ex-o - ra.

The Psalter

Psalm 8

39

Antiphon

How great is your name, O Lord our God,—— through all the earth!

Verses

1.	Your	majesty	is	praised	above	the	heavens;
2.	When I see the heavens,	the		work	of	your	hands,
3.	Yet you have made us	little		less	than		gods;
4.	All	of them,		sheep	and		cattle,
	Give glory to	the		Father	Al	-	mighty,

on the	lips		of	children	and	of	babes
the	moon	and	the	stars	which	you	ar - ranged,
and	crowned	us	with	glory		and	honour,
yes,	even		the	savage			beasts,
to his	Son,	Jesus		Christ,		the	Lord,

you	have found praise		to	foil	your	enemy,
what are	we	that	you	should keep	us	in	mind,
you	gave us	power	over	the	work	of your	hands,
	birds	of	the	air,		and	fish
to the	Spirit		who	dwells	in	our	hearts

to	silence		the	foe	and	the	rebel.
mere	mortals	that	you	care		for	us?
put	all	things	under			our	feet.
that	make	their		way	through	the	waters.
both	now	and	for	ever.		A -	men.

Psalm 15 (16)

40

PRESERVE ME, GOD, I TAKE REFUGE IN YOU.(†)
2a I say to you Lord: 'You are my God.
2b My happiness lies in you alone.' *omit B & C*

3 You have put into my heart a marvellous love
for the faithful ones who dwell in your land.

4 Those who choose other gods increase their
sorrows. (†)
Never will I offer their offerings of blood.
Never will I take their name upon my lips.

5 O Lord, it is you who are my portion and cup,
it is you yourself who are my prize.

6 The lot marked out for me is my delight,
welcome indeed the heritage that falls to me!

7 I will bless you, Lord, you give me counsel,
and even at night direct my heart.

8 I keep you, Lord, ever in my sight,
since you are at my right hand, I shall stand
firm.

9 And so my heart rejoices, my soul is glad;
even my body shall rest in safety.

10 For you will not leave my soul among the
dead,
nor let your beloved know decay.

11 You will show me the path of life,
the fullness of joy in your presence, *omit C*
at your right hand happiness for ever.

*Give praise to the Father, the Son and
Holy Spirit,* *omit B & C*
both now and for ages unending. Amen.

Response 1

Show us, Lord, the path of— life.

Response 2

O— Lord, it is you who are my por - tion and cup.

Response 3

Show us, Lord, the path of life, di-rect our hearts, and guide our foot-steps; keep us e-ver in your sight, for with you at our right hand, you at our right hand, what can we fear?

Psalmtone

Text © The Grail; R.1 and Psalmtone by Fintan O'Carroll. © 1982 Irish Church Music Association (ICMA) Rr. 2 & 3 © Stephen Dean.

SEE OVERLEAF for another setting of this psalm

40b

Response
(may be sung in two-part canon)

Paul Inwood

Keep me safe, O God, I take re-fuge in you.

Keep me safe, O God, I take re-fuge in you.

See the music editions for the setting of the verses accompanying this response.

• **Another setting of Psalm 16:** *Centre of my life (423)*

Psalm 18(19):8-15 {41}

THE LAW OF THE LORD IS PERFECT,
it revives the soul.
    The rule of the Lord is to be trusted,
    it gives wisdom tò the simple.

9 The precepts of the Lord are right,
they gladden the heart.
    The command of the Lord is clear,
    it gives light tò the eyes.

10 The fear of the Lord is holy,
abiding for ever.
    The decrees of the Lord are truth
    and all òf them just.

11 They are more to be desired than gold,
than the purest of gold
    and sweeter are they than honey,
    than honey fròm the comb.

12 So in them your servant finds instruction;
great reward is in their keeping.
13 But can we discern all our errors?
From hidden faults àcquit us.

14 From presumption restrain your servant
and let it not rule me.
    Then shall I be blameless,
    clean fròm grave sin.

15 May the spoken words of my mouth,
the thoughts of my heart,
    win favour in your sight, O Lord,
    my rescuèr, my rock!

Praise the Fáther, the Són, and Holy Spírit,
both nów and for éver,
The God who ís, who wás, and who wíll be,
wórld without énd.

41a   Response 1

The pre-cepts of the Lord glad - den the heart.

Psalmtone

41b   Response 2

May be sung by two alternating groups.

You, Lord, have the mes-sage of e - ter - nal life.

Psalm 22 (23)

1. Lord, you are my shepherd;
2. You guide me a - long the right path;
3. You have pre - pared a banquet for me
4. Surely goodness and kindness shall follow me
5. To the Father and Son give glory,

1. there is nothing I shall want.
2. You are true to your name.
3. in the sight of my foes.
4. all the days of my life.
5. give glory to the Spirit.

1. Fresh and green are the pastures
2. If I should walk in the valley of darkness
3. My head you have a - nointed with oil;
4. In the Lord's own house shall I dwell
5. To God who is, who was and who will be

1. where you give me re - pose. Near restful
2. no evil would I fear. You are there with your
3. [_____
4. [_____
5. [_____

1. waters you lead me, to re - vive my droop-ing spi - rit.
2. crook and your staff; with these you give me com - fort.
3. my cup is o - ver-flow - ing.
4. _____] for e - ver and e - ver.
5. _____] for e - ver and e - ver.

42a
Resp. 1
The Lord is my shep-herd; there is no-thing I shall want.

42b
Resp. 2
My shep-herd is the Lord; no - thing in - deed shall I want.

Text: The Grail. Psalmtone and R 2 by Joseph Gelineau SJ. © The Grail. R.1 by Fintan O'Carroll © 1982 ICMA

Other settings of Psalm 22(23) *Because the Lord is my shepherd (948); Shepherd me, O God (951); The King of love (804); The living God (805); The Lord's my shepherd (806)*

Psalm 23(24) *Fling wide the gates (104)*

Psalm 24 (25)

43

To you, O Lord, I lift up my soul. (†)
² My God, I trust you, let me not be
disappointed;
do not let my enemies triumph.
³ Those who hope in you shall not be
disappointed
but only those who wantonly break faith.

⁴ Lord, make me know your ways.
Lord, teach me your paths.
⁵ Make me walk in your truth, and teach me,
for you are God my saviour.

In you I hope all the day long (†)
⁷ because of your goodness, O Lord.
⁶ Remember your mercy, Lord, (†)
and the love you have shown from of old.
⁷ Do not remember the sins of my youth.
In your love remember me.

⁸ The Lord is good and upright.
showing the path to those who stray,
⁹ guiding the humble in the right path,
and teaching the way to the poor.

¹⁰ God's ways are steadfastness and truth
for those faithful to the covenant decrees.

¹¹ Lord, for the sake of your name
forgive my guilt, for it is great.
¹² Those who revere the Lord (†)
will be shown the path they should choose.
¹³ Their souls will live in happiness (†)
and their children shall possess the land.
¹⁴ The Lord's friendship is for the God-fearing;
and the covenant is revealed to them.

¹⁵ My eyes are always on the Lord,
who will rescue my feet from the snare.
¹⁶ Turn to me and have mercy
for I am lonely and poor.

¹⁷ Relieve the anguish of my heart
and set me free from my distress.
¹⁸ See my affliction and my toil
and take all my sins away.

¹⁹ See how many are my foes, (†)
how violent their hatred for me.
²⁰ Preserve my life and rescue me. (†)
Do not disappoint me, you are my refuge.
²¹ May innocence and uprightness protect me
for my hope is in you, O Lord.

²²(D) Redeem Israel, O God, from all its distress.

Glory be: see after Ps 33 (34)

43a
Response 1

To you, O Lord, I lift up my soul.

Psalmtone

A   B   C   D

43b
Response 2 *See the music editions for the setting of the verses accompanying this response.*

Lord, your ways are faith-ful-ness and love, for those who keep your co-ve-nant.

Another setting of Psalm 24(25): *Remember, remember your mercy Lord (843)*

THE LORD IS MY LIGHT AND MY HELP;
whom shall I fear?
The Lord is the stronghold of my life;
before whom shall I shrink?

2   When evildoers draw near
to devour my flesh,
it is they, my enemies and foes,
who stumble and fall.

3   Though an army encamp against me
my heart would not fear.
Though war break out against me
even then would I trust.

4   There is one thing I ask of the Lord,
for this I long,
to live in the house of the Lord,
all the days of my life,
to savour the sweetness of the Lord,
to behold his temple.

5   For God makes me safe in his tent
in the day of evil.
God hides me in the shelter of his tent,
on a rock I am secure.

6   And now my head shall be raised
above my foes who surround me
and I shall offer within God's tent
a sacrifice of joy.

7   O Lord, hear my voice when I call;
have mercy and answer.

8   Of you my heart has spoken:
'Seek God's face.'

It is your face, O Lord, that I seek;
9   hide not your face.
Dismiss not your servant in anger;
you have been my help.

Do not abandon or forsake me,
O God my help!
10   Though father and mother forsake me,
the Lord will receive me.

11   Instruct me, Lord, in your way;
on an even path lead me.
When they lie in ambush 12 protect me
from my enemies' greed.
False witnesses rise against me,
breathing out fury.

13   I am sure I shall see the Lord's goodness
in the land of the living.
14   In the Lord, hold firm and take heart.
Hope in the Lord!

Praise the Fáther, the Són, and Holy Spírit,
both nów and for éver,
The God who ís, who wás, and who wíll be,
wórld without énd.

(A)   I will sing and make music for the Lord.

Response: The Lord is my light and my help.

Psalmtone

Verses 4, 11

Other settings of Psalm 26 (27) *May the choirs of angels (443); One thing I ask of the Lord (990); Those who seek your face (393)*

RING OUT YOUR JOY TO THE LORD, O YOU JUST
for praise is fitting for loyal hearts. (A & D)

2 Give thanks to the Lord upon the harp
with a ten-stringed lute play your songs.
3 Sing to the Lord a song that is new,
play loudly, with all your skill.

4 For the word of the Lord is faithful
and all his works done in truth.
5 The Lord loves justice and right
and fills the earth with love.

6 By God's word the heavens were made,
by the breath of his mouth all the stars.
7 God collects the waves of the ocean;
and stores up the depths of the sea.

8 Let all the earth fear the Lord,
all who live in the world stand in awe.
9 For God spoke; it came to be.
God commanded, it sprang into being.

10 The Lord foils the designs of the nations,
and defeats the plans of the peoples.
11 The counsel of the Lord stands forever,
the plans of God's heart from age to age.

12 They are happy, whose God is the Lord,
the people who are chosen as his own.
13 From the heavens the Lord looks forth
and sees all the peoples of the earth.
14 From the heavenly dwelling God gazes
on all the dwellers on the earth;
15 God who shapes the hearts of them all
and considers all their deeds.

16 A king is not saved by his army,
nor a warrior preserved by his strength.
17 A vain hope for safety is the horse;
despite its power it cannot save.

18 The Lord looks on those who fear him,
on those who hope in his love,
19 to rescue their souls from death,
to keep them alive in famine.

20 Our soul is waiting for the Lord.
The Lord is our help and our shield.
21 Our hearts find joy in the Lord.
We trust in God's holy name.

22 May your love be upon us, O Lord,
as we place all our hope in you. (A & D)

45a **Response 1**

Glory be: see after Ps 33 (34) opposite

See the music editions for the full setting of the verses accompanying response 2.

Another setting of Psalm 32(33): *Happy the people the Lord has chosen (no 394)*

IWILL BLESS THE LORD AT ALL TIMES,
God's praise always on my lips;

3 in the Lord my soul shall make its boast.
The humble shall hear and be glad.

4 Glorify the Lord with me.
Together let us praise God's name.
5 I sought the Lord and was heard;
from all my terrors set free.

6 Look towards God and be radiant;
let your faces not be abashed.
7 When the poor cry out the Lord hears them
and rescues them from all their distress.

8 The angel of the Lord is encamped
around those who fear God, to rescue them.
9 Taste and see that the Lord is good.
They are happy who seek refuge in God.

10 Revere the Lord, you saints.
They lack nothing, who revere the Lord.
11 Strong lions suffer want and go hungry
but those who seek the Lord lack no blessing.

12 Come, children, and hear me
that I may teach you the fear of the Lord.

13 Who are those who long for life
and many days, to enjoy their prosperity?

14 Then keep your tongue from evil
and your lips from speaking deceit.
15 Turn aside from evil and do good;
seek and strive after peace.

16 The eyes of the Lord are toward the just
and his ears toward their appeal.
17 The face of the Lord rebuffs the wicked
to destroy their remembrance from the earth.

18 They call and the Lord hears
and rescues them in all their distress.
19 The Lord is close to the brokenhearted;
those whose spirit is crushed God will save.

20 Many are the trials of the upright
but the Lord will come to rescue them,
21 keeping guard over all their bones,
not one of their bones shall be broken.

22 Evil brings death to the wicked;
those who hate the good are doomed.
23 The Lord ransoms the souls of the faithful.
None who trust in God shall be condemned.

Give práise to the Fáther Almíghty,
to his Són, Jesus Chríst, the Lórd,
to the Spírit who dwélls in our héarts
both nów and for éver. Amén.

Response

Taste   and   see   that   the   Lord   is   good.

Psalmtone

Response by Francis Duffy (1914-2000). Psalmtone by Stephen Dean.

For Lent, Sunday 4C, sing vv. 2-7. For Ordinary Time, Common Psalm, and Ordinary Sunday 19B:
vv. 2-9. For Sunday 20B: vv. 2-3. 10-15. For Sunday 21B: vv. 2-3. 16-23

Other settings of Psalm 33 (34) *Taste and see (617 & 618), The cry of the poor (892)*

L IKE THE DÉER THAT YÉARNS
for rúnning stréams,
só my sóul is yéarning
for yóu, my Gód.

3 My sóul is thírsting for Gód
the Gód of my lífe;
whén can I énter and sée
the fáce of Gód?

4 My téars have becóme my bréad
by níght, by dáy,
as I héar it said áll the day lóng:
'Whére is your Gód?'

5 Thése things will Í remémber (†)
as I póur out my sóul:
how I would léad the rejóicing crówd (†)
into the hóuse of Gód,
amid críes of gládness and thanksgíving,
the thróng wild with jóy.

6 Why are you cast dówn, my sóul,
why gróan withín me?
Hope in Gód; I will práise yet agáin,
my sáviour and my Gód.

42 (43):3-5

O SÉND FORTH YOUR LÍGHT AND YOUR TRÚTH;
let thése be my gúide.
Let them bríng me to your hóly móuntain,
to the pláce where you dwéll.

4 And I will cóme to your áltar, O Gód,
the Gód of my jóy.
My redéemer, I will thánk you on the hárp,
O Gód, my Gód.

5 Whý are you cast dówn, my sóul,
why gróan withín me?
Hope in Gód; I will práise yet agáin,
my sáviour and my Gód.
Glory be: as after Ps 26 (27)

47a
Response 1
Like the deer that yearns for—— run - ning streams,
so my soul is year - ning for you, my—— God.

Psalmtone
Use underlinings in text.

47b
Response 2
My soul is thirst - ing for the Lord; when shall I see him face to face?—

Psalmtone
A   B   C   D
Use accents in text.

Other settings of these psalms: As the deer longs (214); Like as the deer (219); As longs the deer (450)

Text: The Grail; R.2 and psalmtone by Joseph Gelineau SJ © The Grail. R.1 and psalmtone by Fintan O'Carroll © 1982 ICMA

H AVE MÉRCY ON ME, GÓD, IN YOUR KÍNDNESS.
In your compássion blot óut my offénce.
4 O wásh me more and móre from my gúilt
and cléanse me fróm my sín.

5 My offénces trúly I knów them;
my sín is álways befóre me.
6 Against yóu, you alóne, have I sínned;
what is évil in your síght I have dóne.

That you may be jústified whén you
give séntence
and bé without repróach when you júdge,
7 O sée, in gúilt I was bórn,
a sínner was Í concéived.

8 Indéed you love trúth in the héart,
then in the sécret of my héart teach me
wísdom.
9 O púrify me, thén I shall be cléan;
O wásh me, I shall be whíter than snów.

10 Make me héar rejóicing and gládness
that the bónes you have crúshed may
revíve.
11 From my síns turn awáy your fáce
and blót out áll my gúilt.

12 A púre heart creáte for me, O Gód,
put a stéadfast spírit withín me.
13 Do not cást me awáy from your présence,
nor depríve me of your hóly spírit.

14 Give me agáin the jóy of your hélp;
with a spírit of férvour sustáin me,
15 that I may téach transgréssors your wáys
and sínners may retúrn to yóu.

16 O réscue me, Gód, my hélper,
and my tóngue shall ríng out your góodness.
17 O Lórd, ópen my líps
and my móuth shall decláre your práise.

18 For in sácrifice you táke no delíght,
burnt óffering from mé you would refúse;
19 my sácrifice, a cóntrite spírit,
a húmbled, contrite héart you will not spúrn.

20 In your góodness, show fávour to Zíon;
rebúild the wálls of Jerúsalem.
21 Thén you will be pléased with lawful
sácrifice,†
(burnt ófferings whólly consúmed),
then you will be óffered young búlls on
your áltar.

*Give práise to the Fáther Almíghty,
to his Són, Jesus Chríst, the Lórd,
to the Spírit who dwélls in our héarts
both nów and for éver. Amén.*

48a **Response 1**

A— pure heart cre - ate for me, O God.___

48b **Response 2**

Have mer-cy on us, O Lord, for we__ have sinned.

Psalmtone

Follow accents in the text. Underlinings are for use with a psalmtone such as that on p.27

Other settings of Psalm 50 (51) *Come back to the Lord (194); Give me a new heart (195)*

Text: The Grail; Psalmtone by Joseph Gelineau SJ © The Grail;. Responses 1 & 2 © Stephen Dean

Psalm 62 (63)

49

Response

My soul is thir- sting, my soul is thir- sting, my soul is thir- sting for

you, O Lord my God.

1. O God, you are my God whom I seek:
   O God, you are my God whom I seek:
   for you my flesh pines, my soul thirsts
        like the earth,
   parched, lifeless, without water.

2. Thus have I gazed toward you in your
        holy place
   to see your power and your glory.
   Your kindness is a greater good than life
        itself;
   my lips will glorify you.

3. Thus will I bless you while I live;
   lifting up my hands I will call upon
        your name.
   As with a banquet shall my soul be
        satisfied;
   with exultant lips my mouth shall praise
        you.

4. For you have been my help, you have
        been my help;
   in the shadow of your wings I shout for
        joy.
   My soul clings fast to you: your right
        hand holds me firm:
   in the shadow of your wings I sing for joy.

Text: Ps 63: 2.3-4.5-6.8-9 & Music: Michael Joncas, © 1987 G.I.A. Publications, Inc

Other settings of Psalm 62 (63): *O God, you are my God (4); Your love is finer than life (213).*

Psalm 83(84): *O how holy (454); O how lovely is your dwelling place (457)*

Psalm 84(85): 9-14

50

I WILL HEAR WHAT THE LORD HAS TO SAY,
  a voice that speaks of peace,
peace for his people and friends
    and those who turn to God in their hearts.
¹⁰ Salvation is near for thè God-fearing,
  and his glory will dwell in our land.

¹¹ Mercy and faithfulness have met;
  justice and peace have embraced.
¹² Faithfulness shall spring fròm the earth, and
  justice look down from heaven.
¹³ The Lord will make us prosper
  and our earth will yield its fruit.
¹⁴ Justice shall march in the forefront,
  and peace shall follow the way.

Response

Let us see, O Lord, your mer- cy and— give us your sa- ving help.

Psalmtone

Text © The Grail; Music © 1987 Alan Smith

Those who dwéll in the shélter of the
    Most Hígh
and abíde in the sháde of the Almíghty
2 sáy to the Lórd: 'My réfuge,
  my strónghold, my Gód in whom I trúst!'

3 It is Gód who will frée you from the snáre
  of the fówler who séeks to destróy you;
4 Gód will concéal you with his pínions,
  and únder his wíngs you will find réfuge.

5 You will not féar the térror of the níght
  nor the árrow that flíes by dáy,
6 nor the plágue that prówls in the dárkness
  nor the scóurge that lays wáste at nóon.

7 A thóusand may fáll at your síde,
  ten thóusand fáll at your ríght,
  yóu, it will néver appróach;
4c God's fáithfulness is búckler and shíeld.

8 Your éyes have ónly to lóok
  to sée how the wícked are repáid,
9 yóu who have sáid: 'Lord, my réfuge!'
  and have máde the Most Hígh your dwélling.

10 Upon yóu no évil shall fáll,
  no plágue appróach where you dwéll.
11 For yóu God has commánded the ángels,
  to kéep you in áll your wáys.

12 They shall béar you upón their hánds
  lest you stríke your fóot against a stóne.
13 On the líon and the víper you will tréad
  and trámple the young líon and the drágon.

14 You sét your love on mé so I will sáve you,
  protéct you for you knów my náme.
15 When you cáll I shall ánswer: 'I am wíth you,'
  I will sáve you in distréss and give you glóry.

16 With léngth of dáys I will contént you;
        Psalmtone 2: omit B and C
  I shall lét you sée my saving pówer.

Give práise to the Fáther Almíghty,
to his Són, Jesus Chríst, the Lórd,
to the Spírit who dwélls in our héarts
both nów and for éver. Amén.

51a Response 1

Be with me, O Lord, in my dis-tress.

Psalmtone 1   omit for v.16

Accents in the text are for use with this psalmtone, underlinings with the tone below

51b Response 2

My — re-fuge, my — strong-hold, my — God in whom I trust.

Psalmtone 2   A   B   C   D

For Lent Sunday 1C, Lent Common Psalm: sing vv. 1-2, 10-15

Other settings of Psalm 90 (91):
Night Prayer (31), On eagle's wings (952); Safe in the shadow of the Lord (953)

Psalm 94 (95)

COME, RÍNG OUT OUR JÓY TO THE LÓRD;
háil the róck who sáves us.

2 Let us cóme before Gód, givíng thánks,
with sóngs let us háil the Lórd.

3 A míghty Gód is the Lórd, †
a gréat king abóve all góds,

4 in whose hánds are the dépths of the éarth; †
the héights of the móuntains as wéll.

5 The séa belongs to Gód, who máde it
and the drý land sháped by his hánds.

6 Come ín; let us bów and bend lów;
let us knéel before the Gód who máde us

7 for thís is our Gód and wé †

the péople who belóng to his pásture,
the flóck that is léd by his hánd.

O that todáy you would lísten to Gód's vóice!

8 Hárden not your héarts as at Meríbah, †
as on that dáy at Mássah in the désert

9 when your áncestors pút me to the tést;
when they tríed me, though they sáw
my work.

10 For forty yéars I was wéaried of these péople
and I sáid: "Their héarts are astráy, †
these péople do not knów my wáys."

11 Thén I took an óath in my ánger:
Néver shall they énter my rést."'

52a R. 1 O that to-day you would lis-ten to his voice! Har-den not your_ hearts.

Psalmtone 1

52b R. 2 A migh - ty God is the Lord, come, let us a - dore him!

Psalmtone 2

omit for 4-line stanza

omit for 5-line st.

Other settings of Psalm 94 (95) *To God with gladness sing (3)* **Psalms 96-98:**

Psalm 99 (100)

CRY OUT WITH JÓY TO THE LÓRD, ALL THE ÉARTH.
Sérve the Lórd with gládness.
Come befóre God, sínging for jóy.

3 Knów that the Lórd is Gód,
Our Máker, to whóm we belóng.
We are God's péople, shéep of the flóck.

4 Énter the gátes with thanksgíving,
God's cóurts with sóngs of práise.
Give thánks to God and bléss his náme.

5 Indéed, how góod is the Lórd,
whose mérciful lóve is etérnal;
whose fáithfulness lásts foréver.

Response We are his peo-ple, the sheep of his flock; his peo-ple, the sheep of his flock.

Psalm 102 (103) — 54

M Y SOUL, GIVE THANKS TO THE LORD,
all my being, bless God's holy name.

2 My soul, give thanks to the Lord
and never forget all God's blessings.

3 It is God who forgives all your guilt, †
who heals every one of your ills,

4 who redeems your life from the grave, †
who crowns you with love and compassion,

5 who fills your life with good things,
renewing your youth like an eagle's.

6 The Lord does deeds of justice,
gives judgement for all who are oppressed.

7 The Lord's ways were made known to Moses
the Lord's deeds to Israel's children.

8 The Lord is compassion and love, †
slow to anger and rich in mercy.

9 The Lord will not always chide, †
will not be angry forever.

10 God does not treat us according to our sins
nor repay us according to our faults.

11 For as the heavens are high above the earth
so strong is God's love for the God-fearing,

12 As far as the east is from the west
so far does he remove our sins.

13 As parents have compassion on their children,
the Lord has pity on those who are
God-fearing

14 for he knows of what we are made,
and remembers that we are dust.

15 As for us, our days are like grass;
we flower like the flower of the field;

16 the wind blows and we are gone
and our place never sees us again.

17 But the love of the Lord is everlasting
upon those who fear the Lord.
God's justice reaches out to children's
children †

18 when they keep his covenant in truth,
when they keep his will in their mind.

19 The Lord has set his throne in heaven †
and his kingdom rules over all.

20 Give thanks to the Lord, all you angels,
mighty in power, fulfilling God's word,
who heed the voice of that word.

21 Give thanks to the Lord, all you hosts,
you servants who do God's will.

22 Give thanks to the Lord, all his works, †
in every place where God rules.
My soul, give thanks to the Lord!

Glory be: see after Ps 90 (91), no.51

Response

The__ Lord is com- pas - sion and__ love, slow to an - ger and rich in mer - cy.

Psalmtone

Psalm 114-5 (116)

(114)

ALLELUIA!
I love the Lord, for the Lord has heard
the cry of my appeal.

2 The Lord was attentive to me
in the day when I called.

3 They surrounded me, the snares of death,
with the anguish of the tomb;
they caught me, sorrow and distress.

4 I called on the Lord's name. †

O Lord, my God, deliver me!

5 How gracious is the Lord, and just;
our God has compassion.

6 The Lord protects the simple hearts;
I was helpless so God saved me.

7 Turn back, my soul, to your rest
for the Lord has been good,

8 and has kept my soul from death, †
(my eyes from tears,)
my feet from stumbling.

8 I will walk in the presence of the Lord
in the land of the living.   *(omit B, C)*

(115)

10 I trusted, even when I said:
'I am sorely afflicted,'

11 and when I said in my alarm:
'There is no one I can trust.'

12 How can I repay the Lord
for his goodness to me?

13 The cup of salvation I will raise;
I will call on the Lord's name.

14 My vows to the Lord I will fulfill
before all the people.

15 O precious in the eyes of the Lord
is the death of the faithful.

16 Your servant, Lord, your servant am I;
you have loosened my bonds.

17 A thanksgiving sacrifice I make;
I will call on the Lord's name.

18 My vows to the Lord I will fulfill
before all the people,

19 in the courts of the house of the Lord,
in your midst, O Jerusalem.

Praise the Fáther, the Són, and Holy Spírit,
both nów and for éver,
The God who ís, who wás, and who wíll be,
wórld without énd.

55

Response

I will walk in the presence of the Lord in the land of the li-ving.

Psalmtone

55a
Setting 2

Our blessing cup is a com-mu-nion with the blood of Christ;

and the bread we break, it is a sha-ring in the bo-dy of the Lord.

See music editions for verses

Other settings: *God, our fountain of salvation (459); How can I repay (619); Lord, how can I repay (620)*

Psalm 116 (117)   *Come praise the Lord (700); Praise the Lord (461); Holy is God (699)*

Psalm 117 (118)   *The stone which the builders (258); This is the day (257)*

Psalm 121 (122)   56

I REJOICED WHEN I HEARD THEM SAY:
  'Let us go to God's house.'
2 And now our feet are standing
  within your gates, O Jerusalem.

3 Jerusalem is built as a city
  strongly compact.
4 It is there that the tribes go up,
  the tribes of the Lord.

  For Israel's law it is,
  there to praise the Lord's name.
5 There were set the thrones of judgement
  of the house of David.

6 For the peace of Jerusalem pray:
  'Peace be to your homes!
7 May peace reign in your walls,
  in your palaces, peace.'

8 For love of my family and friends
  I say, 'Peace upon you.'
9 For love of the house of the Lord
  I will ask for your good.

  Praise the Fáther, the Són, and Holy Spírit,
  both nów and for éver,
  The God who ís, who wás, and who wíll be,
  wórld without énd.

I re-joiced when I heard— them say: Let us go to God's house.

Other settings of Psalm 121 (122):   *I rejoiced (992)*   Text © The Grail. Music by Fintan O'Carroll © 1982 ICMA

Psalm 125 (126)   57

WHEN THE LÓRD DELIVERED ZÍON from
      bóndage,
  it séemed like a dréam.
2 Thén was our móuth filled with láughter,
  on our líps there were sóngs.

  The héathens themsélves said: 'What márvels
  the Lórd worked for thém!'
3 What márvels the Lórd worked for ús!
  Indéed we were glád.

4 Delíver us, O Lórd, from our bóndage
  as stréams in dry lánd.
6 Thóse who are sówing in téars
  will síng when they réap.

6 They go óut, they go óut, full of téars,
  carrying séed for the sówing;
  they come báck, they come báck, full of sóng,
  cárrying their shéaves.

      Glory be: see after previous psalm

Responses 1 & 2

What mar - vels the Lord worked for us!— In - deed— we were glad.
⅞ Those who are so - wing in tears— will sing— when they reap.

Psalmtone

Text © The Grail; Music © Stephen Dean

Psalm 127 (128)

OBLESSED ARE YOU WHO FEAR THE LORD
and walk in God's ways!

2 By the labour of your hands you shall eat.
You will be happy and prosper;

3 your wife like a fruitful vine
in the heart of your house;
your children like shoots of the olive,
around your table.

4 Indeed thus shall be blessed
those who fear the Lord.

5 May the Lord bless you from Zion
5c all the days of your life!
6 May you see your children's children†
5b in a happy Jerusalem!

On Israel, peace!

Praise the Fáther, the Són, and Holy Spírit,
both nów and for éver,
The God who ís, who wás, and who wíll be,
wórld without énd.

omit bars 2-3 of psalmtone

O blessed are those who fear the Lord, and walk in his ways, O blessed are those who fear the Lord, and walk in his ways.

Text © The Grail; Music © 1981 P. Inwood, published by OCP. All rights reserved

Psalmtone *if through setting (see other editions) is not used*

omit in doxology

© Stephen Dean

Another setting of Psalm 127 (128):   *Blessed are those who love you (409)*

Psalm 129 (130) first setting

OUT OF THE DEPTHS I CRY TO YOU, O LORD,
2 Lord, hear my voice!
O let your ears be attentive
to the voice of my pleading.

3 If you, O Lord, should mark our guilt,
Lord, who would survive?
4 But with you is found forgiveness:
for this we revere you.

5 My soul is waiting for the Lord.
I count on God's word.
6 My soul is longing for the Lord
more than those who watch for daybreak.
(Let the watchers count on daybreak
7 and Israel on the Lord.)   *(repeat C+D)*

Because with the Lord there is mercy
and fullness of redemption,
8 Israel indeed God will redeem
from all its iniquity.

Response

Doxology as above

With the Lord there is mer - cy and ful-ness of re-demp-tion.

Psalmtone

Text © The Grail. Music by Fintan O'Carroll © 1982 ICMA

Other settings: 60 *opposite; Out of the depths (452); Out of the direst depths (207); Grant them eternal rest (439) (v.1)*

Psalm 129 (130) second setting

60

R. I place all my trust in you, my God, all my hope is in your sa-ving word.

Verses

1. Out of the depths   I   cry   to   you,   O   Lord,
2. If you, O Lord,   should mark   our   guilt,
3. My   soul   is wai-ting for the Lord.
4. Be - cause   with the Lord   there is mercy
   To the   Fa - ther   Al - mighty   give   glory,

Lord,   hear my   voice!   O   let   your
Lord, who would sur - vive?   But with you   is
I   count   on God's word.   My   soul   is
and fullness   of   re - demption,   Israel   in -
give   glo - ry   to   his   Son,   to the   Spirit   most

ears   be   at - tentive   to the voice   of my   plea - ding.
found   for - giveness: for   this   we re - vere   you.
long - ing for   the Lord   more than watch - man for day - break.
deed God will   re - deem   from   all   its   i - ni - quity.
Holy   give   praise,   whose   reign   is for   e - ver.

Words and music by Joseph Gelineau SJ © 1959 The Grail

Psalm 131 (132)   *Like a child rests (453), My soul is longing (950)*
Psalm 132 (133)   *O come, bless the Lord (35, 36)*

Psalm 135 (136)

61

1. O   give   thanks   to   the   LORD   who   is   good,
2. Who   a - lone   has wrought   mar - vel - lous   works,
3. It   was   God   who   made   the   great   lights,
4. The   first - born   of   the   E - gyp - tians   God   smote,
5. God   di - vided   the   Red   Sea   in   two,
6. Through the   de - sert   the   peo - ple   God   led,
7. God   let   Israel   in - he - rit   their   land,
8. And   God   snatched   us   a - way   from   our   foes,

Great   is   God's   love,   love   with - out   end;

Give thanks to the God_____ of gods,
whose wisdom it was made the skies,
the sun to rule in the day,
and brought Israel out from their midst,
and made Israel pass through the midst,
Nations in their great - ness God struck,
the heritage of Is - rael, God's servant;
God gives food to all li - ving things,

Great is God's love, love with - out end;

Give thanks to the Lord_____ of lords,
who fixed the earth firmly on the seas,
the moon and stars in the night,
arm out-stretched, with po - wer - ful hand,
Who flung Pharoah and his force in the sea,
Kings in their splen - dour God slew,
God re - mem - bered us in our dis - tress,
to the God of hea - ven give thanks.

Great is God's love, love with - out end.

Psalm 136 (137)   *By the waters (216)*   Words and music by Joseph Gelineau SJ © 1959 The Grail

Psalm 137 (138)   62

I   Lord, may our prayer___ rise like in-cense in your sight, may this
II In the___ pre-sence of the an - gels, O Lord, may we
III Lord, on the day___ that I called___ out for help, you___

place be___ filled with the fra-grance of Christ.
praise your___ name, may we praise___ your name.
an - swered me, you___ an - swered me.

1 I will thank you, Lord, with all of my heart,
   you have heard the words of my mouth.
   In the presence of the angels I will bless you,
   I will adore before your holy temple.

2 I will thank you, Lord,
   for your faithfulness and love
   beyond all my hopes and dreams.

On the day that I called you answered;
you gave life to the strength of my soul.

3 All who live on earth shall give you thanks
   when they hear the words of your voice.
   And all shall sing of your ways:
   'How great is the glory of God!'
   Psalm 138:1-5, David Haas

Psalm 138 (139)   *O God, you search me (779); O Lord, I know you are near (777);*
You know me, Lord (778)

Psalm 140 (141)   *Let my prayer rise (17, 18)*

Psalm 144 (145)

63

I WILL GIVE YOU GLÓRY, O GÓD MY KÍNG,
I will bléss your náme for éver.   *(omit B, C)*

2 I will bléss you dáy after dáy
and práise your náme for éver.

3 You are gréat, Lord, híghly to be práised,
your gréatness cánnot be méasured.

4 Age to áge shall procláim your wórks,
shall decláre your míghty déeds,

5 shall spéak of your spléndour and glóry,
tell the tále of your wónderful wórks.

6 They will spéak of your térrible déeds,
recóunt your gréatness and míght.

7 They will recáll your abúndant góodness;
age to áge shall ríng out your jústice.

8 You are kínd and fúll of compássion,
slow to ánger, abóunding in lóve.

9 How góod you are, Lórd, to áll,
compássionate to áll your créatures.

10 All your créatures shall thánk you, O Lórd,
and your fríends shall repéat their bléssing.

11 They shall spéak of the glóry of your réign
and decláre your míght, O Gód,

12 to make knówn to áll your mighty déeds
and the glórious spléndour of your réign.

13 Yóurs is an éverlasting kíngdom;
your rúle lasts from áge to áge.

You are fáithful in áll your wórds
and lóving in áll your déeds.

14 You suppórt all thóse who are fálling
and ráise up áll who are bowed dówn.

15 The éyes of all créatures look to yóu
and you gíve them their fóod in due séason.

16 You ópen wíde your hánd,
grant the desíres of áll who líve.

17 You are júst in áll your wáys
and lóving in áll your déeds.

18 You are clóse to áll who cáll you,
who cáll on yóu from their héarts.

19 You gránt the desíres of thóse who féar you,
you héar their cry´ and you sáve them.

20 Lórd, you protéct all who lóve you;
but the wícked you will útterly destróy.

21 Let me spéak your práise, O Lórd,
let all péoples bléss your holy náme
for éver, for áges unénding.   *(omit C)*

Glory be: see after Ps 90 (91), no.51

Text © The Grail. R.1 & Psalm by A. Gregory Murray OSB © McCrimmon Publishing Co. Ltd. R.2 & Psalm © S. Dean

Ps 145(146) God my King (702); Ps 147 Fill your hearts (703); Ps 148 O praise ye (406);
Pss 149-50 Bring to the Lord (705); Ps 150 see nos. 5-6

The Seasons: Advent

Advent Seasonal Music: 64-80
(Advent hymns: 81-117)

64 Litany of the Word

Bernadette Farrell

1. *Word of jus - tice,   Al - le - lu - ia,   Come to dwell here.   Ma - ra - na - tha!*

2 Word of mercy, ...
   live among us, ...
3 Word of power, ...
   live within us, ...
4 Word of freedom, ...
   save your people.
5 Word of healing, ...
   heal our sorrow.
6 Word of comfort, ...
   bring us hope now, ...

7 Word of gladness, ...
   fill our hearts now, ...
8 Word of wisdom, ...
   Come renew us, ...
9 Word we long for, ...
   word we thirst for, ...
10 Key of David, ...
   Son of Mary, ...
11 Promised Saviour, ...
   True Messiah, ...

12 Cry of prophets, ...
   hope of ages, ...
13 Light of nations, ...
   light in darkness, ...
14 Risen Saviour, ...
   Lord of glory, ...
15 You we long for, ...
   you we thirst for, ...
16 Here among us, ...
   living in us, ...

65 Advent Wreath Service

John Schiavone

After the priest's greeting and introduction, he or another minister lights one candle on the Wreath while the cantor or choir sing the first invocation, ending with:

1st: Cantor. 2nd: All

Ky - ri - e,   e - lei - son.
(Lord,____   have   mer - cy.)

After the second invocation:

1st: Cantor. 2nd: All

Chris - te,   e - lei - son.
(Christ,____   have   mer - cy).

After the third invocation Lord, have mercy *is sung, as above. Then the priest gives the Absolution.*

66 Advent Kyrie 1

Missa Emmanuel:Plainsong, arr. Richard Proulx

Each phrase: first time Cantor, repeated by all.

Lord,____ have_ mer-cy. Christ,____ have_ mer - cy.____
Lord,____ have_ mer-cy. Christ,____ have_ mer - cy.____

Repeat: Lord, have mercy....

67 Advent Kyrie 2

Short Mass for Advent & Lent, Stephen Dean

In Penitential Act 3, The Priest, or a Deacon or another minister, sings an invocation before each phrase.

Cantor sings, all repeat

Ky - ri - e, e - le - i - son.   Chris - te, e - le - i - son.
Ky - ri - e, e - le - i - son.   Chris - te, e - le - i - son.

Repeat: Kyrie, eleison

Absolution (Penitential Act 3)

May almighty God have mercy on us,
forgive us our sins,
and bring us to everlasting life.

All (or Cantor then All):

A - men.

Common Responsorial Psalms: *Psalm 24(25), no. 43 ; psalm 84 (85), no. 50*

68 Gospel Acclamation 1 for Advent

Ken Simmons

Refrain

Je - sus is Lord, al - le - lu - ia!   Je - sus shall come, Al - le - lu - ia!

Verses

Cantor   **All**

Pre - pare a way for the Lord.   Je - sus shall come, Al - le - lu - ia!

Cantor   **All**

Make straight the path for him.   Je - sus shall come, Al - le - lu - ia!

Repeat Refrain

69 Gospel Acclamation 2 for Advent

Michael Joncas

Hal - le - lu - ia, hal - le - lu - ia, hal - le - lu - ia, hal - le - lu - ia.

70 Gospel Acclamation 3 for Advent

Howard Hughes

Repeat each phrase after the Cantor

Al - le - lu - ia.   Al - le - lu - ia.   Al - le - lu - ia.

71 Gospel Acclamation 4 for Advent *Christopher Walker*

Al - le - lu - ia, al - le - lu - ia, Al - le - lu - ia, al - le - lu - ia.

72 Advent Gospel Acclamation for younger people *Christopher Walker*

1. Stay a-wake, be_ rea-dy, you do not know the hour when the
Lord is coming. Stay a-wake, be_ rea-dy, the Lord is coming soon!
Al - le - lu - ia, al - le - lu - ia, the Lord is co-ming_ soon.

2a/b, 3c   Change your lives, he's coming,
    the one who will baptise with the Holy Spirit.
    Change your lives, he's coming,   *(3c: to * below)*
    the Lord is coming soon!
    Alleluia, alleluia, the Lord is coming soon.

2c. Prepare! He's coming!
    The one who will give peace to the world is coming.
    Prepare! He's coming!
    * *(+ 3c)* The reign of God is near.
    Alleluia, alleluia! 'The reign of God is near.'

3a. Go back, tell John
    all that you have heard and seen me doing.
    Go back, tell John
    the wonders that you see!
    Alleluia, alleluia! 'The wonders that you see.'

3b. Change your lives, he's coming,
    the one who is the light of the world is coming.
    Change your lives, he's coming,
    the Lord is coming soon!
    Alleluia, alleluia! 'The Lord is coming soon.'

4a/b. By the pow'r of the Spirit,
    Mary will give birth to a son called Jesus.
    By the pow'r of the Spirit,
    Emmanuel is near.
    Alleluia, alleluia! 'Emmanuel is near.'

4c. You are blessed among women.
    Mary you are blessed, you believe God's promise.
    You are blessed among women,
    the mother of my Lord.
    Alleluia, alleluia! 'The Mother of my Lord.'

73 General Intercessions Response for Advent *Christopher Walker*

We pray to the Lord. Come, Lord Je - sus, ma - ra - na-tha!___

➤ *see also no 26*

74 **Eucharistic Acclamations: Holy, Holy, Holy** *Stephen Dean*

Ho - ly,— Ho - ly, Ho-ly Lord— God of hosts, heav'n and earth are

full of your glo - ry. Ho - san - na in the highest, ho -

san-na in the high-est. Blessed is he who comes in the name— of the

Lord. Ho - san - na in the high-est, ho - san-na in the high-est!

75a **Memorial Acclamation 1**

We pro-claim your Death, O Lord, and pro -

fess your Re - sur - rec - tion, and pro - fess your Re - sur -

rec - tion un - til you come a - gain, un - til you come a - gain.

75b **Memorial Acclamation 2**

When we eat this Bread and drink this— Cup, we pro - claim your Death, O

Lord, un - til you come a - gain, un - til you come a - gain.

75c **Memorial Acclamation 3**

Save— us, Sa - viour of the world, for by your

Cross and Re-sur-rec-tion, for by your Cross and Re-sur-rec-tion you have set us free, you have set us free.

76 Amen

A - men, a - men, a - men.

May be sung twice.

77
Lamb of God

Lamb of God, you take a-way the sins of the world,

1, 2
have mer-cy on us, have mer-cy on us.

Last time
grant us peace, grant us peace.

78 Advent Communion Song 1

Bernadette Farrell

Refrain
Bread of life, hope of the world, Je-sus Christ, our bro - ther:

feed us now, give us life, lead us to one a - no-ther.

Advent Verses 1. Be with your peo - ple, Lord, send us your sa - ving Word;
2. Bring to our world of fear the truth we long to hear;

Je-sus Christ, light of glad - ness, come a-mong us now.
Je-sus Christ, hope of a - ges, come to save us now.

Additional verses overleaf

Christmas verses

1 A child is born for us,
  a son is given to us,
  in our midst, Christ, our Lord
    and God
  comes as one who serves.

2 With our own eyes we see,
  with our own ears we hear
  the salvation of all the world,
  God's incarnate Word.

3 You are the hope of all,
  our promise and our call,
  radiant light in our darkness,
  truth to set us free.

Lent verses

1 Our hunger for your Word,
  our thirsting for your truth,
  are the sign of your life in us
  till we rest in you.

2 To those whose eyes
    are blind
  you give a light to see;
  dawn of hope in the
    midst of pain,
  love which sets us free.

General verses

1 As we proclaim your death,
  as we recall your life,
  we remember your promise
  to return again.

2 The bread we break and share
  was scattered once as grain;
  just as now it is gathered,
  make your people one.

3 We eat this living bread,
  we drink this saving cup:
  sign of hope in our broken
    world,
  source of lasting love.

4 Hold us in unity,
  in love for all to see;
  that the world may believe
    in you,
  God of all who live.

5 You are the bread of peace,
  you are the wine of joy,
  broken now for your people,
  poured in endless love.
            Bernadette Farrell

79 **Advent Communion Song 2**   *Stephen Dean*

Come, O come, Lord Je-sus;— come, O come, Lord Je-sus;—
come, O come, Lord Je-sus;— Come, Lord Je-sus, quick-ly come.

The refrain is sung continuously. Cantor verses are added ad lib.

1 You, Lord, have spread a banquet for us,
  you, Lord, have spread a banquet for us,
  you, Lord, have spread a banquet for us,
  Come, Lord Jesus, quickly come.

2 You, Lord, have showered gifts upon us...

3 Your day will dawn in peace and justice...
4 Your day will see all sorrow banished...
5 Darkness will flee away for ever...
6 Come, Lord, into our hearts and heal us...
7 Join us in hope and love together...

80 **Advent Comm. Song 3**
Marty Haugen

God of our jour-neys, day-break to night;
lead us to jus-tice and light.___ Grant us com-passion,
strength for the day, wis-dom to walk in your way.___

Verses: see Now in this banquet *(623). Another refrain:* Lord, you can open *(192)*

81

Come to set us free, come to make us your own.— Come to show the
way to your peo-ple, your cho - sen.— O-pen our lives— to the light
of your pro - mise.— Come to our hearts— with hea - ling,
come to our minds with po-wer, come to us and bring us your life.—

Verse

1 You are light which shines in dark-ness, Mor-ning Star which ne - ver sets.
O-pen our eyes which on - ly dim-ly see the truth which sets us free.

2 You are hope which brings us courage,
you are strength which never fails.
Open our minds to ways we do not know,
but where your Spirit grows.

3 You are promise of salvation,
you are God in human form.
Bring to our world of emptiness and fear
the Word we long to hear.

Bernadette Farrell

82

1 Bright and clear, as a trum-pet blast, a her— -ald shout goes out:
2 Take your stand on a lof - ty place, Mes—sen - ger of God.

drive a path through the wil - der-ness, a high-way for our God;
Shout, O shout with a voice of joy, cast all fear a - side.

hills and moun-tains to be laid low, the val - ley lif - ted high,
Say to all in Je - ru - sa - lem, the ci - ty of the Lord:

ev' - ry na - tion and land shall see the glo - ry of our God.
Look a - round you, the hour has come: See, here is your God.

Refrain opposite

Refrain

Come, Lord, to a world of lon - ging, lis - ten to cre - a-tion's cry;
An - swer na-ture's dee - pest year-ning; ma - ni - fest God's reign.
Come, Lord, shi-ning star of mor-ning, rise up, scat-ter death's dark shade.
Come, Lord, migh - ty King E - ter - nal! Je - sus, Em-ma - nu - el!

3 See, he comes in pow'r and might, Master of all things.
See, the Lord of Victories, he the King of Kings.
Shepherd-like he will feed his flock and take them to his arms,
leading them to a place of rest, Saviour, King and God.   *Peter McGrail*

83

1 Blest be the Lord, the God of Israel,
who brings the dawn and darkest night dispels,
who raises up a mighty saviour from the earth,
of David's line, a son of royal birth.

2 The prophets tell a story just begun
of vanquished foe and glorious vict'ry won,
of promise made to all who keep the law
as guide:
God's faithful love and mercy will abide.

3 This is the oath once sworn to Abraham:
all shall be free to dwell upon the land,
free now to praise, unharmed by the
oppressor's rod,
holy and righteous in the sight of God.

4 And you, my child, this day you shall be called
the promised one, the prophet of our God,
for you will go before the Lord to clear the way,
and shepherd all into the light of day.

5 The tender love God promised from our birth
is soon to dawn upon this shadowed earth,
to shine on those whose sorrows seem to
never cease,
to guide our feet into the path of peace.
The Benedictus (Luke 1:68-79), Owen Alstott

84

1 Like a sea without a shore
love divine is boundless.
God is now and evermore
and his love surrounds us.
Maranatha! Maranatha!
Maranatha!
Come, Lord Jesus, come!

2 So that we could all be free
he appeared among us,
blest are those who have not seen,
yet believe his promise.

3 All our visions, all our dreams,
are but ghostly shadows
of the radiant clarity
waiting at life's close.

4 Death where is your victory?
Death where is your sting?
Closer than the air we breathe
is our risen King.
Estelle White (1926-2011)

➤ *Melody for no. 83: see no. 338*

85

1 Before the earth had yet begun
her journey round the burning sun,
before a seed of life had stirred,
there sounded God's creating word.

2 In that bright dawning of the world,
ere ocean surged or wind unfurled,
the vaults of heaven with praises rang,
the morning stars together sang.

3 Thus when creation's Lord did take
the clay of earth our form to make,
God willed that to our race belong
the gifts of music, word, and song.

4 For us who would this God attend,
no earthly mind can comprehend
Eternal glory; praise alone
is our companion by that throne.
Herbert O'Driscoll

86

1 God is working his purpose out
as year succeeds to year,
God is working his purpose out
and the time is drawing near;
nearer and nearer draws the time,
the time that shall surely be,
when the earth shall be filled with the
glory of God
as the waters cover the sea.

2 From utmost east to utmost west
where human foot hath trod,
by the mouth of many messengers
goes forth the voice of God.
'Give ear to me, ye continents,
ye isles give ear to me,
that the earth may be filled with the
glory of God
as the waters cover the sea.'

3 What can we do to work God's work,
to prosper and increase
the friendship of all humankind,
the reign of the Prince of Peace?

What can we do to hasten the time,
the time that shall surely be,
when the earth shall be filled with the
glory of God
as the waters cover the sea?

4 March we forth in the strength of God
with the banner of Christ unfurled,
that the light of the glorious Gospel of
truth may shine throughout the world.
Fight we the fight with sorrow and sin,
to set their captives free,
that the earth may be filled with the
glory of God
as the waters cover the sea.

5 All we can do is nothing worth
unless God blesses the deed;
vainly we hope for the harvest–tide
till God gives life to the seed;
yet nearer and nearer draws the time,
the time that shall surely be,
when the earth shall be filled with the
glory of God
as the waters cover the sea.
A. C. Ainger (1841–1919)

87

1 Creator of the stars of night
the people's everlasting light,
Redeemer, Saviour of us all
O hear your servants when they call.

2 As once through Mary's flesh you came
to save us from our sin and shame,
so now, Redeemer, by your grace,
come heal again our fallen race.

3 And when on that last judgment day
we rise to glory from decay,
then come again, O Saviour blest,
and bring us to eternal rest.

4 To God the Father, God the Son,
and God the Spirit, three in one,
Praise, honour, might and glory be
from age to age eternally.
Irwin Udulutsch, O.F.M. Cap., from
Conditor alme siderum *(9th C.)*

Taizé chant by Jacques Berthier

Wait for the Lord, whose day is near. Wait for the Lord, keep watch, take heart.

89

1 Keep on looking, go on seeking,
don't stop hoping, He will come.
Keep awake now, watch and pray now,
trust and see that He will come.
Shake off slumber, dawn is breaking,
come with full expectancy!
Years of longing, years of hoping,
all fulfilled when He will come.

2 Blessed angels, saints and sinners,
all rejoice to see this day.
Poor or wealthy, high or lowly,
all must help to clear His way.
Down among us He has chosen
here to taste our cup of life;
Who would guess that He'd be coming
here to share both joy and strife?

3 Hearts will wonder, eyes must open,
ears shall catch his every word;
words of thunder, words of wisdom,
words like these were never heard.
Through the ages we've been waiting,
countless prayers above did fly;
Now he's coming down among us,
here to live and here to die.
Willard F. Jabusch

90

1 When the King shall come again
all his power revealing,
splendour shall announce his reign,
life and joy and healing:
earth no longer in decay,
hope no more frustrated;
this is God's redemption day
longingly awaited.

2 In the desert trees take root
fresh from his creation;
plants and flowers and sweetest fruit
join the celebration:
rivers spring up from the earth,
barren lands adorning;
valleys, this is your new birth,
mountains, greet the morning!

3 Strengthen feeble hands and knees,
fainting hearts, be cheerful!
God who comes for such as these
seeks and saves the fearful:
now the deaf can hear the dumb
sing away their weeping;
blind eyes see the injured come
walking, running, leaping.

4 There God's highway shall be seen
where no roaring lion,
nothing evil or unclean
walks the road to Zion:
ransomed people homeward bound
all your praises voicing,
see your Lord with glory crowned,
share in his rejoicing!
Christopher Idle

91

1 'Wake, awake! For night is dying,'
the watchmen on the heights are crying,
'Awake, Jerusalem, at last!'
Midnight hears the welcome voices,
and at the thrilling cry rejoices:
'Come forth, you virgins, night is past;
the bridegroom comes; awake,
your lamps with gladness take, alleluia!
And for his marriage feast prepare,
for you must go to meet him there.'

2 Sion hears the watchmen singing,
and all her heart with joy is springing;
she wakes, she rises from her gloom:
for her Lord comes down all-glorious,
the strong in grace, in truth victorious;
her star is risen, her light is come.
Now come, O blessed one,
God's own beloved Son; alleluia!
We follow to the festal hall
to feast with you, the Lord of all.

3 Now let earth and heaven adore you,
as men and angels sing before you
with harp and cymbal's joyful tone;
of one pearl each shining portal,
where we join with the choirs immortal
of angels round your dazzling throne.
No eye has seen, nor ear
is yet attuned to hear such great glory;
alleluia, as here we sing
our praise to you, eternal King!
Philipp Nicolai (1556-1608),
tr. Catherine Winkworth (1827-78), alt.

92

1 Hark! a herald voice is calling;
'Christ is nigh!' it seems to say;
'Cast away the dreams of darkness,
waken, children of the day!'

2 Startled at the solemn warning,
let the earth–bound soul arise;
Christ her Sun, all sloth dispelling,
shines upon the morning skies.

3 Lo! the Lamb so long expected,
comes with pardon down from heaven;
let us meet him with repentance,
pray that we may be forgiven.

4 So when next he comes with glory,
wrapping all the earth in fear,
may he then as our Defender
on the clouds of heav'n appear.

5 Honour, glory, praise and blessing,
to the Father and the Son,
with the everlasting Spirit,
while unending ages run.
6th C., tr. E.Caswall (1814–78), alt.

93

Christmas is coming,
the Church is glad to sing,
and let the Advent candles
brightly burn in a ring.

1 The first is for God's promise
to put the wrong things right,
and bring to earth's darkness
the hope of love and light.

2 The second for the prophets,
who said that Christ would come
with good news for many
and angry words for some.

3 The third is for the Baptist,
who cried, 'Prepare the way.
Be ready for Jesus,
both this and every day.'

4 The fourth is for the Virgin,
who mothered God's own son
and sang how God's justice
was meant for everyone.

5 At last we light the candle
kept new for Christmas day,
This shines bright for Jesus,
new-born, and here to stay.

Christ is among us.
The candles in the ring
remind us that our Saviour
will light up everything.
John L. Bell

➤ *See also The Lord's coming (982-989); I rejoiced (992)*

94

1. On Jordan's bank the Baptist's cry
announces that the Lord is nigh;
come then and hearken, for he brings
glad tidings from the King of kings.

2. Then cleansed be every Christian breast,
and furnished for so great a guest!
Yea, let us each our heart prepare,
for Christ to come and enter there.

3. For thou art our salvation, Lord,
our refuge and our great reward;
without thy grace our souls must fade,
and wither like a flower decayed.

4. Stretch forth thy hand to heal our sore,
and make us rise, to fall no more;
once more upon thy people shine,
and fill the world with love divine.

5. All praise, eternal Son, to thee
whose advent sets thy people free,
whom, with the Father, we adore,
and Holy Ghost, for evermore.

Charles Coffin (1676–1749), tr. John Chandler (1808–76)

95

Come Sa - viour, come like dew on the grass;___ break
Ro - ra - te cae - li de - su - per___ et

through the clouds___ like gen - tle rain.
nu - bes plu - ant jus - tum.

1. Be angry, Lord, no more with us;
remember no longer our transgression.
See the city of God laid waste and desolate:
Zion is turned to wilderness,
Jerusalem, ravaged and ruined,
your dwelling place and the Holy of holies,
the house of your glory;
silent are those voices now
that once proclaimed your praise.

2. We have gone astray;
in the multitude of our sins
we have been made unclean,
fallen, fallen,
stricken as the leaves of autumn.
The stormwind carries us away,
the tempest of our evil deeds;
you have turned away from us
the face of your mercy,
and our iniquity has crushed us
like a potter's vessel.

3. O Lord our God, look upon your people
in their affliction:
be mindful of your promises.
Send us the Lamb who will
set up his dominion
from the Rock of the Wilderness to Zion
throned on her mountain.
There is no other whose power
can break our chains and set us free.

4. Be comforted, be comforted,
take heart, my people:
you shall quickly see your salvation.
Why do you waste yourself with grief,
though you have walked so long
    with sorrow?
I am your Saviour, be afraid no more.
For am I not God,
the Lord your God whom you worship,
the Holy One of Israel,
come to redeem you?

Latin, 10th C., tr. Luke Connaughton (1919-76)

96

1 Console my people, the ones dear to me;
speak to the heart of Jerusalem:
the time of your mourning is ended now,
the Lord of life will come.

A voice cries out in the wil-der-ness: Pre-pare a way for the Lord!

A voice cries out in the wil-der-ness: Make straight a high-way for God!

2 Ev'ry valley is made a plain,
ev'ry mountain is levelled;
the glory of God shall then be revealed,
and the nations will sing in praise.

3 A voice shouts: 'Cry!' O what shall I cry?
All flesh is like grass and its flowers;
the grass may wither, the flowers may fade,
but the Word of the Lord is forever.

4 Zion, shout from the mountain-top,
lift up your voice, O Jerusalem,
and say to the people of God's own land,
'Behold, behold your God!'

5 The Lord will appear as a shepherd,
holding his lambs in his arms,
keeping his flock so close to his heart,
leading them all, old and young.
Michael Joncas, based on Isaiah 40:1-11

97

1 Comfort, comfort, now my people,
Speak of peace - so says your God;
comfort all who sit in darkness,
burdened by a heavy load.
To Jerusalem proclaim:
God will take away your shame.
Now get ready to recover,
guilt and suffering are over.

2 Hear the herald's proclamation
in the desert far and near,
calling all to true repentance,
telling that the Lord is near.
Oh, that warning cry obey!
For your God prepare a way.
Let the valleys rise to greet him
and the hills bow down to meet him.

3 Straighten out what has been crooked,
make the roughest places plain;
Let your hearts be true and humble,
as befits God's holy reign.
Soon the glory of the Lord
shall on earth be shed abroad;
Human flesh shall surely see it;
God is ready to decree it.
Is 40:1-8; J. Olearius (1611-84);
tr. Catherine Winkworth (1827-78), altered by John L. Bell

98

Be-hold the Lamb of God,— who comes to take our sins a-way, to bind the bro-ken heart,— and set the captives free:— his king-dom will not end,— his mer-cy will not fal - ter. He comes, the hope of a - ges, the joy of all the world.

Stephen Dean

1 Hear ye the voice:
'Prepare a way for one who comes!'
Make straight his paths,
the Saviour comes with power to heal.

2 Speak to my flock:
'Your time of woe is ended.'

Shout from the heights,
'Jerusalem, your God is near!'

3 See from the heavens,
the Spirit comes to rest on him.
God's voice resounds:
'Behold my well-beloved Son.'

99

1 O comfort my people and calm all their fear,
and tell them the time of salvation draws near.
O tell them I come to remove all their shame.
Then they will forever give praise to my name.

2 Proclaim to the cities of Juda my word:
that gentle yet strong is the hand of the Lord.
I rescue the captives, my people defend
and bring them to justice and joy without end.

3 All mountains and hills shall become as a plain
for vanished are mourning and hunger and pain.
And never again shall these war against you.
Behold I come quickly to make all things new.

Chrysogonus Waddell OCSO (1930-2008), froms Isaiah 40:1-2.4.9

100

1 Come, thou long–expected Jesus,
born to set thy people free,
from our fears and sins release us,
let us find our rest in thee.

2 Israel's strength and consolation,
hope of all the earth thou art;
dear desire of every nation,
joy of every longing heart.

3 Born thy people to deliver,
born a child and yet a king,
born to reign in us for ever,
now thy gracious kingdom bring.

4 By thine own eternal Spirit
rule in all our hearts alone;
by thine all–sufficient merit
raise us to thy glorious throne.

Charles Wesley (1707–88)

101

1 Now watch for God's coming, be
   patient till then;
  like sunshine he'll brighten all women
   and men;
  who hope in the Lord will possess
   fertile land;
  the poor he will welcome and grasp
   by the hand.

2 Our steps are directed, God watches
   our path;
  he guides us and holds us and saves us
   from wrath,
  and though we may fall we will not go
   headlong,
  for God gives sound footing and keeps
   us from wrong.

3 So wait for his coming, be patient
   till then;
  the wicked are armed and would kill
   honest men.
  Their arms shall be broken, no refuge
   they'll see,
  but saved are the needy by God's
   own decree.

4 Now those who do evil will wither
   like grass,
  like green of the springtime they fade
   and they pass,
  so trust in the Lord and to him give
   your life,
  he'll bring heart's desires and peace in
   our strife.
  Willard F. Jabusch

102

1 Hail to the Lord's anointed!
  Great David's greater son!
  Hail, in the time appointed,
  his reign on earth begun!
  He comes to break oppression,
  to set the captive free;
  to take away transgression,
  and rule in equity.

2 He shall come down like showers
  upon the fruitful earth,
  and love, joy, hope, like flowers,
  spring in his path to birth:
  before him on the mountains
  shall peace the herald go;
  and righteousness in fountains
  from hill to valley flow.

3 Kings shall fall down before him,
  and gold and incense bring;
  all nations shall adore him,
  his praise all people sing;
  to him shall prayer unceasing
  and daily vows ascend;
  his kingdom still increasing
  a kingdom without end.

4 O'er every foe victorious,
  he on his throne shall rest,
  from age to age more glorious,
  all–blessing and all–blest;
  the tide of time shall never
  his covenant remove;
  his name shall stand for ever;
  that name to us is love.
  James Montgomery (1771–1854)

103

1 Promised Lord, and Christ is he,
  may we soon his kingdom see.
  Come, O Lord, speedily;
  come in glory, come in glory,
  come in glory, speedily.

2 Teaching, healing once was he,
  may we soon his kingdom see.

3 Dead and buried once was he,
  may we soon his kingdom see.

4 Risen from the dead is he,
  may we soon his kingdom see.

5 Soon to come again is he,
  may we soon his kingdom see.
  Come, O Lord, speedily,
  in our lifetime, in our lifetime,
  in our lifetime may it be.
  Roger Ruston, based on a Passover song

104

Fling wide the gates, un-bar the an-cient doors; sa-lute your king in his tri-um-phant cause!

1 Now all the world belongs to Christ our
      Lord:
   let all creation greet the living Word!

2 Who has the right to worship him today?
   All those who gladly serve him and obey.

   Michael Perry (1942-96) from Psalm 24

3 He comes to save all those who trust
      his name,
   and will declare them free from guilt
      and shame.

4 Who is the victor glorious from the fight?
   He is our King, our life, our Lord, our
      right!

105

1 Lift up your heads, you mighty gates;
   behold the King of glory waits!
   The King of kings is drawing near;
   the Saviour of the world is here.

2 O blest the land, the city blest,
   where Christ the ruler is confessed!
   O happy hearts and happy homes
   to whom this King of triumph comes!

3 Fling wide the portals of your heart;
   make it a temple, set apart
   from earthly use for heav'n's employ,
   adorned with prayer and love and joy.

4 So come, my Sovereign, enter in!
   Let new and nobler life begin;
   your Holy Spirit guide us on,
   until the glorious crown be won.
      George Weissel (1590-1635),
      tr. Catherine Winkworth (1827–1878), alt

106

1 The King shall come when morning dawns
   and light triumphant breaks,
   when beauty gilds the eastern hills
   and life to joy awakes.

2 Not as of old a little child,
   to bear and fight and die,
   but crowned with glory like the sun
   that lights the morning sky.

3 O brighter than the rising morn
   when he, victorious, rose,
   and left the lonesome place of death,
   despite the rage of foes.

4 O brighter than the glorious morn
   shall this fair morning be,
   when Christ our King in beauty comes,
   and we his face shall see!

5 The King shall come when morning dawns
   and light and beauty brings;
   'Hail, Christ the Lord!' your people pray,
   'Come quickly, King of kings!'
      John Brownlie (1859–1925)

107

The King of glory comes, the nation
*   rejoices,*
open the gates before him, lift up your
*   voices.*

1 Who is the King of glory
   how shall we call him?
   He is Emmanuel,
   the promised of ages.

2 In all of Galilee,
   in city and village,
   he goes among his people,
   curing their illness.

3 Sing then of David's Son,
   our Saviour and brother;
   in all of Galilee
   was never another.

4 He gave his life for us,
   the pledge of salvation.
   He took upon himself
   the sins of the nation.

5 He conquered sin and death;
   he truly has risen.
   And he will share with us
   his heavenly vision.
            Willard F. Jabusch

108

1 The voice of God goes out to all the
         world:
   his glory speaks across the universe.
   The Great King's herald cries from star
         to star;
   *with power, with justice, he will walk
         his way.*

2 Give glory to the mystery revealed,
   the voice of God, his image and his Word:
   his word of peace, the image of his grace:

3 The Lord has said: Receive my messenger,
   my promise to the world, my pledge
         made flesh,
   a lamp to every nation, light from light:

4 The broken reed he will not trample down,
   nor set his heel upon the dying flame.
   He binds the wounds, and health is in
         his hand:

5 Anointed with the Spirit and with power,
   he comes to crown with comfort all the
         weak,
   to show the face of justice to the poor:

6 His touch will bless the eyes that
         darkness held,
   the lame shall run, the halting tongue
         shall sing,
   and prisoners laugh in light and liberty:
            Luke Connaughton (1919–79)

109

1 Lo, he comes with clouds descending,
   once for favour'd sinners slain;
   thousand thousand saints attending
   swell the triumph of his train:
       Alleluia! Alleluia! Alleluia!
   God appears on earth to reign.

2 Every eye shall now behold him
   robed in glorious majesty;
   those who set at naught and sold him,
   pierced and nailed him to the tree,
       deeply wailing,
   shall the true Messiah see.

3 Those dear tokens of his passion
   still his dazzling body bears,
   cause of endless exultation
   to his ransomed worshippers:
       with what rapture
   gaze we on those glorious scars.

4 Yea, Amen, let all adore thee,
   high on thine eternal throne;
   Saviour, take the power and glory,
   claim the kingdom for thine own:
       Come, Lord Jesus!
   Everlasting God, come down!
            Charles Wesley (1707–1788)

110

1 The coming of our God
   our thoughts must now employ;
   then let us meet him on the road
   with songs of holy joy.

2 The everlasting Son,
   was born to set us free;
   and he a servant's form put on,
   to gain our liberty.

3 Daughter of Sion, rise
  to greet your infant King,
  nor let your stubborn heart despise
  the pardon he doth bring.

4 In glory from his throne
  again will Christ descend,
  and summon all that are his own
  to joys that never end.

5 Let deeds of darkness fly
  before the approaching morn,
  for unto sin 'tis ours to die,
  and serve the virgin–born.

6 Our joyful praises sing
  to Christ, that set us free;
  like tribute to the Father bring,
  and, Holy Ghost, to thee.

Charles Coffin (1676–1749),
tr. R. Campbell (1814–68), alt.

Refrain

111 For you, O Lord, my soul in still-ness waits; tru-ly my hope is in you.

Verses

1. O Lord of Light, our on-ly hope of glo-ry, your ra-diance shines in all who look to you, come, light the hearts of all in dark and sha-dow.

2. O Spring of Joy, rain down up-on our spi-rits, our thir-sty hearts are year-ning for your Word, come, make us whole, be com-fort to our hearts.

3. O Root of Life, im-plant your seed with-in us, and in your ad-vent, draw us all to you, our hope re-born in dy-ing and in ri-sing.

4. O Key of Know-ledge, guide us in our pil-gri-mage, we ev-er seek, yet un-ful-filled re-main, o-pen to us the path-way of your peace.

5 Come, let us bow before the God who made us,
  let ev'ry heart be opened to the Lord,
  for we are all the people of his hand.

6 Here we shall meet the Maker of the heavens,
  Creator of the mountains and the seas,
  Lord of the stars, and present to us now.

Marty Haugen

112

1 O come, O come, Emmanuel,
and ransom captive Israel,
that mourns in lonely exile here
until the Son of God appear:
Rejoice, rejoice! Emmanuel
shall come to thee, O Israel.

2 O come, thou wisdom from on high,
and order all things mightily;
to us the path of knowledge show,
and teach us in her ways to go.

3 O come, O come, thou Lord of might,
who to thy tribes, on Sinai's height
in ancient times, didst give the law
in cloud and majesty and awe:

4 O come, thou Rod of Jesse, free
thine own from Satan's tyranny;
from depths of hell thy people save,
and give them vict'ry o'er the grave:

5 O come, thou key of David, come
and open wide our heavenly home;
make safe the way that leads on high,
and close the path to misery.

6 O come, thou dayspring, come and cheer
our spirits by thine advent here;
disperse the gloomy clouds of night,
and death's dark shadows put to flight:

7 O come, desire of nations, bind
in one the hearts of humankind;
bid every sad division cease,
and be thyself our Prince of peace.

> *From the 'Great O Antiphons'*
> *(12th–13th C.), tr. J.M. Neale (1818–66)*
> *(vv1,3,5,6); composite (others)*

113

1 The angel Gabriel from heaven came,
his wings as drifted snow, his eyes as flame;
'All hail,' said he, thou lowly maiden
Mary,
most highly favoured lady.' Gloria!

2 For known a blessed Mother thou shalt be,
all generations laud and honour thee,
thy Son shall be Emmanuel, by seers
foretold;
most highly favoured lady.' Gloria!

3 Then gentle Mary meekly bowed her head,
To me be as it pleaseth God,' she said.
'My soul shall laud and magnify his
holy name.'
Most highly favoured lady. Gloria!

4 Of her, Emmanuel, the Christ was born
in Bethlehem, all on a Christmas morn,
and Christian folk throughout the world
will ever say
'Most highly favoured lady.' Gloria!

> *Basque carol, paraphrased by*
> *Sabine Baring–Gould (1834–1924)*

114

1 When the Angel came to Mary,
he said 'Be at peace,
for the Lord God shall be with you,
his love will not cease.'
And Mary bore Jesus Christ,
our Saviour for to be:
and the first and the last
and the greatest is he, is he, is he;
and the first and the last
and the greatest is he.

2 When the Angel came to Mary,
he said 'Do not fear,
for his power shall be upon you,
a child you will bear.'

3 When the Angel came to Mary,
he said 'Hear his name,
for his title shall be Jesus
of kingly acclaim.'

4 When the Angel came to Mary,
she said 'Be it so:
for the Lord God is my master,
his will I must do.'

> *Michael Perry (1942-96)*

➤ *See also Our Lady (Annunciation, 330-4;*
Magnificat: 23-25, 335-340, 880)

115

1 Praise we the Lord this day,
  this day so long foretold,
  whose promise shone with cheering ray
  on waiting saints of old.

2 The prophet gave the sign
  for faithful men to read;
  a virgin, born of David's line,
  shall bear the promised seed.

3 Ask not how this should be,
  but worship and adore;
  like her, whom heaven's majesty
  came down to shadow o'er.

4 Meekly she bowed her head
  to hear the gracious word,
  Mary, the pure and lowly maid,
  the favoured of the Lord.

5 Blessèd shall be her name
  in all the Church on earth,
  through whom that wondrous mercy came,
  the incarnate Saviour's birth.

6 Jesus, the virgin's son,
  we praise thee and adore,
  who art with God the Father one
  and Spirit evermore.
  Anonymous, c.1847

116

1 Long ago, prophets knew
  Christ would come, born a Jew,
  come to make all things new,
  bear his people's burden,
  freely love and pardon.
    Ring, bells, ring, ring, ring!
    Sing, choirs, sing, sing, sing!
    When he comes,
    when he comes,
    who will make him welcome?

2 God in time, God in man,
  this is God's timeless plan:
  he will come, as a man,
  born himself of woman,
  God divinely human:

3 Mary, hail! Though afraid,
  she believed, she obeyed.
  In her womb God is laid,
  till the time expected,
  nurtured and protected:

4 Journey ends: where afar
  Bethlem shines, like a star,
  stable door stands ajar.
  Unborn Son of Mary,
  Saviour, do not tarry.
  Ring, bells, ring, ring, ring!
  Sing, choirs, sing, sing, sing!
  Jesus comes,
  Jesus comes:
  we will make him welcome.
    F. Pratt Green (1903-2000)

117

1 O come, divine Messiah!
  The world in silence waits the day
  when hope shall sing its triumph,
  and sadness flee away.

  Dear Saviour, haste; come, come to earth:
  dispel the night, and show your face,
  and bid us hail the dawn of grace.
  O come, divine Messiah!
  The world in silence waits the day
  when hope shall sing its triumph,
  and sadness flee away.

2 O come, desired of nations,
  whom priests and prophets long foretold,
  will break the captive fetters,
  redeem the long–lost fold.

3 O come in peace and meekness,
  for lowly will your cradle be:
  all clothed in human weakness
  shall we your Godhead see.

    Abbé Simon-Joseph Pellegrin (1663-1745);
    tr. Sr. Mary of St Philip (Mary Frances
    Lescher, 1825-1904), alt.

118 Christmas Gathering Song 1

Piae Cantiones, 1582

Refrain

Gau - de - te, gau de - te, Chris - tus est na - tus ex Ma - ri - a vir - gi - ne. Gau - de te.

Verses

1. Na - ture mar - vels at the sight, an - gels sing the glo - ry:
2. Hail Ma - ry, ev - er blest, Moth - er of the prom - ise.
3. With the wise men from the east, with the stars of heav - en,
4. Now is born Em - ma - nu - el, now is come sal - va - tion.

God be - comes a lit - tle child, shep - herds tell the sto - ry.
By your word the Word - made - flesh came to dwell a - mong us.
with the shep - herd and the sheep, come, let us a - dore him.
Sing we all no - el, no - el! Sing in ex - ul - ta - tion!

English verses by Bob Hurd

119 Christmastide Gathering Song 2

1 Joyful news to you I bring:
Christ the Lord is here on earth,
our Redeemer and our King:
sing with gladness at his birth.
Gloria in excelsis Deo!

2 Joyful news to you I bring:
Jesus Christ is born tonight,
Now let all the heavens ring:
praises to the Lord of light.

3 Joyful news to you I bring:
Jesus Christ, a living sign,
for our human ransoming
comes to us through love divine.

4 Joyful news we sing today:
incarnation, living bread,
passion, taking sin away,
resurrection from the dead.

Paul Inwood

120 Christmastide Gloria

Missa Ubi Caritas, Bob Hurd

Glo - ri - a in ex - cel - sis De - o, et in ter - ra pax ho - mi - ni - bus

bo - nae vo - lun - ta - tis. *After last refrain* *Fine*

A - men. A - men.

121

Psalm for Christmastide Ps. 97(98)1-6

David Haas & Marty Haugen

Responses 1 & 2

R.1 All the ends of the earth have seen the pow-er of God;
R.2 Sing to the Lord a new song, for God has done won-der-ful deeds.

all the ends of the earth have seen the po-wer of God.
Sing to the Lord a new song, for God has done won-der-ful deeds.

Response 3

The Lord comes to the earth to rule the earth with jus-tice. The

Lord comes to the earth to rule the earth with jus tice.

1 Sing to the Lord a new song,
for God has done wondrous deeds;
whose right hand has won the vict'ry for us,
God's holy arm.

2 The Lord has made salvation known,
and justice revealed to all.
Remembering kindness and faithfulness
to Israel.

3 All of the ends of earth have seen
salvation by our God.
Joyfully sing out all you lands,
break forth in song.

4 Sing to the Lord with harp and song,
with trumpet and with horn.
Sing in your joy before the king,
the king, our Lord.

122

Gospel Acclamation for Christmastide

Stephen Dean

Al - le - lu - ia, al - le - lu - ia, al - le - lu - ia.

May be sung in canon.

Midnight Mass verse
I bring you tidings of great joy:
Today a Saviour has been born to us,
he is Christ the Lord.

Christmas Day verse
A hallowed day has dawned upon us.
O come you nations, worship the Lord,
for today a great light has shone down
upon the earth.

Holy Family verse
May the peace of Christ reign in your hearts.
May the message of Christ
find a home with you, alleluia.

Second Sunday of Christmas verse
Glory to you, Lord Jesus Christ,
proclaimed to the nations,
preached to the pagans, believed by the world.

Epiphany verse
We saw his star as it rose,
and we we have come to give him homage,
alleluia.

123

Communion Song for Christmas

➤ *See no. 78, Bread of life*

124

John L.Bell

He became poor that we may be rich, lo-ving the world and lea-ving his throne

King of all kings, and Lord of all lords, flesh of our flesh and bone— of our bone

125

1. A child is born in Beth - le - hem, al - le - lu - ia:
2. Through Ga - bri - el the Word has come, al - le - lu - ia:
3. With - in a man - ger now he lies, al - le - lu - ia:
4. The shep-herds hear the an - gel's word, al - le - lu - ia:

so leap with joy Je - ru - sa - lem, al - le - lu - ia, al - le-lu - ia.
the Vir - gin will con - ceive a son, al - le - lu - ia, al - le-lu - ia.
who reigns on high be - yond the skies, al - le - lu - ia, al - le-lu - ia.
this child is tru - ly Christ the Lord, al - le - lu - ia, al - le-lu - ia.

Refrain

A new song let us sing: for Christ is born, let us a-dore and let our glad-ness ring.

5 From Saba, from the rising sun, *alleluia:*
with incense, gold, and myrrh they come,
alleluia, alleluia.

6 Till with their gifts they enter in,
and kings adore the new–born King,

7 From virgin's womb this child is born,
the Light from Light who brings the dawn,

8 He comes to free us from our strife,
and share with us the Father's life,

9 At this the coming of the Word,
O come, let us adore the Lord,

10 To Father, Son, and Spirit praise,
from all his creatures all their days,
Latin, 14th C., tr. Ralph Wright OSB

126

1 A noble flow'r of Juda
from tender roots has sprung,
a rose from stem of Jesse,
as prophets long had sung;
a blossom fair and bright,
that in the midst of winter
will change to dawn our night.

2 The rose of grace and beauty
of which Isaiah sings
is Mary, virgin mother,
and Christ the flow'r she brings.
By God's divine decree
she bore our loving Saviour
who died to set us free.

3 To Mary, dearest mother,
  with fervent hearts we pray:
  grant that your tender infant
  will cast our sins away,
  and guide us with his love
  that we shall ever serve him
  and live with him above.
German, 15th century, tr. Anthony G Petti

127

1 O little town of Bethlehem,
  how still we see thee lie!
  Above thy deep and dreamless sleep
  the silent stars go by.
  Yet, in thy dark streets shineth
  the everlasting light;
  the hopes and fears of all the years
  are met in thee tonight.

2 O morning stars, together
  proclaim the holy birth,
  and praises sing to God the King,
  and peace to men on earth;
  for Christ is born of Mary;
  and, gathered all above,
  while mortals sleep, the angels keep
  their watch of wondering love.

3 How silently, how silently,
  the wondrous gift is given!
  So God imparts to human hearts
  the blessings of his heaven.
  No ear may hear his coming;
  but in this world of sin,
  where meek souls will receive him, still
  the dear Christ enters in.

4 O holy child of Bethlehem,
  descend to us, we pray;
  cast out our sin, and enter in,
  be born in us today.
  We hear the Christmas angels
  the great glad tidings tell:
  O come to us, abide with us,
  our Lord Emmanuel.
Phillips Brooks (1835–93)

128

1 Once in royal David's city
  stood a lowly cattle shed,
  where a mother laid her baby
  in a manger for his bed;
  Mary was that Mother mild,
  Jesus Christ her little child.

2 He came down to earth from heaven,
  who is God and Lord of all,
  and his shelter was a stable
  and his cradle was a stall;
  with the poor, and mean, and lowly,
  lived on earth our Saviour holy.

3 And through all his wondrous childhood
  he would honour and obey,
  love, and watch the lowly maiden
  in whose gentle arms he lay;
  Christian children all must be
  mild, obedient, good as he.

4 For he is our childhood's pattern,
  day by day like us he grew;
  he was little, weak and helpless,
  tears and smiles like us he knew;
  and he feeleth for our sadness,
  and he shareth in our gladness.

5 And our eyes at last shall see him
  through his own redeeming love,
  for that child so dear and gentle
  is our Lord in heaven above;
  and he leads his children on
  to the place where he is gone.

6 Not in that poor lowly stable,
  with the oxen standing by,
  we shall see him; but in heaven,
  set at God's right hand on high;
  when like stars his children crowned
  all in white shall wait around.
Mrs C.F. Alexander (1818-1895)

129

1 God rest you merry, gentlemen,
  let nothing you dismay,
  for Jesus Christ our Saviour
  was born on Christmas Day,

to save us all from Satan's pow'r
when we were gone astray;
O tidings of comfort and joy,
comfort and joy,
O tidings of comfort and joy.

2 In Bethlehem, in Judah,
this blessed Babe was born,
and laid within a manger,
upon this blessed morn;
the which his Mother Mary,
did nothing take in scorn.

3 From God our heavenly Father,
a blessed angel came;
and unto certain shepherds
brought tidings of the same;
how that in Bethlehem was born
the Son of God by name:

4 'Fear not', then said the angel,
'Let nothing you affright,
this day is born a Saviour
of a pure virgin bright,
to free all those who trust in him
from Satan's power and might.'

5 The shepherds at those tidings
rejoicèd much in mind,
and left their flocks a-feeding,
in tempest, storm and wind;
and went to Bethlehem straightway,
this blessed Babe to find.

6 And when to Bethlehem they came
whereat this infant lay,
they found him in a manger,
where oxen feed on hay;
his mother Mary kneeling,
unto the Lord did pray.

7 Now to the Lord sing praises,
all you within this place,
and with true love and fellowship
each other now embrace;
this holy tide of Christmas
all others doth deface.
English Traditional Carol (18th cent.)

130

1 Angels we have heard in heaven
sweetly singing o'er our plains,
and the mountain tops in answer
echoing their joyous strains.
Gloria in excelsis Deo.
Gloria in excelsis Deo.

2 Shepherds, why this exultation?
Why your rapturous strain prolong?
Tell us of the gladsome tidings,
which inspire your joyous song.

3 Come to Bethlehem, and see him
o'er whose birth the angels sing,
come, adore, devoutly kneeling,
Christ the Lord, the new–born king.

4 See him in a manger lying
whom the choir of angels praise!
Mary, Joseph, come to aid us
while our hearts in love we raise.
James Chadwick (1813–82)

131

1 Angels from the realms of glory,
wing your flight o'er all the earth;
you who sang creation's story,
now proclaim Messiah's birth:
Come and worship,
come and worship,
worship Christ, the new-born King.

2 Shepherds, in the fields abiding,
watching o'er your flocks by night,
God on earth is now residing,
yonder shines the infant light:

3 Sages, leave your contemplations,
brighter visions beam afar;
seek the great Desire of nations,
you have seen his morning star:

4 Though an infant now we view him,
he shall fill his heav'nly throne,
gather all the nations to him;
every knee shall then bow down.
Vv. 1-3, James Montgomery (1771-1854);
v.4 from 'Christmas Box', 1825

132

1 'Twas in the moon of wintertime,
   when all the birds had fled,
   that God the Lord of all the earth
   sent angel choirs instead.
   Beofre their light the stars grew dim,
   and wandering hunters heard the hymn:
   Jesus your King is born, Jesus is born,
   in excelsis gloria!

2 The earliest moon of wintertime
   is not so round and fair
   as was the ring of glory round
   the helpless infant there.
   The chiefs from far before him knelt
   with gifts of fox and beaver pelt.
   Jesus your king is born, ...

3 Oh, children of the forest free,
   the angel song is true:
   the holy child of earth and sky
   is born this day for you;
   come kneel before the radiant boy,
   who brings you beauty, peace and joy.
   Jesus your king is born, ...
       St. Jean de Bréboeuf (1593-1649),
       tr. Jesse E. Middleton (1872-1960)

133

1 While shepherds watched their flocks
        by night,
   all seated on the ground,
   the angel of the Lord came down,
   and glory shone around.

2 'Fear not,' said he, (for mighty dread
   had seized their troubled mind)
   'Glad tidings of great joy I bring
   to all of humankind.'

3 'To you in David's town this day
   is born of David's line
   a Saviour, who is Christ the Lord;
   and this shall be the sign:

4 'The heavenly Babe you there shall find
   to human view displayed,
   all meanly wrapped in swathing bands,
   and in a manger laid.'

5 Thus spoke the Seraph; and forthwith
   appeared a shining throng
   of angels praising God, who thus
   addressed their joyful song:

6 'All glory be to God on high,
   and on the earth be peace,
   goodwill henceforth from heaven to all
   begin and never cease.'
       Nahum Tate (1652–1715)

134

1 On Christmas night all Christians sing,
   to hear the news the angels bring:
   on Christmas night all Christians sing,
   to hear the news the angels bring:
   news of great joy, news of great mirth,
   news of our merciful King's birth.

2 Then why should we on earth be so sad,
   since our Redeemer made us glad?
   Then why should we on earth be so sad,
   since our Redeemer made us glad?
   When from our sin he set us free,
   all for to gain our liberty?

3 When sin departs before his grace,
   then life and health come in its place;
   when sin departs before his grace,
   then life and health come in its place;
   angels and men with joy may sing,
   all for to see the new–born King.

4 All out of darkness we have light,
   which made the angels sing this night:
   all out of darkness we have light,
   which made the angels sing this night:
   'Glory to God and peace to men,
   now and for evermore. Amen.'
       The Sussex Carol. Traditional

135

1 It came upon the midnight clear,
   that glorious song of old,
   from angels bending near the earth
   to touch their harps of gold;
   'Peace on the earth, good will to all,
   from heaven's all gracious King!'
   The world in solemn stillness lay
   to hear the angels sing.

2 Yet with the woes of sin and strife
the world has suffered long;
beneath the angel–strain have rolled
two thousand years of wrong;
and man, at war with man, hears not
the love song which they bring:
O hush the noise, ye men of strife,
and hear the angels sing!

3 For lo, the days are hastening on,
by prophets seen of old,
when with the ever–circling years
shall come the time foretold,
when the new heaven and earth shall own
the Prince of Peace their king,
and all the world repeat the song
which now the angels sing.
E. H. Sears (1810–76)

136

1 Silent night, holy night,
all is calm, all is bright,
round yon virgin mother and child;
holy infant, so tender and mild:
sleep in heavenly peace,
sleep in heavenly peace.

2 Silent night, holy night.
Shepherds quake at the sight,
glories stream from heaven afar,
heavenly hosts sing alleluia;
Christ, the Saviour is born,
Christ, the Saviour is born.

3 Silent night, holy night.
Son of God, love's pure light
radiant beams from thy holy face,
with the dawn of redeeming grace:
Jesus, Lord, at thy birth,
Jesus, Lord, at thy birth.
Joseph Mohr (1792–1848), tr. J. Young

137

1 Away in a manger, no crib for a bed,
the little Lord Jesus laid down his sweet
head,
the stars in the bright sky looked down
where he lay,
the little Lord Jesus asleep on the hay.

2 The cattle are lowing, the baby awakes,
but little Lord Jesus no crying he makes.
I love thee, Lord Jesus! Look down from
the sky,
and stay by my side until morning is nigh.

3 Be near me, Lord Jesus; I ask thee to stay
close by me for ever, and love me, I pray.
Bless all the dear children in thy tender
care,
and fit us for heaven, to live with thee there.
Vv. 1 & 2 Anon;
v. 3 J.T. McFarland (1851–1913)

138

1 Infant holy, infant lowly,
for his bed a cattle stall;
oxen lowing, little knowing
Christ the babe is Lord of all.
Swift are winging angels singing,
nowells ringing, tidings bringing:
Christ the babe is Lord of all;
Christ the babe is Lord of all!

2 Flocks were sleeping, shepherds keeping
vigil till the morning new,
saw the glory, heard the story
tidings of a gospel true.
Thus rejoicing, free from sorrow,
praises voicing, greet the morrow:
Christ the babe was born for you;
Christ the babe was born for you!
From a Polish Carol,
tr. E. M. G. Reed (1885–1933)

139

Come, come, come to the manger,
children, come to the children's King:
sing, sing, chorus of Angels,
stars of morning o'er Bethlehem sing.

1 He lies 'mid the beasts of the stall,
who is Maker and Lord of us all;
the wintry wind blows cold and dreary,
see, he weeps, the world is weary;
Lord, have pity and mercy on me!

2 He leaves all his glory behind;
to be born and to die for mankind.

With grateful beasts his cradle chooses,
thankless man his love refuses;
Lord, have pity and mercy on me!

3 To the manger of Bethlehem come,
to the Saviour Emmanuel's home;
the heav'nly hosts above are singing,
set the Christmas bells a–ringing;
Lord, have pity and mercy on me!

19th C., Anonymous

140

1 Sleep, holy babe,
upon thy mother's breast;
great Lord of earth and sea and sky,
how sweet it is to see thee lie
in such a place of rest.

2 Sleep, holy babe;
thine angels watch around,
all bending low, with folded wings,
before th'incarnate King of kings,
in reverent awe profound.

3 Sleep, holy babe,
while I with Mary gaze
in joy upon that face awhile,
upon the loving infant smile,
which there divinely plays.

4 Sleep, holy babe,
ah, take thy brief repose,
too quickly will thy slumbers break,
and thou to lengthen'd pains awake,
that death alone shall close.

5 O lady blest,
sweet Virgin, hear my cry;
forgive the wrong that I have done
to thee, in causing thy dear Son
upon the cross to die.

Edward Caswall (1814–78)

141

1 Child in the manger, infant of Mary;
outcast and stranger, Lord of all;
child who inherits all our transgressions,
all our demerits on him fall.

2 Once the most holy child of salvation
gently and lowly lived below;
now as our glorious mighty Redeemer,
see him victorious o'er each foe.

3 Prophets foretold him, infant of wonder;
angels behold him on his throne:
worthy our Saviour of all their praises;
happy for ever are his own.

Mary Macdonald (1789–1872),
tr. Lachlan MacBean (1853–1931)

142

1 Jesus, Saviour, holy child, sleep tonight,
slumber deep till morning light.
Lullaby, our joy, our treasure,
all our hope and all our pleasure:
at the cradle where you lie
we will worship lullaby!

2 From your Father's home you come
   to this earth,
by your lowly manger birth:
Child of God, our nature sharing,
Son of Man, our sorrows bearing;
rich, yet here among the poor:
Christ the Lord, whom we adore!

3 Now to heaven's glory song we reply
with a Christmas lullaby.
Hush, the eternal Lord is sleeping
close in Mary's tender keeping:
babe on whom the angels smiled
Jesus, Saviour, holy child.

Michael Perry (1942-96)

143

1 Who is the baby an hour or two old,
looked for by shepherds far strayed from
   their fold,
lost in the world though more precious
   than gold?
This is God with us in Jesus.

2 Who is the woman with child at her breast,
giving her milk to earth's heavenly guest,
telling her mind to be calm and at rest?
Mary, the mother of Jesus.

3 Who is the man who looks on at the door,
   welcoming strangers, some rich but
        most poor,
   scanning the world as if somehow unsure?
   Joseph, the father of Jesus.

4 Who are the people come in from the street,
   some to bring presents and some just to meet,
   joining their song to what angels repeat?
   These are the new friends of Jesus.

5 Will you come with me, even though I
        feel shy,
   come to his cradle and come to his cry,
   give him your nod or your yes
        or your aye,
   give what you can give to Jesus?
        John L. Bell

144

1 In the bleak midwinter,
   frosty wind made moan,
   earth stood hard as iron,
   water like a stone;
   snow had fallen, snow on snow,
   snow on snow,
   in the bleak midwinter
   long ago.

2 Our God, heaven cannot hold him
   nor earth sustain;
   heaven and earth shall flee away,
   when he comes to reign.
   In the bleak midwinter
   a stable–place sufficed
   the Lord God Almighty,
   Jesus Christ.

3 Enough for him, whom Cherubim
   worship night and day,
   a breastful of milk,
   and a mangerful of hay:
   enough for him, whom angels
   fall down before,
   the ox and ass and camel
   which adore.

4 Angels and archangels
   may have gathered there,
   Cherubim and Seraphim
   thronged the air –
   but only his mother
   in her maiden bliss
   worshipped the beloved
   with a kiss.

5 What can I give him,
   poor as I am?
   If I were a shepherd
   I would bring a lamb;
   if I were a wise man
   I would do my part;
   yet what I can I give him –
   give my heart.
        Christina G. Rossetti (1830–94)

145

1 What child is this, who, laid to rest,
   on Mary's lap is sleeping?
   Whom angels greet with anthems sweet,
   while shepherds watch are keeping?
   This, this is Christ the King,
   whom shepherds guard and angels sing:
   come, greet the infant Lord,
   the Babe, the Son of Mary!

2 Why lies he in such mean estate,
   where ox and ass are feeding?
   Good Christian, fear: for sinners here
   the silent Word is pleading.
   Nails, spear, shall pierce him through,
   the cross be borne for me, for you:
   hail, hail the Word made flesh,
   the Babe, the Son of Mary!

3 So bring him incense, gold and myrrh,
   come peasant, king, to own him.
   The King of kings salvation brings,
   let loving hearts enthrone him.
   Raise, raise the song on high,
   the Virgin sings her lullaby:
   joy, joy for Christ is born,
   the Babe, the Son of Mary!
        W. C. Dix (1837-1898)

146

1 Angel voices richly blending,
shepherds to the manger sending,
sing of peace from heav'n descending!
Shepherds, greet your Shepherd King.

2 Lo! a star is brightly glowing!
Eastern Kings their gifts are showing
to the King whose gifts pass knowing!
Gentiles, greet the Gentiles' King!

3 To the manger come adoring,
hearts in thankfulness outpouring
To the child, true peace restoring,
Mary's Son, our God and King!
German, 15th C., tr. James Quinn SJ (1919-2010)

147

1 What shall we give to the child in the
manger?
What shall we give him that he will enjoy?
Milk and wild honey for this little stranger,
food to give strength to a new little boy.

2 What shall we give to the firstborn of Mary,
things what will nourish a new life begun?
Fruits of the forest and figs from the fig-tree
nurtured in soil and ripened by sun.

3 This Child must grow to inherit a kingdom,
blossom and ripen like fields of good corn,
bearing a seed that will fall and lie buried,
springing up new in the bright Easter morn.

4 What shall we give to the child in the manger?
What shall we give him that he will enjoy?
Give of the best to the one who will save us,
food to give strength to this man still a boy.
Catalan carol, adapted by Stephen Dean

148

1 Holy Child within the manger,
long ago yet ever near;
come as friend to every stranger,
come as hope for every fear.
As you lived to heal the broken,
greet the outcast, free the bound,
as you taught us love unspoken,
teach us now where you are found

2 Once again we tell the story -
how the Father's love shone forth
when the Image of his glory
became his image here on earth.
Come, enlighten us with wisdom,
come, and fill us with your grace,
may the fire of your compassion
kindle ev'ry land and race.

3 Holy Child within the manger,
lead us ever in your way,
so we see in ev'ry stranger
how you come to us today.
In our lives and in our living
give us strength to live as you,
that our hearts might be forgiving
and our spirits strong and true.
Marty Haugen

149

1 Let us bring to him the lonely,
let us bring to him the poor,
for salvation lies in a manger,
God's Son lies wrapped in straw.
Do you hear all the heavenly singing?
See the light in a Bethlehem cave?
For the light that shines in the darkness
is Christ the Lord who will save.

2 Let us bring to him the children,
let us bring to him the old,
for one look from him will bring comfort
and strength to brave the cold.

3 Let us bring the tired people
who have never time to pray.
for his love is stronger than sorrow
and freedom is his way.

4 Let us bring to him the suffering,
people sick in heart and mind,
for his touch is gentle and healing
their pain he can unbind.

5 Let us bring to him the hungry,
those who thirst, in prison dwell,
if we care for the least of his children
we care for him as well.
Christopher Walker

150

1 The first Nowell the angel did say
was to certain poor shepherds in fields
     as they lay;
in fields where they lay keeping their
     sheep,
on a cold winter's night that was so deep.
Nowell, Nowell, Nowell, Nowell,
born is the King of Israel!

2 They lookèd up and saw a star,
shining in the east, beyond them far,
and to the earth it gave great light,
and so it continued both day and night.

3 And by the light of that same star,
three wise men came from country far.
To seek for a king was their intent,
and to follow the star wherever it went.

4 This star drew nigh to the north–west,
o'er Bethlehem it took its rest,
and there it did both stop and stay
right over the place where Jesus lay.

5 Then entered in those wise men three,
full reverently upon their knee,
and offered there in his presence,
their gold and myrrh and frankincense.

6 Then let us all with one accord
sing praises to our heavenly Lord,
that hath made heaven and earth of nought,
and with his blood mankind hath bought.
Traditional English carol

151

1 See, amid the winter's snow,
born for us on earth below,
see, the tender lamb appears,
promised from eternal years.
  Hail, thou ever–blessèd morn,
  hail, redemption's happy dawn!
  Sing through all Jerusalem,
  Christ is born in Bethlehem.

2 Lo, within a manger lies
he who built the starry skies;

he who, throned in heights sublime,
sits amid the cherubim.

3 Say, ye holy shepherds, say,
what your joyful news today?
Wherefore have ye left your sheep
on the lonely mountain steep?

4 'As we watched at dead of night,
lo, we saw a wondrous light;
angels, singing peace on earth,
told us of the Saviour's birth.'

5 Sacred infant, all divine,
what a tender love was thine,
thus to come from highest bliss,
down to such a world as this!

6 Virgin mother, Mary blest,
by the joys that fill thy breast,
pray for us, that we may prove
worthy of the Saviour's love.
  Edward Caswall (1814–78)

152

The last line of each verse is repeated

1 Unto us is born a Son,
King of quires supernal;
see on earth his life begun,
of lords the Lord eternal.

2 Christ, from heav'n descending low,
comes on earth a stranger:
ox and ass their owner know
becradled in a manger.

3 This did Herod sore affray,
and grievously bewilder:
so he gave the word to slay,
and slew the little childer.

4 Of his love and mercy mild
this the Christmas story,
and O that Mary's gentle Child
might lead us up to glory!

5 O and A and A and O
cum cantibus in choro,
let the merry organ go,
Benedicamus Domino.
  15th C., tr. G.R. Woodward (1848-1934)

153

1 Ding dong! merrily on high
   in heav'n the bells are ringing,
   ding dong! verily the sky
   is riv'n with angels singing.
   Gloria, hosanna in excelsis!

2 E'en so here below, below,
   let steeple bells be swungen,
   and io, io, io,
   by priest and people sungen.

3 Pray you, dutifully prime
   your matin chime, ye ringers;
   may you beautifully rime
   your evetime song, ye singers.
   G.R.Woodward (1848–1934)

154

1 Good Christians all, rejoice
   with heart and soul and voice!
   Give ye heed to what we say:
   Jesus Christ is born today.
   Ox and ass before him bow,
   and he is in the manger now:
   Christ is born today,
   Christ is born today

2 Good Christians all, rejoice
   with heart and soul and voice!
   Now ye hear of endless bliss;
   Jesus Christ was born for this.
   He hath opened heaven's door,
   and we are blessed for evermore:
   Christ was born for this,
   Christ was born for this.

3 Good Christians all, rejoice
   with heart and soul and voice!
   Now ye need not fear the grave;
   Jesus Christ was born to save,
   calls you one, and calls you all,
   to gain his everlasting hall:
   Christ was born to save,
   Christ was born to save.
   German, 14th C., tr. J. M. Neale (1818–66)

155

1 Hark! the herald angels sing,
   glory to the new–born King;
   peace on earth and mercy mild,
   God and sinners reconciled:
   joyful, all ye nations, rise,
   join the triumph of the skies;
   with the angelic host proclaim:
   'Christ is born in Bethlehem'.
   Hark, the herald Angels sing,
   glory to the new–born King.

2 Christ, by highest heaven adored,
   Christ, the everlasting Lord,
   late in time behold him come,
   offspring of a Virgin's womb.
   Veiled in flesh the Godhead see!
   Hail the incarnate Deity!
   Pleased as man with man to dwell,
   Jesus, our Emmanuel:

3 Hail the heaven–born Prince of Peace!
   Hail the Sun of righteousness!
   Light and life to all he brings,
   risen with healing in his wings.
   Mild he lays his glory by,
   born that man no more may die,
   born to raise the sons of earth,
   born to give them second birth:
   Charles Wesley (1707-88), alt.

156

1 Joy to the world, the Lord has come!
   Let earth receive her King;
   let every heart prepare Him room,
   and heaven and nature sing,
   and heaven and nature sing,
   and heaven, and heaven and nature sing.

2 Joy to the earth, the Saviour reigns!
   Let all their songs employ
   while fields and floods, rocks, hills and
   plains
   repeat the sounding joy,
   repeat the sounding joy,
   repeat, repeat the sounding joy.

3 No more let sin and sorrows grow,
  nor thorns infest the ground;
  he comes to make his blessings flow
      far as the curse is found,
      far as the curse is found,
  far as, far as the curse is found.

4 He rules the world with truth and grace,
  and makes the nations prove
  the glories of his righteousness,
      the wonders of his love,
      the wonders of his love,
  the wonders, wonders of his love.
      Isaac Watts (1674–1748) based on Psalm 98

157

1 Awake! awake, and greet the new morn,
  for angels herald its dawning,
  sing out your joy, for now he is born,
  Behold! the Child of our longing.
  Come as a baby weak and poor,
  to bring all hearts together,
  he opens wide the heav'nly door
  and lives now inside us for ever.

2 To us, to all in sorrow and fear,
  Emmanuel comes a-singing,
  his humble song is quiet and near,
  yet fills the earth with its ringing;
  music to heal the broken soul
  and hymns of loving kindness,
  the thunder of his anthems rolls
  to shatter all hatred and blindness.

3 In darkest night his coming shall be,
  when all the world is despairing,
  as morning light so quiet and free,
  so warm and gentle and caring.
  Then shall the mute break forth in song,
  the lame shall leap in wonder,
  the weak be raised above the strong,
  and weapons be broken asunder.

4 Rejoice, rejoice, take heart in the night,
  though dark the winter and cheerless,
  the rising sun shall crown you with light,
  be strong and loving and fearless;

love be our song and love our prayer,
and love, our endless story,
may God fill every day we share,
and bring us at last into glory.
      Marty Haugen

158

1 In deepest night we hear the story:
  the morning star has risen plain:
  for us an infant has been born,
  'the Lord-shall-save-us' is his name.
  Open your hearts, believe your senses,
  and trust in what you plainly see;
  how God's own word from highest
      heaven
  is wrought in us so humanly.

2 To us no other sign is given,
  no other light comes breaking through:
  this man alone is our companion,
  a God who is our brother, too.
  Sing for your God who has unfolded
  in Jesus his great love for all.
  The world becomes a new creation,
  all flesh receives his saving call.

3 The way the sun comes up in glory,
  a bridegroom shedding light and fire,
  so comes the king of peace to join us,
  and, once for all, has come his hour.
  And joining ev'ryone together,
  his love doled out as nourishment,
  he gives his body to our keeping
  that we may live his covenant.
      Huub Oosterhuis, tr. David Smith

159

1 O come, all ye faithful,
  joyful and triumphant.
  O come ye, O come ye to Bethlehem;
  come and behold him,
  born the king of angels:
      O come, let us adore him,
      O come, let us adore him,
      O come, let us adore him,
      Christ the Lord.

2 God of God,
light of light,
lo! he abhors not the virgin's womb;
very God, begotten not created:

3 Sing, choirs of angels,
sing in exultation,
sing all ye citizens of heaven above;
glory to God in the highest:

4 Yea, Lord, we greet thee,
born this happy morning,
Jesu, to thee be glory given;
word of the Father,
now in flesh appearing:

Attributed to John F. Wade (c.1711-1786),
tr. Frederick Oakeley (1802–80), alt.

159a

1 Adeste fideles,
laeti triumphantes,
venite, venite in Bethlehem.
Natum videte regem angelorum.
Venite adoremus
venite adoremus,
venite adoremus Dominum.

2 Deum de Deo,
lumen de lumine
gestant puellae viscera.
Deum verum, genitum non factum.

3 Cantet nunc io,
chorus angelorum,
cantet nunc aula caelestium.
gloria in excelsis Deo.

4 Ergo qui natus
die hodierna
Jesu tibi sit gloria.
Patris aeternae
verbum caro factum.

Attributed to John F. Wade (c.1711-1786)

160

1 Of the Father's love begotten,
ere the worlds began to be,

he is Alpha and Omega,
he the source, the ending he,
of all things that are and have been
and that future years shall see:
evermore and evermore.

2 By his word was all created;
he commanded, it was done:
heaven and earth and depth of ocean,
universe of three in one,
all that grows beneath the shining
of the light of moon and sun:
evermore and evermore.

3 Blessed was the day for ever
when the virgin, full of grace,
by the Holy Ghost conceiving,
bore the Saviour of our race,
and the child, the world's Redeemer,
first revealed his sacred face:
evermore and evermore.

4 O, ye heights of heaven, adore him,
angels and archangels sing!
Every creature bow before him
singing praise to God our King;
let no earthly tongue be silent,
all the world with homage ring:
evermore and evermore.

5 He, by prophets sung, is here now,
promised since the world began,
now on earth in flesh descended
to atone for sins of man.
All creation praise its Master,
see fulfilment of his plan:
evermore and evermore.

6 Glory be to God the Father,
glory be to God the Son,
glory to the Holy Spirit,
persons three, yet Godhead one.
Glory be from all creation
while eternal ages run:
evermore and evermore.

Aurelius Prudentius (348–c.413) tr. J.M. Neale
(1818–66), H.W. Baker (1823–77), and others

161

1 Jesus the Word has lived among us,
  sharing his fullness, truth and grace,
  God's only Son, the Father's loved one
  reveals him to the human race.
  Jesus the Word has lived among us
  sharing his fullness, truth and grace.

2 He was with God from the beginning
  and through him all things came to be.
  He lightens darkness, conquers evil,
  gives life for living, glad and free.
  He was with God from the beginning
  and through him all things came to be.

3 Sing praise to God who sent Christ Jesus
  to be his sign of endless love;
  sent him to live his life among us,
  lifting our hearts to things above.
  Sing praise to God who sent Christ Jesus
  to be his sign of endless love!

John 1, par. by Keith D. Pearson

162

1 I wonder as I wander out under the sky,
  how Jesus the Saviour did come for
    to die
  for poor ord'n'ry people like you and
    like I.
  I wonder as I wander out under the sky.

2 When Mary birthed Jesus,'twas in a
    cow's stall
  with wise men and farmers and shepherds
    and all.
  But high from God's heaven a star's light
    did fall,
  and the promise of ages it did then recall.

3 If Jesus had wanted for any wee thing,
  a star in the sky, or a bird on the wing,
  or all of God's angels in heav'n for to
    sing,
  he surely could have it,'cause he was
    the king.

*J.J. Niles (1892-1980), possibly from an
Appalachian carol*

163

1. Long ago in depths of winter
   Gospels tell us of a mother
   in an overcrowded stable,
   overjoyed with a newborn Son.
   And some shepherds heard in wonder
   angels tearing the sky asunder
   singing 'Glory to God in heaven
   and on earth peace to everyone.'

2. Eastern wise men saw the shining
   of a star on far horizon
   and they knew it was a herald
   of the birth of a mighty Lord.
   Bringing gifts they made a journey
   till they found what they had been
     seeking
   and they knelt down in adoration
   though a baby was all they saw.

3. Child of Mary, hailed by prophets,
   seen by shepherds, sung by angels
   by your coming here among us
   you have brought us to life and hope.
   Born to serve and to be humble,
   born to give wisdom to the simple:
   born to bind up the broken hearted
   and to free us from fear and woe.

Stephen Dean

164

*Go, tell it on the mountain,
over the hills and ev'rywhere.
Go, tell it on the mountain
that Jesus Christ is born.*

1 While shepherds kept their watching
  o'er silent flocks by night,
  behold, throughout the heavens
  there shone a holy light.

2 The shepherds feared and trembled
  when lo! throughout the earth
  rang out the angel chorus
  that hailed our Saviour's birth.

3 And lo, when they had seen it,
   they all bowed down and prayed,
   they travelled on together
   to where the Babe was laid.

4 Down in a lowly manger
   the humble Christ was born
   and God sent us salvation
   that blessed Christmas morn.
   Afro-American spiritual (19th C.) adapted
   by John Wesley Work Jr (1872-1925)

New Year

165

1 The God of all eternity
   unbound by space yet always near,
   is present where his people meet
   to celebrate the coming year.

2 What shall we offer God today -
   our dreams of what we cannot see,
   or, with eyes fastened to the past,
   our dread of what is yet to be?

3 God does not share our doubts and fears,
   nor shrinks from the unknown or strange:
   the one who fashioned heaven and earth
   makes all things new and ushers change.

4 Let faith or fortune rise or fall,
   let dreams and dread both have their day;
   those whom God loves walk unafraid
   with Christ their guide and Christ their
       way.

5 God grant that we, in this new year,
   may show the world the Kingdom's face,
   and let our work and worship thrive
   as signs of hope and means of grace.
   John L. Bell

Epiphany

166

1 As with gladness men of old
   did the guiding star behold,
   as with joy they hailed its light,
   leading onward, beaming bright,
   so, most gracious God, may we
   evermore be led to thee.

2 As with joyful steps they sped
   to that lowly manger–bed,
   there to bend the knee before
   him whom heaven and earth adore,
   so may we with willing feet
   ever seek thy mercy–seat.

3 As they offered gifts most rare
   at that manger rude and bare,
   so may we with holy joy,
   pure, and free from sin's alloy,
   all our costliest treasures bring,
   Christ, to thee our heavenly King.

4 Holy Jesus, every day
   keep us in the narrow way;
   and, when earthly things are past,
   bring our ransomed souls at last
   where they need no star to guide,
   where no clouds thy glory hide.

5 In the heavenly country bright
   need they no created light,
   thou its Light, its Joy, its Crown,
   thou its Sun which goes not down;
   there for ever may we sing
   alleluias to our King.
   W.C.Dix (1837–98)

167

1 Bethlehem! of noblest cities
   none can once with thee compare;
   thou alone the Lord from heaven
   didst for us incarnate bear.

2 Fairer than the sun at morning
was the star that told his birth,
to the lands their God announcing,
hid beneath a form of earth.

3 By its shining beauty guided,
see the eastern kings appear;
see them bend, their gifts to offer –
gifts of incense, gold and myrrh.

4 Solemn things of mystic meaning!
Incense doth the God disclose;
gold a royal child proclaimeth;
Myrrh a future tomb foreshows.

5 Holy Jesu, in thy brightness
to the gentile world display'd,
with the Father and the Spirit,
endless praise to thee be paid.

Aurelius Prudentius (348–c. 413),
tr. E. Caswall (1814–78), alt.

168

1 The race that long in darkness pined
has seen a glorious light:
the people dwell in day, who dwelt
in death's surrounding night.

2 To hail thy rise, thou better sun,
the gathering nations come,
joyous as when the reapers bear
the harvest treasures home.

3 To us a child of hope is born,
to us a Son is given;
him shall the tribes of earth obey,
him all the hosts of heaven.

4 His name shall be the Prince of Peace
for evermore adored,
the Wonderful, the Counsellor
the great and mighty Lord.

5 His power increasing still shall spread,
his reign no end shall know;
justice shall guard his throne above,
and peace abound below.

John Morison (1749–98)

169

1 O worship the Lord in the beauty of
holiness!
Bow down before him, his glory proclaim;
with gold of obedience, and incense of
lowliness,
kneel and adore him, the Lord is his name!

2 Low at his feet lay thy burden of
carefulness,
high on his heart he will bear it for thee,
comfort thy sorrows, and answer thy
prayerfulness,
guiding thy steps as may best for thee be.

3 Fear not to enter his courts in the
slenderness
of the poor wealth thou wouldst reckon
as thine:
truth in its beauty, and love in its
tenderness,
these are the offerings to lay on his shrine.

4 These, though we bring them in
trembling and fearfulness,
he will accept for the name that is dear;
mornings of joy give for evenings of
tearfulness,
trust for our trembling and hope for our
fear.

5 O worship the Lord in the beauty of
holiness!
Bow down before him, his glory proclaim;
with gold of obedience, and incense of
lowliness,
kneel and adore him, the Lord is his name!

J.S. Monsell (1811–75)

170

1 We three Kings of Orient are;
bearing gifts we traverse afar,
field and fountain, moor and mountain,
following yonder star.
O Star of wonder, star of night,
star with royal beauty bright,
westward leading, still proceeding,
guide us to thy perfect light.

2 Born a King on Bethlehem plain,
  gold I bring, to crown him again,
  King for ever, ceasing never,
  over us all to reign.

3 Frankincense to offer have I,
  Incense owns a Deity nigh.
  Prayer and praising, all are raising,
  worship him, God most high.

➤ *See also Angel voices (146), The first nowell (150)*

4 Myrrh is mine, its bitter perfume
  breathes a life of gathering gloom;
  sorrowing, sighing, bleeding, dying,
  sealed in the stone–cold tomb.

5 Glorious now behold him arise,
  King and God and sacrifice.
  'Alleluia, alleluia!'
  earth to heaven replies.
  John Henry Hopkins (1822–1900)

The Baptism of the Lord

171

1 When Jesus comes to be baptised,
  he leaves the hidden years behind,
  the years of safety and of peace,
  to bear the sins of all mankind.

2 The Spirit of the Lord comes down,
  anoints the Christ to suffering,
  to preach the word, to free the bound,
  and to the mourner, comfort bring.

3 He will not quench the dying flame,
  and what is bruised he will not break,
  but heal the wound injustice dealt,
  and out of death his triumph make.

4 Our everlasting Father, praise,
  with Christ, his well-beloved Son,
  who with the Spirit reigns serene,
  untroubled Trinity in One.
  The Benedictines of Stanbrook

172

1 Songs of thankfulness and praise,
  Jesu, Lord, to you we raise,
  manifested by the star
  to the sages from afar;
  branch of royal David's stem,
  in your birth at Bethlehem;
  anthems be to you addressed,
  God in flesh made manifest.

2 Manifest at Jordan's stream,
  prophet, Priest and King supreme;
  and at Cana wedding–guest,
  in your Godhead manifest;
  manifest in power divine,
  changing water into wine;
  anthems be to you addressed,
  God in flesh made manifest.

3 Manifest in making whole
  palsied limbs and fainting soul;
  manifest in valiant fight,
  quelling all the devil's might;
  manifest in gracious will,
  ever bringing good from ill;
  anthems be to you addressed,
  God in flesh made manifest.

4 Sun and moon shall darkened be,
  stars shall fall, the heavens shall flee;
  Christ will then like lightning shine,
  all will see his glorious sign;
  all will then the trumpet hear,
  all will see the judge appear;
  you by all will be confessed;
  God in flesh made manifest.

5 Grant us grace to see you, Lord,
  mirrored in your holy word;
  may we imitate you now,
  and on us your grace endow;
  that we like to you may be
  at your great Epiphany,
  and may praise you, ever blest,
  God in flesh made manifest.
  Christopher Wordsworth (1807–85), alt.

173

1 When John baptised by Jordan's river
in faith and hope the people came,
that John and Jordan might deliver
their troubled souls from sin and shame.
They came to seek a new beginning,
the human spirit's ageless quest,
repentance, and an end of sinning,
renouncing every wrong confessed.

2 There as the Lord, baptised and praying,
rose from the stream, the sinless one,
a voice was heard from heaven saying,
'This is my own beloved Son.'

There as the Father's word was spoken,
not in the power of wind and flame,
but of his love and peace the token,
seen as a dove, the Spirit came.

3 O Son of Man, our nature sharing,
in whose obedience all are blest,
Saviour, our sins and sorrows bearing,
hear us and grant us this request:
Daily to grow, by grace defended,
filled with the Spirit from above;
in Christ baptised, beloved, befriended,
children of God in peace and love.

Timothy Dudley–Smith

➤ *See also The light of Christ (747); Advent hymns, e.g. 94-99*

The Presentation of the Lord

174 Processional Antiphon

Christ is the light of the na-tions, and the glo-ry of Is-ra-el his peo-ple.

1. At last, all-powerful Master, you give leave to your servant to go in peace,
2. For my eyes have seen your sal-vation
3. The light to enlighten the Gentiles

according to your pro-mise.
which you have prepared for all na-tions.
and give glory to Isra-el your peo-ple.

174a Latin version

Lu-men ad re-ve-la-ti-o-nem gen-ti-um, et glo-ri-am ple-bis tu-ae Is-ra-el.

175

1 In his temple now behold him,
see the long-expected Lord;
ancient prophets had foretold him,
God has now fulfilled his word;
now to praise him, his redeemèd
shall break forth with one accord.

2 In the arms of her who bore him,
Virgin pure, behold him lie,
while his aged saints adore him
ere in faith and hope they die.
Alleluia! Alleluia!
See, th'incarnate God most high.

3 Jesus, by your presentation,
    when they blessed you, weak and poor,
    make us see our great salvation,
    seal us with your promise sure,
    and present us in your glory
    to your Father, cleansed and pure.

4 Prince and author of salvation,
    be your boundless love our theme!
    Jesus, praise to you be given,
    by the world you did redeem,
    with the Father and the Spirit,
    Lord of majesty supreme.

Vv. 1-3 Henry J. Pye (1825-1903);
v.4 William Cooke (1821-94)

176

A light, a light to the Gen-tiles and the glo-ry of Is-ra-el!

Lord, let your servant now die in peace,
  for you kept your promise.
With my own eyes I see the salvation
  you prepared for all peoples.

A light of revelation for the Gentiles
and glory to your people Israel.

Luke 2:29-32. Text: ICEL.
Music by Peter McGrail

177

1 Now let your servant go in peace;
    for praise and blessing here increase;
    for in our midst your word is done
    and you have sent your Promised One.

2 Before the peoples you prepare
    your way of life which all may share.
    your saving power is now made known;
    among the nations love is shown.

3 Child, you are chosen as a sign
    to test the human heart and mind;
    for secrets hidden in the night
    shall be revealed in piercing light.

4 Now let us sing our Saviour's praise,
    and tell God's goodness all our days,
    while breath is ours, let praise be heard
    for God's own faithful, saving word.

Luke 2:29-32, versified by Ruth M. Duck

Another setting of the Nunc Dimittis, no. 37

178 *Alleluia*

Hal-le, hal-le, hal - le - lu - jah! Hal-le, hal-le, hal - le -
lu - jah! Hal-le, hal-le, hal - le - lu -
jah! Hal-le - lu-jah! Hal - le - lu - jah!

Traditional Caribbean, arr. John L. Bell

Alleluia is not sung between Ash Wednesday and the Easter Vigil.
Gospel Acclamations for Lent are found at nos. 184-187, 1004

Lent

Seasonal Music: 179-192. Lent Hymns: 193-237

179 Call to Worship

James Chepponis

This is the time of ful - fil - ment! The reign of God is at hand.

Cantor/Choir sings a sentence appropriate to the day, then this refrain is repeated

180 Gathering Song 1

1 Led by the Spirit of our God,
we go to fast and pray
with Christ into the wilderness;
we join his paschal way.
'Rend not your garments, rend your hearts.
Turn back your lives to me.'
Thus says our kind and gracious God,
whose reign is liberty.

2 Led by the Spirit, we confront
temptation face to face,
and know full well we must rely
on God's redeeming grace.
on bread alone we cannot live,
but nourished by the Word
we seek the will of God to do:
this is our drink and food.

3 Led by the Spirit, now draw near
the waters of rebirth
with hearts that long to worship God
in spirit and in truth.
'Whoever drinks the drink I give
shall never thirst again.'
Thus says the Lord who died for us,
our Saviour, kin and friend.

4 Led by the Spirit, now sing praise
to God the Trinity:
the Source of Life, the living Word
made flesh to set us free,
the Spirit blowing where it will
to make us friends of God:
this myst'ry far beyond our reach,
yet near in healing love.

Bob Hurd

181 Lent Penitential Rite 1

Bob Hurd

1,3 Ky - ri - e, e - le - i - son,   Ky - ri - e, e - le - i - son.
2. Chris - te, e - le - i - son,   Chris - te, e - le - i - son.

➤ *See also: Advent Kyrie 2 (67)*

182 Gathering Song 2

1 From ashes to the living font
your Church must journey, Lord;
baptised in grace, in grace renewed
by your most holy word.

2 Through fasting, prayer, and charity
your voice speaks deep within,
returning us to ways of truth
and turning us from sin.

3 *Sundays I & II*
From desert to the mountaintop
in Christ our way we see,
so, tempered by temptation's might
we might transfigured be.

3 *Sunday III*
For thirsting hearts let waters flow
our fainting souls revive;
and at the well your waters give
our everlasting life.

3 *Sunday IV*
   We sit beside the road and plead,
   'Come, save us, David's son!'
   Now with your vision heal our eyes,
   the world's true Light alone.

3 *Sunday V*
   Our graves split open, bring us back,
   your promise to proclaim:
   to darkened tombs call out 'Arise!'
   and glorify your name.

4. From ashes to the living font
   your Church must journey still;
   through cross and tomb to Easter joy,
   in Spirit-fire fulfilled.
           Alan J.Hommerding

183 Penitential Litany

Parce Domine, *arr. Gary Daigle*

Introduction: Repeat after Cantor

Hold us   in your mer - cy.   Hold us   in your mer - cy.
Hold us   in your mer - cy.   Hold us   in your mer - cy.

Verses

1. Ma - ker's love poured out from hea - ven.   Hold us in your mer - cy.
2. Born as one of home - less pil - grims.
3. You who shared the sin - ner's ta - ble.

Mer - cy's word made flesh a - mong us.   Hold us in your mer - cy.
Sent to bring the poor good news.
You who cleansed the le - per's flesh.

4 You who shared our life and labour.
   You who chose to walk our roads.

5 You who silence raging demons.
   you who bid the storm be silent.

6 You whose cross has gone before us.
   you who bear our cross with us.

7 Innocent, you faced the guilty.
   one in death with us for ever.

8 Come and break the chains that bind us.
   Free us from addiction's prison.

9 Break the power of the darkness.
   Let us rise to life with you.

10 Kyrie, eleison!
    Christe, eleison!

11 Hold us in your mercy!
    Hold us in your mercy!
           repeat as required

Common Responsorial Psalms for Lent
Pss 50 (51), no.48; 90 (91) no.51; 129 (130) nos. 59-60 - and see Psalm Index, p.420

184 Gospel Acclamation 1 for Lent

James Walsh

Praise to you, O Christ, king of e-ter-nal glo-ry!
Glo-ry to you, O Christ, you are the Word of God!

185 Gospel Acclamation 2 for Lent

Martin Foster

Praise to you, Lord Je-sus Christ, Word of the Fa-ther, Son of God.

186 Gospel Acclamation 3 for Lent

Chris O'Hara

Glo-ry and praise to you, Lord! You are the Word of Life.

187 Gospel Acclamation 4 for Lent

Stephen Dean

Glo-ry to you, O Christ;— glo-ry to you, O Christ, you are the
word of God, the word of God: glo-ry to you, O Christ!

✂ *See also: Word of God (197); Praise to you, O Christ (200)*

188

Gospel Responses for Sundays of Lent

Delores Dufner OSB

1st Sunday, A, B & C

 O Spirit-filled Christ Jesus,
 in fasting and in prayer
 you went into the desert
 and you were tempted there.

 O Jesus, like us, tempted
 to glory, wealth, and pow'r,
 make us, like you, unyielding,
 strong in temptation's hour.

2nd Sunday, A, B & C

 O Christ who shares our nature,
 in whom God found delight,
 you stood in radiant glory,
 transfigured by the light.

 Resplendent in God's favour,
 O Christ in beauty bright,
 illumine all who seek you,
 transform us by your light.

3rd Sunday, A

O source of living water
athirst at your own well,
You promised to the woman
a gift no tongue can tell.

Christ, lead us to the fountain,
that we may be immersed.
Give us the living water,
that we may never thirst.

4th Sunday, A

Christ, when you saw your brother,
you healed his blinded eyes.
from isolation's darkness
you summoned him to rise.

O Jesus, heal our blindness
with clarity of sight.
lead us from sin and evil
to walk the way of light.

5th Sunday, A

Christ, when you came in sorrow
to Lazarus, your friend,
you loosed the linen binding
and gave him life again.

Now see the chains that bind us
and all humanity.
from sin and every bondage
untie us, set us free!

Passion (Palm) Sunday, A, B & C

Christ, human in your weakness,
by nature yet divine,
your love is undefeated,
your death, its saving sign.

O Jesus, suff'ring servant,
your death has set us free.
may we who share your dying
share Easter's victory.

189 Gospel Responses for Year B

1st and 2nd Sunday, *as Year A*

3rd Sunday, B

Christ, when you saw the temple
with merchants everywhere,
you drove them out in anger:
this is a house of prayer!

Christ Jesus, see this temple,
keep it a holy place.
cleanse every heart of evil,
transform us by your grace.

4th Sunday, B

You came, the gift of God's love,
not to condemn but save.
to win our joy eternal,
your life you freely gave.

Your cross, O Christ, was lifted
for all who would believe.
Let us, with hearts of welcome,
your gift of life receive.

5th Sunday, B

Unless a grain of wheat dies,
a single seed remains,
but when for love surrendered,
that seed new life attains.

Christ, sow us in your wheat field
where, buried, we may root.
So will the seed, by dying,
bring forth abundant fruit.

Passion (Palm) Sunday *as Year A*

190 Gospel Responses for Year C

1st and 2nd Sunday, *as Year A*

3rd Sunday, C

The owner of the fig tree
had hoped its fruit to share,
he tasted not of harvest,
but disappointment there.

Have mercy, vineyard keeper,
on every barren tree,
till roots and branches tended
bear fruit abundantly.

4th Sunday, C

The spendthrift son, returning,
was pardoned all his wrong,
was welcomed home with feasting,
with ring and robe and song.

God, spendthrift in your mercy,
rejoicing our return,
guide all your children homeward,
your lavish love to learn.

5th Sunday, C

A woman stood before you
in silent shame, alone.
But you did not condemn her,
they dared not cast a stone.

Our sins accuse us, Jesus,
but hear our heartfelt plea:
toward weakness show compassion,
forgive us, set us free.

Passion (Palm) Sunday, *as Year A*

191 Lent Communion Song 1

Stephen Dean

Not on bread a-lone are we nou-rished, but on ev-ery word from the mouth of God.

192 Lent Communion Song 2

Marty Haugen

Lord, you can o-pen hearts that are stone; live in our flesh and our bone.

Lead us to won-der, mys-t'ry and grace, one in your lo-ving em-brace.

Verses: no. 623

Lent Communion Song 3: *Bread of Life (78) with seasonal verses*

Lent Hymns

193

Re - turn to God with all your heart, the source of grace and mer - cy; come seek the ten - der faith-ful-ness of God.

1 Now the time of grace has come,
the day of salvation:
come and learn now the way of our God.

2 I will take your heart of stone
and place a heart within you,
a heart of compassion and love.

3 If you break the chains of oppression,
if you set the pris'ner free;
if you share your bread with the hungry,
give protection to the lost;
give a shelter to the homeless,
clothe the naked in your midst,
then your light shall break forth like the dawn

Marty Haugen

194

Refrain

Come back to the Lord with all your heart, leave the past in as-hes; and turn to God with tears and fas-ting, for God is slow to an-ger and rea-dy to for-give.

Verses

1. Have mér-cy on me, Gód, for your kínd-ness, in com-pás-sion, blot óut my of-fénce. O wásh me from áll my gúilt; make me cléan from áll my sín.

2 I know my sins, every one,
   they stand before me in reproach,
   It is you alone I have offended,
   I have done what is evil in your sight.

3 You are just, O God, when you speak,
   your judgments are true and upright.
   In guilt I have languished since my birth,
   a sinner, even in the womb.

4 Truth in the heart is what you seek,
   plant your wisdom deep within me,
   Purify me, Lord, make me clean;
   wash me from all my sin.

5 A pure heart create within me,
   put a spirit renewed in my breast,
   Cast me not away from your presence,
   nor withhold your Spirit from me.

6 Deliver me from death, O God,
   and my tongue shall sing of your goodness
   Open my lips, O Lord,
   and my mouth shall sing your praise.

7 Sacrifice gives you no delight,
   burnt-offerings from me you would spurn.
   The sacrifice I bring you is my spirit,
   a broken, contrite heart you will befriend.

Psalm 50 (51), versified by Stephen Dean

195

Refrain

Give me a new heart, O God. Put your Spi - rit in me. Keep me with you, give me joy. Give me a new heart, O God.

1 God in your love, have mercy on me.
   in your compassion cleanse me.
   All of my guilt, wash it away,
   Lord, make me clean from my sin.

2 All of my faults, I know them so well.
   All of my sins, I know them.
   For against you alone have I sinned,
   evil in your sight have I done.

3 Truth in the heart you love most of all,
now fill my mind with wisdom.
Wash me from sin and I shall be clean,
I shall be pure as the snow.

Give me a new heart, O God,
put your Spirit in me.
Keep me with you, give me joy,
give me a new heart, O God.

4 Give me again the joy of your help.
Put a new spirit in me,

that I may teach sinners your ways,
that they will turn back to you.

5 You do not want a sacrifice made.
You would refuse burnt offerings.
My spirit is humble, offered to you.
You will not spurn my humble heart.

6 O spare my life and save me, O God.
I will proclaim your goodness.
Open my lips and help me to speak
and I will praise you with joy.

Psalm 50 (51), versified by Christopher Walker

196 Attende, Domine

Refrain

Hear us, al-migh-ty Lord, show us your mer-cy, sin-ners we stand here be-fore＿ you.
At - ten-de Do - mi - ne et mi-se - re - re qui - a pec - ca - vi-mus ti - bi.

Verses

1 Je - sus our Sa - viour,＿ Lord of all the na - tions, Christ our Re - dee-mer,
2 Word of the Fa - ther,＿ key-stone of God's buil - ding, source of our glad-ness

hear the prayers we of - fer, Spare us and save us, com-fort us in sor - row.
gate-way to the King-dom, free us in mer - cy from the sins that bind＿us.

3 God of compassion, Lord of might and
splendour,
graciously listen, hear our cries of anguish,
touch us and heal us where our sins have
wounded.

4 Humbly confessing that we have offended,
stripped of illusions, naked in our sorrow,
pardon, Lord Jesus, those your blood has
ransomed.

5 Innocent captive, you were led to slaughter,
sentenced by sinners when they brought false witness.
Keep from damnation those your death has rescued.

Latin, 10th C., tr. Ralph Wright OSB

197 Gospel Processional

Refrain

Word of God, Je-sus our Lord! O-pen our hearts to your Truth and Love.

Verses opposite

Verses

p Word of Peace, hope for our world, cas-ting a-side all fear:
Word of Joy, Mes-sage of life, glad-den the wea-ry heart:
Word of Hope, com-fort in pain, light in the dar-kest grief:
Word of God, Li-ving and True, pier-cing the stub-born mind:

Peter McGrail

1–4. Speak, and we shall live!

➣ *See also: Lent Gospel Acclamations (184-7); Praise to you, O Christ (200)*

198

1. We rise a-gain from ash-es, from the good we've failed to do. We rise a-gain from ash-es, to cre-ate our-selves a-new. If all our world is ash-es, then must our lives be true, an of-fer-ing of ash-es, an of-fer-ing to you.
2. We of-fer you our fai-lures, we of-fer you at-tempts, the gifts not ful-ly gi-ven, the dreams not ful-ly dreamt. Give our stum-bl-ings di-rec-tion, give our vi-sions wi-der view, an of-fer-ing of ash-es, an of-fer-ing to you.
3. Then rise a-gain from ash-es, let hea-ling come to pain, though spring has turned to win-ter, and sun-shine turned to rain. The rain we'll use for grow-ing, and cre-ate the world a-new, from an of-fer-ing of ash-es, an of-fer-ing to you.
4. Thanks be to the Fa-ther, who made us like him-self. Thanks be to his Son, who saved us by his death. Thanks be to the Spi-rit, who cre-ates the world a-new, from an of-fer-ing of ash-es, an of-fer-ing to you.

Tom Conry

199

1 Again we keep this solemn fast,
a gift of faith from ages past,
this Lent which binds us lovingly
to faith and hope and charity.

2 The law and prophets from of old
in figured ways this Lent foretold,
which Christ, all ages' Lord and Guide,
in these last days has sanctified.

3 More sparing, therefore, let us make
   the words we speak, the food we take,
   our sleep, our laughter, every sense;
   learn peace through holy penitence.

4 Let us avoid each harmful way
   that lures the careless mind astray;

by watchful prayer our spirits free
from scheming of the Enemy.

5 We pray, O blessed Three in One,
   our God while endless ages run,
   that this, our Lent of forty days,
   may bring us growth and give you praise.
   Ascribed to St Gregory the Great, c.540-604;
   tr. Peter J. Scagnelli

200

Bernadette Farrell

Refrain

Praise to you, O Christ our— Sa-viour, Word of the Fa-ther, cal-ling us to life;

Son of God who leads us to free-dom: glo - ry to you, Lord Je sus Christ.

Verses

1. You are the Word who calls us out of dark - ness, you are the
2. You are the Word whom pro - phets hoped and longed for; you are the

Word who leads us in - to light; you are the Word who
one who speaks to us to - day; you are the one who

brings us through the de - sert: glo - ry to you, Lord Je - sus Christ!
leads us to our fu - ture: glo - ry to you, Lord Je - sus Christ!

3. You are the Word who calls us to be
      servants;
   you are the Word whose only law is love;
   you are the Word-made-flesh who lives
      among us:
   glory to you, Lord Jesus Christ!

4 You are the Word who binds us and
      unites us,
   you are the Word who calls us to be one;
   you are the Word who teaches us
      forgiveness;
   glory to you, Lord Jesus Christ!
   Bernadette Farrell

➤ SEE ALSO: Lent Gospel Acclamations (184-7), Word of God (197)

201

1. When Sa - tan speaks_____ in an - gel tones and
2. When stones to bread_____ means more for us and
3. When clim - bing high_____ at - tracts a crowd and

san - cti - fies the road to ru - in; if on that path we're
more for us seems most al - lu - ring;
cheap ac - claim per - verts our cal - ling;

asked to go, Oh Je - sus, give us then the cou-rage to say No.—

4 When bowing down to serve the worst
   brings all we want but breaks our
      conscience
   if on that path we're asked to go, Oh Jesus,
   give us then the courage to say No.

5 When Satan speaks in angel tones
   and sanctifies the road to ruin;
   if on that path we're asked to go,
      Oh Jesus,
   give us then the courage to say No.

John L. Bell

202

1 Lord Jesus, as we turn from sin
   with strength and hope restored,
   receive the homage that we bring
   to you our risen Lord.

2 We call on you whose living word
   has made the Father known,
   O Shepherd, we have wandered far,
   find us and lead us home.

3 Your glance at Peter helped him know
   the love he had denied,
   now gaze on us and heal us, Lord,
   of selfishness and pride.

4 Reach out and touch with healing pow'r
   the wounds we have received,
   that in forgiveness we may love
   and may no longer grieve.

5 Then stay with us when ev'ning comes
   and darkness makes us blind,
   O stay until the light of dawn
   may fill both heart and mind.

Ralph Wright OSB

203

1 As earth that is dry and parched in the sun
   lies waiting for rain,
   my soul is a desert, arid and waste;
   it longs for your Word, O Lord.

*Come to the waters, all you who thirst;
come now, and eat my bread.*

2 Though you have no money, come, buy
      my corn,
   and drink my red wine.
   Why spend precious gold on what will
      not last?
   Hear me, and your soul will live.

3 As one on a journey strays from the road
   and falls in the dark,
   my mind is a wanderer, choosing
      wrong paths
   and longing to find a star.

4 The Lord is your light, the Lord is your
      strength;
   turn back to him now.
   For his ways are not the ways you
      would choose,
   and his thoughts are always new.

5 As rain from the mountains falls
      on the land
   and brings forth the seed,
   the word of the Lord sinks deep in our
      hearts,
   creating the flower of truth.

Anne Conway, from Isaiah 55:1, 2, 6, 9 & 12

204

1 Lord Jesus, think on me,
and purge away my sin;
from earthborn passions set me free,
and make me pure within.

2 Lord Jesus, think on me,
with care and woe oppressed;
let me thy loving servant be,
and taste thy promised rest.

3 Lord Jesus, think on me
amid the battle's strife;
in all my pain and misery
be thou my health and life.

4 Lord Jesus, think on me,
nor let me go astray;
through darkness and perplexity
point thou the heavenly way.

5 Lord Jesus, think on me,
when flows the tempest high:
when on doth rush the enemy,
O Saviour, be thou nigh.

6 Lord Jesus, think on me,
that, when the flood is past,
I may the eternal brightness see,
and share thy joy at last.
Synesius of Cyrene (c.375–430)
tr. A. W. Chatfield (1808–96)

205

1 Lord, who throughout these forty days
for us didst fast and pray,
teach us with thee to mourn our sins,
and close by thee to stay.

2 As thou with Satan didst contend,
and didst the victory win,
O give us strength in thee to fight,
in thee to conquer sin.

3 As thirst and hunger thou didst bear,
so teach us, gracious Lord,
to die to self, and daily live
by thy most holy word.

4 And through these days of penitence,
and through thy Passiontide,
yea, evermore, in life and death,
Lord Christ, with us abide.
Claudia F. Hernaman (1838–98)

206

1 Forty days and forty nights
thou wast fasting in the wild;
forty days and forty nights
tempted still, yet unbeguiled:

2 Sunbeams scorching all the day,
chilly dew–drops nightly shed,
prowling beasts about thy way,
stones thy pillow, earth thy bed.

3 Let us thy endurance share
and from earthly greed abstain
with thee watching unto prayer,
with thee strong to suffer pain.

4 Then if evil on us press,
flesh or spirit to assail,
victor in the wilderness,
help us not to swerve or fail!

5 So shall peace divine be ours;
holier gladness ours shall be,
come to us angelic powers,
such as ministered to thee.

6 Keep, O keep us, Saviour dear,
ever constant by thy side,
that with thee we may appear
at the eternal Eastertide.
G.H. Smyttan (1822–70)
& Francis Pott (1832–1909)

207

1 Out of the direst depths
I make my deepest plea.
O graciously bow down your ear
and listen, Lord, for me.

2 If you kept note of sins,
before you who could stand?
But since forgiveness is your right,
our reverence you command.

3   My soul longs for the Lord,
    and hopes to hear God's word.
    More keenly than some watch for dawn,
    I wait and watch for God.

4   Yes, with the Lord is grace
    and power to free and save.
    Redemption from their every sin
    God's people yet shall have.
Psalm 130, versified by John L. Bell

Transfiguration (cf 2 Sunday of Lent)

208

1   O raise your eyes on high and see
    there stands our sovereign Lord,
    his glory is this day revealed,
    his Word a two–edged sword.

2   We glimpse the splendour and the power
    of him who conquered death,
    the Christ in whom the universe
    knows God's creating breath.

3   Of every creed and nation King
    in him all strife is stilled;
    the promise made to Abraham
    in him has been fulfilled.

4   The prophets stand and with great joy
    give witness as they gaze;
    the Father with a sign has sealed
    our trust, our hope, our praise.

5   This glory that today our eyes
    have glimpsed of God's own Son
    will help us ever sing with love
    of Three who are but One.
Ralph Wright OSB

209

1   How good, Lord, to be here!
    Your glory fills the night;
    your face and garments, like the sun,
    shine with unborrowed light.

2   How good, Lord, to be here,
    your beauty to behold,
    where Moses and Elijah stand,
    your messengers of old.

3   Fulfiller of the past,
    promise of things to be:
    we hail your body glorified,
    and our redemption see.

4   Before we taste of death,
    we see your kingdom come;
    we still would hold the vision bright,
    and make this hill our home.

5   How good, Lord, to be here!
    Yet we may not remain;
    but since you bid us leave the mount,
    come with us to the plain.
J. Armitage Robinson (1858-1933), alt.

210

We behold the splendour of God
shining on the face of Jesus.
We behold the splendour of God
shining on the face of the Son.

1   And oh, how his beauty transforms us,
    the wonder of Presence abiding.
    Transparent hearts give reflection
    of Tabor's light within;
    of Tabor's light within.

2   Jesus, Lord of Glory,
    Jesus beloved Son.
    Oh how good to be with you;
    how good to share your light,
    how good to share your light.
Carey Landry

➤ *See also no. 215*

211

1   Our Father, we have wandered
    and hidden from your face,
    in foolishness have squandered
    your legacy of grace.
    But now, in exile dwelling,
    we rise with fear and shame,
    as distant but compelling,
    we hear you call our name.

2   And now at length discerning
    the evil that we do,
    behold us Lord, returning
    with hope and trust to you.

In haste you come to meet us
and home rejoicing bring.
In gladness there to greet us
with calf and robe and ring.

3 O Lord of all the living,
both banished and restored,
compassionate, forgiving
and ever caring Lord,
grant now that our transgressing,
our faithlessness may cease.
Stretch out your hand in blessing
in pardon and in peace.

Kevin Nichols (1929-2006)

212

1 All ye who seek a comfort sure
in trouble and distress,
whatever sorrow vex the mind,
or guilt the soul oppress:

2 Jesus, who gave himself for you
upon the cross to die,
opens to you his sacred heart,–
oh, to that heart draw nigh!

3 Ye hear how kindly he invites;
ye hear his words so blest:
'All ye that labour, come to me,
and I will give you rest.'

4 Jesus, thou joy of saints on high!
Thou hope of sinners here!
Attracted by those loving words,
to thee I lift my prayer.

5 Wash thou my wounds in that dear blood
which forth from thee doth flow;
new grace, new hope inspire; a new
and better heart bestow.

18th century, tr. Edward Caswall (1814–78

213

Refrain
Oh God, I seek you, my soul thirsts for you, Your love is fi-ner than life.

Verses
1. As a dry and wea - ry __ de - sert land, so my soul is thirs - ting for my God, and my flesh is faint for the God I seek, for your love is more to me than life. __
2. ʼ I think of you when at night I rest, I re- flect u - pon your stead-fast love. I will cling to you, oh __ Lord my God, in the sha - dow of your wings I sing. __
3. I will bless your name all the days I live, I will raise my hands and call on you. My joy-ful lips shall __ sing your praise, you a - lone have filled my hun - gry soul. __

Psalm 62 (63), adapted by Marty Haugen

214

Refrain

As the deer longs for run - ning streams, so I— long,
so I— long,——— so I— long for you.

Verses

1. A - thirst my soul— for you the God who is my life! When shall I
2. ⁊ Ech - oes meet— as deep is cal - ling un - to deep, o - ver my
3. Con - ti - nual - ly— the foe de - lights in taun ting me: 'Where is God,—
4. De - fend me, God,— send forth your light— and your truth, they will lead
5. Then I shall go— un - to the al - tar of my God. Prai - sing you,—

see, when shall I— see,——— see the face of God?
head, all your migh-ty wa - ters, swee - ping o - ver me.
—— where is your— God?'—— Where, O where, are you?
me to your ho - ly moun-tain, to your dwel - ling place.
—— O my joy and glad - ness, I shall praise your name.

Bob Hurd, based on Psalm 41 (42)

215

Transfigure us, O Lord,
transfigure us, O Lord.
Break the chains that bind us;
speak your healing word,
and where you lead we'll follow.
Transfigure us, O Lord.

1. Down from heights of glory
   into the depths below,
   the love of God selfemptied,
   the love of God to show.
   You light the path before us,
   the way that we must go.

2. Light for those in darkness,
   the hungry have their fill,
   glad tidings for the humble,
   the healing of all ills;
   in these we glimpse your glory,
   God's promises fulfilled.

3. Pardon for the sinner,
   a shepherd for the sheep,
   a drink of living water
   for all who thirst and seek,
   and feasting at your table,
   the lowly and the least.

4. To the holy city,
   Jerusalem, you go;
   your face set t'ward the ending,
   the cross to be your throne,
   Shall we journey with you
   and share your paschal road?

Bob Hurd

➤ *See also nos. 211-212*

216

1. By the waters, the waters of Babylon,
2. On the willows, the willows of Babylon,
3. There our captors, our captors from Babylon,
4. Should I not remember Jerusalem.

we sat down and wept, and wept for thee, Zion;
we hung up our harps, our harps, for thee, Zion;
tried to make us sing, and sing, of thee, Zion;
Let my right hand wither, my tongue cleave to my mouth.

we remember thee, remember thee, remember thee, Zion.
how can we sing, can we sing, sing of thee, Zion.
but we could not sing, we could not sing, we could not sing, Zion.
Should I prize not thee, I prize not thee, my joy, Jerusalem.

Anon, based on Psalm 136 (137). V. 4 editorial

217

1 Gift of love, dawning bright,
pierces through endless night:
God of life, sharing might,
all creation holding,
earth and sky enfolding.
Gift of love, love, love,
gift of love, love, love.
Glory be, Lord to thee,
God of our salvation.

2 Thus you spoke from on high:
choose to live or to die,
love to give or deny -

life and love now blending;
love is life unending.

3 Then you came on the earth,
gift of love from your birth;
shared our life, gave us worth;
to yourself inviting,
God with us uniting.

4 For our sake you were killed;
once foretold, now fulfilled;
love so great, be not stilled!
Beams of love you lifted,
and with life were gifted.

Robert C. Trupia

218

Refrain

Deep within I will plant my law, not on stone, but in your heart. Follow me, I will bring you back, you will be my own, and I will be your God.

1 I will give you a new heart, a new spirit within you,
for I will be your strength.

2 Seek my face, and see your God,
for I will be your hope.

3 Return to me, with all your heart,
and I will bring you back.

David Haas, from Jeremiah 31:33,
Ezekiel 36:26, Joel 2:12

219

Refrain

Like as the deer that yearns for flowing wa-ters, so longs my soul for God, the li-ving God.

1 Like the deer that yearns
for flowing waters:
so my soul is yearning
for you, my God.

2 My soul is thirsting for God,
the God of my life:
when can I enter and see
the face of God?

3 These things will I remember
as I pour out my soul:
how I would lead the rejoicing crowd
into the house of God.

4 Send forth your light and truth,
let these be my guide:
let them bring me to your holy mountain,
to the place where you dwell.

5 And I will come to the altar of God,
the God of my joy!
My redeemer, I will thank you on the harp,
O God, my God.

Text: Psalm 41 (42), The Grail. Music from the Abbey of Tamié

220

*Grant to us, O Lord, a heart renewed;
recreate in us your own spirit, Lord!*

1 Behold, the days are coming,
says the Lord our God,
when I will make a new covenant
with the house of Israel.

2 Deep within their being
I will implant my law;

I will write it in their hearts.

3. I will be their God,
and they shall be my people.

4. And for all their faults
I will grant forgiveness;
never more will I remember their sins.

*Lucien Deiss CSSp (1921-2007),
from Jeremiah 31:31-34*

221 God is forgiveness

Chant from Taizé

God is for-give-ness. Dare to for-give and God will be with you.

God is for-give-ness. Love and do not fear.

222 Crucem tuam/O Lord, your cross

Taizé chant by Jacques Berthier (1923–94)

Cru-cem tu - am a-do-ra-mus Do-mi-ne, re-sur-rec-ti-o-nem
O Lord, your cross we a-dore and glo-ri - fy, for your ho-ly re-sur-

tu-am lau-da-mus Do-mi-ne. Lau-da-mus et glo-ri-fi-ca-mus.
rec-tion we praise you Lord of life. We praise you and we glo-ri-fy you.

Re-sur-rec-ti-o-nem tu-am lau-da-mus Do-mi-ne.
For your ho-ly re-sur-rec-tion we praise you, Lord of life.

223

1 At the cross her station keeping,
stood the mournful mother weeping,
close to Jesus to the last;

2 Through her heart his sorrow sharing,
all his bitter anguish bearing,
now at length the sword has pass'd.

3 Oh, how sad and sore distress'd
was that mother highly blest,
of the sole–begotten One.

4 Christ above in torment hangs;
she beneath beholds the pangs
of her dying glorious Son.

5 Is there one who would not weep,
'whelm'd in miseries so deep,
Christ's dear mother to behold?

6 Can the human heart refrain
from partaking in her pain,
in that mother's pain untold?

7 Bruised, derided, cursed, defiled,
she beheld her tender child,
all with bloody scourges rent;

8 For the sins of his own nation,
saw him hang in desolation,
till his spirit forth he sent.

9 O thou mother! Fount of love!
Touch my spirit from above,
make my heart with thine accord:

10 Make me feel as thou hast felt;
make my soul to glow and melt
with the love of Christ my Lord.

11 Holy Mother, pierce me through,
in my heart each wound renew
of my Saviour crucified.

12 Let me share with thee his pain
who for all my sins was slain,
who for me in torments died.

13 Let me mingle tears with thee,
mourning him who mourn'd for me,
all the days that I may live:

14 By the cross with thee to stay,
there with thee to weep and pray,
is all I ask of thee to give.

15 Virgin of all virgins best,
listen to my fond request:
let me share thy grief divine;

16 Let me, to my latest breath,
in my body bear the death
of that dying Son of thine.

17 Wounded with his every wound
    steep my soul till it hath swoon'd
    in his very blood away.

18 Be to me, O Virgin, nigh,
    lest in flames I burn and die,
    in his awful judgement day.

19 Christ, when thou shalt call me hence,
    be thy mother my defence,
    be thy cross my victory.

20 While my body here decays,
    may my soul thy goodness praise,
    safe in paradise with thee.

Ascribed to Jacopone da Todi (d 1306). tr. Edward Caswall (1814–78)

224

We a - dore you, O Je - sus Christ;
for by your cross you re - deemed the world.

Suzanne Toolan, RSM

225

1 Were you there when they crucified my
     Lord?
   Were you there when they crucified my
     Lord?
   *Oh sometimes it causes me to tremble,
     tremble, tremble.*
   *Were you there when they crucified my
     Lord?*

2 Were you there when they nailed him to
     a tree? …

3 Were you there when they pierced him
     in the side? …

4 Were you there when the sun refused to
     shine? …

5 Were you there when they laid him in
     the tomb? …

6 Were you there when they rolled the
     stone away?
           Afro–American Spiritual

226

1 O come and mourn with me awhile;
   see, Mary calls us to her side;
   O come and let us mourn with her;
     *Jesus our love, Jesus our love
       is crucified.*

2 Have we no tears to shed for him,
   while soldiers scoff and men deride?
   Ah! look how patiently he hangs;

3 How fast his feet and hands are nailed;
   his blessed tongue with thirst is tied;
   his failing eyes are blind with blood;

4 Seven times he spoke, seven words of
     love,
   and all three hours his silence cried
   for mercy on humanity;

5 O love of God! O human sin!
   In this dread act your strength is tried;
   and victory remains with love;
           F.W. Faber (1814–63), alt.

227 Hosanna

Taizé chant by Jacques Berthier (1923-94)

Ho - san - na, ho-san - na, ho-san - na in ex - cel - sis. Ho -

228

Sing ho - san - na, sing ho-san - na to the King, Son of Da - vid!

Here he comes! Fol - low the Mas - ter for he comes to save us all.

Bles sings on the King who comes in the name of the Lord!

They came run-ning down the street so ex - ci- ted were the chil-dren as they came, (singing:)

The chil-dren came with ol - ive bran-ches. They tried to touch him as he came:

for they loved him, they be-lieved him, and they fol-lowed him to Je - ru- salem; (The)

Christopher Walker

229

All glory, laud and honour,
to thee, Redeemer King,
to whom the lips of children
made sweet hosannas ring.

1 Thou art the King of Israel,
   thou David's royal Son,
   who in the Lord's name comest,
   the King and blessed one.

2 The company of angels
   are praising thee on high,
   and mortal folk, with all things
   created, make reply.

3 The people of the Hebrews
   with palms before thee went:
   our praise and prayer and anthems
   before thee we present.

4 To thee before thy passion
   they sang their hymns of praise;
   to thee now high exalted
   our melody we raise.

5 Thou didst accept their praises,
   accept the prayers we bring,
   who in all good delightest,
   thou good and gracious king.

St Theodulph of Orleans (d. 821), tr. J.M. Neale (1818–66)

230

1 Ride on! Ride on in majesty!
Hark, all the tribes hosanna cry;
thy humble beast pursues his road
with palms and scattered garments strowed.

2 Ride on! Ride on in majesty!
In lowly pomp ride on to die;
O Christ, thy triumphs now begin
o'er captive death and conquered sin.

3 Ride on! Ride on in majesty!
The wingèd squadrons of the sky
look down with sad and wondering eyes,
to see the approaching sacrifice.

4 Ride on! Ride on in majesty!
Thy last and fiercest strife is nigh;
the Father, on his sapphire throne,
expects his own anointed Son.

5 Ride on! Ride on in majesty!
In lowly pomp ride on to die;
bow thy meek head to mortal pain,
then take, O God, thy power, and reign.
H. H. Milman (1791–1868)

232

1 Ah, holy Jesus, how have you offended?
that man to judge you has in hate pretended?
by foes derided, by your own rejected,
O most afflicted!

2 Who was the guilty? Who brought this
upon you?
It is my treason, Lord, that has undone you.
And I, O Jesus, I it was denied you,
I crucified you.

231

Come to Jerusalem, rejoicing before him
Greet him with loud hosannas,
bow down, adore him!

1 All peoples clap your hands,
cry out to your Maker!
God is the Lord of all,
O tremble and fear him!

2 God mounts the throne with joy,
with blaring of trumpets!
Sing praise to God almighty,
king of all nations!

3 God is the king of all the nations,
O praise him!
Praise him with all your skill,
enthroned in his temple!

4 Peoples and princes come
in homage to meet him.
God is the mighty one,
the world is his kingdom!
Stephen Dean, based on Psalm 46 (47)

---

3 See how the shepherd for the sheep is
offered,
the slave has sinned and yet the son has
suffered;
for our atonement hangs the Saviour
bleeding,
God interceding.

4 For me, kind Jesus, was your incarnation,
your dying sorrow and your life's oblation;
your bitter passion and your desolation,
for my salvation.

5 O mighty Saviour, I cannot repay you;
I do adore you and will here obey you;
recall your mercy and your love unswerving,
not my deserving.
Robert Bridges (1844-1930), after J. Heerman (1585-1647).
Revised by Jubilate Hymns

233 **All you who pass this way** *Taizé chant by Jacques Berthier (1923-94)*

All you who pass this way, look and see.
Sung between cantor's verses

234

Refrain — Stephen Dean

Fa - ther,___ if this cup may not pass me by___ but I must

drink it; your will be done,___ your will be done.

Sung between cantor's verses, or as a 2-part canon

235

Refrain

As pro-phets fore-told long a - go,___ God's ser-vant, the

Christ, would suf - fer and die.___ By his wounds we are healed.___

Verses

1. He com - mit - ted no sin, on his lips was no guile.___ When re -
2. Bo - dy bro - ken in pain, yet he ut - tered no threat,___ but
3. He him - self bore our sins in his pas - sion and pain,___ so that

viled and ab - used he was sil - ent,___ he was si - lent.___
trus - ted the judgement of God,___ and God's jus - tice.___
dy - ing to sin we might live,___ we might live.___

Peter Jones (1951-2016), from 1 Peter 2:21-24.

236

1. See, Christ was wounded for our sake
   and bruised and beaten for our sin,
   so by his suff'rings we are healed,
   for God has laid our guilt on him.

2. Look on his face, come close to him
   - see, you will find no beauty there;
   despised, rejected, who can tell
   the grief and sorrow he must bear?

3. Like sheep that stray we leave God's path
   to choose our own and not his will,
   like lamb to slaughter he has gone,
   obedient to his Father's will.

4. Cast out to die by those he loved,
   reviled by those he died to save,
   see how sin's pride has sought his death,
   see how sin's hate has made his grave.

5. For on his shoulders God has laid
   the weight of sin that we should bear;
   so by his passion we have peace,
   through his obedience and his prayer.

Brian Foley (1919-2000)

237

1 O sacred head ill-uséd,
   by reed and bramble scarred;
   that idle blows have bruiséd
   and mocking lips have marred:
   how dimmed that eye so tender,
   how wan those cheeks appear,
   how overcast the splendour
   that angel hosts revere!

2 What marvel if thou languish,
   vigour and virtue fled,
   wasted and spent with anguish
   and pale as are the dead?
   O by thy foes' derision,
   that death endured for me,
   grant that thy open vision
   a sinner's eyes may see.

3 Good Shepherd, spent with loving,
   look on me, who have strayed,
   oft by those lips unmoving
   with milk and honey stayed;
   spurn not a sinner's crying
   now from thy love out cast,
   but rest thy head in dying
   on these frail arms at last.

4 In this thy sacred Passion
   O, that some share had I!
   O, may thy Cross's fashion
   o'erlook me when I die!
   For these dear pains that rack thee
   a sinner's thanks receive;
   O, lest in death I lack thee,
   a sinner's care relieve.

5 Since death must be my ending,
   in that dread hour of need,
   my friendless cause befriending,
   Lord, to my rescue speed;
   thyself, dear Jesus, trace me
   that passage to the grave,
   and from thy Cross embrace me
   with arms outstretched to save.

   P. Gerhardt (1607–76), tr. R.A Knox (1888-1957)

The Easter Triduum
Maundy Thursday

238

1 The glory of the cross we sing
   the cross of Jesus Christ our Lord,
   who died and rose to set us free
   our way from death to life secured.

2 As once God's people rested safe,
   protected by a lamb's own blood,
   so we acclaim the sacrifice
   of Jesus Christ the Lamb of God.

3 As once the Chosen People passed
   from pain to freedom through the sea,
   so now baptismal water saves
   the chosen, called to liberty.

4 At passover before he died
   Christ Jesus took the bread and wine:
   'This is my body, this my blood,
   do this as my memorial sign.'

5 What once by Jesus was achieved
   we celebrate with heart and soul,
   recalling and effecting now
   the saving work that makes us whole.

   John Ainslie

239

1 The heav'nly Word, proceeding forth
   yet leaving not the Father's side,
   accomplishing his work on earth
   had reached at length life's eventide.

2 By false disciple to be giv'n
   to foemen for his life athirst,
   himself, the very bread of heav'n,
   he gave to his disciples first.

3 He gave himself in either kind,
   he gave his flesh, he gave his blood;
   in love's own fullness thus designed,
   to be, for humankind, the food.

4 O saving victim, opening wide
   the gate of heav'n to all below,
   our foes press on from every side;
   thine aid supply, thy strength bestow.

5 To thy great name be endless praise,
    Immortal Godhead, one in three:
    O grant us endless length of days
    in our true native land with thee.

St. Thomas Aquinas (1227–74), tr. J. M. Neale (1818–66)

240 Reception of the Oils

1 Behold the oil of the sick, blessed by our Bishop,
    sent to us for the anointing of all who suffer illness *(Refrain A or B)*

Ref.A: Thanks_ be to God!_____ Thanks_ be to God!_____
Ref.B: Bless'd be God for e - ver! Bless'd be God for e - ver!

2 Behold the oil of the catechumens, blessed by our Bishop
    send to us for the anointing of our catechumens
    in preparation for their baptism.

3 Behold the sacred chrism, oil mixed with sweet perfume,
    and consecrated by our Bishop, sent to us for the anointing
    of the baptized who are to be sealed with the Holy Spirit.

John Schiavone

241

Jesu, Jesu, fill us with your love,
show us how to serve
the neighbours we have from you.

1 Kneels at the feet of his friends,
    silently washes their feet,
    Master who pours out himself for them.

2 Neighbours are rich folk and poor,
    neighbours are black folk and white,
    neighbours are nearby and far away.

3 These are the ones we should serve,
    these are the ones we should love,
    all these are neighbours to us and you.

4 Kneel at the feet of our friends,
    silently washing their feet,
    this is the way we should live with you.

Ghana folk song, adapted by Tom Colvin

242

God is love, and where true love is
God himself is there.

1 Here in Christ we gather, love of Christ
    our calling.
  Christ, our love, is with us, gladness be
    his greeting.
  Let us love and serve him, God of all
    the ages.
  Let us love sincerely, seeing Christ in
    others.

2 When we Christians gather, members of
    one Body,
  Christ, our God, be present, loving and
    beloved.
  Let there be no discord, banished every
    quarrel.
  Let there be one Spirit, bond of peace
    among us.

3 Grant us love's fulfillment, joy with all
    the blessed,
  when we see your glory, risen Lord and
    Saviour
  bathe us in your splendour, Light of all
    creation,
  be our bliss forever as we sing your
    praises.

Ubi Caritas, arr. James Quinn SJ (1919-2010)

243

1 Into one we all are gathered through the
     love of Christ.
  Let us then rejoice with gladness. In him
     we find love.
  Let us fear and love the living God,
  and love and cherish humankind.
  Where charity and love are, there is God.

2 Therefore, when we are together in the
     love of Christ,
  let our minds know no division, strife or
     bitterness,
  may the Christ our God be in our midst.
  Through Christ our Lord all love is found.

3 May we see your face in glory, Christ our
     loving God.
  With the blessed saints of heaven give us
     lasting joy.
  We will then possess true happiness,
  and love for all eternity.

  Ubi Caritas, versified by Michael Cockett

244a

U - bi ca - ri - tas et a - mor,____ De-us i - bi est.
(est ve - ra)*____ *Either wording may be sung*

1 Congregavit nos in unum Christi amor.
  Exsultemus et in ipso iucundemur.
  Timeamus et amemus Deum vivum.
  Et ex corde diligamus nos sincero.

2 Simul ergo cum in unum congregamur:
  ne nos mente dividamus, caveamus.

  Cessent iurgia maligna, cessent lites.
  Et in medio nostri sit Christus Deus.

3 Simul quoque cum beatis videamus
  glorianter vultum tuum, Christe Deus:
  gaudium quod est immensum, atque
     probum,
  saecula per infinita saeculorum.

  Latin, 9th Century

244b *Taizé chant by Jacques Berthier (1923-94)*

U-bi ca-ri - tas et a - mor, U-bi ca-ri - tas De - us i - bi est.

245a

Faith, hope and love,
these three shall remain,
but the greatest of all is love.

1. On the night of his betrayal,
   Jesus took a towel and water,
   washed the feet of his disciples,
   Faithful and betrayer likewise,
   this is how God loves.

2. Jesus came to Simon Peter,
   Peter could not understand him;
   said that Jesus was his master
   'And a master should not do this,
   only servants kneel.'

3. Jesus said 'Unless I wash you,
   you will have no place beside me;
   now you do not see the reason,
   Later you will understand me,
   why I choose to kneel.'

4. Love is patient, love is kindly;
   never envious or boasting;
   love lays down its life for others;
   this is what the master taught us
   when he washed our feet.

245b Ubi Caritas text (refrain as 245a)

1. Christ has gathered us together
   filled our hearts with joy and gladness,
   Let us love our God sincerely,
   loving one another likewise,
   God is truly love.

2. Therefore when we are assembled,
   Banished be all sad divisions;
   Let all bitterness be ended
   Strife and quarrels be forgotten
   For the Lord is here.

3. Grant us, loving Lord, hereafter,
   Sight of your eternal glory,
   Joy with all the saints in heaven,
   peace and happiness unbounded,
   as we sing your praise.

Paraphrased by Stephen Dean

246

1 Of the glorious body telling,
   O my tongue, its myst'ries sing,
   and the blood, all price excelling,
   which the world's eternal king,
   in a noble womb once dwelling,
   shed for this world's ransoming.

2 Giv'n for us, for us descending,
   of a virgin to proceed,
   man with man in converse blending,
   scattered he the gospel seed,
   till his sojourn drew to ending,
   which he closed in wondrous deed.

3 At the last great supper lying,
   circled by his brethren's band,
   meekly with the law complying,
   first, he finished its command.
   Then, immortal food supplying,
   gave himself with his own hand.

4 Word made flesh, by word he maketh
   very bread his flesh to be;
   man in wine Christ's blood partaketh,
   and if senses fail to see,
   faith alone the true heart waketh,
   to behold the mystery.

5 Therefore, we before him bending,
   this great sacrament revere;
   types and shadows have their ending,
   for the newer rite is here;
   faith, our outward sense befriending,
   makes the inward vision clear.

6 Glory let us give, and blessing,
   to the Father and the Son;

honour, might and praise addressing,
   while eternal ages run;
   ever too his love confessing,
   who from both, with both is one.

St. Thomas Aquinas (1227–74), tr. J. M. Neale,
(1818–66) E. Caswall (1814–78), and others

247

1 Pange, lingua, gloriosi
   corporis mysterium,
   sanguinisque pretiosi,
   quem in mundi pretium
   fructus ventris generosi
   Rex effudit gentium.

2 Nobis datus, nobis natus
   ex intacta Virgine;
   et in mundo conversatus,
   sparso verbi semine,
   sui moras incolatus
   miro clausit ordine.

3 In supremae nocte coenae
   recumbens cum fratribus,
   observata lege plene
   cibis in legalibus:
   cibum turbae duodenae
   se dat suis manibus.

4 Verbum caro, panem verum
   Verbo carnem efficit:
   fitque sanguis Christi merum;
   et si sensus deficit,
   ad firmandum cor sincerum
   sola fides sufficit.

5 Tantum ergo Sacramentum
   veneremur cernui:
   et antiquum documentum
   novo cedat ritui:
   præstet fides supplementum
   sensuum defectui.

6 Genitori, genitoque
   laus, et jubilatio,
   salus, honor, virtus quoque
   sit et benedictio:
   procedenti ab utroque
   compar sit laudatio. Amen.

St Thomas Aquinas (1227–74)

248

1 An upper room did our Lord prepare
for those he loved until the end:
and his disciples still gather there,
to celebrate their Risen Friend.

2 A lasting gift Jesus gave his own:
to share his bread, his loving cup.
Whatever burdens may bow us down,
he by his cross shall lift us up.

3 And after Supper he washed their feet,
for service, too, is sacrament.
In him our joy shall be made complete –
sent out to serve, as he was sent.

4 No end there is! We depart in peace.
He loves beyond the uttermost:
in every room in our Father's house
he will be there, as Lord and Host.

F. Pratt Green (1903-2000)

249 Stay with me

Taizé chant by Jacques Berthier (1923-94)

Stay with me, re-main here with me, watch and pray, watch and pray.

Good Friday

250

1 Sing, my tongue, the song of triumph,
tell the story far and wide;
tell of dread and final battle,
sing of Saviour crucified;
how upon the cross a victim,
vanquishing in death he died.

2 God in pity saw us fallen,
shamed and sunk in misery,
when we fell on death by tasting
fruit of the forbidden tree;
then another tree was chosen
which the world from death should free.

3 Thirty years among us dwelling
his appointed time fulfilled,
born for this, he meets his Passion,
for that this he freely willed,
on the Cross the Lamb is lifted
where his life-blood shall be spilled.

4 He endured the nails, the spitting,
vinegar, and spear, and reed;
from that holy body broken
blood and water forth proceed:

earth and stars, and sky, and ocean
by that flood from stain are freed.

5 Faithful cross! Above all other,
one and only noble tree!
None in foliage, none in blossom,
none in fruit your peer may be;
sweetest wood and sweetest iron!
Sweetest weight is hung on thee.

6 Bend your boughs, O tree of glory!
All your rigid branches, bend!
For a while the ancient temper
that your birth bestowed, suspend;
and the king of earth and heaven
gently on your bosom tend.

7 Praise and honour to the Father,
praise and honour to the Son,
praise and honour to the Spirit,
ever three and ever one,
one in might and one in glory,
while eternal ages run.

Venantius Fortunatus (530–609),
tr. J. M. Neale (1818–66), and others

251

O— my peo-ple, what have I done to of-fend— you so? Tell me, give an swer, tell me.

252

Sung between choir verses

1. The royal banners forward go,
   the cross shines forth in mystic glow,
   where he in flesh, our flesh who made,
   our sentence bore, our ransom paid.

2. There whilst he hung, his sacred side
   by soldier's spear was open'd wide,
   to cleanse us in the precious flood
   of water mingled with his blood.

3. Fulfill'd is now what David told
   in true prophetic song of old,
   how God the heathen's king should be;
   for God is reigning from the tree.

4. O tree of glory, tree most fair,
   ordain'd those holy limbs to bear,
   how bright in purple robe it stood,
   the purple of a saviour's blood!

5. Upon its arms, like balance true,
   he weigh'd the price for sinners due,
   the price which none but he could pay:
   and spoil'd the spoiler of his prey.

6. To thee, eternal Three in One,
   let homage meet by all be done,
   as by the cross thou dost restore,
   so rule and guide us evermore. Amen.

Venantius Fortunatus (530–609), tr. J. M. Neale (1818–66), and others

253 Jesus, remember me

Taizé chant by Jacques Berthier (1923-94)

Je-sus, re-member me when you come in-to your King-dom.

Je-sus, re-member me when you come in-to your King-dom.

The Easter Vigil

Canticle after the Third Reading. Exodus 15

Stephen Dean

254

I will sing to the Lord, glor-ious his tri-umph,

glo-rious his tri-umph! I will sing to the Lord.

Easter

Seasonal Service Music 255-66; Hymns 267-88

Chorus

255

Hail, O fes-ti-val day! Blest day that is hal-lowed for e-ver;

day when our Lord a-rose, brea-king the king-dom of death.

Verses 1, 3, 5, 7

1. All the fair beau-ty of earth from the death of the win-ter a-ri-sing!
3. Dai-ly the love-li-ness grows, a - dorned with the glo-ry of blos-som;
5. God the Al-migh-ty, the Lord, the__ ru - ler of earth and the hea-vens,
7. Spi - rit of life and of power, now__ flow in us, fount of our be - ing,

To chorus

Ev' - ry good_ gift of the year__ now with its Ma-ster re - turns.
hea - ven her_ gates un - bars,__ fling-ing her in-crease of light:
guard us from_ harm with - out,__ cleanse us from e - vil with - in:
light that en - ligh - tens_ all,__ life that in all may a - bide:

Verses 2, 4, 6, 8

2. He who was nailed to the cross is__ Lord and the ru - ler of all things;
4. Rise from the grave now, O Lord, who art au - thor of life and cre - a - tion.
6. Je - sus the health of the world, en - ligh - ten our minds, great Re - dee-mer,
8. Praise to the Gi - ver of good! O__ Lo - ver and au - thor of con-cord,

To chorus

all things cre - a - ted on earth sing to the glo - ry of God:__
Trea - ding the path-way of death, new life you give to us all:__
Son of the Fa - ther su - preme, on - ly be - got - ten of God:__
pour out your balm on our souls, or - der our ways in your peace:__

Salve festa dies, Venantius Fortunatus (530-609).
Tr. composite. Music by R. Vaughan Williams (1872-1958)

256 Blessing of Water

Stephen Dean

I saw streams of water flowing from the temple's right side,
healing power and life bestowing from the one who had died: Allelu - ia, al - le - lu - ia, from our Sa - viour glo - ri - fied.

1 Into day from deepest night,
out of darkness into light,
Christ our Saviour comes once more,
opens wide salvation's door!

2 He has healed us with his blood,
led us safe through Jordan's flood,

on the further bank we stand,
gazing on the promised land!

3. He has raised us from the grave,
from the Red Sea's mighty wave.
Dead to sin we rise with Christ,
paschal Lamb now sacrificed.
Stephen Dean

➤ SEE ALSO: *You have put on Christ (400)*

257 Psalm/Gathering Song (Ps 117 (118))

Michael Joncas

This is the day the Lord— has made, let us re-joice and be glad.—

This is the day the Lord— has made, let us re-joice and be glad.—

1 Give thanks to the Lord for he is good,
his mercy endures for ever;
let the house of Israel say:
'His mercy endures for ever.'

2 The Lord's right hand has struck with
pow'r,
the Lord's right hand is exalted;
I shall not die, but live
and declare the works of the Lord.

3 The stone which the builders rejected
has become the cornerstone.
By the Lord this has been done;
it is wonderful in our eyes!
Michael Joncas

*Psalm 118: Response, ICEL; verses,
Confraternity of Christian Doctrine, alt.*

258 Psalm/Gathering Song (Ps 117 (118)) *Bernadette Farrell*

The stone which the buil-ders re-jec-ted has become the cor-ner-stone;__ al-le-lu - ia,__ al-le-lu - ia,__ has be-come the cor-ner-stone.__

1 Let the family of Israel say:
'God's love has no end, God's love has
no end.'
Let the family of Aaron say:
'God's love has no end, God's love has
no end.'
And let all who fear God, and let all who
fear God
say his love is without end.
Alleluia, alleluia, say his love is without
end.

2 I called to the Lord in my distress,
he answered me and set me free.
God is at my side, God is at my side,
God is here to help me now.
Alleluia, alleluia, God is here to help me
now.

3 Open to me the gates of holiness;
I will enter and give thanks.
This is the Lord's own gate,
the gate where the just may enter in.
I will thank you, Lord, I will thank
you, Lord.
for you hear and answer me.
Alleluia, alleluia, for you hear
and answer me.

4 Go forward with branches, go forward
processing,
go to the altar of the Lord
and give thanks to God,
and give thanks to God
for his love is without end.
Alleluia, alleluia, for his love is
without end.

259 Sequence: Victimae paschali laudes *(Original version overleaf)*

1 O Flock of Christ, your homage bring
to Christ the Lamb, your glorious King!
His Easter praise in triumph sing!
Alleluia, alleluia, alleluia!

2 Peace has come down from God on high!
The King of peace in death did lie!
To save the sheep the Lamb did die!

3 Never on earth was stranger sight:
life fought with death in darkest night,
yet lives to reign in endless light!

4 What saw you, Mary, on your way?
'I saw the tomb where Life once lay,
whose glory shone this Easter Day!

5 Angels their joyful tidings spread!
Grave-clothes I saw where none lay
dead,
the cloth that once had veiled his head!

6 'Christ is my hope, who rose for me!
Soon will you all his glory see!
Christ bids you go to Galilee!'

7 Christ lives again, whose blood was shed,
the Lord of life, our living Bread,
the Firstborn risen from the dead!
Alleluia, alleluia, alleluia!

Ascribed to Wipo of Burgundy, d.1048;
tr. James Quinn SJ (1919-2010)

➤ SEE ALSO Christ the Lord is risen today (273)

260 Sequence: Victimae paschali laudes (original version)

1. Vic - ti - mae pas - cha - li lau - des im - mo - lent Chri - sti - a - ni.
1. *Christians, praise the pas - chal vic - tim! Of - fer thank - ful sa - cri-fice.*

2. Ag - nus re - de - mit o - ves, Chri - stus in - no - cens Pa - tri re - con-
3. Mors et vi - ta du - el - lo con - fli - xe - re mi - ran - do: dux vi -
2. *Christ the Lamb has saved the sheep, Christ the just one paid the price re - con-*
3. *Death and life fought bit - ter - ly for this won-drous vic - to - ry; the Lord*

ci - li - a - vit pec - ca - to - res. 4. Dic no - bis, Ma - ri - ia,_____
tae mor - tu - us re - gnat vi - vus. 6. An - ge - li - cos tes - tes,_____
ci - ling sin - ners to the Fa - ther. 4. O Ma - ry come and say_____
of life who died reigns glo - ri - fied! 6. Bright an - gels tes - ti - fied,_____

quid vi - dis - ti in vi - a? 5. Se - pul - chrum Chri - sti vi -
su - da - ri - um et ves - tes. 7. Sur - rex - it Chri - stus spes
what you saw at break of day. 5. The emp - ty tomb of my
shroud and grave - clothes side by side! 7. Yes, Christ my hope rose glo -

ven - tis, et glo - ri - am vi - di re - sur - gen - tis:
me - a: prae - ce - det su - os in Ga - li - lae - am.
li - ving Lord! I saw Christ Je - sus ri - sen and a - dored!
ri - ous - ly. He goes be - fore you in - to Ga - li - lee.

8. Sci - mus Chri - stum sur - re - xis - se a mor - tu - is ve - re:
8. *Share the good news, sing joy - ful - ly: his death is vic - to - ry!*

tu no - bis, vic - tor Rex, mi - se - re - re. (A - men.___ Al - le - lu - ia.)
Lord Je - sus, vic - tor King, show us mer - cy.

Ascribed to Wipo of Burgundy, d. 1048; English translation by Peter J. Scagnelli

Gospel Acclamations for Easter

261 *Traditional melody*

Al - le - lu - ia, al - le-lu - ia,— al - le - lu - ia.

262 *Refrain* — *Bernadette Farrell*

Al - le - lu - ia, al - le - lu - ia, Je - sus, ri - sen Lord of life!

Al - le - lu - ia, al - le - lu - ia, al - le - lu - ia!

1. Word of the Fa - ther: Je - sus Christ! Hope of the world: Je - sus Christ!
2. Light of the na - tions: Je - sus Christ! Way, truth and life: Je - sus Christ!
3. Li - ving a-mong us: Je - sus Christ! Word in our flesh: Je - sus Christ!

Bro - ken and bur - ied: Je - sus Christ! Ri - sen to life: Je - sus Christ!
Bea-ring our sor - row: Je - sus Christ! With us through time: Je - sus Christ!
Ser - vant of oth - ers: Je - sus Christ! Friend of the poor: Je - sus Christ!

263 *Verses Cantor:* *All:* *Stephen Dean*

1. Did not our hearts burn with - in us, Al-le-lu - ia, al-le-lu - ia.
2. Come, ri - sen Lord, walk be - side us.
3. O - pen our hearts, ri - sen Je - sus.

Cantor: *All:*

As we heard the ri - sen Je - sus? Al - le - lu - ia.
May your gos - pel e - ver guide us.
May your Spi - rit ne - ver leave us.

Refrain *All:*

Al - le - lu - ia, praise the Lord, praise his Word!

Al - le - lu - ia, praise the ri-sen Lord!

264

Refrain

O filii et filiae, French 15th cent.

Al - le - lu - ia,—— al - le - lu - ia, al - le - lu - ia!

Verses

1. O sons and daugh - ters, let—— us sing; the King of hea - ven, the
2. Glo - ry and praise—— to you,—— O Christ, who shed for us—— your

glo - rious King, this day from death rose tri - um - phing: al - le - lu - ia!
blood—— un - priced, pass - o - ver Lamb now sa - cri - ficed: al - le - lu - ia!

➢ *See also nos. 280-281*

Processional Chants/Communion Songs

265 **Christus resurrexit**

Taizé chants by Jacques Berthier (1923-94)

Mmm....

Christus re - sur - re - xit, Chris - tus re - sur - re - xit,

Mmm....

al - le - lu - ia, al - le - lu - ia!

266 **Surrexit Christus**

A1   B

(hum)—— Sur - re - xit Chris - tus, al - le - lu - ia!

A2   C

(hum)—— Can - ta - te Do - mi - no, al - le - lu - ia!

267

1 Jesus Christ is ris'n today, alleluia!
Our triumphant holy day, alleluia!
Who did once, upon the cross, alleluia!
Suffer to redeem our loss, alleluia!

2 Hymns of praise then let us sing, alleluia!
Unto Christ, our heavenly king, alleluia!
Who endured the cross and grave, alleluia!
Sinners to redeem and save, alleluia!

3 But the pains that he endured, alleluia!
Our salvation have procured; alleluia!
Now above the sky he's king, alleluia!
Where the angels ever sing, alleluia!
Lyra Davidica (1708)

268

Alleluia, alleluia,
give thanks to the risen Lord.
Alleluia, alleluia,
give praise to his name.

1 Jesus is Lord of all the earth.
He is the King of creation.

2 Spread the good news o'er all the earth.
Jesus has died and has risen.

3 We have been crucified with Christ.
Now we shall live for ever.

4 God has proclaimed the just reward.
Life for us all, alleluia.

5 Come, let us praise the living God,
joyfully sing to our Saviour.
Don Fishel

269

1 At the Lamb's high feast we sing
praise to our victorious king,
who hath washed us in the tide
flowing from his piercèd side.
Praise we him whose love divine
gives the guests his blood for wine,
gives his body for the feast,
love the victim, love the priest.

2 Where the paschal blood is poured,
Death's dark angel sheathes his sword;
Israel's hosts triumphant go
through the wave that drowns the foe.
Christ the Lamb, whose blood was shed.
Paschal victim, paschal bread;
with sincerity and love
eat we manna from above.

3 Mighty victim from the sky,
powers of hell beneath thee lie;
death is conquered in the fight;
thou hast brought us life and light,
now thy banner thou dost wave;
vanquished Satan and the grave;
angels join his praise to tell –
see o'erthrown the prince of hell.

4 Paschal triumph, paschal joy,
only sin can this destroy;
from the death of sin set free
souls re–born, dear Lord, in thee.
Hymns of glory, songs of praise,
Father, unto thee we raise.
Risen Lord, all praise to thee,
ever with the Spirit be.
Ad regias agni dapes, Anonymous, 7th
century, tr. Robert Campbell (1814–68)

270

1 Christ is alive, with joy we sing;
we celebrate our risen Lord,
praising the glory of his name.
Alleluia, alleluia, alleluia.

2 He is the grain of wheat that died;
sown in distress and reaped in joy,
yielding a harvest of new life.

3 He is the sun which brings the dawn:
he is the light of all the world,
setting us free from death and sin.

4 He is the vine set in the earth,
sharing our life, becoming man,
that we might share in God's own life.

5 Christ is alive, with joy we sing;
we celebrate our risen Lord,
praising the glory of his name.
Pamela Stotter

271

1 Battle is o'er, hell's armies flee:
raise we the cry of victory
with abounding joy resounding,
alleluia, alleluia.

2 Christ who endured the shameful tree,
o'er death triumphant welcome we,
our adoring praise outpouring,
alleluia, alleluia.

3 On the third morn from death rose he,
clothed with what light in heaven shall be,
our unswerving faith deserving,
alleluia, alleluia.

4 Hell's gloomy gates yield up their key,
paradise door thrown wide we see;
never–tiring be our choiring,
alleluia, alleluia.

5 Lord, by the stripes they laid on thee,
grant us to live from death set free,
this our greeting still repeating,
alleluia, alleluia.
Simphonia Sirenum (1695)
tr. R.A. Knox (1888–1957)

272

1 Christ is alive! Let Christians sing;
the cross stands empty to the sky:
let streets and homes with praises ring.
Love, drowned in death, shall never die.

2 Christ is alive! No longer bound
to distant years in Palestine,
but saving, healing, here and now,
and touching every place and time.

3 In every insult, rift and war,
where colour, scorn or wealth divide,
Christ suffers still, yet loves the more,
and lives, where even hope has died.

4 Women and men, in age and youth,
can feel the Spirit, hear the call,
and find the way, the life, the truth,
revealed in Jesus, freed for all.

5 Christ is alive, and comes to bring
good news to this and every age,
till earth and sky and ocean ring
with joy, with justice, love and praise.
Brian A. Wren

273

1 Christ the Lord is risen today!
Christians, haste your vows to pay,
offer ye your praises meet
at the paschal victim's feet;
for the sheep the Lamb hath bled,
sinless in the sinner's stead.
Christ the Lord is ris'n on high;
now he lives, no more to die.

2 Christ, the victim undefiled,
all to God hath reconciled
when in strange and awful strife
met together death and life;
Christians, on this happy day
haste with joy your vows to pay.
Christ the Lord is ris'n on high;
now he lives, no more to die.

3 Say, O wond'ring Mary, say
what thou sawest on thy way.
'I beheld, where Christ had lain,
empty tomb and angels twain,
I beheld the glory bright
of the rising Lord of light;
Christ my hope is ris'n again;
now he lives, and lives to reign.'

4 Christ, who once for sinners bled,
now the first–born from the dead,
throned in endless might and power,
lives and reigns for evermore.
Hail, eternal hope on high!
Hail, thou king of victory!
Hail, thou Prince of life adored!
Help and save us, gracious Lord.
Victimae paschali, tr. Jane E. Leeson (1809–81)

274

1. Dark - ness is gone,_____ day - light is come: God's
2. See now the cross,_____ see__ now the grave: they,

heir to heaven and earth a - ri - ses__ with the dawn. Death
va - cant, ce - le - brate how God's foo-lish-ness can save. The

lo - ses its si - ni-ster sting, God's pro - mise to do a new thing is
cri - mi - nal nailed as a fraud is raised by the po-wer of God and

done, and Hal - le - lu - jah, earth joins__ heaven to sing._____
lives. So Hal - le - lu - jah! Scat - ter the news a - broad._____

3 Greener the grass, brighter the sun,
   the God-loved world proclaims a new
      age has begun.
   Creation is decked for her guest
   who, free from his grave clothes is dressed
   in light and, Hallelujah!
   tells that the earth is blessed.

4 The needed trust, the longed-for peace
   are passed as hands from sword and
      shackle are released.
   The violence of hate reigns no more:
   the victory of love is the core
   of hope and, Hallelujah!
   Love means an open door.

5 'The kingdom comes!' the King proclaims:
   Justice and joy abound where Christ-
      filled faith pertains.
   Religion, remote and typecast,
   is gone, and the future is vast.
   New tongues sing 'Hallelujah!
   God is for us at last!'

6 Enrol the drum, enlist the gong
   to celebrate in sound that right has
      conquered wrong.
   Join hands with the neighbour unknown,
   unite through the love that is shown
   in Christ, for, Hallelujah!
   Christ is our Lord alone.

        John L. Bell & Graham Maule

275

1 The strife is o'er, the battle done;
   the victory of life is won:
   the song of triumph has begun:
    Alleluia, alleluia, alleluia!

2 On the third morn he rose again
   glorious in majesty to reign;
   O let us swell the joyful strain:

3 He closed the yawning gates of hell,
   the bars from heaven's high portals fell;
   let hymns of praise his triumphs tell:

4 Lord, by your death on Calvary,
   from death's dread sting your people
      free,
   that we may live eternally!
        17th C., tr. Francis Pott (1832-1909) alt.

276

1 He is risen, tell the story
to the nations of the night;
from their sin and from their blindness,
let them walk in Easter light.
Now begins a new creation,
now has come our true salvation.
Jesus Christ, the Son of God!

2 Mary goes to tell the others
of the wonders she has seen;
John and Peter come a'running
what can all this truly mean?
O Rabboni, Master holy,
to appear to one so lowly!
Jesus Christ, the Son of God!

3 He has cut down death and evil,
he has conquered all despair;
he has lifted from our shoulders,
all the weight of anxious care.
Risen Brother, now before you,
we will worship and adore you.
Jesus Christ, the Son of God!

4 Now get busy, bring the message,
so that all may come to know
there is hope for saint and sinner,
for our God has loved us so.
Ev'ry church bell is a'ringing,
ev'ry Christian now is singing.
Jesus Christ, the Son of God!
Willard F. Jabusch

277

1. Easter glory fills the sky! *Alleluia!*
Christ now lives, no more to die! *Alleluia!*
Darkness has been put to flight! *Alleluia!*
By the living Lord of light! *Alleluia!*

2 See, the stone is rolled away
from the tomb where once he lay!
He has risen as he said,
glorious Firstborn from the dead!

3 Mary, Mother, greet your Son
radiant from his triumph won!
By his cross you shared his pain,
so for ever share his reign!

4 Magd'len, wipe away your tears!
He has come who calms your fears!
Hear the Master speak your name;
turn to him with heart aflame!

5 Shepherd, seek the sheep that strayed!
Come to contrite Peter's aid!
Strengthen him to be the rock;
make him shepherd of your flock!

6 Seek not life within the tomb;
Christ stands in the upper room!
Risen glory he conceals,
risen Body he reveals!

7 Though we see his face no more,
he is with us as before!
Glory veiled, he is our Priest,
his true flesh and blood our feast!

8 Christ, the Victor over death,
breathes on us the Spirit's breath!
Paradise is our reward,
endless Easter with our Lord!
James Quinn SJ (1919-2010)

278

1 Now the green blade riseth from the
    buried grain,
wheat that in dark earth many days
    has lain;
love lives again, that with the dead
    has been:
love is come again like wheat that
    springeth green.

2 In the grave they laid him, Love whom
    men had slain,
thinking that never he would wake again,
laid in the earth like grain that sleeps
    unseen:
love is come again like wheat that
    springeth green.

3 Forth he came at Easter, like the risen
     grain,
  he that for three days in the grave had lain,
  quick from the dead my risen Lord is seen:
  love is come again like wheat that
     springeth green.

4 When our hearts are wintry, grieving or
     in pain,
  thy touch can call us back to life again,
  fields of our heart that dead and bare
     have been:
  love is come again like wheat that
     springeth green.
           J. M. C. Crum (1872-1958)

279

1 Ye choirs of new Jerusalem,
  your sweetest notes employ,
  the Paschal victory to hymn
  in strains of holy joy.

2 How Judah's Lion burst his chains,
  and crushed the serpent's head;
  and brought with him, from death's
     domain,
  the long–imprisoned dead.

3 From hell's devouring jaws the prey
  alone our leader bore;
  his ransomed hosts pursue their way
  where he hath gone before.

4 Triumphant in his glory now
  his sceptre ruleth all:
  earth, heaven, and hell before him bow
  and at his footstool fall.

5 While joyful thus his praise we sing,
  his mercy we implore,
  into his palace bright to bring,
  and keep us evermore.

6 All glory to the Father be,
  all glory to the Son,
  all glory, Holy Ghost, to thee,
  while endless ages run.
           St. Fulbert of Chartres (c. 1000),
           tr. R. Campbell (1814–68)

280

Alleluia, alleluia, alleluia!

1 O sons and daughters, let us sing!
  the King of heav'n, the glorious King,
  o'er death today rose triumphing,
  Alleluia!

2 That Easter morn, at break of day,
  the faithful women went their way
  to seek the tomb where Jesus lay.

3 An angel clad in white they see,
  who sat, and spoke unto the three,
  'Your Lord has gone to Galilee.'

4 That night th'apostles met in fear
  amidst them came their Lord most dear
  and said, 'My peace be on all here.'

5 When Thomas first the tidings heard,
  how they had seen the risen Lord,
  he doubted the disciples' word.

6 'My wounded side, O Thomas, see;
  behold my hands, my feet', said he,
  and doubt not, but believe in me.'

7 When Thomas saw that wounded side,
  the truth no longer he denied:
  'You are my Lord and God!' he cried.

8 How blest are they who have not seen,
  and yet whose faith has constant been,
  for they eternal life shall win.

9 On this most holy day of days,
  to God your hearts and voices raise,
  in laud, and jubilee and praise.
           O filii et filiae, Jean Tisserand, d.1494,
           tr. J.M.Neale (1818–66), alt.

281

Alleluia, alleluia, alleluia!

1 Glory to God who does wondrous things,
  let all the people God's praises now sing,
  all of creation in splendour shall ring:
  Alleluia!

2 See how salvation for all has been won,
  up from the grave our new life has begun.
  Life now perfected in Jesus, the Son:

3 Now in our presence the Lord will appear,
shine in the faces of all of us here,
fill us with joy and cast out all our fear:

4 Call us, Good Shepherd, we listen for you,
wanting to see you in all that we do,
we would the gate of salvation pass
   through:

5 Lord, we are open to all that you say,
ready to listen and follow your way,
you are the potter and we are the clay:

6 If we have love, then we dwell in the Lord,
God will protect us from fire and
   sword,
fill us with love and the peace of his word:
Marty Haugen

➤ *See also no. 264*

282

Sing to the mountains, sing to the sea.
Raise your voices, lift your hearts.
This is the day the Lord has made.
Let all the earth rejoice.

1 I will give thanks to you, my Lord.
You have answered my plea.
You have saved my soul from death.
You are my strength and my song.

2 Holy, holy, holy Lord.
Heaven and earth are full of your glory.

3 This is the day that the Lord has made.
Let us be glad and rejoice.
He has turned all death to life.
Sing of the glory of God.
Robert J. Dufford SJ

283

1 The day of resurrection!
Earth, tell it out abroad;
the Passover of gladness
the Passover of God!
From death to life eternal,
from earth unto the sky,
our Christ hath brought us over
with hymns of victory.

2 Our hearts be pure from evil,
that we may see aright
the Lord in rays eternal
of resurrection–light;
and listening to his accents,
may hear so calm and plain
his own 'All hail' and, hearing,
may raise the victor strain.

3 Now let the heavens be joyful,
and earth her song begin,
the round world keep high triumph,
and all that is therein;
let all things seen and unseen
their notes of gladness blend,
for Christ the Lord hath risen,
our joy that hath no end.
St. John Damascene (c. 750),
tr. J. M. Neale (1818–66)

284

1 We walk by faith, and not by sight:
no gracious words we hear
of him who spoke as none e'er spoke,
but we believe him near.

2 We may not touch his hands and side,
nor follow where he trod;
yet in his promise we rejoice,
and cry 'My Lord and God!'

3 Help then, O Lord, our unbelief,
and may our faith abound;
to call on you when you are near,
and seek where you are found:

4 That when our life and faith is done
in realms of clearer light
we may behold you as you are
in full and endless sight.

5 We walk by faith, and not by sight:
no gracious words we hear
of him who spoke as none e'er spoke,
but we believe him near.
Henry Alford (1810–71), alt.

285

1 Sing of one who walks beside us
and this day is living still,
one who now is closer to us
than the thoughts our hearts distill.
One who once upon a hilltop
raised against the power of sin,
died in love as his own creatures
crucified their God and King!

2 Strangers we have walked beside him
the long journey of the day,
and have told him of the darkness
that has swept our hope away.
He has offered words of comfort,
words of energy and light,
and our hearts have blazed within us
as he saved us from the night.

3 Stay with us, dear Lord, and raise us,
once again the night is near.
Dine with us and share your wisdom,
free our hearts from every fear.
In the calm of each new evening,
in the freshness of each dawn,
if you hold us fast in friendship
we will never be alone.

Ralph Wright OSB

Tune: American, 19th C.

286

1 This joyful Eastertide,
away with sin and sorrow,
my love, the Crucified,
hath sprung to life this morrow:
Had Christ, that once was slain,
ne'er burst his three–day prison,
our faith had been in vain:
but now hath Christ arisen.

2 My flesh in hope shall rest,
and for a season slumber:
till trump from east to west
shall wake the dead in number:

3 Death's flood hath lost his chill,
since Jesus crossed the river:
lover of souls, from ill
my passing soul deliver:

G.R. Woodward (1848–1934)

287

1 Thine be the glory, risen conquering Son,
endless is the victory thou o'er death hast won;
angels in bright raiment rolled the stone away,
kept the folded grave–clothes, where thy body lay.
Thine be the glory, risen, conquering Son,
endless is the victory thou o'er death hast won.

2 Lo, Jesus meets us, risen from the tomb;
lovingly he greets us, scatters fear and gloom;
let the church with gladness hymns of triumph sing,
for her Lord is living, death has lost its sting.

3 No more we doubt thee, glorious Prince of life;
life is nought without thee; aid us in our strife;
make us more than conquerors, through thy deathless love;
bring us safe through Jordan to thy home above.

E.L. Budry (1854–1932),
tr. R.B. Hoyle (1875–1939)

288

1. On the journey to Emmaus with our hearts cold as
2. And our hearts burned within us as we talked on the

stone— the— One who would save us had left us a - lone. Then a
way, how— all that was pro - mised was ours on that day. So we

stran - ger walks— with us and,— to our sur - prise, he—
begged him, 'Stay— with us and— grant us your word.' We—

o - pens our— sto - ries and he o - pens our eyes.
wel - comed the— stran - ger and we wel - comed the Lord.

3 And that evening at table
as he blessed and broke bread,
we saw it was Jesus
aris'n from the dead;
though he vanished before us
we knew he was near -
the life in our dying
and the hope in our fear.

4 On our journey to Emmaus,
in our stories and feast,
with Jesus we claim that the
greatest is least:
and his words burn within us -
let none be ignored -
who welcomes the stranger
shall welcome the Lord.

Marty Haugen

The Ascension

289

1 Praise him as he mounts the skies,
    alleluia!
  Christ, the Lord of paradise, *alleluia!*
  Cry hosanna in the height, *alleluia!*
  as he rises out of sight, *alleluia!*

2 Now at last he takes his throne,
  from all ages his alone!
  with his praise creation rings:
  'Lord of lords and King of kings!'

3 Hands and feet and side reveal
  wounds of love, high priesthood's seal!
  Advocate, for us he pleads;
  Heavenly Priest, he intercedes!

4 Christians, raise your eyes above!
  He will come again in love,
  on that great and wondrous day
  when this world will pass away!

5 At his word new heavens and earth
  will in glory spring to birth!
  Risen Lord, our great Amen,
  come Lord Jesus, come again!
      James Quinn SJ (1919-2010)

290

1 The head that once was crowned with
      thorns
  is crowned with glory now:
  a royal diadem adorns
  the mighty victor's brow.

2 The highest place that heaven affords
  is his, is his by right.
  The King of kings and Lord of lords,
  and heaven's eternal light;

3 The joy of all who dwell above,
  the joy of all below,
  to whom he manifests his love,
  and grants his name to know.

4 To them the cross, with all its shame
  with all its grace is given;
  their name an everlasting name,
  their joy the joy of heaven.

5 They suffer with their Lord below,
  they reign with him above,
  their profit and their joy to know
  the mystery of his love.

6 The cross he bore is life and health,
  though shame and death to him;
  his people's hope, his people's wealth,
  their everlasting theme.
      Thomas Kelly (1769–1854)

291

1 Hail the day that sees him rise, *alleluia!*
  To his throne above the skies; *alleluia!*
  Christ, the Lamb for sinners given,
      alleluia!
  Enters now the highest heaven,
      alleluia!

2 There for him high triumph waits;
  lift your heads, eternal gates!
  He hath conquered death and sin;
  take the king of glory in!

3 Circled round with angel–powers,
  their triumphant Lord and ours;
  wide unfold the radiant scene,
  take the king of glory in!

4 Lo, the heaven its Lord receives,
  yet he loves the earth he leaves;
  though returning to his throne,
  he calls humankind his own.

5 See! He lifts his hands above.
  See! He shows the prints of love;
  hark! His gracious lips bestow,
  blessings on his Church below.

6 Still for us he intercedes,
  his prevailing death he pleads;
  near himself prepares our place,
  he the first–fruits of our race.

7 Lord, though parted from our sight,
  far above the starry height,
  grant our hearts may thither rise,
  seeking thee above the skies.

8 Ever upward let us move,
  wafted on the wings of love;
  looking when our Lord shall come,
  longing, sighing after home.

*Charles Wesley (1707–88), Thomas
Cotterill (1779–1823), and others*

292

1 New praises be given to Christ newly crowned,
  who back to his heaven a new way hath found;
  God's blessedness sharing before us he goes,
  what mansions preparing, what endless repose!

2 His glory still praising on thrice holy ground
  the apostles stood gazing, his mother around;
  with hearts that beat faster, with eyes full of love,
  they watched while their master ascended above.

3 'No star can disclose him', the bright angels said;
  Eternity knows him, your conquering head;
  those high habitations, he leaves not again,
  till, judging all nations, on earth he shall reign.'

4 Thus spoke they and straightway, where legions defend
  heaven's glittering gateway, their Lord they attend,
  and cry, looking thither, 'Your portals let down
  for him who rides hither in peace and renown.'

5 They asked, who keep sentry in that blessed town,
  'Who thus claimeth entry, a king of renown?'
  'The Lord of all valiance', that herald replied,
  'Who Satan's battalions laid low in their pride.'

6 Grant, Lord, that our longing may follow thee there,
  on earth who are thronging thy temples with prayer;
  and unto thee gather, Redeemer, thine own
  where thou with thy Father dost sit on the throne.

St. Bede (673–735) tr. R. A. Knox (1888–1957)

293

1 Abba, Father, send your Spirit.
  Glory, Jesus Christ.
  Abba, Father, send your Spirit.
  Glory, Jesus Christ.

  *Glory hallelujah, glory, Jesus Christ.
  Glory hallelujah, glory, Jesus Christ.*

2 I will give you living water …

3 If you seek me you will find me …

4 If you listen you will hear me …

5 Come, my children, I will teach you …

6 I'm your shepherd, I will lead you …

7 Peace I leave you, peace I give you …

8 I'm your life and resurrection …

9 Glory Father, glory Spirit …

Sister Virginia Vissing SSMN

Pentecost

294 Gospel Acclamation & Song of Praise

James Walsh

Je-sus is Lord, Al-le-lu - ia! Je-sus is Lord, Al-le-lu - ia!

1. Come,– Ho - ly Spi - rit of God, come, re - new the face of the earth.
2. Send— forth your light and your truth. Guide us with your pow-er- ful love.
3. Ho - ly Spi - rit, make— us one. Al - le - lu - ia, al - le- lu - ia!

295 Litany of the Spirit

Music: Paul Inwood

Refrain

Spi - rit of God, come in - to our hearts, make us your new cre - a - tion.

1. Spirit of light: let your wisdom shine on us.
2. Spirit of silence: make us aware of God's presence.
3. Spirit of courage: dispel the fear in our hearts.
4. Spirit of fire: inflame us with Christ's love.
5. Spirit of peace: help us be still and listen to God's word.
6. Spirit of joy: inspire us to proclaim the good news.
7. Spirit of love: help us to open ourselves to the needs of others.
   Confirmation only:
8. Spirit of power: give your help and strength to those who are to be confirmed.
9. Spirit of power: give us all your help and strength.
10. Spirit of truth: guide us all in the way of Christ.

Words: Paul Inwood & Michael Shaw (1949-2012)

296

1 Come, Holy Ghost, Creator, come
from thy bright heavenly throne,
come, take possession of our souls,
and make them all thine own.

2 Thou who art called the Paraclete,
best gift of God above,
the living spring, the living fire,
sweet unction and true love.

3 Thou who art sev'nfold in thy grace,
finger of God's right hand;
his promise, teaching little ones
to speak and understand.

4 O guide our minds with thy blest light,
with love our hearts inflame;
and with thy strength, which ne'er decays,
confirm our mortal frame.

5 Far from us drive our deadly foe;
true peace unto us bring;
and through all perils lead us safe
beneath thy sacred wing.

6 Through thee may we the Father know,
through thee th'eternal Son,
and thee the Spirit of them both,
thrice–blessèd Three in One.

last verse overleaf

7 All glory to the Father be,
   with his co–equal Son:
   the same to thee, great Paraclete,
   while endless ages run.

Veni Creator Spiritus. Ascribed to
Rabanus Maurus (776–856), tr. Anon.

297

1. Ve - ni, Cre__ a - tor__ Spi - ri - tus, men - tes tu - o - rum__
2. Qui di - ce - ris Pa - ra - cli - tus, al - tis - si - mi do -
3. Tu sep - ti for - mis__ mu - ne - re, digi - tus pa - ter - nae__
4. Ac - cen - de lu - men__ sen - si - bus, in - fund*e* a - mo - rem__
5. Hostem re pel - las__ lon - gi - us, pa - cem - que do - nes__
6. Per te sci__ a - mus, da, Pa - trem, nos - ca - mus at - que

vi - si - ta, im - ple__ su - per na gra - ti - a
num De - i, fons vi - vus, ig - nis, ca - ri - tas
dex - te - rae, tu ri - te pro mis__ sum Pa - tris,
cor - di - bus, in - fir - ma nos - tri cor - por - is,
pro - ti - nus: duc to__ re sic te__ prae - vi - o,
Fi - li - um, te u - tri - us - que__ Spi - ri - tum

quae__ tu cre__ as - ti__ pec - to - ra. A - men.__
et__ spi - ri - ta - lis__ unc - ti - o.
ser__ mo - ne__ di - tans__ gut - tu - ra.
vir - tu - te__ fir - mans__ per - pe - ti.
vi__ te - mus__ om - ne__ no - xi - um.
cre - da - mus__ om - ni__ tem - po - re.

Ascribed to Rabanus Maurus (776–856)

298 **Veni Creator Spiritus**

Taizé chant by Jacques Berthier

Ve - ni cre - a - tor Spi - ri - tus.

299 **Responsorial Psalm for Pentecost** (Ps 103 (104))

Christopher Walker

Send forth your Spi - rit, O Lord, and re - new the face of the earth!

Opposite: Pentecost Sequence   *and see also 301, 304, 307*

300

1. Ve - ni san - cte spi - ri - tus et e - mit - te cae - li - tus
2. Ve - ni pa - ter pau - pe - rum, ve - ni da - tor mu - ne - rum,
Ho - ly Spi - rit, Lord of light, from the clear ce - les - tial height,
Come, thou Fa - ther of the poor, come with trea - sures which en - dure;

lu - cis tu - ae ra - di - um. 3. Con - so - la - tor op - ti - me,
ve - ni lu - men cor - di - um. 4. In la - bo - re re - qui - es,
thy pure bea - ming ra - diance give; Thou, of all con - sol - ers best,
come, thou Light of all that live! Thou in toil art com - fort sweet;

dul - cis hos - pes a - ni - mae, dul - ce re - fri - ge - ri - um.
in ae - stu tem - pe - ri - es, in fle - tu so - la - ti - um.
thou, the soul's de - light - some guest, dost re - fre - shing peace bes - tow:
plea - sant cool - ness in the heat; sol - ace in the midst of woe.

5. O lux be - a - tis - si - ma, re - ple cor - dis in - ti - ma
6. Si - ne tu - o nu - mi - ne, ni - hil est in ho - mi - ne,
Light im - mor - tal, light div - ine, vis - it thou these hearts of thine,
If thou take thy grace a - way, no - thing pure in us will stay;

tu - o - rum fi - de - li - um; 7. La - va quod est sor - di - dum,
ni - hil est in - no - xi - um. 8. Fle - cte quod est ri - gi - dum,
and our in - most be - ing fill: Heal our wounds, our strength re - new;
all our good is turned to ill. Bend the stub - born heart and will;

ri - ga quod est a - ri - dum, sa - na quod est sau - ci - um.
fo - ve quod est fri - gi - dum, re - ge quod est de - vi - um.
on our dry - ness pour thy dew; wash the stains of guilt a - way:
melt the fro - zen, warm the chill; guide the steps that go a - stray.

9. Da tu - is fi - de - li - bus in te con - fi - den - ti - bus
10. Da vir - tu - tis me - ri - tum, da sa - lu - tis e - xi - tum,
Thou, on those who e - ver - more thee con - fess and thee a - dore,
Give them com - fort when they die; give them life with thee on high;

sa - crum sep - te - na - ri - um; A - men.
da pe - ren - ne gau - di - um.
in thy seven - fold gifts des - cend:
give them joys that ne - ver end.

Ascribed to Stephen Langton (c.1160-1228)
tr. Edward Caswall (1814–78)

301

1 Holy Spirit, Lord of light,
from the clear celestial height,
thy pure beaming radiance give;
come, thou Father of the poor,
come with treasures which endure;
come, thou Light of all that live!

2 Thou, of all consolers best,
thou, the soul's delightsome guest,
dost refreshing peace bestow:
thou in toil art comfort sweet;
pleasant coolness in the heat;
solace in the midst of woe.

3 Light immortal, light divine,
visit thou these hearts of thine,
and our inmost being fill:
if thou take thy grace away,
nothing pure in us will stay;
all our good is turned to ill.

4 Heal our wounds, our strength renew;
on our dryness pour thy dew;
wash the stains of guilt away:
bend the stubborn heart and will;
melt the frozen, warm the chill;
guide the steps that go astray.

5 Thou, on those who evermore
thee confess and thee adore,
in thy sevenfold gifts descend:
give them comfort when they die;
give them life with thee on high;
give them joys that never end.
Ascribed to Stephen Langton (c.1160-1228)
tr. Edward Caswall (1814–78)

302

1 Breathe on me, Breath of God,
fill me with life anew,
that I may love what thou dost love,
and do what thou wouldst do.

2 Breathe on me, Breath of God,
until my heart is pure:
until with thee I have one will
to do and to endure.

3 Breathe on me, Breath of God.
till I am wholly thine,
until this earthly part of me
glows with thy fire divine.

4 Breathe on me, Breath of God,
so shall I never die,
but live with thee the perfect life
of thine Eternity.
Edwin Hatch (1835–89)

303

1 Come down, O love divine,
seek thou this soul of mine,
and visit it with thine own ardour
glowing;
O comforter, draw near, within my heart
appear,
and kindle it, thy holy flame bestowing.

2 O let it freely burn,
till earthly passions turn
to dust and ashes in its heat consuming;
and let thy glorious light shine ever on
my sight,
and clothe me round, the while my path
illuming.

3 Let holy charity
mine outward vesture be,
and lowliness become mine inner
clothing;
true lowliness of heart, which takes the
humbler part,
and o'er its own shortcomings weeps
with loathing.

4 And so the yearning strong,
with which the soul will long,
shall far outpass the power of human
telling,
for none can guess its grace,
till he become the place
wherein the Holy Spirit makes a
dwelling.
Bianco da Siena (d. 1434),
tr. R.F. Littledale (1833-90)

304

Come, Ho-ly Spi-rit, come, Ho-ly Spi-rit; come, Ho-ly Spi-rit, set our hearts on fire.

Verses may be sung by cantor over refrain

1. Come. Spirit. Lord of Light,
   Come from your heavenly height
   Come and restore our sight,
   Come, O Spirit.

2. Consoler, Spirit blest,
   the soul's most welcome guest,
   our ease in toil and stress,
   Come, O Spirit.

3. Blest Spirit, guide our way;
   Without your help we stray;
   come to our hearts today,
   Come, O Spirit.

4. Come set our hearts on fire;
   make goodness our desire;
   our weakening souls inspire,
   Come, O Spirit.

5. Come to us from above,
   and fill our hearts with love;
   Descend, O heavenly Dove,
   Come, O Sprit.

6. Give comfort when we die,
   give life with you on high,
   unending joys supply,
   Come, O Spirit.   *Stephen Dean*

305

1. She sits like a bird, broo-ding on the wa-ters,— hov'-ring on the
2. She wings o-ver earth, res-ting where she wi-shes,— lighting close at

cha-os of the world's first day; she sighs and she sings, mo-the-ring cre-
hand or soar-ing through the skies; she nests in the womb, wel-com-ing each

a-tion,— wai-ting to give birth to all the Word— will say.
won-der,— nou-rish-ing po-ten-tial hid-den to— our eyes.

3 She dances in fire, startling her spectators,
  waking tongues of ecstasy where
     dumbness reigned;
  she weans and inspires all whose hearts
     are open,
  nor can she be captured, silenced or
     restrained.

4 For she is the Spirit, one with God in
     essence,
  gifted by the Saviour in eternal love;

she is the key opening the scriptures,
enemy of apathy and heavenly dove.

John L. Bell and Graham Maule

306

Spirit of the living God, fall afresh on me.
Spirit of the living God, fall afresh on me.
Break me, melt me, mould me, fill me.
Spirit of the living God, fall afresh on me.

Daniel Iverson (1890-1972)

307

Ve - ni sanc - te Spi - ri-tus, ve - ni sanc - te Spi - ri-tus,

ve - ni, ve - ni sanc-te Spi- ri - tus, ve - ni sanc - te Spi-ri-tus.

308

1. The Spi - rit of the Lord has brought new life to earth,
2. Bap-tized in God's own breath, made pure by fire and oil,

whose breath, as seed out - poured, now calls all things to birth.
our hope of life in death, our strength in thirst and toil.

God's Spi - rit now re - vives, our hearts of stone it thaws,
Who knows from where it flows, this gen - tle light so warm,

re - buil-ding bro - ken lives, our shat-tered world res - tores.
which deep with - in us glows, to heal and make us one.

3 The Spirit finds a home in every human breast,
   that God's own chosen Son may guide us to our rest,
   may save us from the storm, and raise us from the dust.
   Creator Spirit, come, complete your work in us.

Huub Oosterhuis, tr. Tony Barr. Dutch melody, arr. Bernard Huijbers (1922-2003)

309

Refrain

Spi - rit of God, rest on your peo - ple:

wa - ken your song deep in our hearts.

1. Spirit of the quiet earth,
  spirit breathing hope to birth:
  sustain in us the fire of your love.

2. Spirit blowing through creation, love
  that cannot be contained: bring forth for
  us the wonders you proclaim.

3. Song that echoes through our story,
  music of our restless souls:
  resound with joy in those you call your
  own.

4. Spirit moving through our lives,
  work in our mem-'ries: *continues overlea*

healing and restoring,
teaching and revealing,
strengthening and bringing to life.

5 Spirit breaking through our selfhood,
   spirit tearing down our walls:
   challenge and disturb us;
   be the voice that questions and calls.

Bernadette Farrell

310

1. Spi - rit of God with - in me, pos - sess my hu - man frame;
2. Spi - rit of truth with - in me, pos - sess my thought and mind;

fan the dull em - bers of my heart, stir up the liv - ing— flame:
ligh-ten a - new the in - ward eye by Sa - tan ren - dered— blind:

strive till that im - age A - dam lost, new min - ted and res-tored,
shine on the words that wis - dom speaks and grant me power to see

in shi - ning splen-dour bright-ly bears the like-ness of the Lord.
the truth made known to all in Christ, and in that truth be free.

3 Spirit of love within me,
   possess my hands and heart;
   break through the bonds of self-concern
   that seeks to stand apart:
   grant me the love that suffers long,
   that hopes, believes and bears,
   the love fulfilled in sacrifice
   that cares as Jesus cares.

4 Spirit of life within me,
   possess this life of mine;
   come as the wind of heaven's breath,
   come as the fire divine!
   Spirit of Christ, the living Lord,
   reign in this house of clay,
   till from its dust with Christ I rise
   to everlasting day.

Timothy Dudley-Smith. Music: Michael Joncas

311

1 Holy Spirit, come confirm us
   in the truth that Christ makes known;
   we have faith and understanding
   through your promised light alone.

2 Holy Spirit, come, console us,
   come as Advocate to plead;
   loving Spirit from the Father,
   grant in Christ the help we need.

3 Holy Spirit, come renew us,
   come yourself to make us live;
   holy through your loving presence,
   holy through the gifts you give.

4 Holy Spirit, come possess us,
   you the love of Three in One,
   Holy Spirit of the Father,
   Holy Spirit of the Son.

Brian Foley (1919-2000)

The Holy Trinity

312 312a

1 I bind unto myself today
the strong name of the Trinity
by invocation of the same,
the Three in One, and One in Three.

2 I bind this day to me forever,
by power of faith, Christ's incarnation;
his baptism in the Jordan river;
his death on cross for my salvation;
his bursting from the spicèd tomb;
his riding up the heavenly way;
his coming at the day of doom;
I bind unto myself today.

3 I bind unto myself today
the power of God to hold and lead,
his eye to watch, his might to stay,
his ear to hearken to my need,
the wisdom of my God to teach,
his hand to guide, his shield to ward,
the word of God to give me speech,
his heavenly host to be my guard.

312a

4* Christ be with me, Christ within me,
Christ behind me, Christ before me,
Christ beside me, Christ to win me,
Christ to comfort and restore me,

Christ beneath me, Christ above me,
Christ in quiet, Christ in danger,
Christ in hearts of all that love me,
Christ in mouth of friend and stranger.

---

5 I bind unto myself the name,
the strong name of the Trinity,
by invocation of the same,
the Three in One, and One in Three,
of whom all nature hath creation,
eternal Father, Spirit, Word.
Praise to the Lord of my salvation:
salvation is of Christ the Lord. Amen.

*Attributed to St Patrick (c. 386–c.460),
tr. Cecil Frances Alexander (1818–95)*

313

1 Father in heaven,
grant to your children
mercy and blessing,
songs never ceasing,
love to unite us,
grace to redeem us,
Father in heaven,
Father our God.

2 Jesus, Redeemer,
may we remember
your gracious Passion,
your resurrection.
Worship we bring you,
praise we shall sing you
Jesus, Redeemer,
Jesus our God.

3 Spirit descending
whose is the blessing -
strength for the weary,
help for the needy,
sealed in our service
yours be our worship -
Spirit unending,
Spirit adored.   *D. T. Niles (1908-70)*

314

1 Father, Lord of earth and heaven
King to whom all gifts belong,
give your greatest Gift, your Spirit,
God the holy, God the strong.

2 Son of God, enthroned in glory,
send your promised Gift of grace,
make your Church your holy Temple,
God the Spirit's dwelling-place.

3 Spirit, come, in peace descending
as at Jordan, heav'nly Dove,
seal your Church as God's anointed,
set our hearts on fire with love.

4 Stay among us, God the Father,
stay among us, God the Son,
stay among us, Holy Spirit,
dwell within us, make us one.

James Quinn SJ (1919-2010)

315

1 Lead us, heav'nly Father, lead us
o'er the world's tempestuous sea:
guard us, guide us, keep us, feed us,
for we have no help but thee;
yet possessing ev'ry blessing
if our God our Father be.

2 Saviour, breathe forgiveness o'er us,
all our weakness thou dost know,
thou didst tread this earth before us,
thou didst feel its keenest woe;
lone and dreary, faint and weary,
through the desert thou didst go.

3 Spirit of our God, descending,
fill our hearts with heavenly joy,
love with every passion blending,
pleasure that can never cloy;
thus provided, pardoned, guided,
nothing can our peace destroy.
James Edmeston (1791–1867)

316

*How great is our God,
how great is his name!
How great is our God,
for ever the same!*

1 He rolled back the waters
of the mighty Red Sea,
and he said 'I'll never leave you.
Put your trust in me.'

2 He sent his son, Jesus,
to set us all free,
and he said 'I'll never leave you.
Put your trust in me.'

3 He gave us his Spirit,
and now we can see.
And he said 'I'll never leave you.
Put your trust in me.'
Author unknown

317

1 Father, in my life I see,
you are God, who walks with me.
You hold my life in your hands:
close beside you I will stand.
I give all my life to you:
help me, Father, to be true.

2 Jesus, in my life I see …

3 Spirit, in my life I see …
Frank Anderson MSC

CORPUS CHRISTI

318

1 At this great feast of love
let joyful praise resound,
let heartfelt homage now ascend
to heaven's height:
ring out the reign of sin;
ring in the reign of grace;
a world renewed acclaims its King,
though veiled from sight.

2 Recall that night when Christ
proclaims his law of love,
and shows himself as Lamb of God
and great high priest:
the sinless One, made sin,
for sinners gives his all,
and shares with us his very self
as Paschal feast.

3 The bread that angels eat
becomes our food on earth,
God sends his manna, living Bread,
from heav'n above;
what wonders now we see:
those who are last and least
receive their Lord as food and drink,
his pledge of love.

4 Three persons, yet one God,
   be pleased to hear our prayer:
   come down in pow'r to seek your own,
   dispel our night;
   teach us your word of truth:
   guide us along your way;
   bring us at last to dwell with you
   in endless light.

> *St Thomas Aquinas (1227-74)*
> *tr. James Quinn SJ (1919-2010)*

➤ *Communion Processional songs (613-635);*
Post-Communion (636-653); and Eucharistic
Devotion (654-667). Psalm 114/5 (55).

ChRIST The KING

319

1 Christ is King of earth and heaven!
   Let his subjects all proclaim,
   in the splendour of his temple,
   honour to his holy name.

2 Christ is King! No soul created
   can refuse to bend the knee
   to the God made man who reigneth
   as 'twas promised, from the tree.

3 Christ is King! Let humble sorrow
   for our past neglect atone,
   for the lack of faithful service
   to the Master whom we own.

4 Christ is King! Let joy and gladness
   greet him; let his courts resound
   with the praise of faithful subjects
   to his love in honour bound.

5 Christ is King! In health and sickness,
   till we breathe our latest breath,
   till we greet in highest heaven,
   Christ the victor over death.

> *Ivor J. E. Daniel (1883–1967)*

320

1 Hail, Redeemer, King divine!
   Priest and Lamb, the throne is thine,
   King, whose reign shall never cease,
   Prince of everlasting peace.
   Angels saints and nations sing:
   'Praised be Jesus Christ, our King;
   Lord of life, earth, sky and sea,
   King of love on Calvary.'

2 King whose name creation thrills,
   rule our minds, our hearts, our wills,
   till in peace each nation rings
   with thy praises, King of kings.

3 King most holy, King of truth,
   guide the lowly, guide the youth;
   Christ thou King of glory bright,
   be to us eternal light.

4 Shepherd–King, o'er mountains steep,
   homeward bring the wandering sheep,
   shelter in one royal fold
   states and kingdoms, new and old.

> *Patrick Brennan CSsR (1877–1952)*

321

1 Crown him with many crowns,
   the Lamb upon his throne;
   hark, how the heav'nly anthem drowns
   all music but its own:
   awake, my soul, and sing
   of him who died for thee,
   and hail him as thy matchless King
   through all eternity.

2 Crown him the Virgin's Son,
   the God incarnate born,
   whose arm those crimson trophies won,
   which now his brow adorn;
   fruit of the mystic rose,
   as of that rose the stem,
   the root, whence mercy ever flows,
   the babe of Bethlehem.

3 Crown him the Lord of love;
  behold his hands and side,
  rich wounds, yet visible above,
  in beauty glorified:
  no angel in the sky
  can fully bear that sight,
  but downward bends his burning eye
  at mysteries so bright.

4 Crown him the Lord of peace,
  whose powers a sceptre sways,
  from pole to pole, that wars may cease,
  absorbed in prayer and praise:
  his reign shall know no end,
  and round his piercèd feet
  fair flowers of Paradise extend
  their fragrance ever sweet.

5 Crown him the Lord of heaven,
  one with the Father known,
  and the blest Spirit through him given
  from yonder triune throne:
  all hail, Redeemer, hail,
  for thou hast died for me;
  thy praise shall never, never fail
  throughout eternity.
     Matthew Bridges (1800–94)

322

1 Jesus shall reign where'er the sun
  does his successive journeys run;
  his kingdom stretch from shore to shore,
  till moons shall wax and wane no more.

2 People and realms of ev'ry tongue
  dwell on his love with sweetest song,
  and infant voices shall proclaim
  their early blessings on his Name.

3 Blessings abound where Jesus reigns;
  the prisoner leaps to lose his chains;
  the weary find eternal rest,
  and all who suffer want are blessed.

4 To him shall endless prayer be made,
  and praises throng to crown his head;
  his Name like incense shall arise
  with ev'ry morning sacrifice.

5 Let all creation rise and bring
  blessing and honour to our King;
  angels descend with songs again,
  and earth repeat the loud Amen.
     Isaac Watts (1674-1748), alt.
     Based on Psalm 72

323

1 All hail the pow'r of Jesus' name!
  let angels prostrate fall;
  bring forth the royal diadem
  To crown him, crown him, crown him,
  crown him Lord of all.

2 Crown him, ye martyrs of your God,
  who from his altar call;
  praise him whose way of pain ye trod,
  and crown him Lord of all.

3 Ye prophets who our freedom won,
  ye searchers, great and small,
  by whom the work of truth is done,
  now crown him Lord of all.

4 Sinners, whose love can ne'er forget
  the wormwood and the gall,
  go spread your trophies at his feet,
  and crown him Lord of all.

5 Bless him, each poor oppressèd race
  that Christ did upward call;
  his hand in each achievement trace,
  and crown him Lord of all.

6 Let every tribe and every tongue
  to him their hearts enthral:
  lift high the universal song,
    and crown him Lord of all.
     Edward Perronet (1726–92) and others

324

1 Jesus is Lord! Creation's voice
   proclaims it,
 for by his power each tree and flower
   was planned and made.
 Jesus is Lord! The universe declares it–
 sun, moon and stars in heaven cry:
   'Jesus is Lord!'
 Jesus is Lord, Jesus is Lord!
 Praise him with alleluias, for Jesus is Lord.

2 Jesus is Lord! Yet from his throne eternal
 in flesh he came to die in pain on
   Calvary's tree.
 Jesus is Lord! From him all life
   proceeding –
 yet gave his life a ransom thus setting
 us free.

3 Jesus is Lord! O'er sin the mighty conqueror;
 from death he rose and all his foes shall
   own his name.
 Jesus is Lord! God sends his Holy Spirit
 to show by works of power that
   Jesus is Lord.
   D.J. Mansell

325

Christ is our king, let the whole world
   rejoice!
May all the nations sing out with one voice!
Light of the world, you have helped us to see
that we are one people and one day we all
   shall be free.

1 He came to open the eyes of the blind,
 letting the sunlight pour into their minds.
 Vision is waiting for those who have hope.
 He is the light of the world.

2 He came to speak tender words to the poor,
 he is the gateway and he is the door.
 Riches are waiting for all those who hope.
 He is the light of the world.

3 He came to open the doors of the jail,
 he came to help the downtrodden and frail.
 Freedom is waiting for all those who hope.
 He is the light of the world.

4 He came to open the lips of the mute,
 letting them speak out with courage
   and truth.
 His words are uttered by all those
   who hope.
 He is the light of the world.

5 He came to heal all the crippled and lame
 sickness took flight at the sound
   of his name.
 Vigour is waiting for all those who hope.
 He is the light of the world.

6 He came to love everyone on this earth
 and through his Spirit he promised rebirth
 New life is waiting for all those who hope.
 He is the light of the world.
   Estelle White (1926-2011)

326

1 Rejoice! The Lord is King!
 Your Lord and King adore;
 mortals, give thanks and sing,
 and triumph evermore:
   Lift up your heart, lift up your voice;
   rejoice, again I say, rejoice.

2 Jesus the Saviour reigns,
 the God of truth and love;
 when he had purged our stains,
 he took his seat above:

3 His kingdom cannot fail;
 he rules o'er earth and heaven;
 the keys of death and hell
 are to our Jesus given:

4 He sits at God's right hand
 till all his foes submit,
 and bow to his command,
 and fall beneath his feet:

5 Rejoice in glorious hope:
 Jesus the Judge shall come,
 and take his servants up
 to their eternal home:
   We then shall hear th'Archangel's voice,
   the trump of God shall sound, Rejoice!

   Charles Wesley (1707–88)

Plainsong, 8th-9th century

Refrain 1 Cantors 2 All
Chri stus _ vin - cit: Chri stus _ re - gnat: Chri-stus _ im - pe - rat.

Cantor ... **All**
Ex - au - di Chri - ste. Ex - au - di Chri - ste.

C: ... **A:**
Sum-mo Pon-ti - fi-ci et u - ni-ver-sa-li Pa pae vi - ta. _

Sal-va-tor _ mun - di: _____ tu il-lum _ ad - ju - va.

San-cta Ma-ri - a: _____ tu il-lum _ ad - ju - va.
San-cte Pe - tre: _____
San-cte Pau - le: _____
San-cte Gre-go - ri: _____

Refrain (All)
Chri stus vin - cit: Chri-stus re - gnat: Chri-stus im - pe - rat.

Cantor **All**
Rex _ re - gum! Chri stus _ vin - cit. Rex _ no - ster! Chri stus _ re - gnat

Glor - ri-a _ no - stra! Chri-stus _ im - pe - rat. Ip-si so-li im - pe - ri - um

glo ri - a et po - tes - stas, per im-mor ta - li - a sae-cu-la sae cu - lo rum. A-men.

Final Refrain (All): Christus vincit: Christus regnat, Christus imperat.

Mary

Conceived Immaculate

328

1 Holy light on earth's horizon,
   hope to us the fallen, bring;
   light amid a world of shadows,
   dawn of God's redemption, sing.

2 Chosen from eternal ages,
   you alone of all our race,
   by your Son's atoning merits
   were conceived in perfect grace.

3 Mother of the world's redeemer,
   promised from the dawn of time;
   how could one so highly favoured
   share the guilt of Adam's crime?

4 Sun and moon and stars adorn you,
   sinless Eve, triumphant sign;
   you are she who crushed the serpent,
   Mary, pledge of life divine.

5 Earth below and highest heaven
   praise the splendour of your state:
   you who now are crowned in glory
   were conceived immaculate.

6 Hail, beloved of the Father,
   Mother of his only Son,
   Mystic bride of Love eternal,
   Hail, most fair and spotless one.
   Fabian Duggan OSB (1930-2013)

Chosen One

329

1 Oh Mary, when our God chose you
   to bring his dear Son to birth,
   a new creation made in you
   gave joy to all the earth.
   Alleluia, alleluia, alleluia, alleluia,
   A new creation made in you
   gave joy to all the earth.

2 When he was born on Christmas night
   and music made the rafters ring,
   the stars were dancing with delight;
   now all God's children sing.

3 One winter's night, a heap of straw
   becomes a place where ages meet
   when kings come knocking at the door
   and kneeling at your feet.

4 In you, our God confounds the strong
   and makes the crippled dance with joy
   and to our barren world belong
   his mother and her boy.

5 In empty streets and broken hearts
   you call to mind what he has done;
   where all his loving kindness starts
   in sending you a son.

6 And Mary, while we stand with you,
   may once again his Spirit come,
   and all his brothers follow you
   to reach our Father's home.
   Damian Lundy (1944-1997)

The Promise and Annunciation

➤ *See also Advent section (113-115)*

330

1 An angel came from heaven,
   from heaven, from heaven,
   an angel came from heaven
      to bring good news.
   The angel's name was Gabriel,
   the angel's name was Gabriel,
   the angel's name was Gabriel
      to bring good news.

2 He came to see a lady..
   the lady's name was Mary..

3 He said, 'You'll have a baby...'
   The baby's name was Jesus.

(Christmas) 4 And Mary had a baby...
                  The baby's name was Jesus.
   Christopher Walker

331

1 For Mary, mother of the Lord
   God's holy name be praised,
   who first the Son of God adored
   as on her child she gazed.

2 The angel Gabriel brought the word
she should Christ's mother be;
Our Lady, handmaid of the Lord,
made answer willingly.

3 The heavenly call she thus obeyed,
and so God's will was done;
The second Eve love's answer made
which our redemption won.

4 She gave her body for God's shrine,
her heart to piercing pain,

and knew the cost of love divine
when Jesus Christ was slain.

5 Dear Mary, from your lowliness
and home in Galilee,
there comes a joy and holiness
to every family.

6 Hail, Mary, you are full of grace
above all women blest;
blest in your Son, whom your embrace
in birth and death confessed.

J.R. Peacey (1896-1971)

332

Cantor: *Like rivers in the desert,
like springs from the rock,
new hope came through Mary,*

*when the Word became flesh
and our humanity
regained its former glory.*

Refrain (All)

Bles-sed Ma-ry, spring of new hope, from your Son spring the wa ters of life.

1 *The song of the spring
will glorify the Lord.*
All: Blessed Mary....

2 *The freshness of the clear cooling spring
will quench our burning thirst.*
All: Blessed Mary....

3 *This river in our desert
will fill our hearts with joy.*
All: Blessed Mary....

C: *Like rivers in the desert...*
All: Blessed Mary....

Abbey of Tamié tr, Pamela Stotter

333

*Hail, Mary, full of grace,
the Lord is with you;
Mother of God's own word,
Ave, Maria, Ave, Maria.*

1. Disciple of the Lord,
who Gabriel's message heard,
and bore the eternal Word,
Mary most favoured. *Gratia plena!
Hail, Mary, full of grace....*

2. Blest those who hear God's voice,
and in that call rejoice,
Blest her who was God's choice,
Mary most faithful. *Gratia plena!
Hail, Mary, full of grace....*

3. Praise Mary's prompt reply,
whose soul did magnify
and sang to God on high,
See me, your servant. *Gratia plena!
Hail, Mary, full of grace....*

4. Her eyes with love ablaze,
did on her Saviour gaze
now saints and angels praise
Mary most humble. *Gratia plena!
Hail, Mary, full of grace....*

5. Great God to whom we pray
who sends the rich away,
whose mercy lights our way,
Make us like Mary: *Gratia plena!
Hail, Mary, full of grace....*

Stephen Dean

334

A - ve Ma - ri - a, gra - ti - a ple - na, Do - mi - nus te - cum,

be - ne - dic-ta tu in— mu - li - e - ri - bus, et be - ne - dic-tus fruc-tus ven-tris

tu - i,— Je - sus.— Sanc-ta Ma - ri - a, Ma-ter De - i, o - ra pro no - bis

pec - ca - to - ri - bus, nunc— et in ho - ra mor-tis nos - trae.— A-men.

Plainsong

The Magnificat (Luke 1:46-55)

335 **Magnificat (Canon)**   *Taizé chant by Jacques Berthier*

A   B

Mag-ni - fi-cat, mag-ni-ficat, mag-ni - fi-cat a - ni-ma me-a Do-mi-num

C   D

Mag - ni - fi-cat, mag-ni - fi-cat, mag - ni - fi-cat a - ni-ma me - a!

336 **Refrain**

My soul re - joi - ces——— in God my— Sa - viour.

My spi - rit finds its joy in God, the li - ving God.

Verses

1. My soul pro-claims your migh-ty deeds. My spi - rit sings the great-ness of your name.

2 Your mercy flows throughout the land
   and ev'ry generation knows your love.

3 You cast the mighty from their thrones
   and raise the poor and lowly to new life.

4 You fill the hungry with good things.
   With empty hands you send the rich away.

5 Just as you promised Abraham,
   you come to free your people, Israel.
   Owen Alstott

337

Refrain *repeat as required*   *Peter Jones*

The Al - migh-ty works mar - vels for me.

Ho - ly his name, ho - ly his name.

338

1. My soul pro - claims the great-ness of the Lord, my spi-rit
sings to God, my sa-ving God, who on this day a-bove all oth-ers fa-voured
me and raised me up, a light for all to see.

2 Through me great deeds will God make manifest,
and all the earth will come to call me blest.
Unbounded love and mercy sure will I proclaim
for all who know and praise God's holy name.

3 God's mighty arm, protector of the just,
will guard the weak and raise them from the dust.
But mighty kings will swiftly fall from thrones corrupt,
the strong brought low, the lowly lifted up.

4 Soon will the poor and hungry of the earth
be richly blest, be given greater worth:
and Israel, as once foretold to Abraham,
will live in peace throughout the promised land.

5 All glory be to God, Creator blest,
to Jesus Christ, God's love made manifest,
and to the Holy Spirit, gentle Comforter,
all glory be, both now and evermore.

Owen Alstott. Music by Bernadette Farrell

339

1 My soul is filled with joy
as I sing to God my Saviour:
he has looked upon his servant,
he has visited his people.
And holy is his name
through all generations!
everlasting is his mercy
to the people he has chosen,
and holy is his name!

2 I am lowly as a child,
but I know from this day forward
that my name will be remembered,
for all men will call me blessed.

3 I proclaim the pow'r of God!
He does marvels for his servants;
though he scatters the proud-hearted
and destroys the might of princes.

4 To the hungry he gives food,
  sends the rich away empty.
  In his mercy he is mindful
  of the people he has chosen.

5 In his love he now fulfills
  what he promised to our fathers.
  I will praise the Lord, my saviour.
  Everlasting is his mercy.
            Anonymous

340

1 My soul proclaims you, mighty God,
  my spirit sings your praise.
  You look on me, you lift me up,
  and gladness fills my days.

➤ *See also Tell out, my soul (880); Magnificat for Evening Prayer (23-25)*

2 All nations now will share my joy;
  your gifts you have outpoured.
  Your little one you have made great;
  I magnify my God.

3 For those who love your holy name,
  your mercy will not die.
  Your strong right arm puts down the prou
  and lifts the lowly high.

4 You fill the hungry with good things,
  the rich you send away.
  The promise made to Abraham
  is filled to endless day.

5 Then let all nations praise our God,
  the Father and the Son,
  the Spirit blest who lives in us,
  while endless ages run.
            Anne Carter (1944-1993)

Mary's life and sorrows

341

1 Sing of Mary, pure and lowly
  Virgin-Mother undefiled,
  Sing of God's own Son most holy,
  who became her little child.
  Fairest child of fairest mother,
  God the Lord who came to earth,
  Word made flesh, our very brother,
  Takes our nature by his birth.

2 Sing of Jesus, Son of Mary,
  in the home at Nazareth.
  Toil and labour cannot weary
  Love enduring unto death.
  Constant was the love he gave her,
  though it drove him from her side,[1]
  forth to preach, and heal, and suffer,
  till on Calvary he died.

3 Sing of Mary, sing of Jesus,
  holy Mother's holier Son.
  From his throne in heaven he sees us,
  thither calls us ev'ry one.

Where he welcomes home his mother
to a place at his right hand,
there his faithful servants gather,
there the crownèd victors stand.

4 Joyful Mother, full of gladness,
  in your arms your Lord was borne.
  Mournful Mother, full of sadness,
  all your heart with pain was torn.
  Glorious Mother, now rewarded
  with a crown at Jesus' hand,
  Age to age your name recorded
  shall be blest in every land.

5 Glory be to God the Father;
  Glory be to God the Son;
  Glory be to God the Spirit;
  Glory to the Three in One.
  From the heart of blessèd Mary,
  From all saints the song ascends,
  And the Church the strain re-echoes
  Unto earth's remotest ends.
            Roland F. Palmer SSJE (1891-1985)

---

[1] *cf. Mark 1:12*

342

Refrain

Mag - ni - fi - cat! Mag ni - fi - cat! Your song proclaims the glo ry of the Lord.

Verses

1. Wo - man asked to bear a son; a child who would com - pare with___
2. Wo - man in the tem - ple stands;___ old man takes the child in his
3. Wo - man at the wed - ding meal,___ see the mi - ra - cle re -

[v.5: of the]

none.___ Did you know the pain that lay a - head?
hands.___ Did his words breathe fear in - to your heart?
veal the glo - ry of your Son to all a - round.

4 Woman waiting at the door;
your Son is now your Son no more;
to all the world he gives his life.

5 Woman standing by the cross
with those around you mourn the loss
of the child that you had once borne in
your womb.

6 Woman in the upper room;
in the frightened air and gloom,
see your Son in glory now appear.

7 Woman standing on the rock,
through the child who tends the flock
speak to the world that we may know
your Son.

Anne Ward

343

Where are you bound, Mary, Mary?
Where are you bound, Mother of God?

1 Beauty is a dove sitting on a sunlit bough,
beauty is a pray'r without the need of words.
Words are more than sounds falling off
    an empty tongue:
let it be according to his word.

2 Mary heard the word spoken in her
    inmost heart;
Mary bore the Word and held him in her
    arms.
Sorrow she has known, seeing him upon
    the cross
– greater joy to see him rise again.

3 Where are we all bound, carrying the
    Word of God?
Time and place are ours to make his
    glory known.
Mary bore him first, we will tell the
    whole wide world;
let it be according to his word.
    John Glynn

344

1. Sing we of the blessèd Mother
who received the angel's word,
and obedient to his summons
bore in love the infant Lord;
sing we of the joys of Mary
at whose breast that child was fed
who is Son of God eternal
and the everlasting Bread.

2 Sing we, too, of Mary's sorrows,
of the sword that pierced her through,
when beneath the cross of Jesus
she his weight of suffering knew,
looked upon her Son and Saviour
reigning high on Calvary's tree,
saw the price of our redemption
paid to set the sinner free.

3 Sing again the joys of Mary
when she saw the risen Lord,
and in prayer with Christ's apostles,
waited on his promised word:
from on high the blazing glory

of the Spirit's presence came,
heavenly breath of God's own being,
manifest through wind and flame.

4 Sing the chiefest joy of Mary
when on earth her work was done,
and the Lord of all creation
brought her to his heavenly home:
virgin Mother, Mary blessèd,
raised on high and crowned with grace,
may your Son, the world's redeemer,
grant us all to see his face.

G. B. Timms (1910-1993)

345

Music by Christopher Willcock

1. There is nothing told about this woman but that she had once become engaged, and an angel addressed her and said: You are blessed among all your kind. *On this day all earth and all paradise join in naming you happy and blessed, Virgin Mary, blessed are you.*

2. There is nothing told about this woman but that she had brought into the world in the land of Judea, her son; for some shepherds have passed on this tale. *On this day all earth and all paradise join in naming you happy and blessed, Virgin Mary, blessed are you.*

3 There is nothing told about this woman
but that she had searched for three long
   days
for her child who was busy elsewhere,
and her heart then did not understand.

4 There is nothing told about this woman
but that she at Cana was a guest,
and that Jesus changed water to wine,
so that all might believe who he was.

5 There is nothing told about this woman
but that she was standing by the cross
when her son stretched his arms out on
   high,
and met death with a thief on each side.

6 There is nothing told about this woman
but that she was one in prayer with those
upon whom tongues of fire did descend,
and the Spirit baptised them with flame.

Didier Rimaud SJ (1921-2007),
tr. Christopher Willcock SJ

346

1. Maiden, the angel spoke to you
   with words of reverence and grace;
   you, in reply said, 'Let it be!'
   and gave to God a human face.

2. Virgin-with-child, you went to meet
   Elizabeth who carried John:
   held in his mother's womb, he leapt
   in recognition of your son.

3. Mary, you trudged to Bethlehem
   and there you brought a child to birth;
   One, for whom all creation groaned,
   as helpless infant came to earth.

4. Lady, you heard from Simeon
   the prophecy of joy and pain:
   words, which you treasured in your heart,
   of Israel's hope and gentiles' gain.

5. Mother, you stood beside your Son
   while he was stripped and crucified;
   born of your labour, there you shared
   the agony as Jesus died.

6. Queen, you rejoiced to see the Lord
   who first had risen from your womb,
   triumphing over sin and death,
   now rise in glory from the tomb.

Patrick Lee (1930-2004)

Melody by Stephen Dean

1. Mai-den, the an-gel spoke to you with words of re-ve-rence and grace;
you, in re-ply, said 'Let it be!' and gave to God a hu-man face.

Motherhood of Mary

347

1. O purest of creatures! Sweet mother, sweet maid;
   the one spotless womb wherein Jesus was laid.
   Dark night hath come down on us, mother, and we
   look out for thy shining, sweet star of the sea.

2. Deep night hath come down on this rough–spoken world.
   And the banners of darkness are boldly unfurled;
   and the tempest–tossed Church, all her eyes are on thee.
   They look to thy shining, sweet star of the sea.

3. He gazed on thy soul, it was spotless and fair;
   for the empire of sin, it had never been there;
   none ever had owned thee, dear mother, but he,
   and he blessed thy clear shining, sweet star of the sea.

4. Earth gave him one lodging; 'twas deep in thy breast,
   and God found a home where the sinner finds rest,
   his home and his hiding–place, both were in thee;
   he was won by thy shining, sweet star of the sea.

5. Oh, blissful and calm was the wonderful rest
   that thou gavest thy God in thy virginal breast;
   for the heaven he left he found heaven in thee,
   and he shone in thy shining, sweet star of the sea.

F.W. Faber (1814–63)

348

1 The God whom earth, and sea, and sky,
adore and praise and magnify,
whose might they claim, whose love
    they tell,
in Mary's body comes to dwell.

2 The God whose will by moon and sun,
and all things in due course is done,
is borne upon a maiden's breast
by fullest heavenly grace possessed.

3 O mother blest! the chosen shrine
wherein the Architect divine,
whose hand contains the earth and sky,
has come in human form to lie!

4 Blest in the message Gabriel brought;
blest by the work the Spirit wrought;
most blest, to bring to human birth
the long desired of all the earth.

5 O Lord, the Virgin–born, to you
eternal praise and laud are due,
whom with the Father we adore
and Spirit blest for evermore.
Ascribed to Venantius Fortunatus (530–609),
tr. J. M. Neale (1818–66), alt.

Mary in Glory

349

1 Mother of God's living Word
glorifying Christ your Lord;
full of joy, God's people sing,
grateful for your mothering.

2 Virgin soil, untouched by sin,
for God's seed to flourish in;
watered by the Spirit's dew,
in your womb the Saviour grew.

3 Sharing his humility,
Bethlehem and Calvary,
with him in his bitter pain,
now as queen with him you reign.

4 We are God's new chosen race,
new-born children of his grace,
citizens of heaven who
imitate and honour you.

5 We, God's people on our way,
travelling by night and day,
moving to our promised land,
walk beside you hand in hand.

6 Christ, your Son, is always near,
so we journey without fear,
singing as we walk along:
Christ our joy and Christ our song!

7 Sing aloud to Christ with joy,
who was once a little boy:
sing aloud to Mary, sing,
grateful for her mothering.
Damian Lundy (1944-1997)

350

1 A sign is seen in heaven,
a maiden–mother fair;
her mantle is the sunlight,
and stars adorn her hair.
The maiden's name is Mary;
in love she brings to birth
the Lord of all the ages,
the King of all the earth.

2 Like moonlight on the hilltops
she shines on all below,
like sunlight on the mountains
her Child outshines the snow.
O Mary, Queen of mothers,
still smile on young and old;
bless hearth and home and harvest,
bless farm and field and fold.

3 Pray, Mother, Queen in glory,
before the Father's throne;
praise God's eternal Wisdom,
the Child who is your own;
rejoice in God the Spirit,
whose power let you conceive
the Child of Eden's promise,
O new and sinless Eve.
James Quinn SJ (1919-2010)

351

1 This is the image of the Queen
who reigns in bliss above;
of her who is the hope of men,
whom men and angels love.
Most holy Mary, at thy feet
I bend a suppliant knee;
in this thy own sweet month of May,
do thou remember me.

2 The homage offered at the feet
of Mary's image here
to Mary's self at once ascends
above the starry sphere.
Most holy Mary, at thy feet
I bend a suppliant knee;
in all my joy, in all my pain,
do thou remember me.

3 How fair so ever be the form
which here your eyes behold,
its beauty is by Mary's self
excell'd a thousandfold.
Most holy Mary, at thy feet,
I bend a suppliant knee;
in my temptations each and all,
do thou remember me.

4 Sweet are the flow'rets we have culled,
this image to adorn;
but sweeter far is Mary's self,
that rose without a thorn.
Most holy Mary, at thy feet
I bend a suppliant knee;
when on the bed of death I lie,
do thou remember me.

5 O lady, by the stars that make
a glory round thy head;
and by the pure uplifted hands,
that for thy children plead;
when at the judgement–seat I stand,
and my dread saviour see;
when waves of night around me roll
O then remember me.
Edward Caswall (1814-78)

352

1 Hail, Mary, our icon of trust in God's
Word;
in faith you conceived, and God's life in
you stirred.
O woman of wisdom, now show us the way:
Let our hearts be open to God day by day.

2 Hail, mother of Jesus, of all mothers blest,
to you joyful praises and prayers are
addressed.
The saints and the angels your glory
proclaim;
the faithful in confidence call on your
name.

3 We pray you, O woman of all women blest
to care for the homeless, the poor and
oppressed.
Be with us, your people, in joy and in pain;
be near us to cheer us till heaven we gain.

4 To God, your creator, glad hymns with us
raise.
To Jesus, your Son, and the Spirit, give
praise.
And pray for the churches, that all may be
one:
On earth as in heaven, may God's will be
done!
Delores Dufner OSB

Praise of Mary

353

1 Daily, daily, sing to Mary,
sing my soul, her praises due;
all her feasts, her actions honour,
with the heart's devotion true.
Lost in wond'ring contemplation
be her majesty confessed:
call her Mother, call her Virgin,
happy Mother, Virgin blest.

2 Sing, my tongue, the Virgin's trophies,
   who for us her Maker bore;
   for the curse of old inflicted,
   peace and blessings to restore.
   Sing in songs of praise unending,
   sing the world's majestic Queen;
   weary not nor faint in telling
   all the gifts she gives to men.

3 All my senses, heart, affections,
   strive to sound her glory forth;
   spread abroad the sweet memorials,
   of the Virgin's priceless worth,
   where the voice of music thrilling,
   where the tongues of eloquence,
   that can utter hymns beseeming
   all her matchless excellence?

4 All our joys do flow from Mary,
   all then join her praise to sing;
   trembling sing the Virgin Mother,
   Mother of our Lord and King,
   while we sing her awful glory,
   far above our fancy's reach,
   let our hearts be quick to offer
   love the heart alone can teach.
        Ascribed to Bernard of Cluny (12th C.),
        tr. Henry Bittleston (1818–1886)

354

1 O Mary, conceived in the grace of your
       Son,
   the firstfruits of vict'ry on Calvary won!
   He chose you as Mother to bring him
       to birth,
   the one fitting shrine for his dwelling
       on earth!

2 Immaculate Virgin, with motherhood
       blest,
   true God is the child that in your womb
       did rest!
   With you shall we ever Magnificat sing,
   whose Son is our Maker and Saviour
       and King!

3 O Mother, who stood by your Son till
       his death,
   still stand by your children till life's
       dying breath!
   O pray for us all as in glory you share
   your Son's resurrection, his
       masterpiece fair!
        James Quinn SJ (1919-2010)

355

1 I'll sing a hymn to Mary,
   the Mother of my God,
   the Virgin of all virgins,
   of David's royal blood.
   O teach me, holy Mary,
   a loving song to frame,
   O may I imitate thee
   and magnify God's name.

2 O noble Tower of David,
   of gold and ivory,
   the Ark of God's own promise,
   the gate of heav'n to me,
   to live and not to love thee,
   would fill my soul with shame;
   O may I imitate thee
   and magnify God's name.

3 The Saints are high in glory,
   with golden crowns so bright;
   but brighter far is Mary,
   upon her throne of light.
   O that which God did give thee,
   let mortal ne'er disclaim;
   O may I imitate thee
   and magnify God's name.

4 But in the crown of Mary,
   there lies a wondrous gem,
   as Queen of all the Angels,
   which Mary shares with them:
   no sin hath e'er defiled thee,
   so doth our faith proclaim;
   O may I imitate thee
   and magnify God's name.
        John Wyse (1825–98)

356

1 Hail, Queen of heav'n, the ocean star!
 Guide of the wand'rer here below!
 Thrown on life's surge, we claim thy care;
 save us from peril and from woe.
 Mother of Christ, star of the sea,
 pray for the wanderer, pray for me.

2 O gentle, chaste and spotless maid,
 we sinners make our prayers through thee;
 remind thy son that he has paid
 the price of our iniquity.
 Virgin most pure, star of the sea,
 pray for the sinner, pray for me.

3 Sojourners in this vale of tears,
 to thee, blest advocate, we cry;
 pity our sorrows, calm our fears,
 and soothe with hope our misery.
 Refuge in grief, star of the sea,
 pray for the mourner, pray for me.

4 And while to him who reigns above,
 in Godhead One, in Persons Three,
 the source of life, of grace, of love,
 homage we pay on bended knee,
 do thou, bright Queen, star of the sea,
 pray for thy children, pray for me.
 John Lingard (1771–1851)

357

1 Star of sea and ocean,
 gateway to God's haven,
 Mother of our Maker,
 hear our prayer, O maiden.

2 Welcoming the Ave,
 Gabriel's simple greeting,
 you have borne a Saviour
 far beyond all dreaming.

3 Loose the bonds that hold us
 bound in sin's own blindness
 that with eyes now opened
 God's own light may guide us.

4 Show yourself our mother;
 he will hear your pleading
 whom your womb has sheltered
 and whose hand brings healing.

5 Gentlest of all virgins,
 that our love be faithful
 keep us from all evil,
 gentle, strong and grateful.

6 Guard us through life's dangers,
 never turn and leave us.
 May our hope find harbour
 in the calm of Jesus.

7 Sing to God our Father
 through the Son who saves us,
 joyful in the Spirit,
 everlasting praises.
 Anon, 9th C., tr. Edward Caswall (1814-78)

358

1 Ave maris stella
 Dei Mater alma,
 atque semper virgo,
 felix caeli porta.

2 Sumens illud Ave
 Gabrielis ore,
 funda nos in pace,
 mutans Hevae nomen.

3 Solve vincla reis,
 profer lumen caecis,
 mala nostra pelle,
 bona cuncta posce.

4 Monstra te esse matrem,
 sumat per te preces,
 qui pro nobis natus
 tulit esse tuus.

5 Virgo singularis,
 inter omnes mitis,
 nos culpis solutos
 mites fac et castos.

6 Vitam praesta puram,
 iter para tutum,
 ut videntes Jesum,
 semper collaetemur.

7 Sit laus Deo Patri,
  summo Christo decus,
  Spiritui sancto,
  tribus honor unus.
> *Anon, 9th Century*

359

1 All who keep the faith of Jesus,
  sing the wonders that were done,
  when the love of God the Father
  o'er our sin the vict'ry won,
  when he made the Virgin Mary
  Mother of his only Son.
> *Hail, Mary, full of grace!*

2 Blessèd were the chosen people
  out of whom the Lord did come,
  blessèd was the land of promise
  fashioned for his earthly home;
  but more blessèd far the Mother,
  she who bore him in her womb.

3 Wherefore let all faithful people
  tell the honour of her name,
  let the Church in her foreshadowed
  part in her thanksgiving claim;
  what Christ's Mother sang in gladness
  let Christ's people sing the same.

4 May the Mother's intercessions
  on our homes a blessing win,
  that the children all be prospered,
  strong and fair and pure within,
  following our Lord's own footsteps,
  firm in faith and free from sin.

5 For the sick and for the agèd,
  for our dear ones far away,
  for the hearts that mourn in secret,
  all who need our prayers today,
  for the faithful gone before us,
  may the holy Virgin pray:

6 Praise, O Mary, praise the Father,
  praise your Saviour and your Son,
  praise the everlasting Spirit,
  who has made you ark and throne;
  o'er all creatures high exalted,
  lowly praise the Three in One.
> *V.S.S. Coles (1845-1929)*

360

1 As I kneel before you,
  as I bow my head in prayer,
  take this day, make it yours
  and fill me with your love.
> *Ave Maria, gratia plena,*
> *Dominus tecum, benedicta tu.*

2 All I have I give you,
  ev'ry dream and wish are yours;
  mother of Christ, mother of mine,
  present them to my Lord.

3 As I kneel before you,
  and I see your smiling face,
  ev'ry thought, ev'ry word
  is lost in your embrace.
> *Maria Parkinson*

361

1 Blessed Virgin Mother,
  daughter of your Son,
  highest of all women,
  humbler there is none.
  When you bore the Saviour
  by divine decree,
  you gave all creation
  new nobility.

2 When the Source of Hope sprang
  forth against Despair,
  and the God of Love was
  nourished by your care,
  Then the fire of grace did
  flourish and increase,
  spreading through the nations
  news of heavenly peace.

3 You are loving kindness,
  ever know our need;
  you are all compassion,
  gladly intercede,
  you are all perfection
  in the human race,
  through your mediation
  we can share God's grace.
> *from Dante's* Paradiso, *Canto 33,*
> *paraphrased by A. G. Petti (1932-1985)*

362

1. Of one that is so fair and bright, *ve - lut ma - ris stel - la,*
2. In sor - row, coun - sel thou art best, *fe - lix fe - cun - da - ta:* for

bright - er than the day is light, *pa - rens et pu - el - la;* I
all the wea - ry thou art rest, *ma - ter ho - no - ra - ta:* be -

cry to thee to turn to me, La - dy, pray thy Son for me, *tam*
seech him in thy mil - dest mood, who for us did shed his blood *in*

pi - a, that I may come to thee,____ *Ma - ri - a.*
cru - ce, that we may come to him____ *in lu - ce.*

3 All this world was forlorn,
  Eva peccatrice,
till our Saviour Lord was born
  de te genetrice;
with thy ave sin went away,
dark night went and in came day
  salutis.
The well of healing sprang from thee,
  virtutis.

4 Lady, flower of everything,
  rosa sine spina,
thou borest Jesus, heaven's king,
  gratia divina.
Of all I say thou bore the prize,
Lady, Queen of Paradise,
  electa;
maiden mild, Mother
  es effecta.
      Anon., medieval.
      Music by Francis Duffy (1914-2000)

363

1 Mary immaculate, star of the morning,
  chosen before the creation began,
  chosen to bring, for thy bridal adorning,
  woe to the serpent and rescue to man.

2 Here, in an orbit of shadow and sadness
  veiling thy splendour, thy course thou
    hast run;
  now thou art throned in all glory and
    gladness,
  crowned by the hand of thy saviour and Son.

3 Sinners, we honour thy sinless perfection,
  fallen and weak, for thy pity we plead;
  grant us the shield of thy sovereign
    protection,
  measure thine aid by the depth of our need.

4 Frail is our nature, and strict our
    probation,
  watchful the foe that would lure us to
    wrong,
  succour our souls in the hour of
    temptation,
  Mary immaculate tender and strong.

5 Bend from thy throne at the voice of
    our crying;
  bend to this earth which thy footsteps
    have trod;
  stretch out thine arms to us living and
    dying,
  Mary immaculate, mother of God.
      F.W. Weatherell

364

1 O Mother blest, whom God bestows
on sinners and on just,
what joy, what hope thou givest those
who in thy mercy trust.
 Thou art clement, thou art chaste,
 Mary, thou art fair;
 of all mothers sweetest, best;
 none with thee compare.

2 O heavenly mother, mistress sweet!
It never yet was told
that suppliant sinner left thy feet
unpitied, unconsoled.

3 O mother pitiful and mild,
cease not to pray for me;
for I do love thee as a child,
and sigh for love of thee.

4 Most powerful mother, we all know
thy Son denies thee nought;
thou askest, wishest it, and lo!
His power thy will hath wrought.

5 O mother blest, for me obtain
ungrateful though I be,
to love that God who first could deign
to show such love for me.
 St. Alphonsus Liguori (1699–1787),
 tr. Edmund Vaughan (1827–1908)

365

1 Immaculate Mary!
Our hearts are on fire,
that title so wondrous
fills all our desire.
Ave, ave, ave Maria!
Ave, ave, ave Maria!

2 We pray for God's glory,
may his kingdom come!
We pray for his vicar,
our father, and Rome.

3 We pray for our mother
the church upon earth,
and bless, sweetest Lady,
the land of our birth.

4 For poor, sick, afflicted
thy mercy we crave;
and comfort the dying
thou light of the grave.

5 In grief and temptation,
in joy or in pain,
we'll ask thee, our mother,
nor seek thee in vain.

6 In death's solemn moment,
our mother, be nigh;
as children of Mary –
help us when we die.

7 And crown thy sweet mercy
with this special grace,
to behold soon in heaven
God's ravishing face.

8 To God be all glory
and worship for aye,
and to God's virgin mother
an endless Ave.
 Traditional

366

1 Holy Virgin, by God's decree,
you were called eternally;
that he could give his Son to our race.
Mary, we praise you, hail full of grace.
 Ave, ave, ave, Maria.

2 By your faith and loving accord,
as the handmaid of the Lord,
you undertook God's plan to embrace.
Mary, we thank you, hail full of grace.

3 Joy to God you gave and expressed,
of all women none so blessed,
when in mankind your Son took his place.
Mary, we love you, hail full of grace.

4 Refuge for your children so weak,
sure protection all can seek.
Problems of life you help us to face.
Mary, we trust you, hail full of grace.

5 To our needy world of today
love and beauty you portray,
showing the path to Christ we must trace.
Mary, our mother, hail, full of grace.
 J. P. Lécot, tr. W. Raymond Lawrence

367

Author unknown, 11th C. (attr. to Herman the Lame, 1013-54)

Sal - ve Re - gi - na, Ma - ter mi - se - ri - cor - di - æ, vi - ta, dul - ce - do,

et spes nos-tra, sal - ve. Ad te cla-ma-mus, ex - u - les fi - li - i He-væ.

Ad te sus - pi - ra - mus, ge-men-tes et flen-tes, in hac la-cri-ma-rum val-le.

E - ia er-go, Ad-vo-ca-ta nos-tra, il - los tu - os mi - se - ri-cor-des o - cu -

los ad nos con-ver - te. Et Je - sum be-ne-dic-tum fruc-tum ven-tris tu - i,

no - bis post hoc ex - si - li - um os-ten - de. O—— cle - mens,

O—— pi - a, O—— dul - cis Vir-go Ma - ri - a.

367a

➤ *See also nos. 38a and 38b*

1 Hail, our Queen and Mother blest!
Joy when all was sadness,
life and hope you brought to birth,
Mother of our gladness!
Children of the sinful Eve,
sinless Eve, befriend us,
exiled in this vale of tears:
strength and comfort send us!

2 Pray for us, O patroness,
be our consolation!
Lead us home to see your Son,
Jesus, our salvation!
Gracious are you, full of grace,
loving as none other,
Joy of heaven and joy of earth,
Mary, God's own Mother!

Salve Regina, tr. James Quinn SJ (1919-2010)

368

Re - gi - na Cae-li lae-ta - re, al - le - lu - ia; qui-a quem me-ru - i - sti por-ta-re, al-le-lu - ia,

re - sur - re - xit si - cut di - xit, al - le - lu - ia, O - ra pro no - bis De-um, al - le - lu - ia.

368a

Joy fill your heart, O Queen most high, alleluia!
Your Son who in the tomb did lie, alleluia!
Has risen as he did prophesy, alleluia!
Pray for us, Mother, when we die,
　Alleluia, alleluia, alleluia!
Regina coeli (author and date unknown), tr. James Quinn SJ (1919-2010)

The Saints

369

Saints of God, come to our aid! Pray for us, O pray for us all!

Saints of God, come to our aid, hear us when we call.

This refrain is sung between spoken invocations of the saints.

James Walsh

---

370 REFRAIN

As a tree plan-ted by streams of wa-ter is the

one who de-lights in the word of the Lord.

1　Blessed are the poor in spirit,
　theirs is the Kingdom of heaven;
　blessed are the ones who mourn,
　for they shall be comforted.

2　Blessed are the meek and lowly,
　they shall inherit the earth;
　blessed are those who thirst for good,
　for they shall be satisfied.

3　Blessed are the merciful,
　for they shall have mercy shown them;
　blessed are the pure in heart,
　for they shall see their God.

4　Blessed are the peaceful hearts,
　for they shall be called God's children;
　bless'd those suff'ring for righteousness,
　the Kingdom of heaven is theirs.
　　Matt 5:1-12, versified by Marty Haugen

➢ *The Beatitudes: see also 615, 814-*

371

1　For all the saints who from their labours
　　rest,
　who thee by faith before the world
　　confessed,
　thy name, O Jesus be for ever blest.
　　Alleluia!

2　Thou wast their rock, their fortress, and
　　their might;
　thou, Lord, their captain in the
　　well–fought fight;
　thou in the darkness drear their one
　　true light.

3 O may thy soldiers, faithful, true and bold,
 fight as the saints who nobly fought
  of old,
 and win, with them, the victor's crown
  of gold.

4 O blest communion! Fellowship divine!
 We feebly struggle, they in glory shine;
 yet all are one in thee, for all are thine.

5 And when the strife is fierce, the
  warfare long,
 steals on the ear the distant triumph–song,
 and hearts are brave again, and arms are
  strong.

6 The golden evening brightens in the west;
 soon, soon to faithful warriors cometh rest:
 sweet is the calm of paradise the blest.

7 But lo! There breaks a yet more
  glorious day;
 the saints triumphant rise in bright array:
 the king of glory passes on his way.

8 From earth's wide bounds,
  from ocean's farthest coast,
 through gates of pearl streams in the
  countless host,
 singing to Father, Son and Holy Ghost.
   W.W. How (1823–97)

372

By all your saints still striving,
for all your saints at rest,
your holy Name, O Jesus,
for evermore be blessed.
You rose, our King victorious,
that they might wear the crown
and ever shine in splendour
reflected from your throne.

2 Apostles, prophets, martyrs,
and all the noble throng
who wear the spotless raiment
and raise the ceaseless song:
For them and those whose witness
is only known to you
By walking in their footsteps
we give you praise anew.
  or appropriate verse from selection opposite

3 Then let us praise the Father
and worship God the Son
and sing to God the Spirit,
eternal Three in One.
Till all the ransomed number
who stand before the throne
ascribe all pow'r and glory
and praise to God alone.

————————————

Substitute one of the following as v.2 as appropriate:

JANUARY 25: Conversion of Paul
 Praise for the light from heaven
 and for the voice of awe:
 praise for the glorious vision
 the persecutor saw.
 O Lord, for Paul's conversion,
 we bless your Name today.
 Come shine within our darkness
 and guide us in the Way.

February 22: Chair of Peter
 We praise you, Lord, for Peter,
 so eager and so bold:
 thrice falling, yet repentant,
 thrice charged to feed your fold.
 Lord, make your pastors faithful
 to guard your flock from harm
 and hold them when they waver
 with your almighty arm.

March 19: Joseph, Husband of Mary
 All praise, O God, for Joseph,
 the guardian of your Son,
 who saved him from King Herod,
 when safety there was none.
 He taught the trade of builder,
 when they to Naz'reth came,
 and Joseph's love made 'Father'
 to be, for Christ, God's name.

March 25: Annunciation of Our Lord
 We sing with joy of Mary
 whose heart with awe was stirred
 when, youthful and unready,
 she heard the angel's word;
 Yet she her voice upraises
 God's glory to proclaim,
 as once for our salvation
 your mother she became.

April 25: Mark

For Mark, O Lord, we praise you,
the weak by grace made strong:
his witness in his Gospel
becomes victorious song.
May we, in all our weakness,
receive your power divine,
and all, as faithful branches,
grow strong in you, the Vine.

May 3: Philip and James

We praise you, Lord, for Philip,
blest guide to Greek and Jew,
and for young James the faithful,
who heard and followed you,
O grant us grace to know you,
the victor in the strife,
that we with all your servants
may wear the crown of life.

June 24: Birth of John the Baptist

All praise for John the Baptist,
forerunner of the Word,
Our true Elijah, making
a highway for the Lord.
The last and greatest prophet,
he saw the dawning ray
of light that grows in splendor
until the perfect day.

June 29: Peter and Paul

We praise you for Saint Peter;
we praise you for Saint Paul.
They taught both Jew and Gentile
that Christ is all in all.
To cross and sword they yielded
and saw the kingdom come:
O God, your two apostles
won life through martyrdom.

July 3: Thomas

All praise, O Lord, for Thomas
whose short-lived doubtings prove
your perfect twofold nature,
the depth of your true love.
To all who live with questions
a steadfast faith afford;
and grant us grace to know you,
made flesh, yet God and Lord.

July 22: Mary Magdalene

All praise for Mary Magd'lene,
whose wholeness was restored
by you, her faithful Master,
her Saviour and her Lord.
On Easter morning early,
a word from you sufficed:
her faith was first to see you,
her Lord, the risen Christ.

July 25: James

O Lord, for James, we praise you
who fell to Herod's sword.
He drank the cup of suff'ring
and thus fulfilled your word.
Lord, curb our vain impatience
for glory and for fame,
equip us for such suff'rings
as glorify your Name.

September 21: Matthew

We praise you, Lord, for Matthew
whose gospel words declare
that, worldly gain forsaking,
your path of life we share.
From all unrighteous mammon,
O raise our eyes anew,
that we, whate'er our station
may rise and follow you.

October 18: Luke

For Luke, beloved physician,
all praise, whose Gospel shows
the healer of the nations,
the one who shares our woes.
Your wine and oil, O Saviour,
upon our spirits pour,
and with true balm of Gilead
anoint us evermore.

November 30: Andrew

All praise, O Lord, for Andrew,
the first to follow you;
he witnessed to his brother,
'This is Messiah true.'
You called him from his fishing
upon Lake Galilee;
he rose to meet your challenge,
'Leave all and follow me'.

December 26: Stephen

All praise, O Lord, for Stephen
who, martyred, saw you stand
to help in time of torment,
to plead at God's right hand.
Like you, our suff'ring Saviour,
his enemies he blessed,
with 'Lord, receive my spirit,'
his faith, in death, confessed.

December 27: John

For John, your loved disciple
exiled to Patmos' shore,
and for his faithful record,
we praise you evermore;
praise for the mystic vision
his words to us unfold.
Instill in us his longing,
your glory to behold.

Jerry D. Godwin, based on H. Nelson (1823-1913)

373

Jerusalem, my happy home
when shall I come to thee?
When shall my sorrows have an end?
Thy joys when shall I see?

Thy saints are crowned with glory great;
they see God face to face;
they triumph still, they still rejoice
in that most happy place.

There David stands with harp in hand
as master of the choir:
ten thousand times would one be blest
who might this music hear.

Our Lady sings Magnificat
with tunes surpassing sweet,
and all the virgins join the song
while sitting at her feet.

There Magdalene has left her tears,
and cheerfully doth sing
with blessed saints, whose harmony
doth ring in every street.

6 Jerusalem, Jerusalem,
God grant that I may see
thine endless joy, and of the same
partaker ever be!
'F.B.P.' (c. 16th C.), alt.

Apostles

374

1 The eternal gifts of Christ the King,
the apostles' glory, let us sing,
and all with hearts of gladness, raise
due hymns of thankful love and praise.

2 Their faith in Christ, the Lord, prevailed;
their hope, a light that never failed;
their love ablaze o'er pathways trod
to lead them to the eternal God.

3 In them the Father's glory shone,
in them the will of God the Son,
in them exults the Holy Ghost,
through them rejoice the heavenly host.

4 To you, Redeemer, now we cry,
that you would join to them on high
your servants, who this grace implore
for ever and for evermore.
St Ambrose (c.340-397), tr. J.M.Neale (1818-66), alt.

Martyrs

375

1 Blessed feasts of blessed martyrs,
holy women, holy men,
with our love and admiration
greet we your return again.
Worthy deeds are theirs, and wonders,
worthy of the name they bore;
we, with joyful praise and singing
honour them for evermore.

2 Faith prevailing, hope unfailing,
loving Christ with single heart,
thus they, glorious and victorious,
bravely bore the martyr's part,
by contempt of every anguish,
by unyielding battle done;
victors at the last, they triumph,
with the host of angels one.

3 Therefore, all that reign in glory,
  strong and sure with Christ on high,
  join to ours your supplication
  when before him we draw nigh,
  praying that, this life completed,
  all its fleeting moments past,
  by his grace we may be worthy
  of eternal bliss at last.

  Latin, 12th C., tr. J.M.Neale (1818-66), alt.

St Joseph

376

1 Come now, and praise the humble saint
  of David's house and line;
  the carpenter whose life fulfilled
  our gracious God's design.

2 The Architect's high miracles
  he saw, and what was done,
  the Virgin's spouse, the guardian of
  great David's greater Son.

3 For him there was no glory here,
  no crown or martyr's fame,
  for him there was the patient life
  of faith and humble name.

4 But now within the Father's grace
  where saints and angels throng,
  beside his spouse, before the Son,
  he joins the heavenly song.

  G. W. Williams

377

1 Hail, holy Joseph, hail!
  Husband of Mary, hail!
  Chaste as the lily flower
  in Eden's peaceful vale.

2 Hail, holy Joseph, hail!
  Father of Christ esteemed,
  Father be thou to those
  thy foster Son redeemed.

3 Hail, holy Joseph, hail!
  Prince of the house of God,
  may his blest graces be
  by thy pure hands bestowed.

4 Hail, holy Joseph, hail!
  Comrade of angels, hail:
  cheer thou the hearts that faint,
  and guide the steps that fail.

5 Hail, holy Joseph, hail!
  God's choice wert thou alone;
  to thee the Word made flesh
  was subject as a Son.

6 Mother of Jesus, bless,
  and bless, ye saints on high,
  all meek and simple souls
  that to Saint Joseph cry.

  F.W. Faber (1814–1863)

St John the Baptist

378

1 The great fore-runner of the morn
  the herald of the Word, is born;
  and faithful hearts shall never fail
  with thanks and praise his light to hail.

2 With heavenly message Gabriel came,
  that John should be that herald's name,
  and with prophetic utterance told
  his actions great and manifold.

3 John, still unborn, yet gave aright
  his witness to the coming light;
  and Christ, the sun of all the earth,
  fulfilled that witness at his birth.

4 Of woman born shall never be
  a greater prophet than was he,
  whose mighty deeds exalt his fame
  to greater than a prophet's name.

5 All praise to God the Father be,
  and to the Son eternally,
  whom with the Spirit we adore
  for ever and for evermore.

  Bede the Venerable (673-733),
  tr. J.M.Neale (1818-1866), alt.

➤ *See also On Jordan's Bank (94); When John
baptised (173); Behold the Lamb of God (98);
Benedictus (83)*

379

1 O Peter, you were named by Christ
the guardian-shepherd of his flock:
protect the Church he built on you
to stand unyielding, firm on rock.

2 Your weakness Christ exchanged for
strength;
you faltered, but he made you true:
he knew the greatness of your love,
and gave the keys of heaven to you.

3 Apostle of the gentiles, Paul,
the greatest witness of them all,
you turned to Christ, the risen Lord,
when out of light you heard him call.

4 You journeyed far and wide to tell
that Christ was risen from the dead;
that all who put their faith in him
would live for ever, as he said.

5 Unseen, eternal Trinity,
we give you glory, praise your name:
your love keeps faith with faithless hearts;
through change and stress you are the same.
The Benedictines of Stanbrook

380

1 Into a world of darkness since the fall,
new light had dawned, two champions
heard the call:
Peter the rock, and Paul once known as
Saul,
Alleluia, alleluia.

2 First Peter stared in wonder at the sight,
Jesus, transfigured, clothed in glorious
light,
then heard God praise his Son from
heaven's height.

3 Beside a desert road a different sign,
Saul saw a blinding light in splendour
shine
and Jesus told him, 'These you hurt are
mine!'

4 On each a lifelong mission was
conferred,
'Go tell the nations all that you have
heard
of God made known through Christ,
th'incarnate Word.'

5 Their work accomplished, called to
their reward,
one crucified, one martyred by the
sword,
their deaths bore witness to the risen
Lord:
Alleluia, alleluia!
Patrick Lee (1930-2004)

Saints of Wales

381

1 Lord, who in thy perfect wisdom
times and seasons dost arrange -
working out thy changeless purpose
in a world of ceaseless change;
thou didst form our ancient nation
in remote barbaric days,
to unfold in it thy purpose
to thy glory and thy praise.

2 To our shores remote, benighted,
washed by distant western waves,
tidings in thy love thou sentest,
tidings of the Cross that saves.
Men of courage strove and suffered
here thy holy Church to plant;
glorious in the roll of heroes
shines the name of Dewi Sant.

3 Lord, we hold in veneration
all the saints our land has known,
bishops, priests, confessors, martyrs,
standing now around thy throne;
Dewi, Dyfrig, Deiniol, Teilo -
all the gallant saintly band,
who of old by prayer and labour
hallowed all our fatherland.

4 Still thy ancient purpose standeth
every change and chance above;
still thy ancient church remaineth -
witness to thy changeless love.
Vision grant us, Lord, and courage
to fulfill thy work begun;
in the church and in the nation
Lord of lords, thy will be done.

Timothy Rees, C.R. (1874-1939)

St David

382

1 O Great Saint David, still we hear thee
call us,
unto a life that knows no fear of death;
Yea, down the ages, will thy words
enthral us,
strong happy words: 'Be joyful, keep
the faith.'
On Cambria's sons stretch out thy hands
in blessing;
for our dear land thy help we now
implore.
Lead us to God, with humble hearts
confessing
Jesus, Lord and King for evermore.

2 Christ was the centre rock of all thy
teaching,
God's holy will – the splendour of its
theme.
His grace informed, his love inflamed
thy preaching;
Christ's sway on earth, the substance of
thy dream.

3 In early childhood, choosing Jesus only,
thy fervour showed his yoke was light
and sweet!
And thus for thee, life's journey was not
lonely –
the path made plain by prints of
wounded feet.

4 O glorious saint, we wander in the dark;
with thee we seek our trusted guide in
Rome.

Help him to steer on earth Saint Peter's
barque,
that we may safely reach our heavenly
home.

Archbishop Francis Mostyn (1860–1939)

St Patrick

383

1 Hail, glorious Saint Patrick, dear saint
of our isle,
on us thy poor children bestow a
sweet smile;
and now thou art high in the mansions
above,
on Erin's green valleys look down in
thy love.
On Erin's green valleys,
on Erin's green valleys,
on Erin's green valleys look down in
thy love.

2 Hail, glorious Saint Patrick! Thy word
were once strong
against Satan's wiles and an infidel throng;
not less is thy might where in heaven
thou art;
O, come to our aid, in our battle take part.

3 In the war against sin, in the fight for
the faith,
dear saint, may thy children resist unto
death;
may their strength be in meekness, in
penance, in prayer,
their banner the Cross which they glory
to bear.

4 Thy people, now exiles on many a shore
shall love and revere thee till time be no
more;
and the fire thou hast kindled shall ever
burn bright,
its warmth undiminished, undying its light.

5 Ever bless and defend the sweet land of
our birth,
where the shamrock still blooms as when
thou wert on earth,

and our hearts shall yet burn,
  wheresoever we roam,
for God and Saint Patrick, and our native
  home.
Sister Agnes

➤ *See also : St Patrick's Breastplate (312);*
  Christ be near on either hand (812)

384

1 We praise you and thank you our Father
    above,
  who offer us peace in your kingdom of
    love.
  Your people are saved by the death of
    your Son
  who leads us to glory where all will be
    one.
  Accepting this Gospel we honour Saint
    Patrick,
  who taught in our land what your
    kindness has done.

2 Your Word has revealed what our future
    will be,
  Raised up from earth I draw all men to me.'
  May we, like Saint Patrick, bear witness
    to you,
  reflecting your love in whatever we do.
  He came to our country which once had
    enslaved him,
  to preach the good news that God makes
    all things new.
            Donal Murray

St Andrew

385

1 Great Saint Andrew, friend of Jesus,
  lover of his glorious cross,
  early by his voice effective
  called from ease to pain and loss,
  strong Saint Andrew, Simon's brother,
  who with haste fraternal flew,
  fain with him to share the treasure
  which, at Jesus' lips, he drew.

2 Blest Saint Andrew, Jesus' herald,
  true apostle, martyr bold,
  who, by deeds his words confirming,
  sealed with blood the truth he told.
  Ne'er to king was crown so beauteous,
  ne'er was prize to heart so dear,
  as to him the cross of Jesus
  when its promised joys drew near.

3 Loved Saint Andrew, Scotland's patron,
  watch thy land with heedful eye,
  rally round the cross of Jesus
  all her storied chivalry!
  To the Father, Son, and Spirit,
  fount of sanctity and love,
  give we glory, now and ever,
  with the saints who reign above.
        Frederick Oakeley (1802–80)

St George

386

1 Leader now on earth no longer,
  soldier of th'eternal king,
  victor in the fight for heaven,
  we thy loving praises sing.
  Great Saint George, our patron, help us,
  in the conflict be thou nigh;
  help us in that daily battle,
  where each one must win or die.

2 Praise him who in deadly battle
  never shrank from foeman's sword,
  proof against all earthly weapon,
  gave his life for Christ the Lord.

3 Who, when earthly war was over,
  fought, but not for earth's renown;
  fought, and won a nobler glory,
  won the martyr's purple crown.

4 Help us when temptation presses,
  we have still our crown to win,
  help us when our soul is weary
  fighting with the powers of sin.

5 Clothe us in thy shining armour,
  place thy good sword in our hand;
  teach us how to wield it, fighting
  onward towards the heavenly land.

6 Onward, till, our striving over,
on life's battlefield we fall,
resting then, but ever ready,
waiting for the angel's call.
Joseph W. Reeks (1849–1900)

Everyday Saints

387

1 For all the saints who showed your love
in how they lived and where they moved,
for mindful women, caring men,
accept our gratitude again.

2 For all the saints who loved your name,
whose faith increased the Saviour's fame,
who sang your songs and shared your
word,
accept our gratitude, good Lord.

3 For all the saints who named your will,
and saw your kingdom coming still
through selfless protest, prayer and praise,
accept the gratitude we raise.

4 Bless all whose will or name or love
reflects the grace of heaven above.
Though unacclaimed by earthly powers,
your life through theirs has hallowed ours.
John L.Bell & Graham Maule

Holy Souls

388

1 Help, Lord, the souls that thou hast made,
the souls to thee so dear,
in prison for the debt unpaid
of sin committed here.

2 These holy souls, they suffer on,
resigned in heart and will,
until thy high behest is done,
and justice has its fill.

3 For daily falls, for pardoned crime
they joy to undergo
the shadow of thy cross sublime,
the remnant of thy woe.

4 Oh, by their patience of delay,
their hope amid their pain,
their sacred zeal to burn away
disfigurement and stain;

5 Oh, by their fire of love, not less
in keenness than the flame;
oh, by their very helplessness,
oh, by thy own great name;

6 Good Jesus, help! Sweet Jesus, aid
the souls to thee most dear,
in prison for the debt unpaid
of sins committed here.
J.H. Newman (1801–90)

The Triumph of the Cross (14 September)

389

*Lift high the cross, the love of Christ
proclaim
till all the world adore his sacred name.*

1 Come, Christians, follow where the
Master trod,
our King victorious, Christ the Son of God:

2 Each new–born soldier of the Crucified
is signed with the cross, the seal of him
who died:

3 This is the sign which Satan's armies fear,
and angels veil their faces to revere:

4 Saved by the cross on which their Lord
was slain,
see Adam's children their lost home regain:

5 From north and south, from east and
west they raise
in growing unison their songs of praise:

6 Let every race and every language tell
of him who saves our souls from death
and hell:

7 O Lord, once lifted on the tree of pain,
draw all the world to seek you once again:

8 So shall our song of triumph ever be:
praise to the Crucified for victory!
*G.W. Kitchin (1827–1912) & M.R. Newbolt (1874–
1956) alt. by Jubilate Hymns and others*

Christian Initiation

The passage of a person into the Christian community takes place over an extended period of time. The members of the local church, the catechists and sponsors, the clergy and the bishop, all take part in the journey from inquiry through the catechumenate to baptism, confirmation and the eucharist.

The journey is marked by liturgical rites: Acceptance into the Order of Catechumens (celebrated in the parish), the Rite of Election (usually in the Cathedral), Scrutinies and other rites with the elect, and finally the celebration of the Sacraments of Initiation (baptism, confirmation, first eucharist), ideally at the Easter Vigil.

Acceptance into the Order of Catechumens

Introductory Rites
The priest greets the assembly. The candidates are asked what it is they seek and each replies. After each candidate has responded, an acclamation such as the following may be sung.

390

Marty Haugen

We praise you, Lord, we praise you, Lord, we praise you, Lord, and we bless you.

Signing of the Candidates with the Cross
The priest signs each candidate with the cross on the forehead, praying that the catechumens may share in the cross's saving power. Sponsors and others may also sign them. Ears, eyes and other senses may also be signed. An acclamation such as the following may be sung.

391 Refrain 1

Marty Haugen

In the cross of Christ, our glo - ry, Christ, our sto - ry, Christ our song.

Refrain II

Marty Haugen

Glo - ry and praise to you, Lord Je - sus Christ.

392

Stephen Dean

ff Glo - ry and praise to you, Lord Je - sus Christ!

*Sing this note only the last time

Response to the Intercessions   *See nos. 547-551; 928*

The Rite of Election

This is celebrated by the Bishop on the 1st Sunday of Lent, and the readings are those of the mass of the day.
Psalms: Year A: Psalm 50(51), no. 48; B: Psalm 24 (25), no. 43; C: Psalm 90 (91), no. 51

The Scrutinies

The Scrutinies occur on the 3rd, 4th & 5th Sundays of Lent. The elect are called before the community for
exorcism and prayer. This rite may conclude with a refrain or a psalm, sung prior to dismissal of the elect, e.g.
25(26) nos.43 or 393; 32(33), nos.45 or 394; 50(51), no.48; 129(130), no.59; 138(139), nos. 777-779

Celebration of the Sacraments of Initiation
outside the Easter Vigil

Responsorial Psalms

22(23), The Lord is my shepherd, no. 42; 41(42) Like the deer, no. 47; 50(51), R. A pure heart create for
me, no. 48; 62(63), My soul is thirsting, no. 49; 125(126) When the Lord delivered Zion, no. 57

Baptismal Acclamations

Up from the waters, no. 396; You have put on Christ, no. 400; Awake from your sleep, no. 403

The Baptism of Infants

22(23), The Lord is my shepherd, no. 42; 32(33), nos. 45 or 394; 26 (27), R. The Lord is my light and my
help. ACCLAMATIONS no. 396, 400, 403

Reception into Full Communion with the Church

Responsorial Psalms

26(27), The Lord is my light, no. 44; 41(42), Like the deer, no. 47; 62(63), My soul is thirsting, no. 49

Confirmation

Responsorial Psalms

22 (23), The Lord is my shepherd, no. 42; 103(104), Send forth your spirit, no.299; 144 (145), I will bless
your name for ever, no. 62

Psalms for Initiation

Christopher Walker

393 Those who seek your face, Lord, with a pure heart shall stand in your ho-ly place.

Psalm 26 (27) (Acceptance Rite)

1 Lord, you are my light and my help.
  With you there is no-one I fear.
  For you are the stronghold of my life.
  I will not be afraid.

2 My God, there is one thing I ask:
  to live in your house all my life.
  To savour your sweetness and to ask you
  Lord, to guide my ways.

3. O Lord, hear my voice when I call.
O Lord, in your mercy give answer.
Of you I have spoken in my heart,
O God, I seek your face.

4. O Lord, do not turn me away,
O Lord, do not leave me alone!
Teach me, to do what is your will
and lead me in your paths.

5. I know in this life I will see
the goodness of God all around me.
Have trust in the Lord, do not despair
but have faith in your God.

6. To you our Creator we pray;
to you, God the Son, we give glory.
To you, Holy Spirit, we give praise
both now and evermore.

Verses: Psalm 32 (33) (Scrutinies)

1. O happy are those you forgive,
the people whose sin you have pardoned,
O happy the guiltless for their hearts
are free from all deceit.

2. O God, when I grieved at my guilt
my days were exhausted with crying;
your hand was upon me night and day,
my strength drained away.

3. But then I confessed all my sins,
I did not conceal my wrongdoings.
To you I confessed them and in love
you have forgiven me.

4. God, you are the place where I hide.
When I am in trouble you save me.
Aloud I will sing of your salvation.
God, protect my soul.

Adapted by Christopher Walker

394 *Psalm 32 (33), no. 45, with response* May your love be upon us O Lord, *or :*

Hap-py the peo-ple the Lord   has cho-sen,   cho - sen as   his   own.

Sung twice each time   *Stephen Dean*

395

In   love you sum-mon,   in   love I   fol - low,   li - ving to -

day for   your to - mor - row,   Christ   to   re - lease me, Christ   to en -

fold   me,   Christ   to re - strain   me,   Christ___   to   up - hold   me.

395, 395a: John L. Bell

395a

Take,   O   take me   as   I   am,   sum-mon out what   I shall

be;   set   your   seal   u - pon   my   heart   and   live   in   me.

396 Acclamation

{Priest: I baptise you in the name of the Father, and of the Son, and of the Holy Spirit..}
All: *(music below)* Praise to the One who called and named you up from the waters into life.
Baptismal or Sprinkling song

Up from the wa-ters God has claimed you, up— from the wa-ters, child of light.

Praise to the One who called and named you up— from the wa-ters in-to life.

1 Always proclaim the wonderful story:
Up from the waters, child of light.
How you were raised from death into glory:
Up from the waters into life.

2 Now you have crossed the River of Jordan:
Now you behold God's mercy and pardon:

3 No more shall sin have power to hold you:
now let the grace of Jesus enfold you:

4 Come and praise the God of the living:
Now let your song ring out with
thanksgiving:

5 Water of life and grace and salvation:
Water that heals the heart of creation:

6 This is the life that rains down from
heaven:
this is the new life Jesus has given:

Marty Haugen

397

Refrain

No lon-ger I, but Christ who lives with-in— me:

this po-ver-ty, a trea-sure rich be-yond com - pare.

Last time: repeat

1. The life we live is not our own.
Christ lives within us, the seed that must
be sown.
Formed in the pattern of God's love,
we die to rise with the Lord.

2 We have been clothed in Christ,
children of freedom of justice and new life.

To him whose dying set us free,
we give our lives, our liberty.

3 Then may we bear the cross of Christ,
and wear the brandmarks of Jesus in
our flesh;
as wounded healers we become
images of the risen one.
Bob Hurd

398

*Neither death, nor life, nor angels nor rulers,
nor trials in the present, nor any trials to
come:
neither height, nor depth, nor all of creation
can ever separate us from the love of God
poured out in Christ Jesus, our Lord.*

1. Dwell in the One who raised Christ
from the dead;
though your body shall die, in Christ
you shall rise
through the Spirit who brings you to life.

2. All who are led by the Spirit shall live
   as children of God, and heirs with
      Christ Jesus,
   God's adopted and chosen and loved.

3 All of the suff'ring we now must endure
   is nothing to the glory so soon to be
      revealed
   when creation itself is set free.

4. All of creation awaits the new birth,
   the fullness of redemption,
   through labour pains of love,
   and so we wait in patience and hope.

5. All things work for good
      for the ones who love God,
   and if God is for us,
      then who can be against us?
   God's justified cannot be condemned.

6. Who can separate us from the love of
      Christ?
   Will hardship or distress,
      persecution or famine,
   or nakedness or peril or sword?
   Marty Haugen, from Romans 8:11-19.
   22-25. 28. 35. 38

399

With joy you shall draw wa-ter,___ with joy you shall draw
Fine
wa-ter from the foun-tain of God's mer-cy, from the well-spring of love.

1. Come, all who are thirsty,
   come and drink this living water,
   come and rest beside the river
   of healing love.

2. I saw water flowing
   from the side of God's own temple,
   from the wounded heart of Jesus,
   who died for us.

3 This water I give you
   shall become a flowing river,
   welling up from deep within you,
   eternal life.

4 May this living water
   confirm us in our calling
   to be Christ to one another
   and all the world.
   Bob Hurd

400

You have put on Christ; in him you have been bap -
tized. Al- le - lu - ia, al-le - lu - ia, al-le - lu - ia!

1 We who were dead are now reborn.
   We who were buried now are raised.
   We who were dwelling in the dark
      now see light.

2 For though in Adam all have sinned,
   in Jesus Christ are all made clean.
   The grace abounding of his death
      sets us free.

vv 3-4 overleaf

3 One Lord we serve, who died for us;
  one faith we hold, in life to come;
  one God and Father of us all we proclaim.

4 And this we know, that nothing ill,
  no price nor power, nor death nor sin,
  can separate us from God's love
      shown in Christ.
  Refrain from the Rite of Baptism; Verses
  from Scripture, arr. by Stephen Dean

401

1 God, at creation's dawn,
  over a world unborn,
  your Spirit soared.
  By word and water deign
  that this same Spirit reign
  in those now born again,
  through Christ our Lord.

2 We, who in Adam fell,
  are, as the Scriptures tell,
  saved and restored.
  For, when these rites are done,
  dying we are made one,
  rising we overcome,
  with Christ our Lord.

3 Hear us, your Church, rejoice,
  singing with grateful voice,
  Father adored;

telling our faith anew,
greeting with welcome true
children new born to you,
in Christ our Lord.
    Denis E. Hurley (1915-2004)

402

1 O come let us follow the voice we have
      heard
  for our God is faithful, and faithful
      God's word.
  As pilgrims we journey, by faith
      through the night,
  for God's Son is our sun; we walk in
      the light.

2 Yes, now is the hour to rise from our sleep
  to follow the road, though both narrow
      and steep,
  to leave works of darkness and hasten
      toward day.
  O see how Christ Jesus in love shows
      the way!

3 So let us set out with the gospel as guide
  for God will go with us and stay at our
      side,
  and love shall impel us to climb
      every height,
  our hearts overflowing with joy and deligh
    Delores Dufner OSB

403 **Refrain**

A - wake from your sleep, rise up from the
dead and Christ will shine up - on you.

1 In the beginning, before all creation,
  Christ was the eternal word of God.

2 Born in the flesh, preached to the nations,
  he makes our peace by his death on the
  cross.

3 Risen from the dead, raised up in glory,
  all things created in him are restored.

4 My redeemer, victorious!
  Mighty Saviour, now reigning!
  Where, death, is thy power,
  where, grave, thy sting?
    Stephen Dean, from scripture

404

1. A little child in a bed of night
long, long ago,
convinced the world of its need for light
and how to glow.
Oh, child in the borrowed shed,
clearly you show
how God in splendour reveals for earth
Love from below.

2. A little child from her mother's knee
squeezed through a space
to find herself in a tradesman's arms,
smile on her face.
Oh, child saved from adult scorn,
central your place
when Christ embraces you as the key
to heaven's grace.

3. A little child in a random crowd
tired and unfed,
arrived to place in a stranger's hands
fishes and bread.

Oh, child by your selflessness,
others you've led
to share with all what they called their own,
as Jesus said.

4. A little child to the font we bring
here to entwine
his/her life with that of the Lord of Love,
Jesus, the Vine.
Oh, child as you're christened here
through word and sign,
God's finger writes in your heart the words
'Now you are mine.'

If several children are to be baptised:

[4a These children now to the font we bring
here to entwine
their lives with that of the Lord of Love,
Jesus, the Vine.
On all who are christened here
through word and sign,
God's finger writes in their hearts the words
'Now you are mine.'

John L. Bell

405

(Adults) 1a. Into the family of God we welcome you now.

Into the family of God we welcome this child. Child of the
Into the family of God we welcome you now. People of

promise, child of grace,
promise, filled with grace,
come to the Spirit's dwelling place, come to
Christ's own loving embrace, come to the Lord.

2. Set on a journey of faith with the
people of God;
led into paths that the saints before you
have trod:

Oil of rejoicing grace your head,
At the Lord's feast may you be fed
Christ's own life in wine and bread,
strength for the way.

vv. 3-4 overleaf

3 God who created us all,
    we give thanks for this child.
  Help us to cherish what Christ
    by blood reconciled.
  Help us to teach what he has taught,
  train for the fight which he has fought,
  seek the life his victory bought,
  teach us to strive.

4 Into the family of God we welcome this
    child;
  into the family of God we welcome this
    child;
  risen with Christ and dead to sin
  after new birth, new life begin
  Christ the Saviour welcomes you in:
  come to the Lord!

3a God who created us all,
    we give thanks for this day.
  Help us to cherish new friends
    now sharing our way.
  Help us to teach what Christ has taught,
  strengthen the faith which they have
    sought,
  live the life Christ's victory bought,
  teach us to strive.

4a Into the family of God we welcome
    you now;
  into the family of God we welcome
    you now;
  risen with Christ and dead to sin,
  after new birth, new life begin
  Christ the Saviour welcomes you in:
  come to the Lord!
    Stephen Dean

406

1 O praise ye the Lord!
  Praise him in the height;
  rejoice in his word,
  ye angels of light;
  ye heavens, adore him,
  by whom ye were made,
  and worship before him,
  in brightness arrayed.

2 O praise ye the Lord!
  praise him upon earth,
  in tuneful accord,
  ye sons of new birth.
  Praise him who hath brought you
  his grace from above,
  praise him who hath taught you
  to sing of his love.

3 O praise ye the Lord,
  all things that give sound;
  each jubilant chord
  re–echo around;
  loud organs, his glory
  forth tell in deep tone,
  and, sweet harp, the story
  of what he hath done.

4 O praise ye the Lord!
  Thanksgiving and song
  to him be outpoured
  all ages along;
  for love in creation,
  for heaven restored,
  for grace of salvation,
  O praise ye the Lord!
    H.W. Baker (1821–77)

407

1 Baptised in water, sealed by the Spirit,
  cleansed by the blood of Christ our King:
  trusting his promise, heirs of salvation,
  faithfully now God's praises we sing.

2 Baptised in water, sealed by the Spirit,
  dead in the tomb with Christ our King:
  one with his rising, freed and forgiven,
  thankfully now God's praises we sing.

3 Baptised in water, sealed by the Spirit,
  marked with the sign of Christ our King:
  born of one Father, we are his children,
  joyfully now God's praises we sing.
    Michael Saward

408

1 O let all who thirst,
let them come to the water.
And let all who have nothing,
let them come to the Lord:
without money, without price.
Why should you pay the price
except for the Lord?

2 And let all who seek,
let them come to the water.
And let all who have nothing,
let them come to the Lord:
without money, without strife.
Why should you spend your life,
except for the Lord?

3 And let all who toil,
let them come to the water.
And let all who are weary,
let them come to the Lord:
all who labour, without rest.
How can your soul find rest,
except for the Lord?

4 And let all the poor,
let them come to the water.
Bring the ones who are laden,
bring them all to the Lord:
bring the children without might.
Easy the load and light:
come to the Lord!

John Foley SJ, based on Isaiah 55:1-12

Marriage

409 **Refrain I**
Blest are those who love you, hap - py those who fol - low you,
blest are those who seek you, O God.

from Psalm 127 (128),
Marty Haugen

Refrain II
May the Lord bless us, may the Lord pro - tect us,
all the days, all the days of our life.

1 Happy all those who fear the Lord, and walk in God's pathway;
you will find what you long for: the riches of our God.

2 Your spouse shall be like a fruitful vine in the midst of your home,
your children flourish like olive plants rejoicing at your table.

3 May the blessings of God be yours all the days of your life,
may the peace and the love of God live always in your heart.

➤ see also: The Lord fills the earth with his love, 45; O blessed are those, 58

410 Wedding Acclamation

Repeated after each verse.

Bles-sed be God, bles-sed be God, bles-sed be God for e - ver.

1 Blessed are you, heavenly Father: you give joy to bridegroom and bride.

2 Blessed are you, Lord Jesus Christ: you have brought new life to the world.

3 Blessed are you, Holy Spirit of God: you bring us together in love.

4 Blessed are you, source of all grace, one God to be praised for ever.

From the Rite of Marriage, Alternative Service Book. Music by Paul Inwood

411

Refrain

May God bless you, hold and keep you; may God's mer-cy shine on you,

guide your work and guard your rest-ing, keep your love for ev - er new.

1 May God satisfy your longing, be refreshment at your table,
and provide your daily bread,
guard your going and your coming, be the solace in your silence:
life within the lives you wed.

2 May God join your hopeful spirits, fill your hearts with truth and courage,
trust to share both joy and tears,
teach love to your children's children, may your household learn to witness
living faith through all your years.

3 May God find your home a refuge where you warmly welcome strangers
and the lowly find a place;
make you caring, kind companions, help you meet the needs of neighbours,
finding Christ in ev'ry face.

Michael Joncas

412

1. O let there be songs of— joy on this our day of—
2. His ca - ring hand has led us here, his word un - ites us—
3. May it be con - stant as the stars with love no flood can—

days and for this feast of life and love to God let us— give praise.
now, the Christ that once graced Ca-na's feast will bless our mar - riage vow.
drown, my love a seal up - on your heart and yours for me— a crown.

4 Now where you go I will go,
    and with you I will dwell;
    in laughter, sorrow, rich or poor
    for God does all things well.

5 So let there be songs of joy
    on this our day of days,
    and for this feast of life and love
    to God let us give praise.
        Liam O'Carroll CSsR

413

  Jesus, Lord, we pray,
  be our guest today!
  Gospel story has recorded
  how your glory was afforded
  to a wedding day:
  be our guest, we pray.

2 Lord of love and life,
    blessing man and wife:
    as they stand, their need confessing,
    may your hand take theirs in blessing.
    You will share their life:
    bless this man and wife.

3 Lord of hope and faith,
    faithful unto death:
    let the ring serve as a token
    or a love sincere, unbroken:
    love more strong than death -
    Lord of hope and faith!
        Basil E. Bridge

414

1 God in the planning and purpose of life,
    hallowed the union of husband and wife:
    this we embody where love is displayed,
    rings are presented and promises made.

2 Jesus was found at a similar feast,
    taking the roles of both waiter and priest,
    turning the worldly towards the divine,
    tears into laughter and water to wine.

3 Therefore we pray that his spirit preside
    over the wedding of bridegroom and
        bride,
    fulfilling all that they've hoped will
        come true,
    lighting with love all they dream of and do.

4 Praise then the Maker, the Spirit, the Son,
    source of the love through which two
        are made one.
    God's is the glory, the goodness and grace
    seen in this marriage and known in
        this place.
        John L. Bell and Graham Maule

415

1 O perfect love, all human thought
        transcending,
    lowly we kneel in prayer before thy
        throne.
    That theirs may be the love which
        knows no ending,
    whom thou for evermore dost join in one.

2 O perfect life, be thou their full assurance
    of tender charity and steadfast faith,
    of patient hope, and quiet, brave endurance,
    with childlike trust that fears not pain nor
        death.

3 Grant them the joy which brightens
        earthly sorrow,
    grant them the peace which calms all
        earthly strife;
    and to life's day the glorious unknown
        morrow
    that dawns upon eternal love and life.
        Dorothy Frances Gurney (1858–1932)

416

1 When love is found and hope comes home,
    sing and be glad that two are one.
    When love explodes and fills the sky
    praise God and share our Maker's joy.

2 When love has flow'red in trust and care,
    build both each day that love may dare
    to reach beyond home's warmth and light,
    to serve and strive for truth and right.

3 When love is tried, as loved-ones change,
hold still to hope though all seems strange
till ease returns and love grows wise
through list'ning ears and opened eyes.

4 When love is torn and trust betrayed,
pray strength to love till torments fade,
till lovers keep no score of wrong
but hear through pain love's Easter song.

5 Praise God for love, praise God for life,
in age or youth, in calm or strife,
Lift up your hearts! Let love be fed
through death and life in broken bread.
Brian Wren

417

1 Lord of all loving, we stand before you,
asking your blessing on us today.
Love in our union this day beginning,
life–long communion every new day.

2 Lord of our living, grant in good measure
grace for forgiving each fault we find.
Holding together in time of trouble
strength for each other, loving and kind.

3 Lord of salvation, daily we offer
fresh consecration, blessing and praise.
Find you in work–life, friends for our
sharing,
joy in our home–life through all our days.

4 Lord of all power, joy is our crowning,
faith is our strong tower, hope is our peace.
Love is the promise golden before us,
grant that our gladness never may cease.
Averil Norton

418

1 Surprised by joy no song can tell,
no thought can compass, here we stand
to celebrate eternal Love,
to reach for God's almighty hand.

2 Beyond an angel's mind is this,
best gift, alone to mortals given;
the love of parent, lover, friend
brings straight to earth the bliss of heaven.

3 Faith, hope and love here come alive,
God's very being is made known,
when giving and forgiving all
two are inseparably one.

4 For all this splendour, all this joy
is ours because a Father's care -
large, generous, patient, strong as death
showed us in Christ what love can dare

5 Your banner over us be love,
your grace refresh our travelling days,
your power sustain, your beauty cheer,
our words, our home, our lives be praise.
Erik Routley (1917-82)

419

God of tender mercy, God of love,
God of glorious light from heav'n above
in your light we see light, in your love w
feel love:
Light eternal, love which never ends.

1 Living God, creator of all life,
heav'n and earth proclaim your mighty
pow'r.
Man and woman you have fashioned
in your loving kindness,
setting them to prosper and to grow.

2 Word of God, inviting us to trust,
bidding us to pledge our hope–filled vo
son and daughter by your grace
in one flesh now united,
called to live the sacrament of love.

3 Spirit of our God and bond of peace,
day by day you call us to be one.
Hopes and fears we bring to you
in sorrow and rejoicing,
strengthened by the promise of your lov

4 Age to age shall raise its voice in song,
as your Church rejoices in your name:
singing to the God of life
and source of ev'ry blessing:
praise and glory now and ever more!
Ernest Sands (1949-2016)

420

1 O Father all creating
whose wisdom, love and power
first bound two lives together
in Eden's dawning hour,
today to these your children
your earliest gifts renew:
a home by you kept happy,
a love by you kept true.

2 With good wine, Lord, at Cana
the wedding feast you blessed.
Grant them your saving presence
and be their dearest guest.
Their store of earthly treasure
transform to heav'nly wine,
and teach them in the testing
to know the gift divine.

3 O Spirit, bond of union
breathe on them from above
so mighty in your coming,
so tender in your love,
that guarded by your presence
and kept from strife and sin,
their hearts may sense your guidance
and know you dwell within.

4 Unless you build it, Father,
the house is built in vain;
unless you, Saviour, bless it,
the joy will turn to pain,
but nothing breaks a marriage
of hearts in you made one.
The love your Spirit hallows
is endless love begun.
John Ellerton (1826-1893)

421

1 Hear us now, Our God and Father,
send your Spirit from above
on this Christian man and woman
who here make their vows of love!
Bind their hearts in true devotion
endless as the seashore's sands,
boundless as the deepest oceans,
blest and sealed by your own hands.

2 Give them joy to lighten sorrow!
Give them hope to brighten life!
Go with them to face the morrow,
stay with them in every strife.
As your Word has promised, ever
fill them with your strength and grace,
so that each may serve the other
till they see you face to face.

3 May the grace of Christ, our Saviour,
and the Father's boundless love,
with the Holy Spirit's favour
rest upon them from above.
Thus may they abide in union
with each other and the Lord,
and possess in sweet communion
joys which earth cannot afford.
Vv. 1,2, Harry N. Huxhold (b.1922)
V.3, John Newton (1725-1807), alt

422

1 Father, we come in prayer
to witness to your love,
to make two hearts as one.
Father, we give ourselves to you,
we give our lives anew for all time.
Wherever you must go
I'll be always at your side.
Wherever you live you'll find me there,
for your God is mine.

2 Jesus, we ask your help
to conquer for all time
the darkness in our land.
Jesus, where we live you live too,
unite our hearts with you in your love.

3 Spirit, we feel your pow'r
your presence in our hearts:
be with us in each day,
Spirit, may we be one in you,
make all we say and do give you praise.
Anthony Sharpe. Refrain: Ruth 1:16

➤ *See also: Love for one another (918-927),*
e.g. 918 Where there is love; 919 Not for tongues
of heaven's angels

Ministry, Service, Ordination

423

Refrain

O Lord, you are the centre of my life: I will al-ways praise you, I will al-ways serve you, I will al-ways keep you in my sight.

1. Keep me safe, O God, I take refuge in you.
   I say to the Lord: 'You are my God.
   My happiness lies in you alone;
   my happiness lies in you alone.'

2. I will bless the Lord who gives me counsel,
   who even at night directs my heart.
   I keep the Lord ever in my sight:
   since he is at my right hand, I shall stand
   firm.

3. And so my heart rejoices, my soul is glad;
   even in safety shall my body rest.
   For you will not leave my soul among
   the dead,
   nor let your beloved know decay.

4. You will show me the path of life,
   the fullness of joy in your presence,
   at your right hand, at your right hand
   happiness for ever.

Ps 15 (16) The Grail; Refrain by Paul Inwood

424

Refrain

Go in-to the world,— al-le-lu - ia; make dis-ci-ples of all the na-tions, al-le-lu - ia.

Psalm 95 (96), refrain Matt 28:19. Music: Stephen Dean

➤ *see also: Ps 22 (23), no. 42; Ps 24 (25), no.53; Ps 84 (85), no. 50; Ps 115(116), no. 55*

425

1. You are called to tell the story
   passing words of life along,
   then to blend your voice with others
   as you sing the sacred song.
   Christ be known in all our singing
   filling all with songs of love.

2. You are called to teach the rhythm
   of the dance that never ends,
   then to move within the circle,
   hand in hand with strangers, friends.
   Christ be known in all our dancing,
   touching all with hands of love.

3. You are called to set the table,
   blessing bread as Jesus blessed,
   then to come with thirst and hunger,
   needing care like all the rest,
   Christ be known in all our sharing,
   feeding all with signs of love.

4. May the One whose love is broader
   than the measure of all space
   give us words to sing the story,
   move among us in this place.
   Christ be known in all our living
   filling all with gifts of love.
   Ruth Duck

426

1 Go to the world! Go into all the earth.
Go preach the cross where Christ
   renews life's worth,
baptising as the sign of our rebirth,
   Alleluia.

2 Go to the world! Go into every place.
Go live the Word of Christ's redeeming
   grace.
Go seek God's presence in each time
   and space
   Alleluia.

3 Go to the world! Go struggle, bless and
      pray;
the nights of tears give way to joyous day.
As servant Church, you follow Christ's
   own way.
   Alleluia.

4 Go to the world! Go as the ones I send,
for I am with you 'til the age shall end,
when all the hosts of glory cry 'Amen!'
   Alleluia.

Sylvia Dunstan (1955-93)

➤ *See also Church (777-798); Sending out/
discipleship/commitment (815-841); Laudate
Dominum (730); Out of Darkness (835)*

Healing

Psalms *24(25), To you, O Lord, no.43; 33(34), Taste and see, no. 46; 41(42), Like the deer that yearns, no. 47; 62(63) For you my soul is thirsting, no.49; 102(103) The Lord is compassion and love, no. 54; and other settings of these psalms listed on p.420*

427

Refrain

Hea-ler of our ev'-ry ill, light of each to-mor-row,

give us peace be-yond our fear, and hope be-yond our sor - row.

Verses

1. You who know our fears and sad-ness, grace us with your
2. In the pain and joy be-hol-ding, how your grace is

peace and glad-ness, Spi-rit of all com-fort: fill our hearts.___
still un-fol-ding, give us all your vi-sion: God of love.___

3 Give us strength to love each other,
ev'ry sister, ev'ry brother,
Spirit of all kindness: be our guide.

4 You who know each thought and feeling,
teach us all your way of healing,
Spirit of compassion: fill each heart.

Marty Haugen

428

1 By gracious powers so wonderfully
    sheltered
  and confidently waiting, come what may,
  we know that God is with us night and
    morning,
  and never fails to greet us each new day.

2 Yet is this heart by its old foe tormented
  still evil days bring burdens hard to bear;
  O give our frightened souls the sure
    salvation
  for which, O God, you taught us to prepare.

3 And when this cup you give is filled to
    brimming
  with bitter suffering, hard to understand,
  we take it thankfully and without trembling,
  out of so good, and so beloved, a hand.

4 Yet when again, in this same world, you
    give us
  the joy we had, the brightness of your sun,
  we shall remember all the days we lived
    through,
  and our whole life shall then be yours
    alone.

5 Now, when your silence deeply spreads
    around us,
  O let us hear all your creation says
  that world of sound which soundlessly
    invades us,
  and all your children's highest hymns of
    praise.
  F. Pratt Green (1903-2000), based on the
  German of Dietrich Bonhoeffer (1906-45)

429

1 Great God of mercy, God of consolation,
  look on your people, gathered here to
    praise you!
  Pity our weakness, come in power to
    aid us,
  source of all blessing.

2 Jesus Redeemer, Lord of all creation,
  come as our Saviour, Jesus, friend of
    sinners:

grant us forgiveness, lift our downcast
    spirit,
  heal us and save us.

3 Joygiving Spirit, be our light in darkness,
  come to befriend us, help us bear our
    burdens:
  give us true courage, breathe your
    peace around us,
  stay with us always.

4 God in three persons, Trinity eternal,
  come to renew us, fill your Church with
    glory:
  grant us your healing, pledge of
    resurrection,
  foretaste of heaven.
  James Quinn SJ (1919-2010)

430

1 O Christ, the Healer, we have come
  to pray for health, to plead for friends.
  How can we fail to be restored,
  when reached by love that never ends?

2 From every ailment flesh endures
  our bodies clamour to be freed;
  yet in our hearts we would confess
  that wholeness is our deepest need.

3 How strong, O Lord, are our desires,
  how weak our knowledge of ourselves!
  Release in us those healing truths
  unconscious pride resists or shelves.

4 In conflicts that destroy our health
  we recognise the world's disease;
  our common life declares our ills:
  is there no cure, O Christ, for these?

5 Grant that we all, made one in faith,
  in your community may find
  the wholeness that, enriching us,
  shall reach the whole of human kind.
  F. Pratt Green (1903-2000)

431

1 Your hands, O Lord, in days of old,
  were strong to heal and save;
  they triumphed over pain and death,

fought darkness and the grave.
To you they went, the blind, the mute,
the palsied and the lame,
the leper set apart and shunned,
the sick and those in shame.

2 And then your touch brought life
　　and health,
gave speech, and strength, and sight;
and youth renewed and health restored,
claimed you, the Lord of light:
and so, O Lord, be near to bless,
Almighty now as then,
in ev'ry street, in ev'ry home,
in ev'ry troubled friend.

3 O be our mighty healer still,
O Lord of life and death;
restore and strengthen, soothe and bless,
with your almighty breath;
on hands that work and eyes that see,
your healing wisdom pour,
that whole and sick, and weak and strong
may praise you evermore.
　　　E. H. Plumtree (1821-91), alt.

432

Lay your hands gently upon us,
let their touch render your peace;
let them bring your forgiveness and
　　　healing,
lay your hands, gently lay your hands.

1 You were sent to free the broken hearted.
You were sent to give sight to the blind.
You desire to heal all our illnesses.
Lay your hands, gently lay your hands.

2 Lord, we come to you through one
　　another.
Lord, we come to you in our need.
Lord, we come to you seeking wholeness.
Lay your hands, gently lay your hands.
　　　Carey Landry

433

1 We cannot measure how you heal
or answer every sufferer's prayer,
yet we believe your grace responds

where faith and doubt unite to care.
Your hands, though bloodied on the cross,
survive to hold and heal and warn,
to carry all through death to life
and cradle children yet unborn.

2 The pain that will not go away,
the guilt that clings from things long past,
the fear of what the future holds,
are present as if meant to last.
But present too is love which tends
the hurt we never hoped to find,
the private agonies inside,
the memories that haunt the mind.

3 So some have come who need your help
and some have come to make amends,
as hands which shaped and saved the
　　world
are present in the touch of friends.
Lord, let your Spirit meet us here
to mend the body, mind and soul,
to disentangle peace from pain
and make your broken people whole.
　　　John L. Bell & Graham Maule

434

1 We give God thanks for those who knew
the touch of Jesus' healing love;
they trusted him to make them whole,
to give them peace, their guilt remove.

2 We offer prayer for all who go
relying on his grace and power,
to help the anxious and the ill,
to heal their wounds, their lives restore.

3 We dedicate our skills and time
to those who suffer where we live,
to bring such comfort as we can
to meet their need, their pain relieve.

4 So Jesus' touch of healing grace
lives on within our willing care;
by thought and prayer and gift we prove
his mercy still, his love we share.
　　　Michael Perry (1942-96)

435

1 He healed the darkness of my mind
   the day he gave my sight to me:
   it was not sin that made me blind;
   it was no sinner made me see.

2 Let others call my faith a lie,
   or try to stir up doubt in me:

Look at me now! None can deny
I once was blind, and now I see!

3 Ask me not how! But I know who
   has opened up new worlds to me:
   this Jesus does what none can do –
   I once was blind, and now I see.

F. Pratt Green (1903-2000)

436

Refrain

Jes-us heal us: Je-sus.___ Je-sus, hear us now.___

1 All who fear the Lord:
   wait for God's mercy.
   All who love the Lord:
   come, he will fill you.

2 All who fear the Lord:
   Follow the way.
   All who love the Lord:
   hope in God's goodness.

3. All who fear the Lord:
   Keep your hearts prepared.
   All who love the Lord:
   be humbled in God's presence.

4. All who trust in God:
   God will uphold you.
   Let us cling to our God;
   let us fall in the arms of the Lord!

David Haas

437

Lord Je-sus Christ, lo - ver of all, trail
wide the hem of your gar - ment, bring hea-ling, bring peace.

John L.Bell and Graham Maule

Funerals

438

Re - qui-em ae - ter - nam___ do - na e-
is___ Do - mi - ne, et_ lux___ per-
pe - tu - a lu - ce-at___ e - is.

Te de - cet hym- nus, De - us, in Si- on: et ti - bi red - de -
tur vo-tum in Ie- ru - sa- lem. *Requiem..* Qui au - dis o - ra - ti - o-nem,
ad te om- nis ca- ro ve - ni - et prop-ter in - i - qui - ta- tem.
Requiem..

Owen Alstott

Refrain

439 Grant them e - ter- nal rest, O Lord, and let per - pe - tu-al
light shine up - on them. **Verses** 1. Out of the depths I cry to
2. One thing I ask, just one thing
3. Hear me, O God, hide not your

you, O Lord, I know you are my on - ly hope. Save me, O God!
do I seek: to dwell for - e - ver in your house, Lord, God of Hosts!
face from me. Re - mem - ber that your mer-cies, Lord, are from of old.

Responsorial Psalms
22(23) The Lord's my shepherd, no. 42; 24(25), To you, O Lord, no. 43; 41(42), Like the deer that yearns, no. 47; 62(63) For you my soul is thirsting, no. 49; 121(122) I rejoiced, no. 56; 129(130) nos. 59, 60 or 452. Complete Psalm list: p.409

Gospel Acclamation
Settings of the Alleluia: nos 534-46. Lenten Acclamation: 184-87. A suitable verse:
> I am the resurrection and the life, says the Lord;
> whoever believes in me will never die.

Jn 11:25-26

Songs of Farewell

440

1 I know that my Redeemer lives,
   and on that final day of days
   his voice shall bid me rise again:
   unending joy, unceasing praise.

2 This hope I cherish in my heart:
   to stand on earth, my flesh restored,
   and, not a stranger but a friend
   behold my Saviour and my Lord.

John Hatton (d.1793?)

441

Refrain

I know that my Re-dee-mer lives, and on the last day I will rise a-gain;
I know that my Re-dee-mer lives, and on the last day I will rise a-gain.

Verses

1. With my own eyes I shall gaze on my God, face to face.
2. And this one hope I will che-rish, this pro - mise he gives:

It is my Sa-viour who calls me: I trust in his grace.
that though this bo - dy may pe-rish in Christ I will live.

3 And nothing evil can touch us,
no danger befall;
God watches over his people,
and answers their call.

4 And though we go into darkness
all hidden from sight;
God's arms are open to welcome
and lead us to light.

Stephen Dean

442

In pa - ra - di - sum de - du - cant te an - ge - li: in tu - o ad -
May an-gels guide you and bring you in - to pa - radise: and may all the

ven - tu sus - ci - pi-ant te mar-ty - res,— et per-du-cant te in
mar - tyrs come—forth to wel-come you— home;— and may they lead you in-

ci - vi-ta-tem sanc - tam— Je - ru - sa - lem. Cho - rus an - ge-
to the ho - ly ci - ty,— Je - ru - sa - lem. May— the an - gel

lo - rum te— sus - ci - pi-at, et cum La - za-ro quondam—
cho - rus sing— to— wel-come you, and like La - za-rus, for-got -

pau-pe - re ae - ter - nam— ha-be-as— re-qui-em
ten and poor, you shall— have— e - ver - las ting rest.

From the liturgy, English translation by Owen Alstott

443

Ernest Sands (1949-2016), from Psalm 27

Refrain

May the choirs of an-gels come to greet you. May they speed you to pa-ra-dise.

May the Lord en-fold you in his mer-cy. May you find e - ter - nal life.

1 The Lord is my light and my help;
it is he who protects me from harm.
The Lord is the strength of my days;
before whom should I tremble with fear?

2 There is one thing I ask of the Lord;
that he grant me my heartfelt desire.
To dwell in the courts of our God
ev'ry day of my life in his presence.

3 O Lord, hear my voice when I cry;
have mercy on me and give answer.
Do not cast me away in your anger,
for you are the God of my help.

4 I am sure I shall see the Lord's goodness;
I shall dwell in the land of the living.
Hope in God, stand firm and take heart,
place all your trust in the Lord.

444

1 Go, silent friend,
your life has found its ending;
to dust returns
your weary mortal frame.
God, who before birth
called you into being,
now calls you hence,
his accent still the same.

2 Go, silent friend,
your life in Christ is buried;
for you he lived
and died and rose again.
Close by his side
your promised place is waiting
where, fully known,
you shall with God remain.

3 Go, silent friend,
forgive us if we grieved you;
safe now in heaven,
kindly say our name.
Your life has touched us,
that is why we mourn you;
our lives without you
cannot be the same.

4 Go, silent friend,
we do not grudge you glory;
sing, sing with joy
deep praises to your Lord.
You, who believed
that Christ would come back for you,
now celebrate
that Jesus keeps his word.

John L. Bell and Graham Maule

445

1 May God the Father look on you with love,
and call you to himself in bliss above.
May God the Son, good Shepherd of his
sheep,
stretch out his hand and waken you from
sleep.
May God the Spirit breathe on you his peace,
where joys beyond all knowing never cease.

2 May flights of angels lead you on your way
to paradise, and heaven's eternal day!
May martyrs greet you after death's dark
night,
and bid you enter into Zion's light!
May choirs of angels sing you to your rest,
with once poor Lazarus, now for ever blest.

In paradisum,
tr. James Quinn SJ (1919-2010)

446

1 Jesu, Son of Mary, fount of life alone
here we hail thee present, we who are
thine own.
Think, O Lord, in mercy on the souls of
those
who, in faith gone from us, now in
death repose.

2 Often they were wounded in the deadly
strife;
heal them, Good Physician, with the
balm of life.
Every taint of evil, frailty and decay,
good and gracious Saviour, cleanse and
purge away.

3 Rest eternal grant them, after weary fight;
shed on them the radiance of the
heavenly light.
Lead them onward, upward, to the holy
place,
where thy saints made perfect gaze
upon thy face.
Swahili, tr. E.S. Palmer (1857-1931)

447

1 Word of God from Mary's womb,
born to die for our salvation,
laid to rest within the tomb,
risen Lord of all creation:
bread of life, with new life feed us,
bread from heav'n, to heaven
lead us.

2 Shepherd-King, for us you bled,
guard your sheep in love's safe
keeping:
welcome home your faithful dead,
where no sound is heard of weeping:
Loving Shepherd, walk beside them,
through death's darkness safely
guide them.

3 Living Lord, you conquered death,
come and take away our sadness;
breathe on us the Spirit's breath,
give us hope of heaven's gladness:
word of peace, all sorrow healing,
speak, your Father's love revealing.
James Quinn SJ (1919-2010)

➤ See also no.741

1. Since we are sum-moned to a si-lent place, strug-gling to
2. Since we are sa-vaged by the pain of loss, stopped at a

find some words to fill the space; Christ be be-side us as we
bar-rier we have yet to cross; Christ be be-side us as we

grieve, da - ring to doubt or to be - lieve.
mourn, bro - ken, dis - con - so - late and torn.

3 Since we are forced to face this last
farewell,
saddened to depths we never could foretell;
Christ be beside us as we weep,
loosening our hold on whom you'll keep.

4 Christ be beneath us, Christ be all above,
Christ take the hand of *her* we've lost
and love;
Take *her* to paradise and then
Christ be beside us once again.
John L. Bell and Graham Maule

Remembrance Sunday

449

1. What shall we pray for those who died, those on whose
2. What shall we pray for those who mourn friend-ships and

death our lives re - lied? Si - lenced by war but not de- nied,
love, their fruit un- born? Though years have passed, hearts still are torn;

Verses 1-5

God give them peace.
God give them peace.

Verse 6

wor- king for peace that lasts.

3 What shall we pray for those who live
   tied to the past they can't forgive,
   haunted by terrors they relive?
   God give them peace.

4 What shall we pray for those who know
   nothing of war, and cannot show
   grief or regret for friend or foe?
   God give them peace.

5 What shall we pray for those who fear
   war, in some guise, may reappear
   looking attractive and sincere?
   God give them peace.

6 God give us peace, and, more than this,
   show us the path where justice is;
   and let us never be remiss
   working for peace that lasts.
   John L. Bell & Graham Maule

Songs of Hope

450

1 As longs the deer for cooling streams,
   in parched and barren ways,
   so longs my soul for you, my God,
   and your refreshing grace.

2 For you, my God, the living God,
   my thirsting soul will pine:
   O when shall I behold your face,
   your majesty divine?

3 My tears have been my constant food,
   in sorrow I have prayed,
   I know the taunts: where is your God,
   and where his promised aid?

4 Why restless, why cast down, my soul?
   Hope still, and you shall sing
   the praise of him who is your God,
   your health's eternal spring.

5 To Father, Son and Holy Ghost,
   The God whom we adore,
   be glory as it was, is now,
   and shall be evermore.
   Based on Psalm 42 in the New Version

451

1 Sing with all the saints in glory,
   sing the resurrection song!
   Death and sorrow, earth's dark story,
   to the former days belong.
   All around the clouds are breaking,
   soon the storms of time shall cease;
   in God's likeness we awaken,
   knowing everlasting peace.

2 O what glory, far exceeding
   all that eye has yet perceived!
   Holiest heart for ages pleading,
   never that full joy conceived.
   God has promised, Christ prepares it,
   there on high our welcome waits;
   Ev'ry humble spirit shares it,
   Christ has passed the eternal gates.

3 Life eternal! heaven rejoices:
   Jesus lives who once was dead;
   Shout with joy, O deathless voices!
   Child of God, lift up your head!

Patriarchs from distant ages,
saints all longing for their heaven,
prophets, psalmists, seers and sages,
all await the glory giv'n.

4 Life eternal! O what wonders
   crowd on faith; what joy unknown,
   when, amidst earth's closing thunders,
   saints shall stand before the throne!
   O to enter that bright portal,
   see that growing firmament,
   know, with you, O God immortal,
   'Jesus Christ whom you have sent!'

William J. Irons (1812-83), alt.

452 **Refrain**
Out of the depths I cry— to you, O Lord.

1 From out of the depths, I cry to you, Lord:
   O hear the sound of my voice.
   Lord, open your ears and listen to me;
   I plead for your kindness, O God.

2 If you, O Lord, should number our sins,
   then Lord, who would survive?
   But you are forgiveness for our sins;
   for this we adore you, O God.

3 I trust in you, Lord, my soul looks to yo
   as watchmen wait for the dawn.
   And more than the watchman wait for
     the dawn,
   let Israel wait for the Lord.

4 For with you is found forgiveness of sin
   you show your mercy to all.
   And you will deliver your chosen ones;
   deliver your people, O God.

Psalm 129 (130), adapted by Scott Sope

453 **Refrain**
Like a child rests in its mo-ther's arms, so will I rest in you.

Like a child rests in its mo-ther's arms, so will I rest in you.

Verses
1. My God, I am not proud. I do not look for things too great.
2. My God, I trust in you. You care for me, you give me peace.
3. O Is - rael, trust in God, now and al - ways trust in God.

Psalm 130 (131), adapted by Christopher Walker

➤ *Funerals: See also Trust, Hope Guidance (948-973); Be still my soul (780); One thing I ask
(990). May you walk with Christ (994); Ps 130(131): My soul is longing for your peace (950)*

The House of God, Dedication of a Church

Psalms   *18(19): Your words are spirit, no 41; 83(84) below; 121(122) Let us go to God's house, no. 56*

454

Psalm 84:36.11, adapted by Stephen Dean

Refrain 1
They are hap-py who— dwell in your house,— O— Lord.

Refrain 2
O how ho-ly the house of the Lord; O how ho-ly the house of the Lord.

Ho-ly place where God's people are gath-ered,— joined in one by the love of the Lord.

1 O my soul is longing and yearning,
   is yearning for the courts of the Lord;
   my heart rings out its joy
   to God, the living God.

2 See, the sparrow herself finds a home,
   the swallow a nest for her brood,
   she lays her young by your altars,
   O Lord, my God and King.

3 They are happy who dwell in your temple
   for ever singing your praise,
   whose strength is you, O God,
   who love the road to Sion.

4 Just one day to spend in your courts
   surpasses far a thousand elsewhere,
   the house of God I love,
   the wicked I treat with scorn.

455

1 Christ the rock is our foundation
   on his word we firmly build;
   for in him is God's own wisdom,
   and in him all doubt is stilled.
   Come and praise him for the promise
   that in him has been fulfilled.

2 On this rock that is his temple,
   here was poured the oil of might,
   that the dreams which stirred in Jacob
   in the watches of the night,
   may be found in us his people
   here made holy in God's sight.

3 Here the living stones, his people,
   consecrated to his name,
   burn the incense of their praises,
   offer thanks and then proclaim
   joyfully that Christ is risen
   and one day will come again.

4 Offer praise to God the Father
   in whose love we came to be.
   Praise the Son, whose might is gentle
   and whose power can make us free
   if we live in his own Spirit.
   Praise our God, both One and Three.
   Ralph Wright OSB

456

1 Christ is made the sure foundation,
 Christ the head and corner–stone,
 chosen of the Lord, and precious,
 binding all the Church in one,
 holy Sion's help for ever,
 and her confidence alone.

2 All that dedicated city,
 dearly loved of God on high,
 in exultant jubilation
 pours perpetual melody,
 God the One in Three adoring
 in glad hymns eternally.

3 To this temple where we call you
 come, Almighty Lord, today;
 with your wonted loving kindness
 hear your people as they pray,
 and your fullest benediction
 shed within its walls alway.

4 Grant, we pray, to all your servants
 what they ask of you to gain,
 what they gain of you forever
 with the blessed to retain,
 and hereafter in your glory
 evermore with you to reign.

5 Praise and honour to the Father,
 praise and honour to the Son,
 praise and honour to the Spirit,
 ever Three and ever One,
 consubstantial, coeternal,
 while unending ages run.
 Latin, c. 8th C., tr. J .M. Neale (1818–66), alt.

➤ *see also All are welcome, 458; God, you call
us to this place, 469; and the Church on Earth
section (822-836), e.g. Sing a new church, 836*

457

O how love-ly is your dwel-ling place, dwel-ling of the Lord of hosts! How we long— for your house, O Lord, sing-ing out a song of joy— to the li - ving God!

1 Even sparrows find a home with you,
 and swallows lay their young to rest.
 Blessed are those who dwell in you
 and sing your praise, O God!

2 Bless'd are those who find their strength
 in you,
 whose hearts are highways for your will.
 Bringing joy to those around them,
 they go from strength to strength.

3 Hear our prayer, O Lord God of hosts;
 receive our life into your hands!
 Look into the hearts of those you love
 and grant us all we need!

4 For one day within your house exceeds
 a thousand spent away from you.
 We would rather serve within your hous
 than wealth and power receive.

5 For our God protects us from all harm;
 he gives his favour and his love.
 All good things will come to those
 who love
 the Lord, and walk with him.
 Randall DeBruyn,
 based on Psalm 83(84)

Music for the Eucharist

Gathering

458

1. Let us build a house where love can dwell and all can safe-ly_ live,
a_ place where saints and chil-dren_ tell how_ hearts learn_ to for-give.
Built of hopes and dreams and vi-sions, rock of faith and vault of grace;
here the love of Christ shall end di-vi-sions, All are wel-come,
all are wel-come, all are wel-come in this place.___

2 Let us build a house where prophets
      speak,
   and words are strong and true,
   where all God's children dare to seek
   to dream God's reign anew.
   Here the cross shall stand as witness
   and as symbol of God's grace;
   here as one we claim the faith of Jesus:
   All are welcome, all are welcome,
   all are welcome in this place.

3 Let us build a house where love is found
   in water, wine and wheat:
   a banquet hall on holy ground
   where peace and justice meet.
   Here the love of God through Jesus
   is revealed in time and space;
   as we share in Christ the feast that frees us:

4 Let us build a house where hands will reach
   beyond the wood and stone
   to heal and strengthen, serve and teach,
   and live the Word they've known.
   Here the outcast and stranger
   bear the image of God's face;
   let us bring an end to fear and danger:

5 Let us build a house where all are named,
   their songs and visions heard
   and loved and treasured, taught and claimed
   as words within the Word.
   Built of tears and cries and laughter,
   prayers of faith and songs of grace,
   let this house proclaim from floor to
      rafter:

Marty Haugen

459

God, our foun-tain of sal - va-tion, re - new the spring of your life in us. In li-ving wa - ter wash a-way our sin, that we may come to you__ in ho - li-ness, God, our foun-tain of sal - va - tion.__ God, our foun-tain of sal - va-tion.__

Verses

1. Tru - ly now__ God is my Sa - viour. I have trust, I will__ not fear.
2. Draw with joy from wells of sal - va - tion. Praise the Lord, call on__ God's name.
3. Sing out loud__ praise for God's won - ders, let the whole world hear. the news.

God my song, God my sal-va - tion.__ God a - lone my power__ and strength!
What God does, tell all the na - tions:__ God has done great things_ for us!
Shout and sing, peo-ple of Zi - on:__ God the ho - ly, God__ with us!

(Isaiah 12:2-6)

Lent verses

1 God, my God, I have kept faithful,
   even when in fear I said:
   'God I feel crushed with affliction,
   there is no-one I can trust.'

2 God, my God, how can I thank you!
   All that you have done for me!
   I will raise the cup of salvation,
   thanking you for saving me.

3 Now, before all of your people,
   I will keep my vows to you.
   In your sight precious the death of
   one who has kept faith in you.

4 In my heart I am your servant;
   you, my God, save me from death.
   To you now I bring thanksgiving,
   on my lips I speak your name.

5 Now before all of your people
   I will keep my vows to you.
   In your temple singing your praises,
   even in Jerusalem.

6 Praise to God, Creator almighty,
   praise to God, the only Son.
   Praise to God, the Holy Spirit,
   now and evermore. Amen.

(Psalm 116)

Christopher Walker

Refrain

160 All the earth pro-claim_ the Lord, sing your praise to God.

Verses

1. Serve you the Lord, hearts filled with glad - ness. Come in - to God's pre-sence,
2. Know that the Lord is our cre - a - tor. Yes, he is our Fa - ther;

sing - ing for joy!
we are his own.

We are the sheep of his green pasture,
for we are God's people, chosen by God.

Come to the gates bringing thanksgiving,
O enter the courts while singing in praise.

5 Our Lord is good, with love enduring,
God's word is abiding now with us all.

6 Honour and praise be to the Father,
the Son, and the Spirit, world without end.

*Lucien Deiss CSSp (1921-2007), based
on Psalm 99 (100)*

161

Cantor: Praise the Lord, all_ you na - tions,
All: Praise the Lord, all_ you na - tions,

Cantor: Ac - claim him all_ you peo-ples!
All: Ac - claim him all_ you peo-ples!

*Cantor: Strong is his love for us, he is faithful for ever.
Alleluia, alleluia; alleluia, alleluia.*
    All: Alleluia, alleluia; alleluia, alleluia.

*O sing a new song to the Lord,
sing to the Lord all the earth,
O sing to the Lord, bless his name.
ll: Alleluia, alleluia; alleluia, alleluia.*

*Proclaim his help day by day,
tell among the nations his glory,*

and his wonders among all the peoples.
All: Alleluia, alleluia; alleluia, alleluia.

3 *Bring an offering and enter his courts,
worship the Lord in his temple,
O earth tremble before him.*
All: Alleluia, alleluia; alleluia, alleluia.

Cantor: *Praise the Lord, all you nations!*   All repeat.
            Acclaim him all you peoples!   All repeat.
Cantor: *Strong is his love for us, he is faithful for ever.
            Alleluia, alleluia; alleluia, alleluia.*
All: Alleluia, alleluia; alleluia, alleluia.

Pss. 116 & 96, arr. Fintan O'Carroll (1922-1981)

462

Refrain

Ga-ther your peo ple, O Lord,_____ Ga-ther your peo ple, O Lord. One__ bread, one__ bo - dy, one spi - rit of love._____ Ga - ther your peo - ple, O Lord._____

Verses

1. Draw us forth to the ta - ble of life: bro-thers and sis - ters, each of us called to walk in your light.__
2. We are parts of the bo - dy of Christ, nee - ding each o - ther, each of the gifts the Spi - rit pro - vides.__

3 No more harm on the mountain of God;
swords into ploughshares,
free us, O Lord, from hardness of heart.
Bob Hurd, based on 1 Cor 12, Is 2:3-4, 11:9

Extra verse (as a sprinkling song)
4 Wash us, Lord, in the waters of life;
waters of mercy,
waters of hope that flow from your side

463 **Refrain 1** Cantors then All repeat

Fa - ther, we come to you, God of all power and might. Show us your glo - ry: give us your life.

Cantor You have united us, bound us in love and peace:
God in the midst of us, holy, unseen.

Refrain 2 All

Bles-sed is he who comes, pier-cing our night of sin. O - pen your hearts to him. Great is his name.

Cantor Bread of life shared with us, body of Christ the Lord,
broken and died for us: life for the world.

All: **R1:** Father, we come to you, God
of all power and might.
Show us your glory: give us your life.

R2: Blessed is he who comes piercing our
night of sin.
Open our hearts to you: great is your name.
Open our hearts to you: great is your name!
James Walsh

464

On this day, the first of days,
God the Father's name we praise
who creation's Lord and spring,
did the world from darkness bring.

On this day th'eternal Son
over death his triumph won;
on this day the Spirit came
with the gifts of living flame.

On this day his people raise
one pure sacrifice of praise,
and with all the saints above,
tell of Christ's redeeming love.

Praise, O God, to you be given,
praise on earth and praise in heaven,
Praise to the eternal Son,
who this day our victory won.
*H.W. Baker (1821-77) (vv.1-2), and
editors of The New English Hymnal*

465

This is the day (2)
that the Lord has made. (2)
We will rejoice, (2)
and be glad in it. (2)
This is the day that the Lord has made.
We will rejoice and be glad in it.
This is the day (2)
that the Lord has made.

This is the day.. when he rose again ...

This is the day.. when the Spirit came...
Les Garrett

466

All people that on earth do dwell,
sing to the Lord with cheerful voice;
him serve with fear, his praise forth tell,
come ye before him and rejoice.

2 The Lord, ye know, is God indeed,
without our aid he did us make;
we are his folk, he doth us feed
and for his sheep he doth us take.

3 O enter then his gates with praise,
approach with joy his courts unto,
praise, laud, and bless his name always,
for it is seemly so to do.

4 For why? The Lord our God is good:
his mercy is for ever sure;
his truth at all times firmly stood,
and shall from age to age endure.

5 To Father, Son and Holy Ghost,
the God whom heaven and earth adore,
from us and from the angel–host
be praise and glory evermore.
*W. Kethe (d. 1594), from 'Day's Psalter'
(1560–61)*

467

1 Sing, all creation, sing to God in gladness!
Joyously serve him, singing hymns of
homage!
Chanting his praises, come before his
presence!
Praise the Almighty!

2 Know that our God is Lord of all the ages!
He is our maker, we are all his creatures,
people he fashioned, sheep he leads to
pasture!
Praise the Almighty!

3 Enter his temple, ringing out his praises!
Sing in thanksgiving as you come
before him!
Blessing his bounty, glorify his greatness!
Praise the Almighty!

4 Great in his goodness is the Lord we
    worship;
steadfast his kindness, love that knows
    no ending!
Faithful his word is, changeless, everlasting!
Praise the Almighty!
James Quinn SJ (1919-2000)
from Psalm 99 (100)

468

1 Holy, holy, holy! Lord God almighty!
Early in the morning our song shall rise
    to thee;
holy, holy, holy! Merciful and mighty!
God in three persons, blessed Trinity!

2 Holy, holy, holy! All the saints adore thee.
Casting down their golden crowns
    around the glassy sea;
cherubim and seraphim falling down
    before thee,
God ever living through eternity.

3 Holy, holy, holy! Though the darkness
    hide thee,
though the eye made blind by sin thy
    glory may not see;
only thou art holy, there is none beside thee
perfect in power, in love and purity.

4 Holy, holy, holy! Lord God almighty!
All thy works shall praise thy name, in
    earth, and sky and sea;
holy, holy, holy! Merciful and mighty!
God in three persons, blessed Trinity!
Reginald Heber (1783–1875)

469

1 God, you call us to this place
where we know your love and grace.
Here your hospitality
makes of us one family,
makes our rich diversity
richer still in unity,
makes our many voices one,
joined in praise with Christ your Son.

2 Now assembled in Christ's name,
all your mercies to proclaim -
In the hearing of your word,
in the gospel of the Lord,
in the breaking of the bread,
in the meal where we are fed -
in the Spirit let us be
one in faith and unity.

3 In the water we were born
of the Spirit in the Son.
Now a priestly, royal race
rich in every gift of grace -
called, forgiven, loved and freed,
for the world we intercede:
Gather into unity
all the human family.
Delores Dufner OSB

470

1 Let us go rejoicing,
rejoicing to the house of God.
Let us join together,
who come from near and far,
who seek the holy city,
the new Jerusalem,
rejoicing before the living God.

2 Now our feet are standing
within your gates, Jerusalem.
Gathered as one people
we offer thanks and praise
before the throne of justice,
compassion and all grace,
rejoicing before the living God.

3 Peace reign in this city,
the peace of God within these walls.
May this peace empow'r us
to put an end to war,
to seek the reign of justice
with dignity for all,
rejoicing before the living God.

4. Let us go rejoicing,
rejoicing to the house of God.
Let us sit at table
with Christ, the risen Lord.
Then, guided by his Spirit
as servants we'll go forth,
rejoicing before the living God.
Bob Hurd

471

Jubilate, ev'rybody,
serve the Lord in all your ways, and
come before his presence singing;
enter now his courts with praise.
For the Lord our God is gracious,
and his mercy everlasting.
Jubilate, jubilate, jubilate Deo!
Fred Dunn (1907–1979)

472

1 Open your ears, O Christian people,
open your ears and hear Good News.
Open your hearts, O royal priesthood
God has come to you.
God has spoken to his people, alleluia.
And his words are words of wisdom,
alleluia.

2 Israel comes to greet the Saviour,
Judah is glad to see his day.
From East and West the people travel,
he will show the way.

3 Those who have ears to hear his message;
those who have ears, then let them hear.
Those who would learn the way of wisdom,
let them hear God's words.
W. F. Jabusch

473

We— come to share our sto - ry, we— come to break the
bread, we— come to know our ri - sing from the— dead.

We come as your people,
we come as your own,
united with each other,
love finds a home.

We are called to heal the broken,
to be hope for the poor,
we are called to feed the hungry
at our door.

3 Bread of life and cup of promise,
in this meal we all are one.
In our dying and our rising,
may your kingdom come.

4 You will lead and we shall follow,
you will be the breath of life;
living water, we are thirsting
for your light.

5 We will live and sing your praises,
'Alleluia' is our song.
May we live in love and peace
our whole life long.
David Haas

474

Refrain

Let us go to the al-tar of God, the
God of our glad-ness and joy! Let us en-ter the courts of the
house of the Lord and sing to the glo-ry of God.

1 Give praise with blast of trumpet,
  with noble sound of the horn,
  With the clash of the clanging cymbal,
  give glory to the Lord!

2 Give praise with lyre and timbrel,
  with lute and sound of the harp.
  With the dance of the flute and oboe,
  give glory to the Lord!

3 Give praise with pipe and organ,
  with rousing beat of the drum,
  with the call of bell and bagpipe,
  give glory to the Lord!

4 Give praise, all creatures of heaven,
  and all that dwell on the earth.
  Come to worship the God who made us
  and dance before the Lord!

  Based on Pss 42, 150. Daniel L. Schutte

475

1 Here in this place, new light is
    streaming,
  now is the darkness vanished away,
  see, in this space, our fears and our
    dreamings,
  brought here to you in the light of this
    day.
  Gather us in the lost and forsaken,
  gather us in the blind and the lame;
  call to us now, and we shall awaken,
  we shall arise at the sound of our name.

2 We are the young – our lives are a
    mystery,
  we are the old – who yearn for your face
  we have been sung throughout all of
    history,
  called to be light to the whole human
    race.
  Gather us in the rich and the haughty,
  gather us in the proud and the strong;
  give us a heart so meek and so lowly,
  give us the courage to enter the song.

3 Here we will take the wine and the water,
  here we will take the bread of new birth,
  here you shall call your sons and your daughters,
  call us anew to be salt for the earth.
  Give us to drink the wine of compassion,
  give us to eat the bread that is you;
  nourish us well, and teach us to fashion,
  lives that are holy and hearts that are true.
  Marty Haugen

476

You have called us by our name.
We belong to you.
You have called us by our name
and we are yours.

1. You have chosen us to be
   members of your family.
   In your love you have created us
   to live in unity.

2. You will lead us to your light,
   walk before you through the night.
   You will guide us on our journey.
   You will keep our vision bright.

3. You will hold us when we fall,
   give new strength to hear your call.
   You will never be beyond us.
   for your love is all in all.

4. You will nourish, you will lead,
   giving every gift we need,
   for your reign will be established
   from the smallest of all seeds.

5. Through our sharing here today
   may our faith and life convey
   Christ our light and Christ our vision,
   Christ our purpose, Christ our way.
   Bernadette Farrell

477

1 All who hunger, gather gladly;
   holy manna is our bread.
   Come from wilderness and wand'ring.
   Here in truth, we will be fed.
   You that yearn for days of fullness,
   all around us is our food.
   Taste and see the grace eternal.
   Taste and see that God is good.

2 All who hunger, never strangers,
   seeker, be a welcome guest.
   Come from restlessness and roaming.
   Here in joy we keep the feast.
   We that once were lost and scattered
   in communion's love have stood.
   Taste and see the grace eternal.
   Taste and see that God is good.

3 All who hunger, sing together;
   Jesus Christ is living bread.
   Come from loneliness and longing.
   Here in peace, we have been led.
   Blest are those who from this table
   live their lives in gratitude.
   Taste and see the grace eternal.
   Taste and see that God is good.
   Sylvia Dunstan (1955-93)

478 Laudate omnes gentes

Taizé chant by Jacques Berthier (1923-1984)

Lau - da - te om - nes gen - tes, lau - da - te Do - mi - num. Lau - da - te om - nes gen - tes, lau - da - te Do - mi - num.

The Order of Mass

The Introductory Rites

The Introductory Rites help the faithful come together as one, establish communion and prepare themselves properly to listen to the Word of God and to celebrate the Eucharist worthily.

All stand. The Priest approaches the altar with the ministers and venerates it while the Entrance Song is sung.

Sign of the Cross

All make the Sign of the Cross as the Priest says:

In the name of the Father, and of the Son, and of the Holy Spirit.

The people reply:

A - men.

Greeting

Then the Priest, extending his hands, greets the people, saying:

The grace of our Lord Jesus Christ,
and the love of God,
and the communion of the Holy Spirit
be with you all.

Or:

Grace to you and peace from God our Father
and the Lord Jesus Christ.

Or:

The Lord be with you.

The people reply:

And with your spi - rit.

Penitential Act*

* From time to time on Sundays, especially in Easter time, instead of the customary Penitential Act, the blessing and sprinkling of water may take place as a reminder of Baptism. See nos. 511-515

The Priest invites the faithful to make the Penitential Act:

Brethren (brothers and sisters), let us acknowledge our sins,
and so prepare ourselves to celebrate the sacred mysteries.

After a brief pause for silence, one of the forms of the Penitential Act follows:

All say:

I confess to almighty God
and to you, my brothers and sisters,
that I have greatly sinned,
in my thoughts and in my words,
in what I have done and in what I have failed to do,

And, striking their breast, they say:

> through my fault, through my fault,
> through my most grievous fault;
> therefore I ask blessed Mary ever-Virgin,
> all the Angels and Saints,
> and you, my brothers and sisters,
> to pray for me to the Lord our God.

Or:

The Priest says:

> Have mercy on us, O Lord.

The people reply:

For we have sinned a-gainst you.

The Priest:

> Show us, O Lord, your mercy.

The people:

And grant us your sal-va-tion.

The absolution by the Priest follows:

> May almighty God have mercy on us,
> forgive us our sins,
> and bring us to everlasting life.

The people reply:

A - men.

Or:

The Priest invites the faithful to make the Penitential Act:

> Brethren (brothers and sisters), let us acknowledge our sins,
> and so prepare ourselves to celebrate the sacred mysteries.

There follows a brief pause for silence.

The Priest, a Deacon, or another minister, then says the following or other invocations with Kyrie, eleison (Lord, have mercy):

You were sent to heal the contrite of heart:
> Lord, have mercy. *Or:* Kyrie, eleison.

The people reply:

Lord, have mer - cy.   *Or:*   Kyrie, e - le - i - son.

The Priest:

> You came to call sinners:
> Christ, have mercy. *Or:* Christe, eleison.

The people: *Or:*

The Priest:

> You are seated at the right hand of the Father to intercede for us:
> Lord, have mercy. *Or:* Kyrie, eleison.

The people: *Or:*

The absolution by the Priest follows:

> May almighty God have mercy on us,
> forgive us our sins,
> and bring us to everlasting life.

The people reply:

Kyrie

> *The Kyrie (Lord, have mercy) invocations follow, unless they have just occurred in a formula*
> *of the Penitential Act.* *(Greek version, no. 502)*

Gloria

When indicated this hymn is either sung or said. *(Latin version, no. 503)*

O God, al-migh-ty Fa-ther. Lord Je-sus Christ, On-ly Be-got-ten Son,

Lord God, Lamb of God, Son of the Father, you take a-way the sins of the world,

have mer-cy on us; you take a-way the sins of the world, re-ceive our prayer;

you are sea-ted at the right hand of the Fa-ther, have mer-cy on us.

For you a-lone are the Ho-ly One, you a-lone are the Lord,

you a-lone are the Most High, Je-sus Christ, with the Ho-ly Spi-rit,

in the glo-ry of God the Fa - ther. A - men.

The Collect

When this hymn is concluded, the Priest says:

Let us pray.

And all pray in silence with the Priest for a while.

Then the Priest says the Collect prayer, at the end of which the people acclaim:

A - men.

The Liturgy of the Word

By hearing the word proclaimed in worship, the faithful again enter into the unending dialogue between God and the covenant people, a dialogue sealed in the sharing of the Eucharistic food and drink. The proclamation of the word is thus integral to the Mass and at its very centre. It is appropriate to have a brief time of quiet after the readings for those present to take the word of God to heart and begin to prepare a prayerful response to what they have heard.

All sit

First Reading

To indicate the end of these readings, the reader acclaims:

The word of the Lord.

All reply:

Thanks be to God.

Psalm

After the First Reading the psalmist or cantor sings or says the Psalm, with the people making the response.

Second Reading

On Sundays and certain other days there is a second reading. It concludes with the same responsory as above.

Gospel

The assembly stands to sing the Gospel Acclamation to welcome the Gospel. They remain standing in honour of the Gospel reading, the high point of the Liturgy of the Word.

Dialogue before the Gospel

The Deacon, or the Priest, says or sings:

The Lord be with you.

The people reply:

And with your spi-rit.

A reading from the holy Gospel according to N.

The people acclaim:

Glory to you, O Lord.

At the end of the Gospel, the Deacon, or the Priest, acclaims:

The Gospel of the Lord.

All reply:

Praise to you, Lord Je-sus Christ.

After the proclamation of the Gospel the congregation is seated.

The Homily

At the end of the Homily it is appropriate for there to be a brief silence for recollection. The congregation then stands.

The Creed

On Sundays and Solemnities, the Profession of Faith or Creed will follow. During Lent and Easter Time, especially, the Apostles' Creed may be used.

The Niceno-Constantinopolitan Creed

A musical setting will be found at no. 545.

I believe in one God,
the Father almighty,
maker of heaven and earth,
of all things visible and invisible.

I believe in one Lord Jesus Christ,
the Only Begotten Son of God,
born of the Father before all ages.
God from God, Light from Light,
true God from true God,
begotten, not made, consubstantial
    with the Father;
through him all things were made.
For us men and for our salvation
he came down from heaven,
*At the words that follow, up to and
including* and became man, *all bow.*

and by the Holy Spirit was incarnate
    of the Virgin Mary,
and became man.

For our sake he was crucified under
    Pontius Pilate,
he suffered death and was buried,
and rose again on the third day

in accordance with the Scriptures.
He ascended into heaven
and is seated at the right hand
    of the Father.
He will come again in glory
to judge the living and the dead
and his kingdom will have no end.

I believe in the Holy Spirit, the Lord,
    the giver of life,
who proceeds from the Father
    and the Son,
who with the Father and the Son is
    adored and glorified,
who has spoken through the prophets.

I believe in one, holy, catholic and
    apostolic Church.
I confess one Baptism for the
    forgiveness of sins
and I look forward to the resurrection
    of the dead
and the life of the world to come.
    Amen.

The Apostles' Creed

I believe in God,
the Father almighty,
Creator of heaven and earth,
and in Jesus Christ, his only Son, our
    Lord,
*At the words that follow, up to and
including* the Virgin Mary, *all bow.*

who was conceived by the Holy
    Spirit,
born of the Virgin Mary,
suffered under Pontius Pilate,
was crucified, died and was buried;
he descended into hell;

on the third day he rose again from
    the dead;
he ascended into heaven,
and is seated at the right hand of God
    the Father almighty;
from there he will come to judge the
    living and the dead.

I believe in the Holy Spirit,
the holy catholic Church,
the communion of saints,
the forgiveness of sins,
the resurrection of the body,
and life everlasting. Amen.

The Prayer of the Faithful (Bidding Prayers)

After each intention there is a pause while the faithful pray. This time of silent prayer may simply be followed by the next intention, or may be concluded in some other way such as by a spoken or sung response (see nos. 548-551).

The Liturgy of the Eucharist

For Catholics, the Eucharist is the source and summit of the whole Christian life. It is the vital centre of all that the Church is and does, because at its heart is the real presence of the crucified, risen and glorified Lord, continuing and making available his saving work among us.

During the Offertory Song the faithful usually express their participation by making an offering, bringing forward bread and wine for the celebration of the Eucharist and perhaps other gifts to relieve the needs of the Church and of the poor.

When he has received the bread and wine for the celebration, the Priest offers prayer of blessing quietly at the altar. Sometimes these prayers are said aloud, If the priest says the prayers aloud the assembly's acclamation each time is

Blessed be God for ever.

The Priest completes additional personal preparatory rites, and the people rise as he says or sings:

Pray, brethren (brothers and sisters),
that my sacrifice and yours
may be acceptable to God,
the almighty Father.

The people rise and reply:

May the Lord accept the sacrifice at your hands, for the praise and glory of his name

for our good and the good of all his ho - ly Church.

Then the Priest says the Prayer over the Offerings, at the end of which the people acclaim:

A - men.

THE EUCHARISTIC PRAYER

The Eucharistic Prayer, the centre and summit of the entire celebration, is a memorial proclamation of praise and thanksgiving for God's work of salvation, a proclamation in which the Body and Blood of Christ are made present by the power of the Holy Spirit and the people are joined to Christ in offering his Sacrifice to the Father.

Preface Dialogue

The Lord be with you. And with your spirit. *Lift up your hearts.* We lift them

up to the Lord. *Let us give thanks to the Lord our God.* It is right and just.

The Priest continues with the Preface.

The Priest concludes the Preface with the people, singing or saying aloud:

Ho- ly, Ho- ly, Ho- ly Lord God of hosts. Hea - ven and earth are

full of your glo-ry. Ho-san-na in the highest. Bles-sed is he who comes in the

name of the Lord. Ho- san - na in the high - est. *(Latin version, no.504)*

After the singing of the Sanctus the congregation kneels for the remainder of the Eucharistic Prayer.

Memorial Acclamation

After the words of Consecration the priest sings or says:

The mys - te - ry of faith.

And the people continue, acclaiming:

1

We pro - claim your Death, O Lord, and pro - fess your Re - sur - rec - tion,

un - til you come_ a- gain.

2

When we eat this Bread and drink this Cup, we pro-claim your Death, O Lord, un - til you come a - gain.

3

Save us, Sa - viour of the world, for by your Cross and Re - sur - rec - tion you have set us free.

At the conclusion of the prayer the Priest takes the chalice and the paten with the host and, raising both, he alone sings or says:

Through him, and with him, and in him, O God almighty Father, in the unity of the

The people acclaim:

Ho - ly Spi - rit, all glo - ry and ho - nour is yours, for e - ver and e - ver. Amen.

The Communion Rite

The eating and drinking together of the Lord's Body and Blood in a Paschal meal is the culmination of the Eucharist. The themes underlying these rites are the mutual love and reconciliation that are both the condition and the fruit of worthy communion and the unity of the many in the One.

The Lord's Prayer

The congregation stands and the Priest says:

At the Saviour's command
and formed by divine teaching,
we dare to say:

Together with the people, he continues: *(Latin version, no.506)*

Our Fa-ther, who art in heaven, hal-lowed be thy name; thy king - dom come,

thy will be done on earth as it is in hea ven. Give us this day our dai- ly bread and for-give us our tres-pas-ses, as we for-give those who tres-pass a-gainst us;

and lead us not in-to temp-ta-tion, but de-li-ver us from e-vil.

The Priest alone continues:

Deliver us, Lord, we pray, from every evil,
graciously grant peace in our days,
that, by the help of your mercy,
we may be always free from sin
and safe from all distress,
as we await the blessed hope
and the coming of our Saviour, Jesus Christ.

The people conclude the prayer, acclaiming:

For the king-dom, the power and the glo-ry are yours, now and for e-ver.

Sign of Peace

Lord Jesus Christ,
who said to your Apostles:
Peace I leave you, my peace I give you,
look not on our sins,
but on the faith of your Church,
and graciously grant her peace and unity
in accordance with your will.
Who live and reign for ever and ever.

A - men.

The peace of the Lord be with you always.

And with your spi - rit.

The Deacon, or the Priest, adds:

Let us offer each other the sign of peace.

And all offer one another the customary sign of peace: a handclasp or handshake, which is an expression of peace, communion, and charity.

Breaking of the Bread

During the breaking of the host the following is sung or said: *(Latin version, no. 509).*

Lamb of God, you take a-way the sins of the world, have mer-cy on us.

Lamb of God, you take a-way the sins of the world, grant us peace.

Invitation to Communion

The Priest says or sings:

Behold the Lamb of God,
behold him who takes away the sins of the world.
Blessed are those called to the supper of the Lamb.

All say or sing:

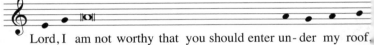

Lord, I am not worthy that you should enter un-der my roof,

but only say the word and my soul shall be healed.

After the priest has reverently consumed the Body and Blood of Christ the communicants come forward in reverent procession, and make a preparatory act of reverence by bowing their head in honour of Christ's presence in the Sacrament. They receive Holy Communion standing.

The Priest says:

The Body of Christ.

The communicant replies: Amen   *and receives communion.*

When Communion is ministered under both kinds the minister of the Chalice offers it to each of the communicants, saying:

The Blood of Christ.

The communicant replies: Amen.

After the distribution of Communion, if appropriate, a sacred silence may be observed for a while, or a psalm or other canticle of praise or a hymn may be sung.

Then, the Priest says:

Let us pray.

All stand and pray in silence. Then the Priest says the Prayer after Communion, at the end of which the people acclaim:

A - men.

The Concluding Rites

The brief Concluding Rites send the people forth to put into effect in their daily lives the Mystery of Christ's Death and Resurrection and the unity in Christ which they have celebrated. Their mission is to witness to Christ in the world and to bring the Gospel to the poor.

Any brief announcements to the people follow here.

Final Blessing and Dismissal

Then the dismissal takes place. Sometimes this takes a more elaborate form than that given below.

The Priest says or sings:

    The Lord be with you.

The people reply:

And with your spi - rit.

The Priest blesses the people, saying or singing:

    May almighty God bless you,
    the Father, and the Son, + and the Holy Spirit.

A - men.

Then the Deacon or Priest says or sings:

    Go forth, the Mass is ended.

Or: Go and announce the Gospel of the Lord.

Or: Go in peace, glorifying the Lord by your life.

The people reply:

Thanks be to God.

Or: Go in peace.

The people reply:

Thanks be to God.

On Easter Sunday, the Octave of Easter, and in the Mass during the day on Pentecost Sunday:

    Go forth, the Mass is ended, alleluia, alleluia.

Or: Go in peace, alleluia, alleluia.

The people reply:

Thanks be to God, al - le - lu - ia, al - le - lu - ia.

The Eucharist: Mass Settings

A Parish Mass

Peter Jones (1951-2016)

Penitential Act

480

In Penitential Act 3 the Priest, a Deacon, or another minister, sings an invocation before each phrase, and all respond Lord, have mercy *or* Christ, have mercy.

Lord,— have— mer - cy, Lord,— have— mer - cy.

Christ, — have— mer - cy, Christ,— have— mer - cy.

Lord, have— mer - cy, Lord, have— mer - cy.

Absolution (Penitential Act 3)

Priest: (sung or spoken)

May almighty God have mercy on us,
forgive us our sins,
and bring us to everlasting life.

A - men.

Gloria

481

Glo-ry to God in the high-est, and on earth peace to

peo-ple of good will. We praise— you, we bless— you, we a-dore— you, we

glo-ri-fy you, we give you thanks for your great glo-ry, Lord God, hea-ven-ly

King, O— God, al-might-y Fa-ther. Lord Jes-us

Christ, On-ly Be-got-ten Son, Lord God, Lamb of God,

Son— of the Fa-ther, you take a-way the sins of the world, have

mer-cy on us; you take a-way the sins of the world, re-

ceive — our prayer; you are seat-ed at the right hand of the Fa-ther, have

mer-cy on us. For you a-lone are the Ho-ly One,

you a-lone are the Lord, you a-lone are the Most High, Je-sus Christ,

— with the Ho-ly— Spir-it, in the glo-ry of God the Fa-ther. A-men.

Sanctus

482

Ho-ly, Ho-ly, Ho-ly Lord God of hosts.

Heav'n and earth, heav'n and earth are full of your glo-ry. Ho-san - na in the high-est. Blessed is he who comes in the

name of the Lord. Ho - san - na in the high-est.

Memorial Acclamation 1

483

We pro-claim your Death, O Lord, and pro - fess your Re - sur -

rec - tion un - til you come a - gain.

Memorial Acclamation 2

484

When we eat this Bread and drink this Cup,

we pro - claim your Death, O Lord, un - til you come a - gain.

Memorial Acclamation 3

485

Save us, save us, Sav - iour of the world, for by your

Cross and Re - sur - rec - tion you have set us free.

Concluding Doxology and Amen

486

A - men, A - men, A - men, A - men.

Agnus Dei

487

Lamb of God, you take a-way the sins of the world, __ have mer-cy on us. Lamb of God, you take a-way the sins of the world, __ have mer-cy on us. Lamb of God, you take a-way the sins of the world, __ grant __ us peace.

Mass of Creation

Marty Haugen

Penitential Act

488

In Penitential Act 3 the Priest, a Deacon, or another minister, sings an invocation before each phrase.

Each phrase: Presider or Cantor, then all

Ky-ri-e, e-le-i-son. Chris-te, e-le-i-son. Ky-ri-e, e-le-i-son.

Absolution (Penitential Act 3)

May almighty God have mercy on us,
forgive us our sins,
and bring us to everlasting life.

Cantor then All

A - men.

Gloria

489

Glo-ry to God in the high-est, __ and on earth peace __ to peo-ple of good will. __

We praise you,	we give you thanks for your great glory,
we bless you,	Lord God, heavenly King,
we adore you,	O God, almighty Father. *(Refrain)*
we glorify you,	

215

Lord Jesus Christ, Only Begotten Son,
Lord God, Lamb of God, Son of the Father,
you take away the sins of the world,
    have mercy on us;
you take away the sins of the world,
    receive our prayer;
you are seated at the right hand of the Father,
    have mercy on us. *(Refrain)*

For you alone are the Holy One,
you alone are the Lord,
you alone are the Most High,
Jesus Christ,
with the Holy Spirit,
in the glory of God the Father.
Amen, amen.   *(Refrain)*

Sanctus

490

Ho-ly, Ho-ly, Ho-ly— Lord, God of hosts.—

Heaven and earth are full of your glo-ry.— Ho-san-na in the high-est.—

Bless-ed is he who comes in the name of the Lord.— Ho-san-na

in the high-est.— Ho-san-na in the high - est.—

Memorial Acclamation 1

491

We pro-claim your Death, O— Lord, and pro-fess your Re-sur-

rec-tion un-til you come a-gain, un-til you come a-gain.

Memorial Acclamation 2

492

When we eat this Bread and drink this Cup, we pro-

claim your Death, O Lord, un - til you come a - gain.

Memorial Acclamation 3

493

Save us, Sa-viour of the world, for by your Cross and Res-ur-rec-tion you have set us free, you have set us free.

Amen

494

A - men, a - men, a - men. *Repeat*

Agnus Dei

495

Cantor or choir: Lamb___ of God,___ *All:* you take a-way the sins of the world,__ have mer-cy on_ us. *Repeat*

Last time *Cantor or choir:* Lamb___ of God,___ *All:* you take a - way the sins of the world, grant us your peace.

See overleaf for a Communion Song to accompany this setting

Communion Song

496

Come and eat this bread, come and drink this cup, come and share the feast our God has spread. You have pro-mised us, you are here with us in the brea-king of the bread.

1. This is the Bread of Life, for all to share,
   Bread of hope and redemption,
   Bread to feed a world of hungers.

2. This is the Cup of Christ's own sacrifice,
   Blood of love and compassion,
   Blood to heal the world's divisions.

3. Just as the scattered grains become one
   bread,
   make us one in your Spirit,
   all one Body in Christ Jesus.

4. And as we share one Cup of covenant
   make us one in communion
   at the table of Christ Jesus.

5. Each time we eat this Bread and drink this Cup,
   we remember your death, Lord
   and we celebrate your rising.

When communion has finished, the refrain changes:

Praise the li-ving God, praise to Christ the Son, praise, O migh-ty Spi-rit, Ho-ly Breath. For our whole life through we shall sing to you God of life be-yond all death.

6. Now from this table to the ends of earth,
   gather all of your people
   in this feast of all creation.

Marty Haugen

Missa de Angelis

Plainsong

Kyrie
Cantor then All

497

Ky-ri - e   e - le - i - son.

Cantor then All

Chris-te   e - le - i - son.

Cantor

Ky-ri - e   e - le-ison. Ky-ri-e

All

e - le - i - son.

Gloria

498

Glo - ri - a in ex - cel - sis De - o. Et in ter - ra pax ho - mi - ni - bus

bo - nae vo - lun - ta - tis. Lau-da - mus te. Be - ne - di - ci-mus te.

A-do-ra - mus te. Glo - ri - fi - ca-mus te. Gra - ti - as a - gi-mus

ti - bi prop-ter mag-nam glo - ri - am tu-am. Do-mi-ne De-us, Rex cae - le - stis,

De - us Pa - ter o - mni - po - tens. Do - mi-ne Fi-li u - ni-ge-ni-te

Je - su Chris - te. Do - mi-ne De-us, Ag-nus De - i, Fi - li - us

Pa - tris. Qui tol - lis pec - ca - ta mun - di___ mi-se-re - re___ no - bis. Qui tol - lis pec-ca-ta mun - di___ sus-ci - pe de-pre-ca-ti - o-nem nos - tram.___ Qui se - des ad dex - te - ram Pa - tris, mi-se-re-re no - bis. Quo-ni-am tu so-lus sanc-tus, tu so-lus___ Do - mi - nus, tu so-lus___ al - tis - si - mus,___ Je - su___ Chris - te. Cum Sanc-to___ Spi - ri - tu, in glo-ri - a De-i Pa - tris.___ A - men.___

Sanctus

499

Sanc - tus, sanc-tus,___ sanc - tus,___ Do - mi - nus De-us Sa - ba - oth. Ple - ni___ sunt cae - li et___ ter - ra___ glo-ri - a tu - a. Ho-san - na___ in ex - cel - sis.___

Be - ne - dic - tus qui ve - nit in no-mi-ne Do - mi-ni.

Ho san - na in ex - cel - sis.

Agnus Dei

500

Ag - nus De - i, qui tol - lis pec-ca-ta mun - di,

mi-se - re - re no - bis. Ag-nus De - i, qui tol - lis

pec ca-ta mun - di, mi se - re - re no - bis. Ag - nus De - i,

qui tol - lis pec ca-ta mun - di, do-na no - bis pa - cem.

Simple Plainchant

Kyrie Orbis Factor

Cantor then All   *Cantor then All*

501

Ky - ri - e e - le - i-son. Chris - te

Cantor then All

e - le - i-son. Ky - ri - e e - le - i-son.

Cantor   *All*

Ky - ri - e e - le - i-son.

Kyrie XVI
502
Cantor then All — Ky-ri - e, e - le - i-son. Cantor then All — Chris-te,— e - le - i-son.
Cantor — Ky-ri - e, e - le - i-son. All — Ky-ri - e, e - le - i-son.—

Gloria XV
503
Glo - ri - a— in ex - cel - sis De - o. Et in ter - ra pax ho - mi - ni - bus
bo-nae vo-lun-ta-tis. Lau-da-mus te. Be-ne - di-ci-mus te. A - do - ra-mus te.
Glo-ri-fi - ca-mus te. Gra-ti - as a - gi-mus ti - bi prop-ter mag-nam glo-ri - am
tu - am. Do - mi - ne De - us, Rex cae-le-stis, De-us Pa-ter o-mni-po-tens.
Do - mi - ne Fi - li u - ni-ge-ni - te Je-su Chris-te. Do-mi-ne De-us, Ag-nus De - i,
Fi - li - us Pa-tris. Qui tol-lis pec-ca - ta mun - di, mi-se - re - re no-bis.
Qui tol-lis pec-ca-ta mun-di, sus-ci - pe de-pre-ca - ti - o - nem no-stram.
Qui se-des ad dex-te-ram Pa-tris, mi-se-re - re no-bis. Quo-ni-am tu so-lus
sanc-tus. Tu so-lus Do-mi-nus. Tu so-lus Al-tis-si-mus, Je-su Chri - ste.

cum Sanc-to Spi-ri-tu, in glo-ri-a De-i Pa-tris. A - men.

Credo III

504 Cre-do in u-num De - um, Pa - trem om - ni - po-ten-tem,

fac-to-rem cae-li et ter-rae, vi-si-bi-li-um om - ni-um et in-vi-si-

bi - li-um. Et in un-um Do-mi-num Ie-sum Chris-tum, Fi-li-um De-i

u - ni-ge-ni-tum. Et ex Pa-tre na - tum an-te om-n-ia sae - cu-la.

De-um de De-o, lu-men de lu-mi-ne, De-um ve-rum de De-o ve-ro. Ge-ni-tum, non

fac - tum, con-sub-stan-ti - a-lem Pa-tri: per quem om-ni - a fa-cta sunt.

Qui prop-ter nos ho-mi-nes, et prop-ter nos-tram sa-lu-tem de-scen-dit de_ cae-lis.

Et in-car-na-tus est de Spi-ri-tu Sanc - to ex Ma-r-ia Vir-gi-ne: et ho-mo fac-tus est.

Cru-ci - fi - xus et-i-am pro no - bis: sub Pon-ti-o Pi-la-to pas-sus, et se-

pul - tus est. Et re-sur-re-xit ter-ti-a di-e, se-cun-dum Scri-ptu-ras.

Et as-cen - dit in cae - lum: se-det ad dex-te-ram Pa - tris. Et i-te-rum ven-tu-rus

est cum glo-ri - a, iu-di-ca-re vi-vos et mor-tu-os: cu-ius reg-ni non e - rit fi-nis.

Et in Spi-ri-tum Sanc-tum, Do-mi-num, et vi-vi-fi-can-tem: qui ex Pa-tre Fi-li - o-que

pro - ce-dit. Qui cum Pa - tre et Fi-li - o si-mul a - do-ra-tur, et con-glo-ri-fi-ca-tur

qui lo - cu-tus est per Pro - phe-tas. Et u - nam san-ctam ca - tho-li-cam

et a - po-sto - li-cam Ec - cle - si - am. Con-fi - te - or un-um bap - tis-ma

in re-mis-si - o-nem pec-ca-tor - um. Et exs-pec-to re-sur-rec-ti-on-em mor-tu-o-rum

Et vi - tam ven-tu-ri sae-cu-li. A - men

Preface Dialogue

505

Priest   All

Do - mi-nus vo - bis - cum. Et cum spi - ri - tu tu - o.

Priest   All   Priest

Sur - sum cor - da. Ha-be - mus ad Do - mi-num. Gra-ti - as

All

ga - mus Do-mi-no De - o nos-tro. Di - gnum et jus-tum est.

Sanctus XVIII

505a

Sanc-tus,— sanc-tus,— sanc-tus Do-mi-nus De-us Sa-ba-oth.

Ple-ni sunt cae-li et ter-ra glo-ri-a tu-a. Ho-san-na in ex-cel sis.

Be ne dictus qui ve-nit in no-mi-ne Do-mi-ni. Hosan - na in ex-cel - sis.—

Memorial Acclamation

506

1   Priest   1 All

Myste - ri-um fi-de-i. Mortem tu-am an-nun-ti-a-mus, Do — mi-ne,

et tu - am re-sur-rec-ti-o-nem con-fi-te - mur, do - nec ve-ni - as.

2

Quo-ti - es-cum-que man-du-ca-mus pa-nem hunc, et ca-li-cem

bi - bi mus, mortem tu - am an-nun-ti-a mus, Do - mine, do - nec ve-ni - as.

3

Sal-va - tor mun-di sal - va nos, qui per cru -

cem et re-sur-rec-ti - o-nem tu - am li-be - ra-sti nos.

Pater Noster

507

Pa-ter nos-ter, qui es in cae-lis: sanc-ti-fi-ce-tur— no-men tu-um;

ad-ve-ni-at reg-num tu um; fi-at vo-lun-tas tu-a, si-cut in cae-lo,— et— in ter-ra.

Pa-nem nos-trum co-ti-di-a-num da no-bis ho-di-e; et di-mit-te no-bis

de-bi-ta nos-tra, si-cut et nos di-mit-ti-mus de-bi-to-ri-bus nos-tris;

et ne nos in-du-cas in ten-ta-ti-o-nem, sed li-be-ra nos a ma-lo.

Acclamation after 'Deliver us, Lord..'

508

Priest ...et ad-ven-tum Sal-va-to-ris nos-tri Ie-su Chris-ti.

Qui-a— tu-um est reg-num, et po-tes-tas,— et glo-ri-a in sae-cu-la.

Agnus Dei XVIII

509

Ag nus De-i, qui tol-lis pec-ca-ta mun-di, mi-se-re-re no-bis.

Repeat

Ag-nus De-i, qui tol-lis pec-ca-ta mun-di, do-na no-bis pa-cem.

Dismissal

510

Deacon or Priest   All

I-te,— mis-sa est. De-o— gra-ti-as.

Rite of Blessing of Water

Marty Haugen

511

Refrain

Springs of wa-ter, bless the Lord! Give him glo-ry and praise for ev-er!

1 Oceans of earth, sing glory to God!
Praise to the one who formed you!
Sound from your depths a hymn that tells
the wonders God has done!
Oh, blessed be God for ever!

All **Blessed be God for ever!**

2 Rivers and lakes, sing glory to God!
Praise, all you ponds and bogs!
Rich with the life that God creates,
now let your song be heard! Oh...

3 Brooks of the hills, sing glory to God!
Praise to the source of life!
Dancing with joy from peak to valley,
laughing and clear your song! Oh...

4 Showers and springs, sing glory to God!
Praise, all you living waters!
Shower the earth with life and goodness,
shower the grace of God! Oh...

---

512 Water of Life

Stephen Dean

Cantors *Litany section (optional)*   All

Springs— of wa-ter, bless— the Lord,   Praise— and glo-ry for e-ver!
Ri-vers and streams,— bless— the Lord,   *Other invocations are sung*

Wa-ter of Life, cleanse and re-fresh us; raise us to life in Christ Je-sus.

All you who thirst, come to the waters,
and you will never be thirsty again.

As rain from heav'n, so is God's word,
it waters the earth and brings forth life.

3 Dying with Christ, so we shall rise with him,
death shall no longer have power over us.

4 Turn to the Lord, cast off your wickedness,
you will find peace in his infinite love.

➤ *See also: Water of Life Gloria (528)*

513

Refrain

O wash— me— in the wa-ter— of re-dee-ming love:

li-ving wa-ter— from the foun-tain of sal-va-tion.——

The water of life renews the soul:
your gift to us all the source of life.
O cleanse us! cleanse us, Lord, and
refresh us!
Renew the spring of your spirit in us.

Creator of life, of all we are:
forgive us our weakness and our fear.

Deliver us from the darkness of evil;
from danger free us body and soul.

3 You stretched out your hand to calm the sea:
the people of Israel you set free.
O Freedom! Lead your people to freedom!
And Liberty, through the water of life.

Chris O'Hara

514

Bernadette Farrell

Refrain

Give us, Lord, a new heart; re-cre-ate your spir-it with-in us.

1 I will cleanse you in living waters,
I will wash away your sin.
I will put a new spirit in you
and you shall live, shall live. *Ez. 36:25.26*

2 I will implant my law deep within you,
I will write it on your hearts.
I will be your God,
and you shall be my people. *Jer. 31:33*

3 For all your faults I will grant forgiveness,
nevermore will I remember your sins. *Jer. 31:34*

515a

As - per - ges me, Do - mi - ne
hys-so - po - et mun-da - bor: la - va - bis me,
et su - per ni - vem de - al - ba - bor.

Ps 50: 1 Miserere mei, Deus, secundum magnam misericordiam tuam.   *Refrain*
Gloria Patri et Filio, et Spiritui Sancto ...   *Refrain*

Purify me, O Lord, with hyssop, and I shall be made clean; wash me, and I shall be clean as new snow
V. Have mercy on me, O God, in your kindness; in your compassion blot out my offence.

515b

lengthen

Vi - di a - quam e-gre - di - en-tem de tem -
plo, a la - te-re dex - tro, al-le -
lu - ia: et om - nes, ad quos per - ve - nit a - qua is -
ta. sal - vi fac - ti sunt.

et di - cent, al - le-lu - ia, al - le - lu - ia.

Ps 117: 1 Confitemini Domino quoniam bonus: quoniam in saecula misericordia ejus. *R.*
Gloria Patri et Filio, et Spiritui Sancto, sicut erat in principio, et nunc, et
semper, et in saecula saeculorum. Amen. *R.*

saw water flowing from the temple, on the right side, alleluia:
nd all to whom that water came were saved, alleluia.

'. Give thanks to the Lord for he is good, for his love has no end.

➤ *See also: Surrexit Christus (266); I saw springs of water (256);*
You have put on Christ (400), We shall draw water joyfully (692).

Penitential Acts & Kyries

Kyrie 1   *Taizé chant by Jacques Berthier (1923-94)*

516

1, 3. Ky - ri - e,   Ky - ri - e,   e - le - i-son,   Ky - ri - e,
2. Christ - te,   Chris - te,   e - le - i-son.   Chris - te,

Ky - ri - e,   e - le - i - son.
Chris - te,   *hmm.*

Cantor:

Kyrie 7   *Taizé chant by Jacques Berthier (1923-94)*

517

1, 3. Ky - ri - e,   e - le - i - son,   Ky - ri - e,   e -
2. Christ - te,   e - le - i - son,   Chris - te,   e

Cantor:

le - i - son.   *hmm*

The New Celtic Liturgy

Christopher Walke

518

In Penitential Act 3, the Priest, or a Deacon or another minister, sings an invocation before each phrase.

Lord, have mer - cy. Christ, have mer - cy. Lord, have mer - cy.

Absolution (Penitential Act 3)

May almighty God have mercy on us,
forgive us our sins,

and bring us to e-ver-las - ting life. A - men.

➤ *See also the Gloria (529), Eucharistic Acclamations (553ff), and Lamb of God (59*

Russian Kyri

1, 3. Ky - ri - e, e - lei - son, Ky - ri - e, e - lei - son,
2. Chris - te, e - lei - son, Chris - te, e - lei - son,

519

Ky - ri - e, e - lei - son.
Chris - te, e - lei - son.

The Revised Gathering Mass

Paul Inwoo

520

(Sung or spoken invocation) *Lord, have mer - cy.* Ky - ri - e, e - le - i - son.

(Invocation) *Christ, have mer - cy.* Chri - ste, e - le - i - son.

(Invocation)   Lord, have mer - cy.   Ky-ri-e, e - le - i-son.

Priest (sung or spoken)

May almighty God have mercy on us,
forgive us our sins,
and bring us to everlasting life.

1st time Cantor. repeated by All:

A - men.

➤ *See also: Eucharistic Acclamations (570ff.)*

Mass of Hope   *Stephen Dean*

521

Cantor then All:

(Sung or spoken invocation)   Ky- ri - e,   e - le - i-son.   *(invocation)*

Chri - ste, e - le - i- son.   *(invocation)*   Ky-ri- e, e - le - i-son.

Priest (sung or spoken)

May almighty God have mercy on us,
forgive us our sins,
and bring us to everlasting life.

Cantor: **All:**

A——— men.   A——— men.

➤ *See also: Gloria no 531*

The Storrington Mass   *Marty Haugen*

522

All: **(sung twice)**

(Sung or spoken invocation)   Lord,— have mer - cy.   *(invocation)*
Ky-ri-e, e - le - i-son.

Christ,— have mer - cy.   *(invocation)*   Lord,— have mer - cy.
Chris-te, e - le - i-son.   Ky-ri-e, e - le - i-son.

Priest (sung or spoken)

May almighty God have mercy on us,
forgive us our sins,
and bring us to

Cantor then All:

e-ver - las - ting life, e-ver- las - ting life: A - men.

➤ *See also: Gloria (532), Eucharistic Acclamations (584ff), Lamb of God (590)*

The Pershore Mass

Alan Smith

523

1, 3. Lord,——— have mer - cy, Lord,———have have mer-cy.

2. Christ,——— have mer - cy, Christ——— have mer - cy.

Glory to God

The Pershore Mass

Alan Smith

524

Refrain **First time: Cantor then All**

Glo - ry to God in the high - est, and on earth— peace to peo-ple of good will.

Verse 1 Cantor

We— praise— you, we bless— you, we a-dore— you, we glo-ri-fy you,

we give you thanks for your great glo - ry, Lord——— God,

heav'n-ly— King, O God, al - migh - ty Fa - ther. *To Refrain*

Verse 2 Cantor

Lord Je - sus Christ, On- ly Be- got- ten Son, Lord— God,

Lamb of God, Son of the Fa- ther, you take a- way the

sins of the world, have mer - cy, have mer - cy on us; you take a way the

sins of the world, re - ceive our prayer, re - ceive_ our_ prayer;

you are sea ted at the right hand of the Fa - ther, have mer - cy on us.

Verse 3 Cantor

For you a-lone are the Ho - ly One, you a - lone are the Lord,

you a - lone are the Most_ High, Je - sus_ Christ, with the

Ho - ly Spirit, in the glo - ry of God the Fa - ther, A - men.

To Refrain (sung twice: Cantor, then All)

525

Anne Ward

Refrain **May be sung twice to begin** **1, 3-5**

Glo - ry to God in the high-est, and on earth peace to peo-ple of good will.

Optional final refrain **To verse 1** **Verse 1**

will. A - men. will. We praise you, we bless you, we a - dore you, we

glo - ri - fy you, we give you thanks for your great glo - ry!

Lord, God, heav-en-ly King, O God, al - migh-ty Fa - ther.

to Refrain

Verse 2

Lord, Je-sus Christ, On - ly-Be-got-ten Son, Lord God, Lamb of God,

Son of the Fa-ther, you take a - way the sins of the world, have

mer - cy on us; you take a - way the sins of the world, re - ceive our——

to Refrain

prayer; you are sea-ted at the right hand of the Fa-ther, have mer - cy on us.

Verse 3

For you a-lone are the Ho - ly One, you a - lone are the Lord,

you a-lone are the Most High, Je-sus Christ, with the Ho-ly Spi-rit,—— in th

glo - ry of God the Fa-ther. A - men. A - men.

to optional Final Refrain

Coventry Gloria

Peter Jones (1951-2016

526

Refrain Cantor then All

Glo - ry to God, glo - ry in the high - est,

and on earth peace to peo - ple of good will.

Cantor: We praise you, we bless you, C: *we glorify you,*
All: Glory in the highest.   *we give you thanks for your great glor*
C: *we adore you,*   *Lord God,*
All: Glory in the highest.   All: Glory in the highest.

: *heavenly King,*
ll: Glory in the highest.
: *O God, almighty Father.*

: Glory to God, glory in the highest,
  and on earth peace to people of good will.

: *Lord Jesus Christ,*
  Only Begotten Son,
  Lord God, Lamb of God,
  Son of the Father,
  you take away the sins of the world,
    have mercy on us;
: have mercy on us;

: *you take away the sins of the world,*
    receive our prayer;
: receive our prayer;

  you are seated at the right hand of the
    Father,

  have mercy on us,
All: have mercy on us.

C: *Glory to God, glory in the highest,*
    and on earth peace to people of good will.

All: Glory to God, glory in the highest,
     and on earth peace to people of good will.

C: *For you alone are the Holy One,*
    you alone are the Lord,
    you alone are the Most High,
    Jesus Christ,
    with the Holy Spirit,
    in the glory of God
    the glory of God the Father.

All: Glory to God, glory in the highest,
     and on earth peace to people of good will.
C: *Amen.*   All: Amen.

27 Refrain

Glo - ri - a, glo - ri - a in ex - cel - sis De - o,

Glo - ri - a, glo - ri - a in ex - cel - sis De - o.

Verses

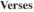

1. Glory to God in the highest, and on earth peace to people of good-will.
2. Lord Jesus Christ, Only Begotten Son, Lord God, Lamb of God, Son of the Father,
3. For you a - lone are the Holy One, you alone are the Lord,

1. We praise you, we bless you, we give you thanks for your great glory,
   we adore you, we glorify you,
2. you take away the sins of the world, have mercy on us;
   Repeat from *
*
[2b] you take away the sins of the world, re - ceive our prayer;
3. you alone are the Most High, Je - sus Christ,

1. Lord God, heavenly King, O God, Almighty Father.
2. you are seated at the right hand of the Father, have mercy on us.
3. with the Holy Spirit, in the glory of God the Father. A - men.

Francis Duffy (1914-2000)

Water of Life Gloria

Stephen Dea

528

Glo-ry to God in the high - est, glo - ry to God in the high - est, and on earth peace_ to peo - ple, to peo - ple of good will.__ We praise_ you,__ we bless_ you, we a - dore_ you,__ we glo - ri-fy you, we give you thanks__ for your great glo - ry, Lord God, hea-ven-ly King, O God, al - migh - ty Fa - ther.__ Lord Je - sus Christ,

**Optional Repeat of 'Glory to God'

On- ly Be-got - ten Son, Lord God, Lamb of God, Son__ of the Fa-ther, you take a - way the sins of the world, have mer - cy on us; you take a - way the sins of the world, re - ceive our prayer; you are sea - ted at the right hand of the Fa - ther, have mer - cy on us. For you a - lone are the Ho - ly One, you_ a - lone are the Lord, you a- lone are the Most High, Je - sus Christ, with the Ho - ly

Spi-rit,___ in the glo-ry of God__ the Fa - ther. A- men.___

Glo-ry to God in the high-est, glo-ry to God in the high - est, and on

earth peace__ to peo - ple, to peo - ple of good will.

529 The New Celtic Liturgy

Christopher Walker

Refrain

Glo ry to God, glo-ry to God, glo-ry to God in the high - est,

and on earth peace, and on earth peace, peace to peo - ple of good will.

Verses

1. We praise you, we bless you, we adore you, we glorify you,
2. Lord Jesus Christ, Only Be-got-ten Son, Lord God, Lamb of God, Son of the Father,
3. For you alone are the Holy One, you alone are the Lord,

we give you thanks for your great glory,
you take away the sins you take away the sins
of the world, have mercy on us; of the world, receive our prayer;
you alone are the Most High, Je - sus Christ, with the Ho - ly Spirit.

Earlier version:
[you alone are the Most High, Jesus Christ, with the Ho - ly Spirit,]

to Refrain

Lord God, hea - ven - ly King, O God, almigh - ty Father.
you are seated at the right hand of the Father, have mercy on us.
in the glory of God the Father. Amen, a - men.

➤ *See also the Kyrie (518), Eucharistic Acclamations (553ff), and Lamb of God (591)*

530 Mass of St Jeanne Jugan

Christopher Walker

Glo-ry to God in the high - est, and on earth peace to peo-ple ___ of good will.

1 We praise you,
   we bless you,
   we adore you,
   we glorify you,
   we give you thanks for your great glory,
   Lord God, heavenly King,
   O God, almighty Father.   *Refrain*

2 Lord Jesus Christ, Only Begotten Son,
   Lord God, Lamb of God, Son of the Father,
                    Refrain (or to verse 3)

3 you take away the sins of the world,
   have mercy on us;

you take away the sins of the world,
   receive our prayer;
you are seated at the right hand of the
   Father,
   have mercy on us.   *Refrain*

4 For you alone are the Holy One,
   you alone are the Lord,
   you alone are the Most High,
   Jesus Christ,
   with the Holy Spirit,
   in the glory of God the Father.
         Refrain, followed by Amen *(below*

A - men, a - men. A - men, a - men.

➣ *See also the Lamb of God (59.*

531 Mass of Hope

Stephen Dea

Refrain *Sung twice each time. To start: Cantor or choir may sing first and all repeat.*

Glo - ri - a in ex-cel-sis De - o; et in ter-ra pax ho - mi - ni-bus

1-3 After 2nd time, to Verses | *Last time* *Much slower* *mp*

bo-nae vo-lun - ta - tis.   ta - tis.   A - men.

Verses *Freely*

1. We praise you, we bless you, we a- dore you, we glorify you, we give you
2. Lord Jesus Christ, Only Be–gotten Son, Lord God,
3. For you alone are the Holy One, you a- lone are the Lord, you a - lone are the

(These bars sung three times in v. 2)

1. thanks for your great glory, Lord God,
2. Lamb of God, Son of the Father, you take a - way the
   you take a - way the
   you are seated at the
3. Most High, Jesus Christ, with the Holy

Verse 2 only   *Refrain*

1. heavenly King, O   God, al-mighty Fa - ther.
2. sins of the world, have   mer-cy on us;
   sins of the world, re -   ceive our prayer;
   right hand of the Father, have   mer - cy, have mercy on us.
3. Spi - rit, in the   glory of God the Father. A-men.

➤ *See also: Kyrie (521), Lamb of God (592)*

532   **The Storrington Mass**   *Marty Haugen*

Refrain

Glo - ry to God in the highest,— and on earth peace to peo-ple of good will.—

Verse 1

We praise you, we bless you, we a-dore—— you, we

glo - ri - fy you, we give— you thanks for— your great glo ry,—

to Refrain

Lord God, hea - ven - ly King, O God, al - migh - ty Fa - ther.—

Verse 2

Lord Je-sus Christ, On-ly Be-got-ten Son, Lord— God,

Lamb— of God, Son of the Fa-ther,—— you take a-way the

sins of the world, have mercy on us;——— you take a-way the

sins of the world, re-ceive— our prayer;— you are sea-ted— at the

to Refrain

right hand— of the Fa-ther,— have— mer - cy on us.

Verse 3

For you a-lone are the Ho - ly One, you a-lone are the

Lord, you a - lone are the Most High, Je - sus Christ, with th

Ho - ly Spi - rit, in the glo-ry of God the Fa-ther.————

Refrain

Glo - ry to God in the high-est,—— and on earth peace to peo - ple of goo

will.—— A - men, a - men, a - men.————

See also: Kyrie (522), Eucharistic Acclamations (584ff), Lamb of God (59

The Plymouth Mass   *Paul Inwood*

533

Refrain

Glo-ry to God in the high-est, and on earth peace to peo-ple of good will.

Verses (cantor or unison choir)

1. We praise you, we bless you, we a - dore___ you,
1a. we give you thanks for your great glo - ry, | Lord God, heavenly King,
2. Lord Jesus Christ, On - ly Be - got - ten Son, | Lord God, Lamb of God,
2a. you take a - way the sins of the world,
2b. you take a - way the sins of the world,
2c. you are seated at the right hand of the Fa - ther,

3. For you alone are the Ho - ly One,
3a. you alone are the Most High, Je - sus Christ,
3b. in the glory of God the Fa - ther.

1. ⁊ we glo - ri - fy___ you,
1a. ⁊ O God, al - might - y Father.

2. ⁊ ⁊ Son___ of the Father,
2a. ⁊ have mer - cy on us;
2b. ⁊ re - ceive___ our___ prayer;
2c. ⁊ have mer - cy on us.

3. you a - lone___ are the Lord,
3a. with the Ho - ly___ Spirit,
3b. ⁊ A - men.

ɟospel Acclamation: Alleluia

Salisbury Alleluia: Christopher Walker

534

Al - le - lu - ia, al - le - lu - ia, al - le - lu - ia.

Al - le - lu - ia, al - le - lu - ia, al - le - lu - ia.

535

Colin Mawby

Al - le-lu - ia, al - le-lu - ia, al - le-lu - ia.

536

Laurence Bévenot OSB (1905-91)

Al - le-lu - ia, al - le - lu - ia, al - le - lu - ia.

537

Stephen Dean

Al - le-lu - ia, al - le - lu-ia, al - le - lu - ia!

Richard Proulx

538

Al - le-lu - ia, al - le - lu - ia,

al - le-lu - ia, al - le-lu - ia, al - le-lu - ia.

Taizé Alleluia 7: Jacques Berthier

539

Al-le - lu-ia, al-le - lu-ia, al-le - lu - ia. Al-le - lu-ia, al-le-

Cantor: verse *(Al - le - lu - ia)*

lu - ia, al-le-lu _ ia.

540

Taizé Alleluia 41: Russian Orthodox

Al-le-lu - ia, al-le-lu - ia, al-le-lu - i - a!

541

Jubilee Alleluia: James Walsh

Al - le - lu - ia! Al - le - lu - ia! Praise to Christ, the Word of Life.

Glo - ry, praise and ju - bi - la - tion, al - le - lu - ia!

542

The Priory Mass, Mick Truman

Al - le - lu - ia, al - le - lu - ia!

543

Stephen Dean

Al - le - lu - ia, al - le - lu - ia, al - le - lu - ia.____

In Lent: Glo-ry to you, O Christ, you are the Word of God. Glo-ry to you.____

544

Russian Alleluia

Al - le - lu - ia, al - le - lu - ia, al - le - lu - ia.

The Choir or Cantor sings the verse, then all sing together:

Al-le - lu - ia, al - le - lu - ia, al - le - lu - ia.

Al - le - lu - ia, al - le - lu - ia, al - le - lu - ia.

The Nicene Creed

545

Stephen Dea

A	I believe in one God, / the Father almighty,
B	maker of heaven and earth,
C	of all things visible and invisible.
A	I believe in one Lord Jesus Christ,
B	the Only Begotten Son of God,
C	born of the Father before all ages.
D	God from God, Light from Light,
E	true God from true_ God,
A	begotten, not made,
B	consubstantial with the Father;
C	through him all things were made.
D	For us men and for our salvation
E	he came down from heaven,

At the words that follow up to and including and became man, all bow.

A	and by the Holy Spirit was incarnate
B	of the Virgin Mary,
C	and became_ man.
A	For our sake he was crucified under Pontius Pilate,
B	he suffered death and was buried,

➤ *See also Credo III (504)*

C	and rose again on the third day / in accordance with the Scriptures.
D	He ascended into heaven
E	and is seated at the right hand of the Father.
A	He will come again in glory
B	to judge the living and the dead
C	and his kingdom will have no end.
A	I believe in the Holy Spirit,
B	the Lord, the giver of life,
C	who proceeds from the Father and the Son,
A	who with the Father and the Son
B	is adored and glorified,
C	who has spoken through the prophets.
D	I believe in one, holy, catholic
E	and apostolic Church.
A	I confess one baptism for the forgiveness of sins
B	and I look forward to the resurrection of the dead
C	and the life of the world to come. A--men.

General Intercessions

546   *Stephen Dean*

Cantor   All

Lord,   hear us: O Lord, hear us; Lord, gra-cious-ly hear us.

547   *Russian chant*

Cantor   All

(Intercessions)   Let us pray to the Lord.   Lord, hear   our prayer.

548   *Paul Inwood*

Cantor   All

Lord,   in your mer - cy,   hear our prayer.

549

Hear our prayer! Hear our prayer! Lord, hear our prayer.

550

God   our   Fa - ther, we make this   prayer,

through our   Sa - viour   and Re - dee - mer,   Je - sus   Christ.
Advent/Christmas [the   co - ming   of   our   Sa - viour,]
Easter   [our   glo - rious   ri - sen   Sa - viour,]

549-550: Stephen Dean

551   *from The Mass of John Carroll, Michael Joncas*

God ev-er- faith-ful, God ev - er mer-ci-ful, God of your peo- ple, hear our prayer.

552   *John L. Bell*

slowly

Through our lives and— by our   prayers, your King-dom come.

See also nos. 9, 26-28, 73 (Advent), 740, 928-930

The Eucharistic Prayer

A New Celtic Liturgy

Christopher Walker

553 Ho - ly, Ho-ly, Ho - ly Lord, Lord God— of hosts.—

Hea-ven and earth are full of your glo-ry. Ho - san - na,—— ho -

san - na—— in the high-est.—— Bles-sed is he who

comes in the name of the Lord.—— Ho - san - na—— in the

high - est,—— ho - san - na—— in the high - est.——

Memorial Acclamation 1

554a We pro-claim your Death, O— Lord, and pro-fess your Re-sur -

May be repeated

rec-tion un-til you come a-gain,—— un - til you come a-gain.

Memorial Acclamation 2

554b When we eat this Bread and drink this

May be repeated.

Cup, we pro-claim your Death, O Lord, un - til you come a - gain.

**Memorial
Acclamation 3**

554c

Save— us, Sa-viour of the world, for by your Cross and

May be repeated.

Re - sur - rec - tion you have set us free, you have set us free.

555

Doxology & Amen

Priest: *for* e - ver and e - ver.

All:

A - men, a - men, a - men,— a - men.

A Mass of Peace

Seóirse Bodley

556

Ho - ly, Ho - ly, Ho - ly Lord

God____ of— hosts. Hea - ven and earth are— full of your

glo - ry. Ho - san - na in the high-est. Bles - sed is— he who—

comes in the name of the Lord. Ho - san - na in the high-est.

Memorial Acclamations

557 a-c

1. We pro-claim your Death, O Lord, and pro -
2. When we eat this Bread and drink this Cup, we pro -
3. Save us, Sa - viour of the world, for by you

fess your Re - sur - rec - tion un - til you come a - gain.
claim your Death, O Lord, un - til you come a - gain.
Cross and Re - sur - rec - tion you have set us free.

558

A - men, a - men, a - men, a - men.

Mass of Hope (Farrell)

Bernadette Farrell

559

Ho-ly Ho-ly, Holy, Ho - ly Lord, Ho - ly Lord,

cresc.

Ho - ly Lord God of hosts. Heav'n and earth are full of your

glo-ry. Ho-san-na in the high - est. Ho-san - na, ho-san - na, ho-

san - na in the high-est. Bles-sed, bles-sed, bles-sed, bles-sed is

cresc.

he who comes in the name, who comes in the name of the Lord

Ho - san - na, ho - san - na, ho - san - na in the high - est. Ho san - na, ho - san - na, ho - san - na— in the high - est.—

Memorial Acclamation 1

660

We pro-claim your Death, O Lord,—

we pro-claim your Death, O Lord,— and pro - fess your

Re - sur - rec - tion— un - til you come a - gain.—

Memorial Acclamations 2 & 3

661a, b

2. When we eat this Bread and drink— this Cup,—
3. Save— us,— Sa - viour of— the world.—

when we eat this Bread and drink— this Cup, we pro - claim your
Save— us,— Sa - viour of— the world, for by your Cross and

Death,— O Lord,— we pro - claim your Death, O Lord—
Re - sur - rec - tion, your Cross and Re - sur - rec - tion

we pro-claim your Death un - til you come— a - gain.—
— you— have— set— us— free.—

Doxology and Amen

562

.... all glo-ry and hon-our is yours,— for ev er, - A -

men. *for ev - er,* A - men. *and ev - er.* A - men.

Simple Amen

A - men, A - men, A - men, A - men.

Community Mass

Richard Proulx

563

Ho-ly, Ho-ly, Ho - ly Lord God of hosts.

Heav'n___ and earth___ are full___ of your glo-ry. Ho-

san - na in the high-est, ho - san-na in the high-est.

Blest is he who comes___ in the name___ of the Lord. Ho-

Repeat Hosann

564a Memorial Acclamation 1

We pro-claim your Death, O Lord,— and pro-fess your Re - sur

rec - tion___ un - til you come a - gain.___

Memorial Acclamation 2

564b

When we eat this Bread—— and drink—— this Cup,
we pro-claim your Death, O Lord, un-til you come a-gain.——

Memorial Acclamation 3

564c

Save us,—— Sa-viour of the world, for by your
Cross and Re-sur-rec-tion you have set—— us— free.

Great Amen

564d

A-men. A-men.. A-men.

St Andrew's Mass   *Stephen Dean*

565

Ho - ly,—— Ho - ly,—— Ho - ly—
Lord God of hosts. Heaven and earth are full of your glo - ry. Ho-
san - na, ho-san - na, ho-san-na in the high-est, ho-
san - na. Blest is he who comes in the name of the Lord.
Blest is he who comes in the name of the Lord. Ho-san - na, ho-
san - na, ho-san-na in the high-est, ho-san - na.

Memorial Acclamation 1

566

We pro-claim your Death, O Lord, and pro-fess your Re-sur-rec-tion un-til you come a-gain, un-til you come a-gain.

Memorial Acclamation 2

567

When we eat this Bread and drink this Cup, we pro-claim your Death, O Lord, un-til you come, un-til— you— come— a - gain.

May be sung twice: 1 Cantor, 2 All

Memorial Acclamation 3

568

Save us, Sa-viour of the world, for by your Cross and— Re-sur - rec-tion you have set us free, for by your Cross and Re-sur-rec - tion you have set— us— free.

569 Concluding Doxology and Amen

Repeat

A - men, a - men, a - men.

The Revised Gathering Mass

570

Paul Inwood

Ho - ly, Ho - ly, Ho - ly Lord, Ho - ly,

Ho - ly Lord God of hosts. Heav-en and earth, heav-en and earth are

full of your glo - ry, Lord God of hosts. Ho - san - na, ho -

san - na, ho - san - na in the high - est. Ho - san -

fine

na, ho - san - na, ho - san - na in the high - est.

Bles-sed, bles-sed is he— who comes, blessed, bles-sed is he— who comes;

Repeat Hosanna

bles-sed is he, bles-sed is he who comes in the name of the Lord.—

571a, 571c Memorial Acclamations 1 & 3

1. We pro-claim— your Death, O Lord, we pro claim— your Death, O Lord,
3. Save us, Sa - viour of—— the world, save us, Sa - viour of—— the world,

To optional Hosanna

and— pro-fess your Re - sur-rec-tion un - til— you come— a-gain.———
for by your Cross and Re - sur-rec - tion you— have set— us free.———

571b
Memorial
Acclamation 2

When we eat this Bread and drink this Cup, we pro-claim your Death, O Lord, we pro-claim your Death, O Lord, un-til you come a-gain.

To optional Hosanna

572 Doxology and Amen

rit.

A - men, a - men.

Coventry Acclamations   Paul Inwood

573

Ho-ly, Ho - ly, Ho-ly Lord, Ho-ly Lord God of hosts. Heav'n and earth are full, heav'n and earth are full, heav'n and earth are full of your glo-ry.

Ho - san - na, ho-san-na, ho-san-na in the high-est; ho-san-na, ho-san-na, ho-san-na in the high-est.

Fine

Blest is he who comes, blest is he who comes in the name of the Lord.

(Choir: Blest is he who comes... is he who

Repeat Hosanna

Memorial Acclamation 1

574a

We pro - claim your Death, O Lord, and pro - fess your Re - sur-

to optional Hosanna

rec - tion un - til you come＿ a - gain. [Ho - san - na....,

Memorial Acclamations 2 & 3

574b, 574c

2. When we eat＿ this＿ Bread and＿ drink＿ this＿Cup, we pro
3. Save us, Sa - viour of the world, save us, Sa - viour of the world, for

to optional Hosanna

claim your Death, your Death, O Lord, un - til you come＿ a - gain.
by your Cross and Re - sur - rec - tion you have set＿ us＿ free.

Amen

575

A - men, a - men, a - men.

The German Mass

Franz Schubert, 1797-1828, arranged by Richard Proulx

mp *Slowly*

576

Ho - ly, Ho - ly, Ho - ly Lord God of hosts. ＿

Ho - ly, Ho - ly, Ho - ly Lord God of hosts. ＿

Heav - en and earth are full,＿ full＿ of your glo - ry. Ho-san - na in the high - est, ho - san - na in the high - est.

f   *mp*

Bless - ed is he who comes___ in the name of the Lord.___ Ho -

dim.

san - na in the high - est, ho - san - na in the high - est.

Memorial Acclamations 1 & 2

577a, 577b

We pro-claim your Death, O Lord,___
When we eat this Bread and drink this Cup,

Either: *and pro-fess___ your___ Re - sur - rec - tion,*

Or: and pro-fess your Re-sur-rec - tion,   } we pro-claim your Death, O
we proclaim___ your___ Death, O Lord,___

Lord,___ un - til___ you___ come a - gain.

Memorial Acclamation 3

577c

Save us, Sav - iour of the world,___

Sav - iour of the world, for by your Cross and Re - sur - rec-tion

p   *pp*

you have___ set us free, you have___ set us free.

Amen

578

mp

A - men, a - men, a - men. A - men, a - men.___

The Pershore Mass *Alan Smith*

79 Ho-ly, Ho-ly, Ho-ly Lord God of hosts, Lord God__ of__ hosts.

Hea-ven and earth are full of your glo-ry. Ho-san-na in the high-est.

rit . . . .

Blessed is he who comes in the name of the Lord. Ho-san-na in the high-est.

Memorial Acclamation 1

80a We pro-claim your Death, O Lord, and pro-fess your Re-sur-

rit . . . .

rec-tion un-til you come__ a - gain.

Memorial Acclamation 2

80b When we eat this__ Bread and drink this__ Cup, we pro-

rit . . . .

claim your Death, O Lord,__ un-til you come__ a - gain.

Memorial Acclamation 3

80c Save us, Sa-viour of the world, for by your

rit . . . .

Cross and Re-sur-rec-tion you have set__ us__ free.

Amen

581

A - men,_ a - men,_ a - men, a - men, a - men.

Eucharistic Acclamations

John Lil

582

Except where marked, each phrase is sung first by Cantor and repeated by All.

Ho - ly, Ho - ly,__ Ho - ly Lord God of hosts.

Heaven and earth are full of your glo-ry. Ho - san - na in_ the

Cantor alone:

high-est. *Bles-sed is he who comes in the name of the*

Cantor first, then All:

Lord. Ho - san - na in_ the high - est.

Memorial Acclamations 1-3

583 a-c

Cantor first, then All:

We pro-claim your Death,__ O__ Lord, and pro
When we eat this Bread and drink this Cup, we pro
Save us, Sa-viour of the world, for by you

fess your Re - sur - rec-tion un - til you come a - gain
claim your Death, O Lord,__
Cross and Re - sur - rec-tion you have set us free

men
583d

Each Amen sung by Cantor first, then All:

A - men. A - men. A - men.

The Storrington Mass

Marty Haugen

584

Ho - ly, Ho - ly, Ho - ly— Lord God of hosts.

Hea-ven and earth are full of your glo-ry. Ho - san-na— in the high - est.

Bles-sed is he who comes—— in the name of the Lord. Ho -

san - na, ho - san - na, ho - san - na—— in the high - est.

Memorial Acclamation 1

585a

We pro - claim your Death,—— O Lord, and pro-

fess your Re - sur - rec-tion un - til you come a - gain.

Memorial Acclamation 2

585b

When we eat this Bread and drink— this Cup, we pro-claim your

Death, O Lord,— un - til you come a - gain, un - til you come a - gain.

Memorial Acclamation 3

585c

Save us, Sa-viour of the world, for by your
Cross and Re - sur - rec - tion___ you have set us free.

Amen

586

A - men, a - men, a - men. A - men, a - men, a - men.

The Lord's Prayer

Nicolai Rimsky-Korsakov (1844 -190

587

Our Fa-ther, who art in heaven, hal-lowed be thy name; thy king-dom come, th

will be done on earth as it is in heaven. Give us this day our dai - ly brea

and for-give us our tres-pas-ses, as we for-give those who tres-pass a-gainst us;

and lead us not in - to temp - ta - tion, but de - li - ver us from e - vil.

At Mass, the Priest continues: Deliver us, Lord, we pray, from every evil...

....and the coming of our Saviour, Jesus Christ.

For the king-dom, the power and the glo - ry are yours now and for e-ver.

588

p Our Fa-ther, who art in hea-ven, hal-lowed be thy name; thy king-dom come,— thy will be done on earth as it is in hea-ven. Give us this day our dai-ly bread, and for-give us our tres-pas-ses,— as we for-give those— who tres-pass a-gainst— us;—— and lead us not— in-to temp-ta-tion, but de-li-ver us from e-vil.—

At Mass, the priest continues with the prayer, which concludes:
and the coming of our Saviour, Jesus Christ.

For the king-dom, the pow-er, and the glo-ry are yours now and for e - ver.

See also the Missal chants (479), Pater noster (507), 1010   *Celtic Mass: Christopher Walker*

Lamb of God

The Pershore Mass   *Alan Smith*

[Cantor or choir:]   **All**

589

Lamb of God, you take a-way the sins—— of the world, have mer - cy, have mer - cy, have mer - cy on us. *Lamb of God, you* take a-way the sins—— of the world, have mer - cy, have mer - cy, have mer - cy on us. *Lamb of God, you take a-way the*

[C:]

All

[C:]

sins___ of the world, grant___ us peace, grant__ us__ peace.

The Storrington Mass *Marty Hauge*

590

Lamb of God, you take a-way the sins of the world, have mercy on us. world, grant___ us peace, grant___ us peace.

Repeat | *Last time*

The New Celtic Liturgy *Christopher Walke*

591

Lamb__ of God, you take a-way the sins of the world, have mer - cy on us. world,___ grant___ us peace,___ grant___ us peace.

1,2 | *Repeat* | *Last time*

Mass of Hope *Stephen Dea*

592

1,3 O Lamb of God, you take a-way the sins of the world, have mer - cy on us,___ { have mer - cy on us. 2 O Lamb of God, yo grant us peace,_ grant us peace,_ grant us__ peace. take a-way the sins of the world, have mer - cy on us, have mer - cy on us.

3. world,___

Mass of St Jeanne Jugan

593

Lamb of God, you take a - way the sins of the

1, 2

Last

world, have mer - cy on us. world, grant us peace.

Mass of Thanksgiving

Stephen Dean

594

Cantor O Lamb of God, *All* you take a - way the

sins of the world, have mer - cy, have mer - cy on us.

Last time: grant us, grant us peace.

Martin Foster

595

Lamb of God, you take a - way the sins of the

1, 2

Repeat

world, have mer - cy, mer - cy on us.

Last time

world, grant us, grant us peace.

96

John Schiavone

Cantor: *Agnus Dei, qui tollis peccata mundi,*

All:

Mi - se - re - re no - bis. Do - na no - bis pa - cem.

The refrain is sung continuously, as required

Preparation of Gifts

597

1, 5 Blest are you who made the universe,
you who see beyond our death.
Blest are you who dwells in each of us.
Blest are you with every breath.
Blest are you with every breath.

2 Through your goodness we have bread
to eat,
seeds that died to bring life new.
As the sep'rate grains become one loaf,
gather us as one in you. (2)

3 Through your goodness we have wine
to drink,
fruit of vineyard, work of hands.
Let the fruits of all we celebrate
spread your love to ev'ry land. (2)

4 Here the stranger is a welcome guest
Here all hungers shall be fed.
Come, and know the one who brings
you life
in the breaking of the bread. (2)

5 Repeat v. 1

Marty Haugen

598

1 O King of might and splendour,
creator most adored,
this sacrifice we render
to thee as sovereign Lord.
May these our gifts be pleasing
unto thy majesty,
from sin, O Lord, release us,
who have offended thee.

2 Thy body thou hast given,
thy blood thou hast outpoured,
that sin might be forgiven,
O Jesus, loving Lord.
As now with love most tender,
thy death we celebrate,
our lives in self–surrender
to thee we consecrate.

German 19th C., tr A. G. Murray OSB (1905–199

599

Refrain

The Lord is now a-bout to en-ter his Tem-ple, he wh
is and who was, and is to come. 'God__ a-mong us'comes to make his dwel-

1 The Word that brings peace is now proclaimed,
the salvation that was promised is now in our midst.
May all strife and hate be banished from our hearts,
may the love of Christ our Lord dwell in them!

2 All you servants of the Lord, give praise to the Lord!
with the heavenly hosts, sing his glory and his holiness.
All you faithful, gathered round the altar of the Holy King,
come, worship Christ among us, with all the saints of heaven.

3 We look up to you, Christ, and we implore you,
remember not our sins, in your love, Lord, have mercy!
With the angels we bless you,
with all the saints, we give you glory!

After the Armenian Liturgy, by André Gouzes OP. Translated by Jean Clément

---

500

All that I am, all that I do,
all that I'll ever have, I offer now to you.
Take and sanctify these gifts
for your honour, Lord.
Knowing that I love and serve you
is enough reward.
All that I am, all that I do,
all that I'll ever have I offer now to you.

All that I dream, all that I pray,
all that I'll ever make, I give to you today.
Take and sanctify these gifts
for your honour, Lord.
Knowing that I love and serve you
is enough reward.
All that I am, all that I do,
all that I'll ever have I offer now to you.

Sebastian Temple (1928-97)

601

Praise to the Lord, the Almighty,
the King of creation;
O my soul, praise him,
for he is your health and salvation:
All you who hear, now to his altar draw
near,
join in profound adoration.

Praise to the Lord, let us offer
our gifts at his altar;
let not our sins and transgressions
now cause us to falter.
Christ, the High Priest,
bids us all join in his feast.
Gathered with him at the altar.

3 Praise to the Lord! O let all that
is in us adore him!
All that has life and breath,
come now in praises before him!
Let the Amen sound from
his people again:
now as we worship before him.

Joachim Neander (1650–80), Vv 1,3 tr.
C. Winkworth (1827–78), v.2 unknown

➤ *See also no 706*

602

1 Almighty Father, Lord most high,
who madest all, who fillest all,
thy name we praise and magnify,
for all our needs on thee we call.

2 We offer to thee of thine own,
ourselves and all that we can bring,
in bread and cup before thee shown,
our universal offering.

3 All that we have we bring to thee,
yet all is naught when all is done,
save that in it thy love can see
the sacrifice of thy dear Son.

4 By this command in bread and cup,
his body and his blood we plead;
what on the cross he offer'd up
is here our sacrifice indeed.

5 For all thy gifts of life and grace,
here we thy servants humbly pray
that thou would'st look upon the face
of thine anointed Son today.

V.S.S. Coles (1845–1929)

603

1 Blest are you, Lord, God of all creation,
thanks to your goodness this bread we
offer:
fruit of the earth, work of our hands,
it will become the bread of life.
Blessed be God! Blessed be God!
Blessed be God forever! Amen!
Blessed be God! Blessed be God!
Blessed be God forever! Amen!

2 Blest are you, Lord, God of all creation,
thanks to your goodness this wine we
offer:
fruit of the earth, work of our hands,
it will become the cup of life.
Aniceto Nazareth

604

1 Lord, accept the gifts we offer
at this Eucharistic feast;
bread and wine to be transformed now
through the action of thy priest.
Take us too, Lord, and transform us,
be thy grace in us increased.

2 May our souls be pure and spotless
as the host of wheat so fine;
may all stain of sin be crushed out,
like the grape that forms the wine,
as we, too, become partakers
in this sacrifice divine.

3 Take our gifts, almighty Father,
living God, eternal, true,
which we give through Christ,
our Saviour,
pleading here for us anew.
Grant salvation to all present,
and our faith and love renew.
Sister M. Teresine Fonder (1897-1988)

605

Take our bread, we ask you,
take our hearts, we love you,
take our lives, oh Father,
we are yours, we are yours.

1 Yours as we stand at the table you set,
yours as we eat the bread our hearts can't
forget.
We are the signs of your life with us yet
we are yours, we are yours.

2 Your holy people stand washed in your
blood,
Spirit filled, yet hungry, we await your
food.
Poor though we are, we have brought
ourselves to you:
we are yours, we are yours.
Joe Wise

606

1 Upon thy table, Lord we place
these symbols of our work and thine,
life's food won only by thy grace,
who giv'st to all the bread and wine.

2 Within these simple things there lie
the height and depth of human life,
the thoughts we own, our tears and toil
our hopes and fears, our joy and strife.

3 Accept them, Lord; from thee they com
we take them humbly at thy hand.
These gifts of thine for higher use
we offer, as thou dost command.

4 All life is thine: O give us faith
to know thee in the broken bread,
and drink with thee the wine of life,
Thou Lord supreme of quick and dead

5 To thee we come; refresh thou us
with food from thy most holy board,
until the kingdoms of this world
become the kingdom of the Lord.
M.F.C. Willson (1884–1944)

607

1 Let all mortal flesh keep silence,
and with fear and trembling stand;
ponder nothing earthly minded:
for with blessing in his hand
Christ our God to earth descendeth,
our full homage to demand.

King of kings, yet born of Mary,
as of old on earth he stood
Lord of lords, in human vesture –
in the Body and the Blood:
he will give to all the faithful
his own self for heavenly Food.

Rank on rank the host of heaven
spreads its vanguard on the way,
as the Light of Light descendeth
from the realms of endless day,
that the powers of hell may vanish
as the darkness clears away.

At his feet the six–winged seraph;
cherubim with sleepless eye
veil their faces to the Presence,
as with ceaseless voice they cry,
Alleluia, alleluia,
alleluia, Lord most high!
Liturgy of St. James, tr. G. Moultrie (1829–85)

608

Take my hands and make them as
    your own,
and use them for your kingdom here on
    earth.
Consecrate them to your care,
anoint them for your service where
you may need your gospel to be sown.

Take my hands, they speak now for my
    heart,
and by their actions they will show their love.
Guard them on their daily course,
be their strength and guiding force
to ever serve the Trinity above.

3 Take my hands, I give them to you, Lord.
Prepare them for the service of your name.
Open them to human need
and by their love they'll sow your seed
so all may know the love and hope you gave.
Take my hands, take my hands, O Lord.
Sebastian Temple (1928-1997)

609

1 In bread we bring you, Lord, our bodies'
    labour.
In wine we offer you our spirits' grief.
We do not ask you, Lord, who is my
    neighbour?
But stand united now, one in belief.
Oh, we have gladly heard your Word,
    your holy Word,
and now in answer, Lord, our gifts
    we bring.
Our selfish hearts make true, our failing
    faith renew,
our lives belong to you, our Lord and King.

2 The bread we offer you is blessed and
    broken,
and it becomes for us our spirits' food.
Over the cup we bring your Word is spoken;
make it your gift to us, your healing blood.
Take all that daily toil plants in our
    heart's poor soil
take all we start and spoil, each hopeful
    dream,
the chances we have missed, the graces
    we resist,
Lord, in thy Eucharist, take and redeem.
Kevin Nichols (1929-2006)

Communion Processional Songs

Be - hold the Lamb of God, be - hold the Lamb_ of God. He takes a - way the sin, the sin____ of the world.

s

611a Communion Song 3

Paul Inwood

1. Je - sus Lamb of God and source of life: Je - sus, lov-ing bear-er of our sins:

Refrain

Hear our prayer, have mer - cy; hear our prayer, have mer - cy; give us your peace.

General

2 Jesus, Son of God and Son of Man;
Jesus, true redeemer of the world:

3 Jesus, Christ, our Way, our Truth, our Life:
Jesus Christ, our living Cornerstone:

4 Jesus, Lord of life and Lord of light:
Jesus, here in form of bread and wine:

Advent

5=1

6 Jesus, coming near to bring us joy:
Jesus, Son of God, Emmanuel:

7 Jesus, bringing hope to all who fear:
Jesus, bringing strength to all who mourn:

8 Jesus, Saviour heralded by John:
Jesus, son of David's house and line:

9=4

Christmas

10 Jesus, Lamb of God, the Word made flesh:
Jesus, Son of God come down on earth:

11 Jesus, King of glory, Prince of Peace:
Jesus, shining in our darkened world:

12 Jesus, King of angels, Lord of joy:
Jesus, born to save the world from sin:

13=4

Lent

14 Jesus, source of everlasting life:
Jesus, source of reconciling love:

15 Jesus, by whose suffering we are healed:
Jesus, man of sorrows, friend of grief:

16 Jesus, crucified, transcending time:
Jesus, Saviour, by whose death we live:

Eucharistic (Maundy Thursday, Corpus Christi)

17 Jesus, Lamb of God and bread of life:
Jesus, blood that cleanses us from sin:

18 Jesus, showing how we ought to serve:
Jesus, teaching how we ought to love:

19 Jesus Christ, our true, eternal priest:
Jesus, food and drink that makes us one:

20=4

Easter

21 Jesus, risen Lord, triumphant King:
Jesus, true redeemer of the world:

22 Jesus, Morning Star which never sets:
Jesus, Paschal Lamb and sacrifice:

23 Jesus, bursting from the shattered tomb:
Jesus, mighty Victor over death:

24=4

Pentecost (Spirit, Healing)

25 Jesus, glorious brightness, flame of love:
Jesus, filling hearts and minds with life:

26 Jesus, healing strength, redeeming power:
Jesus, burning out the mark of sin:

27 Jesus, by whose truth we are inspired:
Jesus, present here among us now:

28=4

611b

Communion Song 4

Paul Inwood

1. Je - sus, Faith - ful Lord, have mer - cy on us.
2. Je - sus, Li - ving Light, have mer - cy on us.
3. Je - sus, Lamb of God, have mer - cy on us.

Can: Tea - ching us your way, help - ing us to serve: **All:** Je - sus, Faith - ful
Way and Truth and Life, source of end - less joy: Je - sus, Li - ving
Je - sus, Son of Man, bea - rer of our sins: Je - sus, Lamb of

v.3
Lord, have mer - cy on us.
Light, have mer - cy on us.
God: give us your peace.

Advent

Jesus, Lamb of God, have mercy on us. *(x2)*
Herald of the dawn, Saviour of the world:
Jesus, Lamb of God, have mercy on us.

Jesus, Word of God, have mercy on us. *(x2)*
Jesus, bringing light; Jesus, bringing peace:
Jesus, Word of God, have mercy on us

Jesus, Saving Lord, have mercy on us. *(x2)*
Hear us when we call; set your people free.
Jesus, Saving Lord, give us your peace.

Christmas

Jesus, Lamb of God, have mercy on us. *(x2)*
Jesus, Word made flesh, bearer of our sins,
Jesus, Lamb of God, have mercy on us.

Jesus, Bread of Life, have mercy on us. *(x2)*
Jesus, Morning Star, Jesus, Prince of
peace:
Jesus, Bread of Life, have mercy on us.

Jesus, Lamb of God, have mercy on us. *(x2)*
Jesus, King of kings, Jesus, Lord of all:
Jesus, Lamb of God, give us your peace.

Lent

1 Jesus, Lamb of God, have mercy on us. *(x2)*
Hear your people's prayer; turn us
back to you.
Jesus, Bread of Life, have mercy on us.

2 Jesus, Lamb of God, have mercy on us. *(x2)*
Tenderness and hope, reconciling love:
Jesus, Bread of Life, have mercy on us.

3 Jesus, Blessed Light, have mercy on us. *(x2)*
Jesus, source of joy, help us to repent.
Jesus, Blessed Light, give us your peace.

Eastertide

1 Jesus, Living Bread, have mercy on us. *(x2)*
Source of life and light, feeding all our
need:
Jesus, Living Bread, have mercy on us.

2 Jesus, Living Lord, have mercy on us. *(x2)*
Victor over death, bursting from the tomb:
Jesus, Living Lord, have mercy on us.

3 Jesus, Mighty King, have mercy on us. *(x2)*
Lord of truth and love, shepherd of
your sheep:
Jesus, Mighty King, give us your peace.

612

1 Jesus, Lamb of God, bearer of our sin;
   Jesus, Saviour:

Hear our prayer, hear our prayer; through this Bread and Cup we share, may we be your sign of peace— ev'- ry - where.

2 Jesus, Lamb of God, bearer of our pain;
   Jesus, healer:

3 Jesus, Lamb of God, broken as our bread,
   here among us:

4 Jesus, Lamb of God, poured our as our wine,
   shared in gladness:

5 Jesus, Word of God, dwelling with the poor;
   Jesus, prophet:

6 Jesus, Word of God, dwelling in our midst;
   Jesus with us.

7 Jesus, Word of God, speaking in our hearts,
   God's compassion:

8 Jesus, Word made flesh, touching each
   one's need,
   Jesus, lover:

9 Kneeling by your friends, washing
   each one's feet,
   Jesus, servant:

10 Hope beyond despair, dawn of fragile
   light,
   Jesus, risen:

11 Tomb of secret hope, open to the dawn,
   Jesus, living:
   Bernadette Farrell

613

Ho - ly gifts for ho - ly peo - ple, come, you hun - gry, and be-lieve; Come and take Christ's bo - dy off - ered, come and be what you receive.

1 This is what we have been told:
   that on the night before he died,
   after thanksgiving spoken,
   bread blest and broken,
   Christ sealed his love with his body
   and blood.

2 This is what we understand:
   that when we eat and drink this feast,
   in this bread which we are breaking,
   Christ we are partaking,
   Christ's death proclaiming until his
   return.

3 This is how we are to live:
   that being joined by Christ's gifts,
   we should be Christ to others,
   sisters and brothers,
   holding them precious, as saved by
   his love.

4 Christ, our way, our truth and life:
   we are not worthy to draw near:
   but take our praise and thanksgiving,
   transform our living,
   give us that food which is healing and
   strength.
   Stephen Dean

514

See this bread; take and eat and live in me.

Fine

See this cup; take and drink, re - mem - ber me.

I am the living bread, come down from heaven.
All who eat my flesh and drink my blood
will live, will live for ever.

I am the living bread: you shall not hunger.
If you believe in me you shall not thirst,
but live, but live for ever.

3 I am the living bread risen among you.
If you believe in me, though you die, you will live,
you will live for ever.

4 You are the living bread, life for the world.
O Lord, to whom shall we go?
Your words, they live for ever.

David Haas

515

Hap- py are those who are in - vi - ted to the feast of the

Cantors sing the Beatitudes (Mt 5:3-12)
Music: Russian chant

King- dom of hea- ven.

516

Come, Christ's be - lo - ved, feed___ on Christ's true flesh,___

Drink your re - demp- tion___ in his pre - cious blood.

Here is salvation, here, the risen Lord,
here God's great banquet: let us thank
  our God.

Christ, in this myst'ry gives his flesh
  and blood,
guiding us safely through death's gates
  to life.

Son of the Father, Lord of all the world,
Christ is our Saviour through his Cross
  and blood.

Christ, priest and victim, gave himself
  for all,
at once the giver and his gift divine.

5 Priests of the old law, off'ring blood
    outpoured,
  did but foreshadow Christ, the victim
    priest.

6 Christ, our salvation, Christ the light
    of all,
  has yet enriched us by this gift sublime.

7 Bring to his banquet faithful hearts
    sincere,
  take now the safeguard of eternal life.
  From the Antiphonary of Bangor (7th Cent.)
  tr. based on J.M. Neale (1818-66)
  Music by James Walsh

617

Taste and see, taste and see that the Lord is good, the Lord is good.

1 I will bless the Lord at all times,
his praise always on my lips.
The Lord shall be the glory of my soul;
the humble shall hear and be glad.

2 Glorify the Lord with me,
together let us praise his name.
I sought the Lord: he answered me;
he set me free from all my fear.

3 Look upon the Lord and be radiant,
hide not your face from the Lord.
He heard the cry of the poor;
he rescued them from all their woes.

4 The angel of the Lord is with his people
to rescue those who trust in him.
Taste and see the goodness of the Lord,
seek refuge in him and be glad.

5 Saints of the Lord, revere him;
those who fear him lack nothing.
Lions suffer want and go hungry,
but those who seek him lack no blessing.

6 Children of the Lord, come and hear,
and learn the fear of the Lord.
Who is he who longs for life,
whose only love is for his wealth?

7 Keep evil words from your tongue,
your lips from speaking deceit.
Turn aside from evil and do good;
seek and strive after peace.
Psalm 34, versified by Stephen Dean

618

Taste and see, taste and see the good-ness of the Lord.___ O
taste and see, taste and see the good-ness of the Lord,___ of the Lord

1 I will bless the Lord at all times.
Praise shall always be on my lips.
my soul shall glory in the Lord
for God has been so good to me.

2 Glorify the Lord with me.
Together let us all praise God's name.
I called the Lord who answered me;
from all my troubles I was set free.

3 Worship the Lord, all you people.
You'll want for nothing if you ask.
Taste and see that the Lord is good;
in God we need put all our trust.
Psalm 34, versified by James Moore

Stephen Dean, from Ps 116

How can I re-pay the Lord for all the good-ness he shows to me?

520

Lord, how can I re-pay all you e-ver give to me? Your end-less love an e-ter-nal flame; Lord, if you say the word, I will take your bles-sing cup and I will call on your ho-ly name.

Last time: repeat 'and I will call on your holy name.'

I trusted, went on trusting
through the night of pain;
in my anguish and affliction
human help was vain.

In the service of your people
I will spend my days,
giving freely of my lifeblood
as I walk your ways.

3 You unbound me, gave me freedom:
you I gladly serve.
In thanksgiving I will offer
praise without reserve.

4 In the service of your people
I will spend my days,
in your temple, in your Church, Lord,
singing endless praise.

John Glynn, from Psalm 116

521

We hold the death of the Lord deep in our hearts. Li-ving, now we re-main with Je-sus, the Christ.

Once we were people afraid,
lost in the night.
Then by your cross we were saved;
dead became living, life from your giving.

Something which we have known,
something we've touched,
what we have seen with our eyes:
this we have heard; life–giving Word.

3 He chose to give of himself,
became our bread.
Broken that we might live.
Love beyond love, pain for our pain.

4 We are the presence of God; this is our call.
Now to become bread and wine:
food for the hungry, life for the weary,
for to live with the Lord, we must die
with the Lord. *David Haas*

622

Bread of Life from heaven,
your blood and body given,
we eat this Bread and drink this Cup
until you come again.

1 Break now the bread of Christ's sacrifice;
giving thanks, hungry ones gather round.
Eat all of you, and be satisfied;
in Christ's presence the loaves will abound.

2 Seek not the food that will pass away;
set your hearts on the food that endures.
Come, learn the true and the living way,
that the fullness of life may be yours.

3 Love as the One who, in love for you,
gave himself for the life of the world.
Live in the One who is food for you,
that your hunger and thirst be no more.

4 Take in the light that will never dim,
taste the life that is stronger than death.
Live in the One who will come, and then
raise you up at the last with the blest.

5 Dwell in the One who now dwells in you;
make your home in the lifegiving Word.
Know only Christ, Holy One of God,
and believe in the truth you have heard.

6 Drink of this cup and declare his death;
eat this bread and believe Easter morn.
Trust his return and, with ev'ry breath,
praise the One in whom you are reborn.
Susan Briehl

623

Now in this banquet, Christ is our Bread;
here shall all hungers be fed.
Bread that is broken, wine that is poured,
love is the sign of our Lord.

1 You who have touched us and graced us
with love,
make us your people of goodness and light.

2 Let our hearts burn with the fire of your
love;
open our eyes to the glory of God.

3 God who makes the blind to see,
God who makes the lame to walk,
bring us dancing into day,
lead your people in your way.

4 Hope for the hopeless, light for the blind
'Strong' is your name, Lord, 'Gentle'
and 'Kind'.

5 Call us to be your light,
call us to be your love,
make us your people again.

6 Come, O Spirit! Renew our hearts!
We shall arise to be children of light.
Marty Hauge
Advent refrain no. 82; Lent refrain no. 19

624

In the breaking of the bread
we have known him; we have been fed.
Jesus the stranger, Jesus the Lord,
be our companion; be our hope.

1 Bread for the journey, strength for our
years,
manna of ages of struggle and tears.
cup of salvation, fruit of the land,
bless and receive now the work of our
hands.

2 Bread of the promise, people of hope,
wine of compassion, life for the world
Gathered at table, joined as his body,
sealed in the Spirit, sent by the Word.
Bob Hurd

625

Bread for the world: a world of hunger
wine for all peoples: people who thirst
May we who eat be bread for others.
May we who drink pour out our love.

1 Lord Jesus Christ, you are the
bread of life,
broken to reach and heal the wounds
of human pain.
Where we divide your people you are
waiting there
on bended knee to wash our feet
with endless care.

2 Lord Jesus Christ, you are the wine of
   peace,
   poured into hearts once broken and
   where dryness sleeps.
   Where we are tired and weary you are
   waiting there
   to be the way which beckons us
   beyond despair.

3 Lord Jesus Christ, you call us to your feast,
   at which the rich and pow'rful have
   become the least.
   Where we survive on others in our
   human greed
   you walk among us begging for your
   ev'ry need.

   Bernadette Farrell

526

One bread we break in the love of Christ, one cup we share in the life of Christ;
one faith we hold, one Lord we serve, one Spi-rit ga-thers us here.

Many the grains but one the bread;
many the grapes but one the wine;
many the gifts, but one same Lord;
many the parts, but all are joined
in Jesus Christ, who makes us One.

We who were scattered on the hills;
we who were shaken by the wind;
we who were wandering and lost
we who were separate and alone
in Jesus Christ are all made One.

3 No longer slaves, we are set free;
   no longer lost, we are redeemed;
   no longer servants, we are friends
   no longer we that live our life
   but Jesus Christ, who lives in us.

4 Open our eyes to see your light;
   open our ears to hear your word;
   open our lips to sing your praise;
   open our hearts to find the love
   of Jesus Christ, who makes us One.

   Stephen Dean

527

This is my body, broken for you,
bringing you wholeness, making
   you free.
Take it and eat it, and when you do,
do it in love for me.

This is my blood poured out for you,
bringing forgiveness, making you free.
Take it and drink it, and when you do,
do it in love for me.

3 Back to my Father soon I shall go.
   Do not forget me; then you will see
   I am still with you, and you will know
   you're very close to me.

4 Filled with my Spirit, how you will grow!
   You are my branches; I am the tree.
   If you are faithful, others will know
   you are alive in me.

5 Love one another – I have loved you,
   and I have shown you how to be free;
   serve one another, and when you do,
   do it in love for me.

   Verses 1 and 2 Jimmy Owens;
   verses 3–5 Damian Lundy (1944-97)

628

1 Draw nigh, and take the body of our Lord;
and drink the holy blood for you
  outpoured;
saved by that body, hallowed by that
  blood,
whereby refreshed we render thanks to
  God.

2 Salvation's giver, Christ the only Son,
who by his cross and blood the victory
  won,
gave his own life for greatest and for least;
himself the Victim, and himself the Priest.

3 Victims were offered by the law of old,
that, in a type, celestial mysteries told.
He, ransomer from death and light
  from shade,
bestows his holy grace his saints to aid.

4 Approach ye then with faithful hearts
  sincere,
and take the safeguard of salvation here,
he that in this world rules his saints and
  shields,
to all believers life eternal yields.

5 With heav'nly bread he makes the
  hungry whole
gives living waters to the thirsty soul,
Alpha and Omega, to whom shall bow
all nations at the doom, is with us now.
From the Antiphonary of Bangor (7th C.)
tr. J. M. Neale (1818–66), alt.

629

1 I am the Bread of life.
You who come to me shall not hunger;
and who believe in me shall not thirst.
No–one can come to me
unless the Father draw him.
And I will raise you up,
and I will raise you up,
and I will raise you up on the last day.

2 The bread that I will give
is my flesh for the life of the world,

and if you eat of this bread,
you shall live for ever,
you shall live for ever.

3 Unless you eat of the flesh of the
  Son of Man,
and drink of his blood,
and drink of his blood,
you shall not have life within you.

4 I am the Resurrection, I am the Life.
If you believe in me,
even though you die,
you shall live for ever.

5 Yes, Lord, I believe,
that you are the Christ,
the Son of God,
who have come into the world.
Suzanne Toolan, R.S.M.

630

1 We come as guests invited
when Jesus bids us dine,
his friends on earth united
to share the bread and wine;
the bread of life is broken,
the wine is freely poured
for us, in solemn token
of Christ our dying Lord.

2 We eat and drink, receiving
from Christ the grace we need,
and in our hearts believing
on him by faith we feed;
with wonder and thanksgiving
for love that knows no end,
we find in Jesus living
our ever-present friend.

3 One bread is ours for sharing,
one single fruitful vine,
our fellowship declaring
renewed in bread and wine –
renewed, sustained and given
by token, sign and word,
the pledge and seal of heaven,
the love of Christ our Lord.
Timothy Dudley-Smith

631

Bread of Life, Truth eternal,
broken now to set us free,
the risen Christ, his saving power,
is here in bread and wine for me.

Lord, I know I am not worthy to
  receive you.
You speak the words and I am healed.
Here at your table, love's mystery,
  one bread, one cup, one family.

Lord, by your cross
you reconciled us to the Father,
We have only to believe.
Your sacrifice, our victory;
now by your blood we are redeemed.

Lord, you gave your people manna in
  the desert;
still you fulfil our every need.
Lord when we hunger,
Lord, when we thirst,
we come to you and we receive the...

Joanne Boyce & Mike Stanley (1965-2013)

632

Come to the feast of heaven and earth!
Come to the table of plenty!
God will provide for all that we need,
here at the table of plenty.

1 O come and sit at my table
   where saints and sinners are friends.
   I wait to welcome the lost and lonely
   to share the cup of my love.

2 O come and eat without money;
   come to drink without price.
   My feast of gladness will feed your
    spirit
   with faith and fullness of life.

3 My bread will ever sustain you
   through days of sorrow and woe.
   My wine will flow like a sea of gladness
   to flood the depths of your soul.

4 Your fields will flower in fullness;
   your homes will flourish in peace.
   For I, the giver of home and harvest,
   will send my rain on the soil.

Daniel L. Schutte

633 Eat this bread

Taizé chant by Jacques Berthier (1923-94)

p Eat this bread, drink this cup, come to me and ne-ver be hun-gry.
(or) Je - sus Christ, bread of life, those who come to you will not hun-ger.

Eat this bread, drink this cup, trust in me and you will not thirst.
Je - sus Christ, Ri - sen Lord, those who trust in you will not thirst.

634

Christ, our peace,
you break down the walls that divide us;
Christ, our peace,
come, make us one body in you.

1. Each time we eat this Bread,
   each time we drink this Cup,
   we share Christ's death and rising,
   until the reign of...

2. One is the bread we break,
   one is the cup we drink,
   one is the body gathered
   here at the feast of...

3. All you with hungry hearts,
   who seek God's gracious reign,
   all you who thirst for justice,
   come to the feast of...

4. And all are welcome here;
   here there is food for all,
   blest meal of grace and mercy,
   gathered as one in...

5. As once he broke the bread,
   and opened eyes and hearts,
   may we now see his presence
   as we remember...

6. No longer Jew or Greek,
   no longer slave or free,
   no longer male or female,
   now you are one in...

Marty Haugen

635

Paul Inwood

Je-sus, Lamb of God, Bread of Life for us; Je-sus, Lamb of God
Source of u - ni - ty;
Bread that makes us one;
Food for hearts and minds;
Build-ing up your Church;

Wine of Joy for us; Je - sus, Lamb of God, bear-ing all our sin
Pre - cious cor - ner - stone;
Wine that heals our pain;
Giv - ing strength to all;
Source of light and love;

have mer - cy on us, give us your peace.

After all the words have been sung, the melody may be hummed while a cantor sings verses of Psalm 34.

636

I receive the living God,
and my heart is full of joy.
I receive the living God,
and my heart is full of joy.

1. Jesus says: I am the Bread,
   sent to you from God Most High.
   Take and eat, and you will live;
   you need never fear to die.

2. Jesus says: I am the Vine,
   far from whom no life can grow.
   If you join yourself to me,
   a rich harvest you will know.

Jesus says: I am the Way,
and my path is straight and true.
Follow me to where I lead;
there my Father waits for you.

Jesus says: I am the Truth.
If you follow close to me,
you will know me in your heart,
and my word shall make you free.

Jesus says: I am the Life,
raised in triumph from the dead.
As one Body now remain,
members joined to me, the Head.

Jesus says: I am the Day,
shining brightly through your night.
Welcome me, and you will walk
by the Spirit's guiding light.

Jesus says: I am the Love
which can bind you close to me.
Those who know this gift I bring
will find true community.

Jesus says: I am the Peace
which the world cannot bestow.
Learn to love and live in me,
and in you my Reign will grow.

Jesus says: I am the Lamb,
and my death set sinners free.
Those who drink the cup I drink
must take up this work with me.
Bernard Geoffroy, tr. Ronald F. Krisman
(v4 anonymous.)

~ *original verses: 636a, see after no 1028*

Communion Thanksgiving

637

Seed, scattered and sown,
wheat, gathered and grown,
bread, broken and shared as one,
the Living Bread of God.
Vine, fruit of the land,
wine, work of our hands.
One cup that is shared by all;
the Living Cup, the Living Bread of God.

1 Is not the bread we break
a sharing in our Lord?
Is not the cup we bless
the blood of Christ out–poured?

2 The seed which falls on rock
will wither and will die.
The seed within good ground
will flower and have life.

3 As wheat upon the hills
was gathered and was grown,
so may the church of God
be gathered into one.
Dan Feiten

638

1 The time was early evening,
the place a room upstairs;
the guests were the disciples,
few in number and few in prayers.

Oh the food comes from the baker,
the drink comes from the vine,
the words come from the Saviour,
'I will meet you in bread and wine.

2 The company of Jesus
had met to share a meal,
but he, who made them welcome,
had much more to reveal.

3 'The bread and body broken
the wine and blood outpoured,
the cross and kitchen table
are one by my sign and word'.

4 On both sides of the table,
on both sides of the grave,
the Lord joins those who love him
to serve them and to save.

5 Lord Jesus, now among us,
confirm our faith's intent,
as, with your words and actions,
we unite in this sacrament.
John L. Bell & Graham Maule

639

1. We have gath-ered round your ta - ble, laid with wine and li- ving bread

now we rise to praise the Gi - ver from whose ri - ches we are fed.

2. Who has laid this banquet for us?
Who has brought us to this feast?
Christ, who seeks out all who hunger,
from the greatest to the least.

3. Love's the lesson, Lord, you gave us,
love the teaching we must learn.
Gifts of love you spread before us,
love you ask us in return.

4. Greater love no one can offer,
more than life no-one can give;
In these symbols we remember:
Jesus died that we might live.

5. Rich ones in a world of hunger,
let us go and do the same:
giving up our lives for others,
feeding them in Jesus's name.

Stephen Dean

640

Plen-ty of *bread* at the feast of life, plen-ty of *bread* to shar

plen - ty of *bread* at the feast of life, there is plen-ty of *bread* to share.

Verses (Cantor and All in alternation)   *sing *bread, fish, wine* or *room* according to previous v

1. Bread for ev'-ry hunger:
you have plenty to share.
the bread of joy and gladness:
you have plenty to share.
the bread of grace and mercy:
you have plenty to share,
you have plenty of bread to share.

Refrain

2. Bread for those who sorrow:
the bread of life and laughter:
the bread of strength and justice:

Refrain

3. Bread for ev'ry sister:
and bread for ev'ry brother:
and bread for freedom's journey:

4. Bread of hope and kindness:
and bread of your compassion:
the bread of love and welcome:

5. Fish for those who hunger:
and joy for all who sorrow:
and faith for unbelievers:

6. Wine of our remembrance:
the wine of dreams and visions:
the wine of celebration:

7. Wine of our forgiveness:
the wine of our redemption:
the wine of our tomorrows:

8. Room for those forgotten:
and room for those rejected:
and room for all the outcasts:

9. Room for all the children:
and room for all the elders:
and room for all the lonely:

10. Room for those who suffer:
and room for all the dying:
and room that sings for new life:

Marty Haugen

541

Come now, the table's spread,
in Jesus' name we break the bread,
here shall we all be fed
within the reign of God.

Come take this holy food:
receive the Body and the Blood,
Grace is a mighty flood
within the reign of God.

Refrain

Bles-sed are they who will feast in the Reign of God! Bles-sed are they who will share the bread of life! Bles-sed are they who are least in the Reign of God! They shall re - joice at the feast of life!

Stand up and do not fear,
for Christ is truly present here.
heaven is truly near
within the reign of God.
Now at this wedding feast,
the greatest here shall be the least.
All bonds shall be released
within the reign of God.
Refrain

Welcome the weak and poor,
the sinner finds an open door,
none judged, and none ignored
within the reign of God.
Here shall the weary rest,
the stranger be a welcome guest.
So shall we all be blest *within the reign...*

All fear and hatred ends
and foes become our faithful friends,
just as our God intends *within the reign...*

All you who seek God's face
are welcome in this holy place;
join in the feast of grace:
within the reign...

5 Sing out the jubilee
when those enslaved are all set free,
children of God are we *within the reign...*
No more can we forget
the ones who bear life's crushing debt;
God's justice guides us yet
within the reign...

6 One earth, one holy band,
one fam'ly as our God has planned,
all share the promised land
within the reign...
Come now, the feast is spread;
in Jesus's name we break the bread.
Here shall we all be fed *within the reign...*
Marty Haugen

542

Praise now your God, every tongue,
ev'ry nation,
tell the good news to the next generation:
Christ, the Redeemer, who rose from the
dead,
stays with his people as life–giving Bread.
Alleluia, God is great!
Alleluia, God is good!

2 Christ gave his word at the multiplication.
Bread and sweet wine are now Christ
our oblation.
Cross and Last Supper are with us today.
Life now abounds, and God's will we obey.
Alleluia, God is great!
Alleluia, God is good!

3 Here is your Saviour, give deep adoration,
sing of his glory in glad celebration.
Come, for his manna is food for the road,
strength for the journey, our glory
    foreshowed.
Alleluia, God is great!
Alleluia, God is good!
                              C.J. Marivoet

643

1 Gifts of bread and wine, gifts we've
    offered,
fruits of labour, fruits of love:
taken, offered, sanctified,
blessed and broken; words of one who
    died:
'Take my body; take my saving blood.'
Gifts of bread and wine: Christ our Lord.

2 Christ our Saviour, living presence here,
as he promised while on earth:
'I am with you for all time,
I am with you in this bread and wine.
Take my body, take my saving blood.'
Gifts of bread and wine: Christ our Lord.

3 To the Father, in the Spirit,
one in union with the Son,
for God's people, joined in prayer
faith is strengthened by the food we
    share.
'Take my body, take my saving blood.'
Gifts of bread and wine: Christ our Lord.
                              Christine McCann

644

1 Alleluia, sing to Jesus,
his the sceptre, his the throne,
alleluia, his the triumph,
his the victory alone:
hark! the songs of peaceful Sion
thunder like a mighty flood;
Jesus, out of every nation,
has redeemed us by his blood.

2 Alleluia, not as orphans
are we left in sorrow now;
alleluia, he is near us,
faith believes, nor questions how;
though the cloud from sight received him
when the forty days were o'er,
shall our hearts forget his promise,
'I am with you evermore'?

3 Alleluia, Bread of Angels,
thou on earth our food, our stay;
alleluia, here the sinful
flee to thee from day to day;
intercessor, friend of sinners,
earth's Redeemer, plead for me,
where the songs of all the sinless
sweep across the crystal sea.

4 Alleluia, King eternal
thee the Lord of lords we own;
alleluia, born of Mary,
earth thy footstool, heaven thy throne;
thou within the veil hast entered,
robed in flesh, our great High Priest;
thou on earth both priest and victim
in the Eucharistic Feast.
                              W. Chatterton Dix (1837–98)

645

1 Father, we give you thanks, who planted
your holy name within our hearts.
knowledge and faith and life immortal
Jesus your Son to us imparts.
Lord, you have made all for your pleasure
and giv'n us food for all our days,
giving in Christ the Bread eternal,
yours is the pow'r, be yours the praise

2 Watch o'er your Church, O Lord, in mercy
save it from evil, guard it still,
And in your love unite, perfect it,
cleanse and conform it to your will.
As grain, once scattered on the hillside
was in the broken bread made one,
so from all lands your Church be gathered
into your kingdom by your Son.
                              F. Bland Tucker (1895-1984), alt.

646

Welcome all you noble saints of old,
as now before your very eyes unfold
the wonders all so long ago foretold.
God with us at table is sat down.
God with us at table is sat down.

Elders, martyrs, all are falling down,
prophets, patriarchs are gath'ring round;
what angels longed to see, now we
    have found.

Who is this who spreads the vict'ry feast?
Who is this who makes our warring cease?
Jesus risen, Saviour, Prince of Peace.

Beggars lame, and harlots also here;
repentant publicans are drawing near;
wayward sons come home without a fear.

Worship in the presence of the Lord
with joyful songs, and hearts in one
    accord,
and let our host at table be adored.

When at last this earth shall pass away,
when Jesus and his bride are one to stay,
the feast of love is just begun that day.
    Robert J. Stamps

647

Now let us from this table rise
renewed in body, mind, and soul;
with Christ we die and rise again,
his selfless love has made us whole.

With minds alert, upheld by grace,
to spread the Word in speech and deed,
we follow in the steps of Christ,
at one with us in hope and need.

To fill each human house with love,
it is the sacrament of care;
the work that Christ began to do
we humbly pledge ourselves to share.

Then give us grace, Companion-God,
to choose again the pilgrim way,
and help us to accept with joy
the challenge of tomorrow's day.
    Fred Kaan

648

1 See us, Lord, about thine altar;
  though so many, we are one;
  many souls by love united
  in the heart of Christ thy Son.

2 Hear our prayers, O loving Father,
  hear in them thy Son, our Lord;
  hear him speak our love and worship,
  as we sing with one accord.

3 Once were seen the blood and water;
  now he seems but bread and wine;
  then in human form he suffered,
  now his form is but a sign.

4 Wheat and grape contain the meaning;
  food and drink he is to all;
  one in him, we kneel adoring,
  gathered by his loving call.

5 Hear us yet; so much is needful
  in our frail, disorded life;
  stay with us and tend our weakness
  till that day of no more strife.

6 Members of his mystic body
  now we know our prayer is heard,
  heard by thee, because thy children
  have received th' eternal word.
    John Greally

649

1 Jesu, the joy of loving hearts,
  true source of life, our lives sustain;
  from the best bliss that earth imparts
  we turn unfilled to you again.

2 Your truth unchanged has ever stood,
  you rescue those who on you call:
  to those yet seeking, you are good,
  to those who find you, all in all.

3 We taste of you, the living bread,
  and long to feast upon you still;
  we drink of you, the fountainhead,
  our thirsty souls from you we fill.

4 Our restless spirits long for you,
  whichever way our lot is cast,
  glad when your gracious smile we view,
  blessed when our faith can hold you fast.

5 Jesus, for ever with us stay,
    make all our moments calm and bright;
    chase the dark night of sin away,
    spread through the world your holy light.
       Jesu, dulcedo cordium, 12th century,
       tr. Ray Palmer 1808-87

650

1 My God, and is thy table spread,
    and does thy cup with love o'erflow?
    Thither be all thy children led,
    and let them all thy sweetness know.

2 Hail, sacred feast, which Jesus makes!
    Rich banquet of his flesh and blood!
    Thrice happy those, who here partake
    that sacred stream, that heavenly food.

3 O let thy table honoured be,
    and furnished well with joyful guests;
    and may each soul salvation see,
    that here its sacred pledges tastes.
       Philip Doddridge (1702–51)

Blessing and Dismissal

651

1 Let us go rejoicing,
    rejoicing from the house of God.
    strengthened by this gath'ring
    to live the Gospel call,
    to be a holy people,
    a sacrament to all,
    rejoicing before the living God.

2. Washed in living water,
    we bear the name of Christ the Lord.
    We receive the mission
    to take Christ to the world,

    to be his healing presence,
    to share his saving word:
    rejoicing before the living God.

3. Standing with the outcast,
    the powerless, the refugee,
    with the bruised and broken
    the Church must ever be,
    a sign of hope and justice
    for all the world to see:
    rejoicing before the living God.
       Bob Hurd

652

1 Go, the Mass is ended,
    children of the Lord.
    Take God's Word to others
    as you've heard it spoken to you.
    Go, the Mass is ended,
    go and tell the world
    the Lord is good, the Lord is kind,
    and loves us ev'ry one.

2 Go, the Mass is ended,
    take God's love to all.
    Gladden all who meet you,
    fill their hearts with hope and courage.
    Go, the Mass is ended,
    fill the world with love,
    and give to all what you've received
    – the peace and joy of Christ.

3 Go, the Mass is ended,
    strengthened in the Lord,
    lighten ev'ry burden,
    spread the joy of Christ around you.
    Go, the Mass is ended,
    take God's peace to all.
    This day is yours to change the world
    – to make God known and loved.
       Sister Marie Lydia Pereira

653

May God bless and keep *you*.* May God's face shine on you. May God be kind to you and give you peace.

    * '*Us*' may be substituted.   *Numbers 6:22-23, music by Christopher Walker*

654

Glory to thee, Lord God!
In faith and hope we sing.
Through this completed sacrifice
our love and praise we bring.
We give thee for our sins
a price beyond all worth,
which none could ever fitly pay
but this thy Son on earth.

Here is the Lord of all,
to thee in glory slain;
of worthless givers, worthy gift
a victim without stain.

Through him we give thee thanks,
with him we bend the knee,
in him be all our life, who is
our one true way to thee.

3 So may this sacrifice
we offer here this day,
be joined with our poor lives in all
we think and do and say.
By living true to grace,
for thee and thee alone,
our sorrows, labours, and our joys
will be his very own.
John Greally

➤ *See also Sending out/Discipleship (852-879)*

Eucharistic Adoration

655

O salutaris hostia,
quae caeli pandis ostium,
bella premunt hostilia,
da robur, fer auxilium.

Uni trinoque Domino
sit sempiterna gloria,
qui vitam sine termino
nobis donet in patria. Amen.
St Thomas Aquinas (1227–74)

655a

1 O saving victim, opening wide,
the gate of heav'n to man below,
Our foes press on from ev'ry side:
thine aid supply, thy strength bestow.

2 To thy great name be endless praise,
Immortal Godhead, one in three;
O grant us endless length of days
in our true native land with thee. Amen.
Translation by J.M. Neale (1818–66),
E. Caswall (1814–78), and others

656

Tantum ergo Sacramentum
veneremur cernui:
et antiquum documentum
novo cedat ritui:
praestet fides supplementum
sensuum defectui.

Genitori, genitoque
laus et jubilatio,
salus, honor, virtus quoque
sit et benedictio;
procedenti ab utroque
compar sit laudatio. Amen.
St Thomas Aquinas (1227–74)

657

1 Come, adore this wondrous presence,
bow to Christ, the source of grace.
Here is kept the ancient promise
of God's earthly dwelling–place.
Sight is blind before God's glory,
faith alone may see his face.

2 Glory be to God the Father,
praise to his co–equal Son,
adoration to the Spirit,
bond of love, in Godhead one.
Blest be God by all creation
joyously while ages run.
Translation by James Quinn SJ (1919-2010)

658

1 O food of travellers, angels' bread,
  manna wherewith the blest are fed,
  come nigh, and with thy sweetness fill
  the hungry hearts that seek thee still.

2 O fount of love, O well unpriced,
  outpouring from the heart of Christ,
  give us to drink of very thee,
  and all we pray shall answered be.

3 O Jesus Christ, we pray to thee
  that this thy presence which we see,
  though now in form of bread concealed,
  to us may be in heaven revealed.
      Maintzisch Gesangbuch, 1661,
      tr. Walter H. Shewring and others

659

1 Father and life–giver,
  grace of Christ impart;
  he, the Word incarnate –
  food for mind and heart.
  Children of the promise,
  homage now we pay;
  sacrificial banquet
  cheers the desert way.

2 Wine and bread the symbols –
  love and life convey,
  offered by your people,
  work and joy portray.
  All we own consigning,
  nothing is retained;
  tokens of our service,
  gifts and song contain.

3 Transformation wondrous
  water into wine;
  mingled in the Godhead
  we are made divine.
  Birth into his body
  brought us life anew,
  total consecration –
  fruit from grafting true.

4 Christ, the head and members
  living now as one,
  offered to the Father
  by this holy Son;
  and our adoration
  will be purified,
  by the Holy Spirit breathing
  through our lives.
      A.J. Newman (adapted)

660

1 Godhead here in hiding, whom I do
    adore,
  masked by these bare shadows, shape
    and nothing more,
  see, Lord, at thy service low lies here a
    heart
  lost, all lost in wonder at the God thou ar

2 Seeing, touching, tasting are in thee
    deceived;
  how says trusty hearing? That shall be
    believed;
  what God's Son hath told me, take for
    truth I do;
  truth himself speaks truly, or there's
    nothing true.

3 On the cross thy Godhead made no sig
    to men;
  here thy very manhood steals from
    human ken;
  both are my confession, both are my
    belief;
  and I pray the prayer of the dying thie

4 I am not like Thomas, wounds I cann
    see,
  but can plainly call thee Lord and Goc
    as he;
  this faith each day deeper be my
    holding of,
  daily make me harder hope and dearer
    love.

5 O thou our reminder of Christ crucifie
  living Bread, the life of us for whom h
    died,

lend this life to me then; feed and feast
    my mind,
there be thou the sweetness man was
    meant to find.

Jesu, whom I look at shrouded here
    below,
I beseech thee send me what I long for so,
some day to gaze on thee face to face in
    light
and be blest for ever with thy glory's sight.

*Adoro te devote, ascr. to St. Thomas Aquinas
(1227–74), tr. G.M. Hopkins (1844–89)*

661

O Godhead hid, devoutly I adore thee,
who truly art within the forms before me;
to thee my heart I bow with bended knee,
as failing quite in contemplating thee.

Sight, touch, and taste in thee are each
    deceived,
the ear alone most safely is believed:
I believe all the Son of God has spoken;
than truth's own word there is no truer
    token.

God only on the cross lay hid from view;
but here lies hid at once the manhood too:
and I, in both professing my belief,
make the same prayer as the repentant
    thief.

Thy wounds, as Thomas saw, I do not see;
yet thee confess my Lord and God to be;
make me believe thee ever more and more,
in thee my hope, in thee my love to store.

O thou memorial of our Lord's own
    dying!
O bread that living art and vivifying!
Make ever thou my soul on thee to live:
ever a taste of heavenly sweetness give.

Jesus, whom for the present veiled I see,
what I so thirst for, oh, vouchsafe to me:
that I may see thy countenance unfolding,
and may be blest thy glory in beholding.

*Adoro te devote, ascr. to St. Thomas Aquinas
(1227–74) tr. E.Caswall (1814–78)*

662

1 O bread of heaven, beneath this veil
    thou dost my very God conceal;
    my Jesus, dearest treasure, hail;
    I love thee and adoring kneel;
    each loving soul by thee is fed
    with thine own self in form of bread.

2 O food of life, thou who dost give
    the pledge of immortality;
    I live; no, 'tis not I that live;
    God gives me life, God lives in me:
    he feeds my soul, he guides my ways,
    and every grief with joy repays.

3 O bond of love, that dost unite
    the servant to his living Lord;
    could I dare live, and not requite
    such love - then death were meet reward:
    I cannot live unless to prove
    some love for such unmeasured love.

4 Belovèd Lord in heaven above,
    there, Jesus, thou awaitest me;
    to gaze on thee with changeless love,
    yes, thus I hope, thus shall it be:
    for how can he deny me heaven
    who here on earth himself hath given?

      *St Alphonsus Liguori (1696–1787),
      tr. Edmund Vaughan (1827–1908)*

663

1 Sweet sacrament divine,
    hid in thy earthly home,
    lo! Round thy lowly shrine,
    with suppliant hearts we come;
    Jesus, to thee our voice we raise,
    in songs of love and heartfelt praise,
    sweet sacrament divine.

2 Sweet sacrament of peace,
    dear home of every heart,
    where restless yearnings cease,
    and sorrows all depart,
    there in thine ear all trustfully
    we tell our tale of misery,
    sweet sacrament of peace.

3 Sweet sacrament of rest,
   Ark from the ocean's roar,
   within thy shelter blest
   soon may we reach the shore,
   save us, for still the tempest raves;
   save, lest we sink beneath the waves
   sweet sacrament of rest.

4 Sweet sacrament divine,
   earth's light and jubilee,
   in thy far depths doth shine
   thy Godhead's majesty;
   sweet light, so shine on us, we pray,
   that earthly joys may fade away,
   sweet sacrament divine.
   Francis Stanfield (1835–1914)

664

1 O praise our great and gracious Lord
   and call upon his name;
   to strains of joy tune every chord,
   his mighty acts proclaim;
   tell how he led his chosen race
   to Canaan's promised land;
   tell how his covenant of grace
   unchanged shall ever stand.

2 He gave the shadowing cloud by day,
   the moving fire by night;
   to guide his Israel on their way,
   he made their darkness light;
   and have not we a sure retreat,
   a Saviour ever nigh,
   the same clear light to guide our feet,
   the dayspring from on high?

3 We, too, have manna from above,
   the bread that came from heaven;
   to us the same kind hand of love
   hath living waters given.
   A rock we have, from whence the spring
   in rich abundance flows;
   that rock is Christ, our priest, our king,
   who life and health bestows.

4 O let us prize this blessèd food,
   and trust our heavenly guide;
   so shall we find death's fearful flood
   serene as Jordan's tide,
   and safely reach that happy shore,
   the land of peace and rest,
   where angels worship and adore,
   in God's own presence blest.
   Harriet Auber (1773–1862)

665

1 Shepherd of souls, in love, come feed us
   life–giving bread for hungry hearts!
   To those refreshing waters lead us
   where dwells that grace your peace
      imparts.
   May we, the wayward in your fold,
   by your forgiveness rest consoled.

2 Life–giving vine, come, feed and nourish
   strengthen each branch with life divine
   Ever in you, O may we flourish,
   fruitful the branches of the vine.
   Lord, may our souls be purified
   so that in Christ we may abide.

3 Following you, O Lord, who led them
   multitudes thronged the mountainside
   filled with compassion, Lord, you fed them
   fed them with loaves you multiplied.
   Come, feed us now, O Lord, we pray:
   life–giving bread give us this day.

4 Father, who fed the Hebrew nation,
   giving them manna from the sky,
   give now the bread of our salvation
   that we who eat shall never die.
   We are your people, God, in need;
   may we on living bread now feed.

5 Help us, dear Lord, prepare a dwelling
   worthy of you who made us all;
   cleanse then our hearts, our guilt dispelling
   purify us who heed your call.
   'Take this and eat' were words you said
   so do we gather for this bread.
   Omer Westendorf (1916-1997)

566

A - ve ve-rum cor-pus na-tum de Ma - ri - a Vir - gi - ne:___
Je - sus' Bo- dy, here we greet you, vir-gin-born of Da - vid's line,___

Ve - re pas-sum im-mo-la-tum in cru - ce pro ho - mi - ne:___
pas - chal vic-tim, giv'n to save us un - der forms of bread__ and wine,___

Cu-jus la-tus per-fo-ra - tum flu-xit___ a - qua__ et__ san-gui-
bo - dy bro-ken, life-blood flo - wing, wa-ter___ strea-ming from__ woun-ded

ne:___ Es-to no-bis prae-gus-ta - tum mor-tis___ in - e -
side:___ ri - sen bo-dy, when we jour - ney home from___ ex - ile,___

xa - mi - ne.___ O___ Je - su dul - cis! O___ Je - su
be our guide! Way___ of truth, lead___ us! Bread of life,

pi - e! O___ Je - su fi - li__ Ma - ri - ae.___
feed__ us! Ma - ry's Son, show us__ your mer - cy!___

Latin, 14th C., tr. James Quinn SJ (1919-2010). Music: plainchant

567 **Adoramus te, Domine/We adore you, Lord, Jesus**

(hum)___ A - do - ra - mus te, Do - mi - ne.
We a - dore you, Lord Je - sus Christ.

With the angels and archangels:

With the patriarchs and prophets:

With the Virgin Mary, mother of God:

With the Apostles and evangelists:

5 With all the martyrs of Christ:

6 With all who witness to the Gospel of the Lord:

7 With all your people of the Church throughout the world:

Taizé chant by Jacques Berthier (1923-94(

See also Communion (613-651), Praise, Church

Morning

668

1. From the night of a-ges wa-king morning comes to heart and min[d]
2. Christ in light im-mortal dwel-ling, Word by whom the worlds were ma[de]

day of grace in splen-dour brea - king, mists and sha-dows fall be-hind;
Light of lights, our dark dis - pel - ling, Lord of lords in light ar-rayed;

in the bright-ness of his glo - ry Christ the Light of life has shined.
in the bright-ness of his glo - ry see the Fa-ther's love dis-played.

3 Risen Lord in radiance splendid,
  Christ has conquered Satan's sway;
  sin and shame and sorrow ended,
  powers of darkness flee away;
    in the brightness of his glory
  walk as children of the day.

4 Light to lighten every nation,
  shining forth from shore to shore,
  Christ who won the world's salvation
  now let all the earth adore;
    in the brightness of his glory
  Light of life for evermore.

Timothy Dudley-Smith. Music by James Walsh

669

1. Lord, as the day be-gins lift up our hearts in praise;
2. Christ be in work and skill, ser-ving each o - ther's need;

take from us all our sins, guard us in all our ways: our ev - ery
Christ be in thought and will, Christ be in word and deed; our minds be

step di - rect and guide that Christ in all be glo - ri - fied!
set on things a - bove in joy and peace, in faith_ and love.

3 Grant us the Spirit's strength,
  teach us to walk his way;
  so bring us all at length
  safe to the close of day:
  from hour to hour sustain and bless
  and let our song be thankfulness.

4 Now as the day begins
  make it the best of days;
  take from us all our sins,
  guard us in all our ways;
  our every step direct and guide
  that Christ in all be glorified!

Timothy Dudley-Smith. Music by Stephen Dea[n]

70

Christ, whose glory fills the skies,
Christ, the true, the only Light,
Sun of Righteousness, arise,
triumph o'er the shades of night;
Day-spring from on high, be near;
day-star, in my heart appear.

Dark and cheerless is the morn
unaccompanied by thee;
joyless is the day's return
till thy mercy's beams I see,
till they inward light impart,
glad my eyes, and warm my heart.

Visit then this soul of mine;
pierce the gloom of sin and grief;
fill me, radiancy divine;
scatter all my unbelief;
more and more thyself display,
shining to the perfect day.
Charles Wesley (1707-88)

71

Morning has broken like the first morning,
blackbird has spoken like the first bird.
Praise for the singing! Praise for the
        morning!
Praise for them, springing fresh from the
        Word!

Sweet the rain's new fall sunlit from heaven,
like the first dewfall on the first grass.
Praise for the sweetness of the wet garden,
sprung in completeness where his feet pass.

3 Mine is the sunlight! Mine is the morning
    born of the one light Eden saw play!
    Praise with elation, praise ev'ry morning,
    God's re–creation of the new day!
        Eleanor Farjeon (1881–1965)

672

1 Lord, when I wake I turn to you,
    yourself my day's first thought and
        prayer:
    your strength to help, your peace to bless,
    your will to guide me everywhere!

2 I live with many in our world -
    their worldly eyes too blind to see -
    who never think what is your will,
    or why you brought this world to be!

3 Your thought for me, your loving care,
    those favours I could never earn,
    call for my thanks in praise and prayer,
    call me to love you in return!

4 There is no blessing Lord, from you
    for those who make their will their way;
    no praise for those who do not praise,
    no peace for those who do not pray!

5 Make then my life a life of love,
    keep me from sin in all I do.
    your way to be my only way,
    your will my will for love of you!
        Brian Foley, from Psalm 5

73

This day God gives me
    strength of high heaven,
sun and moon shining, flame in my hearth,
flashing of lightning, wind in its swiftness,
deeps of the ocean, firmness of earth.

This day God sends me
    strength as my steersman,
might to uphold me, wisdom as guide.
Your eyes are watchful,
    your ears are listening,
your lips are speaking, friend at my side.

3 God's way is my way,
    God's shield is round me,
    God's host defends me, saving from ill.
    Angels of heaven, drive from me always
    all that would harm me, stand by me still.

4 Rising, I thank you, mighty and
        strong One,
    King of creation, giver of rest,
    firmly confessing Threeness of Persons,
    Oneness of Godhead, Trinity blest.
        Adapted from St Patrick's Breastplate,
        by James Quinn SJ (1919-2010)

1. This day God gives me strength of high hea - ven,
sun and moon shi - ning, flame in my hearth, flash-ing of light - ning
wind in its swift - ness, deeps of the o - cean, firm - ness of earth.

Melody by David Ha

Evening

674

1. Now the eve-ning gives way to dark-ness, now the stars of the night ap-pear

shed your light and your peace a - round us; be a - mong us who ga-ther here.

2 For the brightness of passing daylight,
for the fruits of the earth this day,
it is good that we make thanksgiving,
that we praise you in every way.

3 Work is over, the day completed,
in the silence, your word is near;
be the future of all who seek you,
be a stronghold in every fear.

4 As we rest safe within your keeping,
earth is wrapped in the robe of night;
but when daybreak sends out its greeting
we rejoice in the newborn light.

5 Be among us, our promised Daystar,
give your hope to the poor who cry;
be our strength in this world of weakness,
be the light which shall never die.

Tony Barr

675

1. Now it is eve - ning: lights of the ci - ty bid us re
2. Now it is eve - ning: lit - tle ones slee - ping bid us re

mem - ber Christ is our Light. Ma - ny are lone-ly, who will be
mem - ber Christ is our Peace. Some are ne - glected, who will be

neigh-bour? Where there is ca - ring Christ is our Light.
neigh-bour? Where there is ca - ring Christ is our Peace.

Now it is evening:
food on the table
bids us remember
Christ is our Life.
Many are hungry,
who will be neighbour?
Where there is sharing
Christ is our Life.

4 Now it is evening:
here in our meeting
may we remember
Christ is our Friend.
Some may be strangers,
who will be neighbour?
Where there's a welcome
Christ is our Friend.

F. Pratt Green (1903-2000)

576

1. Now the day has drawn to en - ding, and we look u - pon the night;

hear, O God, our glad thanks - gi - ving for the bles-sings— of the light.
(4. friend and com-for-ter)

In the darkness that surrounds us,*
give us calm and quiet sleep,
Guard us safe from every danger,
loving shepherd of the sheep.

3 Every day brings joy and sorrow,
times to dance and times to mourn,
May we rise refreshed tomorrow
fit to work for your kingdom's dawn.

4 Loving Father and Creator,
Jesus Christ, who walked our way;
Holy Spirit, friend and comforter,
be with us till the break of day.

Stephen Dean

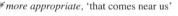 *more appropriate,* 'that comes near us'

577

1. O glad-some light, O grace of God the Fa - ther's face,

the e - ter - nal splen-dour wea - ring; ce - les - tial, ho - ly, blest,

Our Sa - viour, Je - sus Christ, joy - ful in your ap - pear - ing.

As fades the day's last light
we see the lamps of night,
our common hymn outpouring,
O God of might unknown,
you, the incarnate Son,
and Spirit blest adoring.

3 To you of right belongs
all praise of holy songs,
O Son of God, lifegiver;
You, therefore, O Most High,
the world does glorify
and shall exalt for ever.

See also nos. 14, 15

Greek, before 4th Century, tr. Robert Bridges (1844-1930)

678

1 Day is done, but Love unfailing
   dwells ever here;
shadows fall, but hope, prevailing,
   calms every fear.
Loving Father, none forsaking,
take our hearts, of Love's own making,
watch our sleeping, guard our waking,
   be always near!

2 Dark descends, but Light unending
   shines through our night;
you are with us, ever lending
   new strength to sight;
one in love, your truth confessing,
one in hope of heaven's blessing,
may we see, in love's possessing,
   love's endless light!

3 Eyes will close, but you, unsleeping,
   watch by our side;
death may come: in love's safe keeping
   still we abide.
God of love, all evil quelling,
sin forgiving, fear dispelling,
stay with us, our hearts indwelling,
   this eventide!
James Quinn SJ (1919-2010)

679

1 The day thou gavest, Lord, is ended:
the darkness falls at thy behest;
to thee our morning hymns ascended;
thy praise shall sanctify our rest.

2 We thank thee that thy Church
   unsleeping,
while earth rolls onward into light,
through all the world her watch is
   keeping,
and rests not now by day or night.

3 As o'er each continent and island
the dawn leads on another day,
the voice of prayer is never silent,
nor dies the strain of praise away.

4 The sun that bids us rest is waking
our brethren 'neath the western sky
and hour by hour fresh lips are making
thy wondrous doings heard on high.

5 So be it, Lord; thy throne shall never,
like earth's proud empire, pass away;
thy kingdom stands, and grows for ever,
till all thy creatures own thy sway.
John Ellerton (1826–93)

680

1 Sweet Saviour, bless us ere we go,
thy word into our minds instil;
and make our lukewarm hearts to glow
with lowly love and fervent will.
   *Through life's long day
   and death's dark night,
   O gentle Jesus, be our light.*

2 The day is done; its hours have run,
and thou hast taken count of all,
the scanty triumphs grace has won,
the broken vow, the frequent fall.

3 Grant us, dear Lord, from evil ways,
true absolution and release;
and bless us more than in past days
with purity and inward peace.

4 Do more than pardon; give us joy,
sweet fear and sober liberty,
and loving hearts without alloy,
that only long to be like thee.

5 Labour is sweet, for thou hast toiled,
and care is light, for thou hast cared;
let not our works with self be soiled,
nor in unsimple ways ensnared.

6 For all we love – the poor, the sad,
the sinful – unto thee we call;
oh let thy mercy make us glad,
thou art our Jesus and our all.
F.W. Faber (1814–63)

81

1. As the set-ting sun sinks in-to the West, and its
2. On our lips the song all Cre-a-tion sings as it
3. So ac-ross the earth, and in ev-'ry age, count-less

gol-den flame fades a-way: we raise our hearts in thank-ful praise as
yearns to grow in-to birth, to Christ, the First Born in-to life, who
hearts and voi-ces u-nite to sing your praise, O Son of God, for

ev'-ning fol-lows day. When the dy-ing light yields be-
shat-ter'd death's long curse; Christ who trod our path, Christ who
peace and joy and light, till the praise of God through cre-

fore the night and our world is lost in deep shade, then
shared our pain, once in si-lent dark-ness en-tombed: whose
a-tion rings, till the dawn of Life's glo-rious day, when

hear the prayer, O Sa-ving God, of those your hand has made.
ri-sing fills the world with light, and scat-ters sin's dread gloom.
all will be re-newed in light in Love's e-ter-nal Reign.

After v.2,

O Ra-diant light! O Joy-ful light! Our Sa-viour Je-sus Christ! The

glo-rious shi-ning of our God, ar-ise u-pon our night!

To verse 3

Peter McGrail

82

Round me falls the night,
Saviour be my light;
through the hours in darkness shrouded
let me see thy face unclouded.
Let thy glory shine
in this heart of mine.

Earthly work is done,
earthly sounds are none;
rest in sleep and silence seeking,
let me hear thee softly speaking;

in my spirit's ear
whisper: 'I am near'.

3 Blessed heav'nly light
shining through earth's night;
voice that oft of love has told me,
arms, so strong, to clasp and hold me;
thou thy watch wilt keep,
Saviour, o'er my sleep.
William Romanis (1824-99)

God the Creator

683

1 O worship the King
    all glorious above;
O gratefully sing
    his power and his love:
our shield and defender,
    the ancient of days,
pavilioned in splendour,
    and girded with praise.

2 O tell of his might,
    O sing of his grace,
whose robe is the light,
    whose canopy space.
His chariots of wrath
    the deep thunderclouds form,
and dark is his path
    on the wings of the storm.

3 This earth, with its store
    of wonders untold,
almighty, thy power
    hath founded of old;
hath 'stablished it fast
    by a changeless decree;
and round it hath cast,
    like a mantle, the sea.

4 Thy bountiful care
    what tongue can recite?
It breathes in the air,
    it shines in the light;
it streams from the hills,
    it descends to the plain,
and sweetly distils
    in the dew and the rain.

5 Frail children of dust,
    and feeble as frail,
in thee do we trust,
    nor find thee to fail;
thy mercies how tender!
    How firm to the end!
Our maker, defender,
    redeemer, and friend.

6 O measureless might,
    ineffable love,
while angels delight
    to hymn thee above,
thy humbler creation,
    though feeble their lays,
with true adoration
    shall sing to thy praise.
Robert Grant (1779–1838)

684

1 I sing the almighty power of God
that made the mountains rise,
that spread the flowing seas abroad
and built the lofty skies.
I sing the wisdom that ordained
the sun to rule the day;
the moon shines full at God's command
and all the stars obey.

2 I sing the goodness of the Lord
that filled the earth with food;
that formed the creatures with a word
and then pronounced them good.
Lord, how your wonders are displayed
where-e'er I turn my eye;
if I survey the ground I tread,
or gaze upon the sky!

3 There's not a plant or flower below
but makes your glories known;
and clouds arise, and tempests blow,
by order from your throne;
while all that borrows life from you
is ever in your care,
and everywhere that I may be,
O God, be present there.
Isaac Watts (1674-1748), alt.

685

All things bright and beautiful,
all creatures great and small,
all things wise and wonderful,
the Lord God made them all.

1 Each little flower that opens,
each little bird that sings,
he made their glowing colours,
he made their tiny wings.

The purple–headed mountain,
the river running by,
the sunset and the morning,
that brightens up the sky.

The cold wind in the winter,
the pleasant summer sun,
the ripe fruits in the garden,
he made them every one.

The tall trees in the greenwood,
the meadows for our play,
the rushes by the water,
to gather every day.

He gave us eyes to see them,
and lips that we may tell
how great is God Almighty,
who has made all things well.

Cecil Frances Alexander (1818–95)

86

God, beyond our dreams,
you have stirred in us a mem'ry;
you have placed your pow'rful spirit
in the hearts of humankind.
All around us we have known you,
all creation lives to hold you.
In our living and our dying
we are bringing you to birth.

God, beyond all names,
you have made us in your image;
we are like you, we reflect you;
we are woman, we are man.

God, beyond all words,
all creation tells your story;
you have shaken with our laughter,
you have trembled with our tears.

God, beyond all time,
you are labouring within us;
we are moving, we are changing
in your spirit ever new.

God of tender care,
you have cradled us in goodness,
you have mothered us in wholeness,
you have loved us into birth.

Bernadette Farrell

687

1 God in his love for us lent us this
   planet,
   gave it a purpose in time and in space:
   small as a spark from the fire of creation,
   cradle of life and the home of our race.

2 Thanks be to God for its bounty
   and beauty,
   life that sustains us in body and mind:
   plenty for all, if we learn how to share it,
   riches undreamed of to fathom and find.

3 Long have our human wars ruined its
   harvest,
   long has earth bowed to the terror of
   force;
   long have we wasted what others have
   need of,
   poisoned the fountain of life at its source.

4 Earth is the Lord's, it is ours to enjoy it;
   ours, as his stewards, to farm and defend.
   From its pollution, misuse and
   destruction,
   Good Lord, deliver us, world without end!

F. Pratt Green (1903-2000)

688

1 We cannot own the sunlit sky,
   The moon, the wildflow'rs growing,
   For we are part of all that is
   Within life's river flowing.
   With open hands receive and share
   The gifts of God's creation,
   That all may have abundant life
   In ev'ry earthly nation.

2 When bodies shiver in the night
   and weary, wait for morning,
   when children have no bread but tears,
   and warhorns sound their warning,
   God calls humanity to wake,
   to join in common labour,
   that all may have abundant life
   in oneness with their neighbour.

3 God calls humanity to join
    as partners in creating
    a future free from want or fear,
    life's goodness celebrating,

that new world beckons from afar,
invites our shared endeavour,
that all may have abundant life
and peace endure forever.

Ruth Duck

Praise of the creator

689

Bénissez le Seigneur/Let us sing to the Lo...

(Cantor)

Let us sing to the Lord! *(Cantor)*
Bé-nis - sez le Seig-neur!

Let us sing to the Lord!
Bé-nis - sez le Seig-neur! *(Cantor)*

Let us sing to the Lord, let us sing to the Lord!
Bé-nis - sez le Seig-neur, bé-nis - sez le Seig-neur!

Taizé chant b...
Jacques Berthi...
(1923-9...

1 All creation bless the Lord;
    let us sing to the Lord!
    and you, angels of the Lord,
    let us sing to the Lord!
    praise and glorify the Lord.
    let us sing to the Lord,
    let us sing to the Lord!

2 Sun and moon, bless the Lord;
    and you, night and day, bless the Lord;
    and you, light and darkness, bless the Lord.

3 All you heavens, bless the Lord,
    spirits and souls of the just,
    saints and the humble of heart.

4 Praised be Christ, he is our hope.
    He is the joy of our hearts.
    Compassionate and gracious is our God

5 Christ is always with us,
    and loves us before we love him.
    God's love will never pass away.

690

1 Heaven is singing for joy, Alleluia!
    For in your life and mine is shining
    the glory of God.
    Alleluia, alleluia; alleluia, alleluia!

2 Heaven is singing for joy, Alleluia!
    For your life and mine are one

in the love of God.
Alleluia, alleluia; alleluia, alleluia!

3 Heaven is singing for joy, Alleluia!
    For your life and mine will always
    proclaim the Lord.
    Alleluia, alleluia; alleluia, alleluia!

Pablo So...

691 **Jubilate, servite** *canon*   *Taizé chant by Jacques Berthier (1923-9...*

Ju- bi-la-te De-o, om-nis ter - ra, Ser-vi- te Do-mi-no in lae-ti-ti - a.

Al-le-lu-ia, al-le-lu-ia, in lae-ti- ti - a! Al-le- lu-ia, al-le-lu-ia, in lae-ti-ti - a!

Cry out with joy to the Lord, all the earth; serve the Lord with gladness. Ps 100:1.

92 Refrain

Paul Inwood, from Isaiah 12:1-6

We shall draw wa-ter joy - ful - ly, sing-ing joy-ful-ly, singing joy-ful - ly:

we shall draw wa - ter joy - ful - ly from the well-springs of sal - va - tion.

Truly God is our salvation;
we trust, we shall not fear.
For the Lord is our strength,
the Lord is our song;
he became our saviour.

Give thanks, O give thanks to the Lord;
give praise to his holy name!
Make his mighty deeds known
to all of the nations,
proclaim his greatness.

3 Sing a psalm, sing a psalm to the Lord
for he has done glorious deeds.
Make known his works to all of the
earth;
people of Zion, sing for joy,
for great in your midst, great in
your midst
is the Holy One of Israel.

93

Refrain

The heav-ens are tell-ing the glo-ry of God, and all cre-
a-tion is shou-ting for joy. Come, dance in the for-est, come, play in the
field, and sing, sing to the glo-ry of the Lord.

Praise for the sun, the bringer of day,
he carries the light of the Lord in his
rays;
the moon and the stars who light up the
way
unto your throne.

Praise for the wind that blows through
the trees,
the sea's mighty storms, the gentlest
breeze;
they blow where they will, they blow
where they please
to please the Lord.

3 Praise for the rain that waters our fields,
and blesses our crops so all the earth yields;
from death unto life her myst'ry revealed
springs forth in joy.

4 Praise for the fire who gives us his light,
the warmth of the sun to brighten our night;
he dances with joy, his spirit so bright,
he sings of you.

5 Praise for the earth who makes life to grow,
the creatures you made to let your life
show;
the flowers and the trees that help us to know
the heart of love.

6 Praise for our death that makes our life real,
the knowledge of loss that helps us to feel;
the gift of yourself, your presence revealed
to lead us home.

Marty Haugen

694

1 All creatures of our God and King,
lift up your voice and with us sing
   alleluia, alleluia!
Thou burning sun with golden beam,
thou silver moon with softer gleam:
O praise him, O praise him,
alleluia, alleluia, alleluia.

2 Thou rushing wind that art so strong,
ye clouds that sail in heaven along,
   O praise him, alleluia!
Thou rising morn, in praise rejoice,
ye lights of evening, find a voice:

3 Thou flowing water, pure and clear,
make music for thy Lord to hear,
   alleluia, alleluia!
Thou fire so masterful and bright,
that givest us both warmth and light:

4 Dear mother earth, who day by day
unfoldest blessings on our way,
   O praise him, alleluia!
The flowers and fruits that in thee grow
let them his glory also show.

5 And all who are of tender heart,
forgiving others, take your part,
   O sing ye, alleluia!
Ye who long pain and sorrow bear,
praise God and on him cast your care.

6 And thou, most kind and gentle death
waiting to hush our latest breath,
   O praise him, alleluia!
Thou leadest home the child of God,
and Christ our Lord the way hath trod

7 Let all things their Creator bless,
and worship him in humbleness,
   O praise him, alleluia!
Praise, praise the Father, praise the So
and praise the Spirit, Three in One.

W. H. Draper (1855–1933), based on C
tico di Frate Sole (St. Francis of Assisi)

695

Glory and praise to our God,
who alone gives light to our days.
Many are the blessings he bears
to those who trust in his ways.

1 We, the daughters and sons of God
who built the valleys and plains,
praise the wonders our God has done
in ev'ry heart that sings.

2 In his wisdom he strengthens us,
like gold that's tested in fire,
though the power of sin prevails,
our God is there to save.

3 Ev'ry moment of ev'ry day
our God is waiting to save,
always ready to seek the lost,
to answer those who pray.

4 God has watered our barren land
and spent his merciful rain.
Now the rivers of life run full
for anyone to drink.

Daniel L. Schutte, from Pss. 65, 66

696

Refrain

Deep down I know, I must thank God, Oh—
deep down I know, I must thank God!

Sung twice.

Lost in the night, I feel the hand of God;
deep in my soul, I know God is near!
When I awake to greet the sweet morning.
I see the holy light shine before me!
Deep down I know, I must thank God,
Oh, deep down I know, I must thank God.

My heart is glad, leaping for happiness;
my God will walk with me, and I'll
  never die,

for God will destroy the demons that
  haunt me;
forgiving with mercy: giving me peace!

3   Stand up my friends, and feel the power
  of God
stirring within you; answer the call!
Look all around you, and you'll see the
  face of God!
Bound to each other, we will be free!

David Haas

97

Sing a new song unto the Lord;
let your song be sung from mountains
  high.
Sing a new song unto the Lord,
singing alleluia.

Shout with gladness! Dance for joy.
O, come before the Lord!
And play for him on glad tambourines,
and let your trumpet sound.

2   Rise, O children, from your sleep;
your Saviour now has come.
He has turned your sorrow to joy,
and filled your soul with song.

3   Glad my soul for I have seen
the glory of the Lord.
The trumpet sounds; the dead shall be
  raised.
I know my Saviour lives.

Daniel L. Schutte, from Psalm 98

98

Laudate Dominum

Lau- da - te   Do-mi-num,   lau - da - te   Do-mi-num,   om-nes

gen - tes   al - le - lu - ia.   al - le - lu - ia.

Praise the Lord, all you nations. Ps 117:1
Praise the Lord, all you nations,
praise God all you peoples. Alleluia!

Taizé chant by Jacques Berthier (1923-94)
2   Strong is God's love and mercy,
always faithful for ever. Alleluia! *(Ps. 117)*

99

Psalm 117, arr. Paul Inwood

Last time: sing refrain twice

Refrain   1   2

Ho-ly is God,   Ho-ly and strong! God e- ver - li-ving,   al- le-lu - ia.

Verses overleaf

Verses

1. Sing the Lord's praise, ev'-ry na-tion,___ give him all
2. Praise to the Fa-ther al-migh-ty;___ praise to his

ho-nour and glo-ry,___ strong is his love for his peo-ple,
Son, Christ the Lord;___ praise to the life-gi-ving Spi-rit;

_D.

___ his faith-ful-ness___ is e - ter-nal.___
___ both now and for ev - er, A - men.___

700

1 Come, praise the Lord, the almighty,
the King of all nations!
Tell forth his fame, O ye peoples,
with loud acclamations!
His love is sure;
faithful his word shall endure,
steadfast through all generations!

2 Praise to the Father most gracious,
the Lord of creation!
Praise to his Son, the Redeemer
who wrought our salvation!
O heav'nly Dove,
praise to thee, fruit of their love.
Giver of all consolation!

James Quinn SJ (1919-2010), from Ps 1.

701

Con-fi-te-mi-ni Domi-no quo - ni - am bo-nus.

Con - fi-te-mi-ni Do-mi-no, Al-le-lu - ia!

Give thanks to the Lord, who is good, alleluia (Ps 118:1) Taizé chant by Jacques Berthier (1923-9

702

1 God, my King, your might confessing,
ever will I bless your Name;
day by day your throne addressing,
still will I thy praise proclaim.

2 Highest praise to God is fitting;
who his majesty can reach?
Age to age his works transmitting,
age to age his power shall teach.

They shall talk of all your glory,
on your might and greatness dwell,
speak of your dread acts the story,
and your deeds of wonder tell.

Nor shall fail from mem'ry's treasure
works by love and mercy wrought,
works of love surpassing measure,
works of mercy passing thought.

Full of kindness and compassion,
slow to anger, vast in love,
God is good to all creation;
all his works his goodness prove.

All your works, O Lord, shall bless you;
you alone your saints adore:
King supreme shall they confess you,
and proclaim your sovereign power.

R. Mant (1776-1848), from Psalm 145

03

Fill your hearts with joy and gladness,
sing and praise your God and mine!
Great the Lord in love and wisdom,
might and majesty divine!
He who framed the starry heavens
knows and names them as they shine.

Praise the Lord, his people, praise him!
wounded souls his comfort know;
those who fear him find his mercies,
peace for pain and joy for woe;
humble hearts are high exalted,
human pride and power laid low.

Praise the Lord for times and seasons,
cloud and sunshine, wind and rain;
spring to melt the snows of winter
till the waters flow again;
grass upon the mountain pastures,
golden valleys thick with grain.

Fill your hearts with joy and gladness,
peace and plenty crown your days;
love his laws, declare his judgements,
walk in all his words and ways;
he the Lord and we his children -
praise the Lord, all people, praise!

Timothy Dudley-Smith, from Psalm 147

704

1 Praise the Lord! Ye heavens, adore him;
praise him, angels, in the height;
sun and moon, rejoice before him,
praise him, all ye stars and light.
Praise the Lord! For he hath spoken;
worlds his mighty voice obeyed:
laws, which never shall be broken,
for their guidance he hath made.

2 Praise the Lord! For he is glorious;
never shall his promise fail:
God hath made his saints victorious;
sin and death shall not prevail.
Praise the God of our salvation;
hosts on high, his power proclaim;
heaven and earth and all creation,
laud and magnify his name!

3 Worship, honour, glory, blessing,
Lord, we offer to thy name;
young and old, thy praise expressing,
join their Saviour to proclaim.
As the saints in heaven adore thee,
we would bow before thy throne;
as thine angels serve before thee,
so on earth thy will be done.

*Vv. 1-2 from Ps 148, The Foundling Hospital
Collection (1796); v. 3 E. Osler (1798–1863)*

705

1 Bring to the Lord a glad new song,
children of grace extol your king:
your love and praise to God belong -
to instruments of music, sing!
Let those be warned
    who spurn God's name,
let rulers all obey God's word,
for justice shall bring tyrants shame -
let every creature praise the Lord!

2 Sing praise within these hallowed walls,
worship beneath the dome of heaven;
by cymbals' sounds and trumpets' calls
let praises fit for God be given:
with strings and brass and wind rejoice-
then, join our song in full accord
all living things with breath and voice;
let every creature praise the Lord!

Michael Perry (1942-96) from Pss 149/150

706

1 Praise to the Lord, the Almighty,
   the King of creation!
O my soul, praise him, for he is your
   health and salvation.
All you who hear, now to his temple
   draw near,
join in profound adoration.

2 Praise to the Lord, above all things
   so mightily reigning.
Keeping us safe at his side, and so
   gently sustaining.
Have you not seen
   all you have needed has been
met by his gracious ordaining?

3 Praise to the Lord, who will
   prosper our work and defend us;
surely his goodness and mercy
   here daily attend us;
ponder anew what the Almighty can do,
who with his love will befriend us.

4 Praise to the Lord, O let all that
   is in us adore him!
All that has life and breath,
   come now in praises before him.
Let the Amen sound from
   his people again,
now as we worship before him.

Joachim Neander (1650–80),
tr. C. Winkworth (1827–78), alt.

➤ *See also no 601*

707

1 Let us, with a gladsome mind,
praise the Lord, for he is kind:
For his mercies aye endure,
ever faithful, ever sure.

2 Let us blaze his name abroad,
for of gods he is the God;

3 He, with all–commanding might,
filled the new–made world with light;

4 He the golden–tressèd sun
caused all day his course to run:

5 And the hornèd moon at night,
'mid her spangled sisters bright:

6 All things living he doth feed,
his full hand supplies their need:

7 Let us, with a gladsome mind,
praise the Lord, for he is kind.

John Milton (1608–75), from Ps 136

708

1 Holy God, we praise thy name;
Lord of all, we bow before thee!
All on earth thy sceptre own,
all in heaven above adore thee.
Infinite thy vast domain,
everlasting is thy reign.

2 Hark! The loud celestial hymn,
angel choirs above are raising;
cherubim and seraphim,
in unceasing chorus praising,
fill the heavens with sweet accord,
holy, holy, holy Lord.

3 All the apostles join the strain
as thy sacred Name they hallow;
prophets swell the loud refrain,
and the white-robed martyrs follow;
and from morn to set of sun,
through the Church the song goes on.

4 Holy Father, holy Son,
Holy Spirit, three we name thee,
while in essence only one
undivided God we claim thee;
and, adoring, bend the knee
while we own the mystery.

5 Spare thy people, Lord, we pray,
by a thousand snares surrounded;
keep us without sin today;
never let us be confounded.
Lo, I put my trust in thee,
never, Lord, abandon me.

C. A. Walworth (1820–1900) based on
Te Deum Laudamus

'09

1. We praise you O God;___ ac - claim you as Lord.
2. A - pos - tles and proph-ets, the mar - tyrs for Christ,
3. Lord Je - sus the Christ,___ your death brings us life.
4. Lord, grant us sal - va - tion, pro - tect us from harm.

All of cre - a - tion re - sounds to the voice of the
sing of your good - ness while bathed in the beams of your
Come with your judge - ment and grant us a place in the
Free us from e - vil and bless us with mer - cy as

heav - en - ly host, u - ni - ted in song, prai - sing your
in - fi - nite love, your splen - dour and light,
King - dom of God, at one with your saints,
dai - ly in you we trust and we hope,

maj - es - ty, prai - sing your glo - ry. Al - le - lu - ia, al - le -

lu - ia.___ Ho-ly is God, ho - ly and strong. Al - le-lu-

ia, al-le - lu - ia.___ Ho-ly Im - mor - tal One.___

Peter Jones (1951-2016), from Te Deum Laudamus

10

Alleluia, alleluia! Alleluia, alleluia!

Father we praise you as Lord,
all of the earth gives you worship,
for your majesty fills the heavens,
fills the earth.

Blessed apostles sing praise;
prophets and martyrs give glory;
'For your majesty praise the Spirit,
praise the Son!'

3 You are the Christ everlasting,
born for us all of a Virgin,
you have conquered death,
opened heaven to all believers.

4 Help those you saved by your blood,
raise them to life with your martyrs.
Save your people, Lord, as their ruler
raise them up.

Christopher Walker, from Te Deum Laudamus

711

Great is the power we proclaim now, as we worship and praise God's name. For the glory— of God is revealed when we pray — Come, Lord, come Lord,— and live in us to-day.

1 God's people called to serve
   as disciples of the Lord.
     Gifts of the Spirit
     are gifts we inherit
   to build up the body of Christ.

2 God's people called to bring
   to the world, the peace of Christ
     Love for our neighbour,
     and justice in our labour,
   compelled by the love of Christ.

3 God's people called to pray
   for the Church to be made one.
     One Holy Nation
     in hope of salvation,
   brothers and sisters in Christ.

4 God's people called to-day
   to make known the love of God.
     Seeds we are sowing
     with faith that is growing
   strong in the power of Christ.

5 God's people called to share
   in the blessing cup of Christ:
     Bread that is broken,
     and Word that is spoken,
   one in the Body of Christ.
   Christopher Walker

712

1 The God of Abraham praise
   who reigns enthroned above,
   Ancient of everlasting Days,
   and God of love:
   the Lord, the great I AM,
   by earth and heaven confessed;
   we bow and bless the sacred name
   for ever blessed.

2 The God of Abraham praise,
   at whose supreme command
   from earth we rise, and seek the joys
   at his right hand:
   we all on earth forsake
   its wisdom, fame, and power;
   and him our only portion make,
   our shield and tower.

3 The Lord our God has sworn,
   I on that oath depend;
   I shall, on eagle's wings upborne,
   to heaven ascend:
   I shall behold God's face,
   I shall God's power adore,
   and sing the wonders of God's grace
   for evermore.

4 There dwells the Lord our King,
   the Lord our Righteousness,
   triumphant o'er the world of sin,
   the Prince of peace:
   on Sion's sacred height
   his kingdom he maintains,
   and glorious with the saints in light
   for ever reigns.

The God who reigns on high
the great archangels sing,
and 'Holy, Holy, Holy,' cry,
almighty King,
who was, and is the same,
and evermore shall be:
Immortal God, the great I AM,
we worship thee.'
Thomas Olivers (1725-99)
based on the Hebrew Yigdal

13

Sing of the Lord's goodness,
Father of all wisdom,
come to him and bless his name.
Mercy he has shown us, his love is for ever,
faithful to the end of days.
Come then all you nations,
sing of your Lord's goodness,
melodies of praise and thanks to God.
Ring out the Lord's glory,
praise him with your music,
worship him and bless his name.

Power he has wielded,
honour is his garment,
risen from the snares of death.
His word he has spoken,
one bread he has broken,
new life he now gives to all.

Courage in our darkness,
comfort in our sorrow,
Spirit of our God most high;
solace for the weary,
pardon for the sinner,
splendour of the living God.

Praise him with your singing,
praise him with the trumpet,
praise God with the lute and harp;
praise him with the cymbals,
praise him with your dancing,
praise God till the end of days.
Ernest Sands (1949-2016)

714

1 Holy, holy, holy is the Lord;
   holy is the Lord God almighty!
   Holy, holy, holy is the Lord;
   holy is the Lord God almighty!
   Who was, and is, and is to come!
   Holy, holy, holy is the Lord!

2 Jesus, Jesus, Jesus is the Lord...

3 Worthy, worthy, worthy is the Lord..

4 Glory, glory, glory to the Lord;
   glory to the Lord God almighty!
   Author unknown

715

1 King of glory, king of peace,
      I will love thee;
   and that love may never cease,
      I will move thee.
   Thou hast granted my request,
      thou hast heard me;
   thou didst note my working breast,
      thou hast spared me.

2 Wherefore with my utmost art,
      I will sing thee.
   And the cream of all my heart
      I will bring thee,
   though my sins against me cried,
      thou didst clear me;
   and alone, when they replied,
      thou didst hear me.

3 Seven whole days, not one in seven,
      I will praise thee;
   in my heart, though not in heaven,
      I can raise thee.
   Small it is, in this poor sort
      to enrol thee:
   e'en eternity's too short
      to extol thee.
      George Herbert (1593–1633)

716

1 Let all the world in every corner sing,
    my God and King!
The heav'ns are not too high,
God's praise may thither fly;
the earth is not too low,
God's praises there may grow.
Let all the world in every corner sing,
    my God and King!

2 Let all the world in every corner sing,
    my God and King!
The church with psalms must shout,
no door can keep them out;
but, above all, the heart
must bear the longest part.
Let all the world in every corner sing,
    my God and King!
       George Herbert (1593–1633)

717

1 I will sing, I will sing a song unto the Lord.
I will sing, I will sing a song unto the Lord.
I will sing, I will sing a song unto the Lord.
Alleluia, glory to the Lord.
   Allelu, alleluia, glory to the Lord,
   allelu, alleluia, glory to the Lord,
   allelu, alleluia, glory to the Lord,
   alleluia, glory to the Lord.

2 We will come, we will come as one
    before the Lord...
Alleluia, glory to the Lord.

3 If the Son, if the Son shall make you free...
you shall be free indeed.

4 They that sow in tears shall reap in
    joy...
Alleluia, glory to the Lord.

5 Ev'ry knee shall bow and ev'ry tongue
    confess...
that Jesus Christ is Lord.

6 In his name, in his name we have the
    victory...
Alleluia, glory to the Lord.
       Max Dyer

718

1. How shall I sing that Majesty
which angels do admire?
Let dust in dust and silence lie;
Sing, sing, ye heavenly choir.
Thousands of thousands stand around
thy throne, O God most high;
Ten thousand times ten thousand sour
thy praise; but who am I?

2. Thy brightness unto them appears,
whilst I Thy footsteps trace;
A sound of God comes to my ears,
but they behold Thy face.
They sing because Thou art their Sun
Lord, send a beam on me;
For where heaven is but once begun
there alleluias be.

3. Enlighten with faith's light my heart,
inflame it with love's fire;
Then shall I sing and bear a part
with that celestial choir.
I shall, I fear, be dark and cold,
with all my fire and light;
Yet when Thou dost accept their gold,
Lord, treasure up my mite.

4. How great a being, Lord, is Thine,
which doth all beings keep!
Thy knowledge is the only line
to sound so vast a deep.
Thou art a sea without a shore,
a sun without a sphere;
Thy time is now and evermore,
Thy place is everywhere.
       John Mason (1645-1694)

719

1 To God be the glory, great things he h
    done!
So loved he the world that he gave us
    Son.
Who yielded his life in atonement for
and opened the life–gate that all may go
   Praise the Lord! Praise the Lord!
   Let the earth hear his voice!
   Praise the Lord! Praise the Lord!

Let the people rejoice!
O come to the Father through Jesus
*   his Son;*
and give him the glory, great things he
*   has done!*

O perfect redemption, the purchase of
   blood,
to every believer the promise of God!
And every offender who truly believes,
that moment from Jesus a pardon
   receives.

Great things he has taught us, great things
   he has done,
and great our rejoicing through Jesus the
   Son;
but purer, and higher, and greater will be
our wonder, our rapture, when Jesus we see.
Fanny Crosby (1820–1915)

20

Be still, for the presence of the Lord,
   the Holy One is here.
Come, bow before him now,
   with reverence and fear.
In him no sin is found,
   we stand on holy ground.
Be still, for the presence of the Lord,
   the Holy One is here.

Be still, for the glory of the Lord
   is shining all around;
He burns with holy fire,
   with splendour he is crowned.
How awesome is the sight,
   our radiant King of light!
Be still, for the glory of the Lord
   is shining all around.

Be still, for the power of the Lord
   is moving in this place,
He comes to cleanse and heal,
   to minister his grace.
No work too hard for him,
   in faith receive from him;
Be still, for the power of the Lord
   is moving in this place.
David J. Evans

721

1 O Lord, my God, when I in awesome
      wonder
   consider all the worlds thy hand has made,
   I see the stars, I hear the rolling thunder,
   thy power throughout the universe
      displayed.
   Then sings my soul, my Saviour God, to thee:
   how great thou art, how great thou art.
   Then sings my soul, my Saviour God, to thee:
   how great thou art, how great thou art.

2 When through the woods and
      forest glades I wander
   and hear the birds sing sweetly
      in the trees,
   when I look down from lofty mountain
      grandeur
   and hear the brook and feel the gentle
      breeze:

3 And when I think that God, his Son not
      sparing,
   sent him to die, I scarce can take it in
   that on the cross, my burden gladly bearing,
   he bled and died to take away my sin.

4 When Christ shall come with shout of
      acclamation
   and take me home, what joy shall fill my
      heart;
   then I shall bow in humble adoration,
   and there proclaim; my God, how great
      thou art.
   Stuart K. Hine (1898-1989), based on a
   hymn by Carl Boberg (1850–1940)

722

1 Give me joy in my heart, keep me praising,
   give me joy in my heart I pray.
   Give me joy in my heart, keep me praising.
   keep me praising till the break of day.
   Sing hosanna! Sing hosanna!
   Sing hosanna to the King of Kings!
   Sing hosanna! Sing hosanna!
   Sing hosanna to the King!

2 Give me peace in my heart, keep me resting,
  give me peace in my heart I pray.
  Give me peace in my heart, keep me resting,
  keep me resting till the end of day.

3 Give me love in my heart, keep me
    serving,
  give me love in my heart, I pray.

Give me love in my heart, keep me
  serving,
keep me serving till the end of day.

4 Give me oil in my lamp, keep me burnin
  give me oil in my lamp, I pray.
  Give me oil in my lamp, keep me burnin
  keep me burning till the end of day.

  Traditional

723

San - to, san - to, san - to, mi co - ra - zon te a - do - ra! M
Ho - ly, ho - ly, ho - ly, my heart, my heart a - dores you! My

co - ra - zon te sa - be de - cir: san - to e - res, Se - ñor.
heart is glad to say the words: you are ho - ly, Lord.

Holy, holy, holy, my heart, my heart adores you!
My heart is glad to say the words: you are holy, Lord.

Song from Argentina, arranged by Geoff Weaver

724

1 Angel–voices ever singing
  round thy throne of light,
  angel–harps, for ever ringing,
  rest not day nor night;
  thousands only live to bless thee
  and confess thee Lord of might.

2 Thou who art beyond the farthest
  mortal eye can see,
  God almighty, thou regardest
  all our song to thee;
  and we know that thou art near us,
  and wilt hear our ev'ry plea.

3 Yes, we know that thou rejoicest
  o'er each work of thine;
  thou didst ears and hands and voices
  for thy praise design;
  craftsman's art and music's measure
  for thy pleasure all combine.

4 In thy house, great God, we offer
  of thine own to thee;
  and for thine acceptance proffer,
  all unworthily,
  hearts and minds and hands and voice
  in our choicest psalmody.

Honour, glory, might and merit
thine shall ever be,
Father, Son and Holy Spirit,
Blessed Trinity!
Of the best that thou hast given
earth and heaven render thee.
Francis Pott (1832–1909)

25

Immortal, invisible, God only wise,
in light inaccessible hid from our eyes,
most blessed, most glorious, the
    Ancient of Days,
almighty, victorious, thy great name we
    praise.

Unresting, unhasting, and silent as light;
nor wanting, nor wasting, thou rulest in
    might –
thy justice like mountains high–soaring
    above
thy clouds which are fountains of
    goodness and love.

To all life thou givest, to both great and
    small;
in all life thou livest, the true life of all;
we blossom and flourish as leaves on the
    tree,
and wither and perish; but naught
    changeth thee.

Great Father of glory, pure Father of light,
thine angels adore thee, all veiling their
    sight;
all laud we would render: O help us to see
'tis only the splendour of light
    hideth thee.
W. Chalmers Smith (1825–1908)

26

For the beauty of the earth,
for the beauty of the skies,
for the love which from our birth
over and around us lies,
Christ our God, to you we raise
this our sacrifice of praise.

2 For the beauty of each hour
of the day and of the night,
hill and vale, and tree and flower,
sun and moon and stars of light.
Christ our God, to you we raise
this our sacrifice of praise.

3 For the joy of ear and eye,
for the heart and mind's delight,
for the mystic harmony
linking sense to sound and sight.
Christ our God, to you we raise
this our sacrifice of praise.

4 For the joy of human love,
brother, sister, parent, child,
friends on earth and friends above,
pleasures pure and undefiled,
Christ our God, to you we raise
this our sacrifice of praise.

5 For each perfect gift divine
to our race so freely given,
joys bestowed by love's design,
flowers of earth and fruits of heaven,
Christ our God, to you we raise
this our sacrifice of praise.
F. S. Pierpoint (1835–1917)

727

1 My God, how wonderful thou art,
thy majesty how bright
how beautiful thy mercy–seat
in depths of burning light.

2 How dread are thine eternal years
O everlasting Lord!
By prostrate spirits day and night
incessantly adored.

3 How wonderful, how beautiful
the sight of thee must be,
thine endless wisdom, boundless power
and awesome purity!

4 Oh, how, I fear thee, living God!
with deepest, tenderest fears,
and worship thee with trembling hope
and penitential tears.

5 Yet I may love thee too, O Lord,
   almighty as thou art,
   for thou hast stooped to ask of me
   the love of my poor heart.

6 No earthly father loves like thee,
   no mother e'er so mild
   bears and forbears as thou hast done
   with me thy sinful child.

7 Father of Jesus, love's reward,
   what rapture will it be
   prostrate before thy throne to lie,
   and gaze and gaze on thee!
                    F. W. Faber (1814–63)

728

1 O God beyond all praising,
   we worship you today
   and sing the love amazing
   that songs cannot repay;
   for we can only wonder
   at every gift you send,
   at blessings without number
   and mercies without end:
   we lift our hearts before you
   and wait upon your word,
   we honour and adore you,
   our great and mighty Lord.

2 The flower of earthly splendour
   in time must surely die,
   its fragile bloom surrender
   to you, the Lord most high;
   but hidden from all nature
   the eternal seed is sown;
   though small in mortal stature,
   to heaven's garden grown:
   For Christ the man from heaven
   from death has set us free,
   and we through him are given
   the final victory.

3 Then hear, O gracious Saviour,
   accept the love we bring,
   that we who know your favour
   may serve you as our king;
   and whether our tomorrows
   be filled with good or ill,
   we'll triumph through our sorrows
   and rise to bless you still:
   to marvel at your beauty
   and glory in your ways,
   and make a joyful duty
   our sacrifice of praise.
                    Michael Perry (1942-96)

729

1 When, in our music, God is glorified,
   and adoration leaves no room for pride
   it is as though the whole creation cried
      Alleluia!

2 How often, making music, we have found
   a new dimension in the world of sound
   as worship moved us to a more profound
      Alleluia!

3 So has the Church, in liturgy and song
   in faith and love, through centuries of
      wrong,
   borne witness to the truth in every tongue
      Alleluia!

4 And did not Jesus sing a Psalm that night
   when utmost evil strove against the Light
   Then let us sing, for whom he won the
      fight:
      Alleluia!

5 Let every instrument be tuned for praise
   Let all rejoice who have a voice to raise
   and may God give us faith to sing always
      Alleluia!
                    F. Pratt Green (1903-2000)

30

Refrain

Lau - da - te, lau - da - te Do - mi - num, om - nes
We praise you, we praise your ho - ly name, God of

gen - tes, lau - da - te Do - mi - num. Ex - sul - ta - te, ju - bi -
jus - tice, e - ter - nal - ly the same. May our li - ving be thanks-

1 **2**

la - te per an - nos Do - mi - ni, om - nes gen-tes. Lau - gen-tes.
gi - ving, re - joi - cing in your name now and al-ways.

Verses

1. In the faith of Christ we walk hand in hand, light be-fore our path as the
2. In the name of Christ we will spread the seed; share the Word of God with all

Lord has planned; shi - ning the torch of faith in our land:
those in need, faith - ful in thought and word and deed:

in the name, the name of Christ Je - sus.

In the power of Christ we proclaim one
   Lord.
All who put on Christ are by faith
   restored;
sharing new life, salvation's reward.
in the name of Christ Jesus.

In the life of Christ, through the blood
   he shed,
we are justified, and by him are fed,
nourished by word and living bread:
in the name of Christ Jesus.

In the Church of God we are unified,
by the Spirit's power we are sanctified,
temples of grace, where God may abide:
by the pow'r of the Spirit.

6 Praise to God the Father while ages run
praise to Christ the Saviour, God's only
   Son,
praise to the Holy Spirit be sung:
omnes gentes, laudate.
    Christopher Walker

For ordination:
1 In the Church we answer the Saviour's
   call,
serving, as he showed us, both great
   and small.
sharing the Lord's compassion for all:

2 In the name of Christ we baptize and
   teach,
truth upon our lips in the way we preach:
raising the cup of blessing for each:

Harvest

731

1 For the fruits of all creation,
  thanks be to God;
  for these gifts to every nation,
  thanks be to God;
  for the ploughing, sowing, reaping,
  silent growth while we are sleeping,
  future needs in earth's safe keeping,
  thanks be to God.

2 In the just reward of labour,
  God's will is done;
  in the help we give our neighbour,
  God's will is done;
  in our world–wide task of caring
  for the hungry and despairing
  in the harvests we are sharing,
  God's will is done.

3 For the harvests of the Spirit,
  thanks be to God;
  for the good we all inherit,
  thanks be to God;
  for the wonders that astound us,
  for the truths that still confound us,
  most of all, that love has found us,
  thanks be to God.
  F. Pratt Green (1903-2000)

732

1 Loving Father, from your bounty
  choicest gifts unnumbered flow:
  all the blessings of salvation,
  which to Christ thy Son we owe,
  all the gifts that by your bidding
  nature's hands on us bestow!

2 Here your grateful children gather,
  offering gifts of bread and wine;
  these we give to you in homage,
  of your love the loving sign,
  and restore to you creation,
  through this fruit of earth and vine.

3 Soon will come Christ's loving presence
  on our love to set his seal!
  Sacred body, precious life-blood,
  bread and wine will then reveal!
  Bread and wine, though these no long
  flesh and blood will yet conceal.
  James Quinn SJ (1919-2010)

733

1 God whose farm is all creation,
  take the gratitude we give;
  Take the finest of our harvest,
  crops we grow that all may live.

2 Take our ploughing, seeding, reaping,
  hopes and fears of sun and rain,
  all our thinking, planning, waiting,
  ripened in this fruit and grain.

3 All our labour, all our watching,
  all our calendar of care,
  in these crops of your creation,
  take, O God: they are our prayer.
  John Arlott (1914-91)

734

1 Reap me the earth as a harvest to God
  gather and bring it again,
  all that is his, to the Maker of all.
  Lift it and offer it high.
  Bring bread, bring wine,
  give glory to the Lord;
  whose is the earth but God's,
  whose is the praise but his?

2 Go with your song and your music
    with joy,
  go to the altar of God.
  Carry your offerings, fruits of the eart
  work of your labouring hands.

3 Gladness and pity and passion and pai
  all that is mortal in man,
  lay all before him, return him his gift,
  God, to whom all shall go home.
  Peter Icarus

We plough the fields and scatter
the good seed on the land,
but it is fed and watered
by God's almighty hand;
he sends the snow in winter,
the warmth to swell the grain,
the breezes and the sunshine,
and soft refreshing rain.
All good gifts around us
are sent from heav'n above,
then thank the Lord,
O thank the Lord, for all his love.

He only is the maker
of all things near and far;
he paints the wayside flower,
he lights the ev'ning star.
The winds and waves obey him,
by him the birds are fed:
much more to us his children,
he gives our daily bread.

We thank thee then, O Father,
for all things bright and good:
the seed–time and the harvest,
our life, our health, our food.
No gifts have we to offer
for all thy love imparts,
but that which thou desirest,
our humble, thankful hearts.
M. Claudius (1740–1815),
tr. Jane M. Campbell (1817-78)

736

Come, ye thankful people, come,
raise the song of harvest–home!
All be safely gathered in,
ere the winter storms begin;
God, our maker, doth provide
for our wants to be supplied;
come to God's own temple come;
raise the song of harvest–home!

We ourselves are God's own field,
fruit unto his praise to yield;
wheat and tares together sown,
unto joy or sorrow grown;
first the blade and then the ear,
then the full corn shall appear:
grant, O harvest Lord, that we
wholesome grain and pure may be.

3 For the Lord our God shall come,
and shall take his harvest home;
from his field shall purge away
all that doth offend, that day,
give his angels charge at last
in the fire the tares to cast,
but the fruitful ears to store
in his garner evermore.

4 Then, thou Church triumphant, come,
raise the song of harvest–home
all be safely gathered in,
free from sorrow, free from sin,
there for ever purified
in God's garner to abide;
come, ten thousand angels, come,
raise the glorious harvest–home!
Henry Alford (1810–71)

737

Ag Críost an síol; ag Críost an fómhar;
in ioth lainn Dé go dtugtar sinn.
Ag Críost an mhuir; ag Críost an t-iasc,
i líonta Dé go gcastar sinn.
Ó fhás go haois, is ó aois go bás,
Do dhá láimh, a Chríost, anall tharainn.
Ó bhás go críoch, ní críoch ach athfhás,
i bPharthas na nGrást go rabhaimid.
Irish Traditional

The seed is Christ's, the harvest his:
may we be stored within God's barn.

The sea is Christ's, the fish are his:
may we be caught within God's net.

From birth to age, from age to death,
enfold us, Christ, within your arms.

Until the end, the great rebirth,
Christ be our joy in paradise.
English version by James Quinn SJ (1919-2010)

Jesus Christ, The Word made Flesh

Jesus, Word of God

738

1. Be - fore the world be - gan, One Word was there; groun - ded in
2. Life found in him its source, death found its end; light found in

God he was, roo - ted in care; by him all things were made
him its course, dark - ness its friend. For nei - ther death nor doub

In him was love dis - played, through him God spoke, and said, 'I AM FOR YOU
nor dark - ness can put out the glow of God, the shout, 'I AM FOR YOU

3 The Word was in the world
which from him came;
unrecognised he was,
unknown by name;
one with all humankind,
with the unloved aligned,
convincing sight and mind,
'I AM FOR YOU'.

4 All who received the Word
by God were blessed;
sisters and brothers they
of earth's fond guest.
So did the Word of Grace
proclaim in time and space
and with a human face,
'I AM FOR YOU'.

John L. Bell

739

1 In a byre near Bethlehem,
passed by many a wand'ring stranger,
the most precious Word of Life
was heard gurgling in a manger,
for the good of us all.
  And he's here when we call him,
  bringing health, love and laughter
  to life now and ever after
  for the good of us all.

2 By the Galilean Lake
where the people flocked for teaching,
the most precious Word of Life
fed their mouths as well as preaching,
for the good of us all.

3 Quiet was Gethsemane,
camouflaging priest and soldier;
the most precious Word of Life
took the world's weight on his shoulde
for the good of us all.

4 On the hill of Calvary -
place to end all hope of living -
the most precious Word of Life
breathed his last and died, forgiving,
for the good of us all.

5 In a garden, just at dawn,
near the grave of human violence,
the most precious Word of Life
cleared his throat and ended silence,
for the good of us all.

John L. Bell

➤ *see also no.85, Before the earth had yet begu*

40

(Cantor) Word of the Fa-ther, (all)

Hum——— Come, Lord, come; and take our fear a-way,

and take our fear a-way, re-place it with your love.———

Firstborn of Mary,

Healer and helper,

Servant and sufferer,

5 Jesus, redeemer,

6 Christ resurrected,

7 Maranatha!

John L. Bell & Graham Maule

41

Word of God, come down to earth,
living rain from heav'n descending;
touch our hearts and bring to birth
faith and hope and love unending.
Word almighty, we revere you;
Word made flesh, we long to hear you.

Word eternal, throned on high,
Word that brought to life creation,
Word that came from heav'n to die,
crucified for our salvation,
saving Word, the world restoring,
speak to us, your love outpouring.

Word that caused blind eyes to see,
speak and heal our mortal blindness;
deaf we are; our healer be;
loose our tongues to tell your kindness.
Be our Word in pity spoken,
heal the world, by our sin broken.

4 Word that speaks your Father's love,
one with him beyond all telling,
Word that sends us from above
God the Spirit, with us dwelling;
Word of truth, to all truth lead us;
Word of life, with one Bread feed us.

James Quinn SJ (1919-2010)

➤ see also no.447, Word of God from Mary's womb

742

1 God has spoken - by his prophets,
spoken his unchanging word,
each from age to age proclaiming
God, the one, the righteous Lord.
'Mid the world's despair and turmoil
one firm anchor holds us fast:
God is King, his throne eternal.
God the first, and God the last.

2 God has spoken - by Christ Jesus.
   Christ, the everlasting Son,
   brightness of the Father's glory,
   with the Father ever one;
   spoken by the Word incarnate,
   God from God, before time was;
   Light from Light to earth descending.
   He reveals our God to us.

3 God is speaking - by his Spirit,
   speaking to the hearts of all,
   in the age-long word expounding
   God's own message for us all.
   Through the rise and fall of nations
   one sure faith yet standing fast;
   God still speaks, his word unchanging
   God the first, and God the last.

G.W. Briggs (1875-1959), alt.

Jesus Christ: His Ministry

743

1. If you would fol-low me,— fol-low where life will lead;—
2. If you would ho-nour me,— ho-nour the least of these:— yo

do not look for me a-mong the dead,— for I am hid-den in pain,—
will not find me dressed in fi-ne-ry.— My Word cries out to be heard;—

ri-sen in love;— there is no har-vest with-out sow-ing of grain.
breaks through the world:— my Word is on your lips and lives in your heart.

Refrain: All that is hid-den will be made clear.— All that is dark now— will

be re-vealed. What you have heard in the dark— pro-claim in the light

— what you hear in whis-pers— pro-claim from the house— tops.—

3 If you would speak of me
   live all your life in me:
   my ways are not the ways
   that you would choose;
   my thoughts are far beyond yours,
   as heaven from earth:
   if you believe in me my voice will be
   heard.

4 If you would rise with me,
   rise through your destiny:
   do not refuse the death
   which brings you life,
   for as the grain in the earth
   must die for re-birth,
   so I have planted your life deep within
   mine.

Bernadette Farrell

744

Christ is the world's Light, he and no
    other;
born in our darkness, he became our
    brother.
If we have seen him, we have seen the
    Father:
Glory to God on high.

Christ is the world's Peace, he and no
    other;
no–one can serve him and despise
    another.
Who else unites us, one in God the
    Father?

3 Christ is the world's Life, he and no other,
sold once for silver, murdered here, our
    Brother -
he who redeems us, reigns with God the
    Father:

Give God the glory, God and no other;
give God the glory, Spirit, Son and Father;
give God the glory, God in man my
    brother:

F. Pratt Green (1903-2000)

745

O changeless Christ, for ever new,
who walked our earthly ways,
still draw our hearts as once you drew
the hearts of other days.

As once you spoke by plain and hill
or taught by shore and sea,
so be today our teacher still,
O Christ of Galilee.

As wind and storm their master heard
and his command fulfilled,
may troubled hearts receive your word,
the tempest–tossed be stilled.

And as of old to all who prayed
your healing hand was shown,
so be your touch upon us laid,
unseen but not unknown.

5 In broken bread, in wine outpoured,
your new and living way
proclaim to us, O risen Lord,
O Christ of this our day.

6 O changeless Christ, till life is past
your blessing still be given;
then bring us home, to taste at last
the timeless joys of heaven.

Timothy Dudley–Smith

746

1 Jesus the Lord said, 'I am the bread,
the bread of life for mankind am I.'
the bread of life for mankind am I.'
the bread of life for mankind am I.'
Jesus the Lord said, 'I am the bread,
the bread of life for mankind am I.'

2 Jesus the Lord said, 'I am the door,
the way and the door for the poor am I.'..

3 Jesus the Lord said, 'I am the light,
the one true light of the world am I.'..

4 Jesus the Lord said, 'I am the shepherd,
the one good shepherd of the sheep am I.'..

5 Jesus the Lord said, 'I am the life,
the resurrection and the life am I.'..

Urdu hymn, tr. Dermott Monahan (1906-57)

747

The light of Christ has come into the world,
The light of Christ has come into the world.

1 We all must be born again
to see the kingdom of God;
the water and the Spirit
bring new life in God's love.

2 God gave up his only Son
out of love for the world
so that ev'ryone who believes in him
will live for ever.

3 The Light of God has come to us
so that we might have salvation,
from the darkness of our sins, we walk
into glory with Christ Jesus.

Donald Fishel

➤ *See also: He healed the darkness (435), Justice & Peace (887-904)*

The Paschal Mystery: Jesus' suffering & death

748

Un - less a grain of wheat shall fall u - pon the ground__ an
die,__ it re - mains__ but a sin - gle grain__ with no life.__

Verses

1.	If	we	have	died with	him	then	we	shall	live with	him;
2.	If	a - ny - one	serves__	me	then	they	must	fol - low	me;
3.	⁀	Make	your	home in	me	as	I	make	mine in	you;
4.	If	you	re - main in	me	and	my	word	lives in	you;
5.	⁀	Those who	love	me	are	loved by	my	Fa -	ther;
6.	⁀	Peace	I	leave with	you,	my peace	I	give to	you;

if	we	hold	firm	we	shall	reign with	him.__
wher - ev - er	I	am	my	ser - vants	will	be.
those who	re - main in	me	bear	much	fruit.__
then	you	will	be	my	dis - ci - ples.__
we	shall	be	with them and	dwell	in	them.__
peace	which the	world can - not	give	is	my	gift.

Bernadette Farrell. Words adapted from the Gospel of St John

749

1 From heaven You came, helpless babe,
entered our world, Your glory veiled,
not to be served but to serve,
and give Your life that we might live.
  This is our God, the Servant King,
  He calls us now to follow Him,
  to bring our lives as a daily offering
  of worship to the Servant King.

2 There in the garden of tears
my heavy load He chose to bear;
His heart with sorrow was torn,
'Yet not my will but yours,' He said.

3 Come see His hands and His feet,
the scars that speak of sacrifice,
hands that flung stars into space
to cruel nails surrendered.

4 So let us learn how to serve
and in our lives enthrone Him,
each other's needs to prefer,
for it is Christ we're serving.
  Graham Kendrick

750

1 Glory be to Jesus,
who in bitter pains
poured for me the life–blood,
from his sacred veins.

2 Grace and life eternal
in that blood I find:
blest be his compassion,
infinitely kind.

Blest through endless ages
be the precious stream,
which from endless torment
doth the world redeem.

There the fainting spirit
drinks of life her fill;
there as in a fountain
laves herself at will.

Abel's blood for vengeance
pleaded to the skies,
but the blood of Jesus
for our pardon cries.

Oft as it is sprinkled
on our guilty hearts,
Satan in confusion
terror–struck departs.

Oft as earth exulting
wafts its praise on high,
hell with horror trembles;
heaven is filled with joy.

Lift ye, then, your voices;
swell the mighty flood;
louder still and louder,
praise the precious blood.

Italian, 18th century,
tr. Edward Caswall (1814–78)

51

Meekness and majesty,
manhood and deity,
in perfect harmony,
the man who is God.
Lord of eternity
dwells in humanity,
kneels in humility
and washes our feet.

O, what a mystery,
meekness and majesty,
bow down and worship,
for this is your God.
This is your God.

2 Father's pure radiance,
   perfect in innocence,
   yet learns obedience
   to death on a cross.
   Suff'ring to give us life,
   conqu'ring through sacrifice;
   and as they crucify prays
   'Father forgive'.

3 Wisdom unsearchable,
   God the invisible;
   love indestructible
   in frailty appears.
   Lord of infinity,
   stooping so tenderly,
   lifts our humanity
   to the heights of his throne.
   Graham Kendrick

752

1 My song is love unknown,
   my Saviour's love to me,
   love to the loveless shown,
   that they might lovely be.
   O who am I, that for my sake,
   my Lord should take, frail flesh and die?

2 He came from his blest throne,
   salvation to bestow;
   but men made strange, and none
   the longed–for Christ would know,
   but O, my friend, my friend indeed,
   who at my need his life did spend!

3 Sometimes they strew his way,
   and his sweet praises sing;
   resounding all the day
   hosannas to their King;
   then 'Crucify!' is all their breath,
   and for his death they thirst and cry.

4 Why, what hath my Lord done?
   What makes this rage and spite?
   He made the lame to run,
   he gave the blind their sight.
   Sweet injuries! Yet they at these
   themselves displease, and 'gainst him
      rise.

5 They rise, and needs will have
  my dear Lord made away;
  a murderer they save,
  the Prince of Life they slay.
  Yet cheerful he to suffering goes,
  that he his foes from thence might free.

6 In life, no house, no home
  my Lord on earth might have:
  in death no friendly tomb
  but what a stranger gave.
  What may I say? Heaven was his home;
  but mine the tomb wherein he lay.

7 Here might I stay and sing,
  no story so divine,
  never was love, dear King,
  never was grief like thine.
  This is my Friend, in whose sweet praise
  I all my days could gladly spend.
        Samuel Crossman (c.1624–83)

753

1 To Christ, the Prince of peace,
  and Son of God most high,
  the father of the world to come,
  sing we with holy joy.

2 Deep in his heart for us
  the wound of love he bore:
  that love wherewith he still inflames
  the hearts that him adore.

3 O Jesu, victim blest,
  what else but love divine
  could thee constrain to open thus
  that sacred heart of thine?

4 O fount of endless life,
  O spring of water clear,
  O flame celestial, cleansing all
  who unto thee draw near!

5 Hide us in thy dear heart,
  for thither we do fly;
  there seek thy grace through life, in
    death
  thine immortality.

6 Praise to the Father be,
  and sole–begotten Son;
  praise, holy Paraclete, to thee
  while endless ages run.
    Catholicum Hymnolgium Germanicum
    (1587) tr. E. Caswall (1814–78)

754

1 Before the heaven and earth
  were made by God's decree,
  the Son of God all glorious dwelt
  in God's eternity.

2 Though in the form of God
  and rich beyond compare,
  he did not stop to grasp his prize;
  nor did he linger there.

3 From heights of heaven he came
  to this world full of sin,
  to meet with hunger, hatred, hell,
  our life, our love to win.

4 The Son became true man
  and took a servant's role;
  with lowliness and selfless love,
  he came, to make us whole.

5 Obedient to his death
  that death upon the cross,
  no son had ever shown such love,
  nor father known such loss.

6 To him enthroned on high,
  by angel hosts adored,
  all knees shall bow, and tongues confe
  that Jesus Christ is Lord.
    Brian Black, from Philippians 2:6-11

55

Ev-ery knee shall bow be - fore him, ev-ery tongue con-fess his glo - ry, Je - sus Christ is Lord ab - ove ev - ery name.

Verses

1. Though he was in form of God, Je - sus did not flaunt his
2. Be - ing found in hu - man form, he be - came__ hum - bler
3. There-fore God has raised him up; gi - ven him the grea - test

state, but emp - tied him - self, be - came__ as a ser - vant, was
yet; o - be - dient he was, o - be - dient un - to death, he en -
name; All hea - ven and earth con - fess that he is Lord to the

born in the like - ness of a man.__
dured e - ven death__ on a cross.__
glo - ry of God__ the__ Fa - ther.

Stephen Dean, from
Philippians 2:6-11

56

When I survey the wondrous cross
on which the Prince of Glory died,
my richest gain I count but loss,
and pour contempt on all my pride.

Forbid it, Lord, that I should boast,
save in the death of Christ, my God:
all the vain things that charm me most,
I sacrifice them to his blood.

3 See from his head, his hands, his feet,
sorrow and love flow mingled down;
did e'er such love and sorrow meet,
or thorns compose so rich a crown?

4 His dying crimson like a robe,
spreads o'er his body on the Tree;
then I am dead to all the globe,
and all the globe is dead to me.

5 Were the whole realm of nature mine,
that were an offering far too small;
love so amazing, so divine,
demands my soul, my life, my all.
Isaac Watts (1674-1748)

O Christe Domine Jesu   *Taizé chant by Jacques Berthier (1923-94)*

57

O Chris - te Do-mi-ne Je-su, O Chris-te Do-mi-ne Je-su. O

The Paschal Mystery: Jesus risen in glory

758

God, your glo-ry we have seen in your Son, full of truth, full of heav'n

grace; in Christ make us live,— his love shine on our face, and the na-tions

see in us the tri-umph you have won.

1. In the fields of this world his go
2. In his love like a fire that co
3. He was bro-ken for us, God-fo

news he has sown, and sends us out to reap till the har-vest is done.
sumes he passed by: the flame has touched our lips; let us shout: Here am I!'
sa-ken his cry, and still the bread he breaks: to our-selves we must die:

4 He has trampled the grapes
   of new life on his Cross;
   now drink the cup and live:
   he has filled it for us:

5 He has founded a kingdom
   that none shall destroy;
   the corner–stone is laid:
   Go to work, build with joy!

Didier Rimaud SJ (1922-2003), Verses t
Brian Wren, Refrain tr. Ronald Johnson
Music by Jean Langlais (1907-91)

759

Join in the dance of the earth's ju-bi-la-tion! This is th

feast of the love of God. Shout from the heights to the end of cre-a-tion:

Je-sus the Sa-viour is ri-sen from the grave!

1 Wake, O people; sleep no longer:
     greet the breaking day!
   Christ, Redeemer, Lamb and Lion,
     turns the night away!

2 All creation, like a mother,
     labours to give birth.
   Soon the pain will be forgotten,
     joy for all the earth!

Now our shame becomes our glory
    on this holy tree.
Now the reign of death is ended;
    now we are set free!

None on earth, no prince or power,
    neither death nor life,
nothing now can ever part us
    from the love of Christ!

Love's triumphant day of vict'ry
    heaven opens wide.
On the tree of hope and glory
    death itself has died!

Christ for ever, Lord of ages,
    Love beyond our dreams:
Christ, our hope of heaven's glory
    all that yet will be!
    Daniel L. Schutte

760

All heaven declares
    the glory of the risen Lord.
Who can compare
    with the beauty of the Lord?
Forever he will be
    the Lamb upon the throne:
I gladly bow the knee
    and worship him alone.

I will proclaim
    the glory of the risen Lord,
who once was slain
    to reconcile man to God.
Forever you will be
    the Lamb upon the throne:
I gladly bow the knee
    and worship you alone.
    Noel Richards and Tricia Richards

761

He is Lord, he is Lord.
He is risen from the dead and he is Lord.
Ev'ry knee shall bow, ev'ry tongue confess
that Jesus Christ is Lord.

2 He is King, he is King.
He is risen from the dead and he is King.
Ev'ry knee shall bow, ev'ry tongue confess
that Jesus Christ is King.

3 He is love, he is love.
He is risen from the dead and he is love.
Ev'ry knee shall bow, ev'ry tongue confess
that Jesus Christ is love.
    Anonymous

762

1 At the name of Jesus
    every knee shall bow,
every tongue confess him
    King of glory now;
'tis the Father's pleasure
    we should call him Lord,
who from the beginning
    was the mighty Word.

2 At his voice creation
    sprang at once to sight,
all the angel faces,
    all the hosts of light,
thrones and dominations,
    stars upon their way,
all the heavenly orders,
    in their great array.

3 Humbled for a season,
    to receive a name
from the lips of sinners
    unto whom he came,
faithfully he bore it
    spotless to the last,
brought it back victorious
    when from death he passed.

4 Bore it up triumphant
    with its human light
through all ranks of creatures,
    to the central height,
to the throne of Godhead,
    to the Father's breast,
filled it with the glory
    of that perfect rest.

5 Name him, Christians, name him,
    with love as strong as death;
but with awe and wonder,
    and with bated breath;
he is God the Saviour,
    he is Christ the Lord,
ever to be worshipped,
    trusted, and adored.

6 In your hearts enthrone him;
    there let him subdue
all that is not holy,
    all that is not true;
crown him as your captain,
    in temptation's hour
let his will enfold you
    in its light and power.

7 Christians, this Lord Jesus
    shall return again,
with his Father's glory,
    with his angel train,
for all wreaths of empire
    meet upon his brow,
and our hearts confess him
    King of glory now.
        Caroline Maria Noel (1817–77)

763

1 Christ triumphant ever–reigning,
Saviour, Master, King,
Lord of heav'n, our lives sustaining,
hear us as we sing.

> *Yours the glory and the crown,*
> *the high renown,*
> *the eternal name.*

2 Word incarnate, truth revealing,
Son of Man on earth!
Power and majesty concealing
by your humble birth:

3 Suffering servant, scorned, ill–treated,
victim crucified!
Death is through the cross defeated,
sinners justified:

4 Priestly King, enthroned for ever
high in heaven above!
Sin and death and hell shall never
stifle hymns of love:

5 So, our hearts and voices raising
through the ages long,
ceaselessly upon you gazing,
this shall be our song:
        Michael Saward (1932-2015)

764

1. All our hope is in the one who saves us
All our hope is found in Christ the Lord
  O death, where is your power?
  O death, where is your power?

2. He is Lord, he carries all our burdens.
He is Lord, he lifts us from our fear.

3. Sin and death hold us no more in bondage
Sin and death were nailed upon the tree.

4. On the tree he died for our redemption.
On the tree he claimed the victory.

5. Now we live in hope of resurrection.
Now we live in him who set us free.

6. Sign of Life, the empty tomb is glory.
Sign of Life, the Risen Lord is King:
    Sister Paule Freeburg

765

1 I danced in the morning
    when the world was begun,
and I danced in the moon
    and the stars and the sun,
and I came down from heaven and
    I danced on the earth –
at Bethlehem I had my birth.
Dance, then, wherever you may be,
I am the Lord of Dance, said he.
And I'll lead you all, wherever you may be
and I'll lead you all in the dance, said he

2 I danced for the scribe and the pharisee
    but they would not dance
        and they wouldn't follow me,

I danced for the fishermen,
for James and John –
they came with me and the dance went on:

3 I danced on the Sabbath and I cured
the lame;
the holy people said it was a shame.
They whipped and they stripped
and they hung me high,
and they left me there on a Cross to die.

4 I danced on a Friday when the sky
turned black –
it's hard to dance with the devil on your
back.
They buried my body and they thought
I'd gone,
but I am the Dance and I still go on.

5 They cut me down and I leapt up high –
I am the life that'll never, never die
I'll live in you if you'll live in me –
I am the Lord of the Dance, said he.
Sydney Carter (1915-2004)

766

Jesus, you are Lord.
You are risen from the dead
and you are Lord.
Ev'ry knee shall bow,
and ev'ry tongue confess
that Jesus, you are Lord.
You are the Way.

I am the Way.
No one knows the Father but it be
through me.
I am in my Father, and my Father is in me,
and we come in love to live within your
hearts.

I am the Truth.
And I set my spirit deep within your hearts,
and you will know me, and love me,
and the truth I give to you will set you free.

I am the Life.
The living waters I pour out for you.
Anyone who drinks of the waters that I give
will have eternal life.

4 I am the Word,
the true light that shines brightly in the
dark,
a light that darkness could not overpower,
the Word made flesh, risen among you.
Mary Barrett, based on John 14:6

767

Majesty, worship his Majesty;
unto Jesus be glory, honour and praise.
Majesty, kingdom, authority,
flows from his throne unto his own,
his anthem raise.
So exalt, lift upon high,
the name of Jesus,
magnify, come glorify,
Christ Jesus the King.
Majesty, worship his Majesty,
Jesus who died, now glorified,
King of all kings.
Jack W. Hayford

768

1 How lovely on the mountains
are the feet of him
who brings good news, good news,
announcing peace,
proclaiming news of happiness:
our God reigns, our God reigns.
Our God reigns, our God reigns,
our God reigns, our God reigns.

2 You watchmen, lift your voices joyfully
as one,
shout for your king, your king!
See eye to eye, the Lord restoring Sion:
our God reigns, our God reigns.

3 Wasteplaces of Jerusalem,
break forth with joy!
We are redeemed, redeemed,
the Lord has saved
and comforted his people.
our God reigns, our God reigns.

4 Ends of the earth,
see the salvation of our God!
Jesus is Lord, is Lord!

Before the nations,
he has bared his holy arm.
our God reigns, our God reigns.

Leonard E. Smith Jnr.

769

1 Lord, enthroned in heavenly splendour,
first begotten from the dead,
thou alone, our strong defender,
liftest up thy people's head.
    Alleluia, alleluia,
Jesus, true and living bread!

2 Prince of life, for us thou livest,
by thy body souls are healed;
Prince of peace, thy peace thou givest,
by thy blood is pardon sealed;
    alleluia, alleluia,
Word of God, in flesh revealed.

3 Though the lowliest form doth veil thee
as of old in Bethlehem,
here as there thine angels hail thee,
branch and flower of Jesse's stem
    alleluia, alleluia,
we in worship join with them.

4 Paschal Lamb! thine offering, finished
once for all when thou wast slain,
in its fullness undiminished
shall for evermore remain,
    alleluia, alleluia,
cleansing souls from every stain.

5 Life–imparting heavenly manna,
stricken rock, with streaming side,
heaven and earth with loud hosanna
worship thee, the Lamb who died;
    alleluia, alleluia,
risen, ascended, glorified!

G.H. Bourne (1840–1925)

770

1 Lord, the light of your love is shining
in the midst of the darkness, shining;
Jesus, Light of the World, shine upon us,
set us free by the truth you now bring us,
shine on me, shine on me.

*Shine, Jesus, shine,
fill this land with the Father's glory;
blaze, Spirit, blaze,
set our hearts on fire.
Flow, river, flow,
flood the nations with grace and merc*
*send forth your word, Lord,
and let there be light.*

2 Lord, I come to your awesome presenc
from the shadows into your radiance;
by the blood I may enter your brightne
search me, try me, consume all my darkne
Shine on me, shine on me.

3 As we gaze on your kingly brightness
so our faces display your likeness,
ever changing from glory to glory,
mirrored here may our lives tell your stor
Shine on me, shine on me.

Graham Kendrick

771

1 The Spirit lives to set us free,
walk, walk in the light.
He binds us all in unity,
walk, walk in the light.
    *Walk in the light,
    walk in the light,
    walk in the light,
    walk in the light of the Lord.*

2 Jesus promised life to all,
the dead were wakened by his call.

3 He died in pain on Calvary,
to save the lost like you and me.

4 We know his death was not the end,
He gave his Spirit to be our friend.

5 By Jesus' love our wounds are healed,
the Father's kindness is revealed.

6 The Spirit lives in you and me,
His light will shine for all to see.

Damian Lundy (1943-97)

72

Lord, Jesus Christ,
you have come to us
you are one with us, Mary's son.
Cleansing our souls from all their sin,
pouring your love and goodness in,
Jesus our love for you we sing,
living Lord.

Lord Jesus Christ,
now and ev'ry day
teach us how to pray, Son of God.
You have commanded us to do
this in remembrance, Lord, of you
into our lives your pow'r breaks through,
living Lord.

3 Lord Jesus Christ,
you have come to us,
born as one of us, Mary's Son.
Led out to die on Calvary,
risen from death to set us free,
living Lord Jesus, help us see
you are Lord.

4 Lord Jesus Christ,
I would come to you,
live my life for you, Son of God.
All your commands I know are true,
your many gifts will make me new,
into my life your pow'r breaks through,
living Lord.

Patrick Appleford

73

Keep in mind that Je-sus Christ has died for us and is ri-sen from the
dead. He is our sa-ving Lord, he is joy for all a-ges.

Verses *Refrain*

1. — If we die with the Lord, we shall live with the Lord.
   If we en-dure with the Lord, we shall reign with the Lord.

Refrain

2. In him all our sor-row, in him all our joy.
   In him hope of glo-ry, in him all our love.

3. In him our re-demp-tion, in him all our grace.
   In him our sal-va-tion, in him all our peace.

Lucien Deiss CSsP (1921-2007), from 2 Tim 1:8, 11

God's Love & Mercy

774

Lord, your love has drawn us near; per - fect love which casts out fear;

love has sought us, home-ward brought us, joined us in com-mu-nion here.___

1 How can I repay the Lord,
  who feeds us with his word,
    with bread and wine?
  Sing in homage all your days,
  a sacrifice of praise
    will be our sign.

Lord, your love has drawn us near,
perfect love which casts out fear,
  love has sought us,
    homeward brought us,
joined us in communion here.

2 He who calls us to be here,
  who calms us in our fear,
    will guide our way;
  He who gave his very life,
  who conquered in the strife,
    will light our day.

3 Every creature that God feeds,
  praise him who fills your needs,
    lift up your voice;
  every creature that has breath,
  praise him who conquered death,
    and still rejoice!

Stephen Dean

775

I have loved you with an e - ver - las - ting love, I have

called you___ and you are mine; I have loved you with an e - ver - las - ting

love, I have called you___ and you are mine. 1–3. Seek the face of the

Lord and long for him;

2. he will bring you his light and his peace.
    2. he will bring you his joy and his hope.
    3. he will bring you his care and his love.

Michael Joncas, from Jeremiah 31:3, Ps 24:

76

I will come to you in the silence,
I will lift you from all your fear.
You will hear my voice,
I claim you as my choice,
be still and know I am here

I am hope for all who are hopeless,
I am eyes for all who long to see.
In the shadows of the night,
I will be your light,
come and rest in me.
Do not be afraid, I am with you;
I have called you each by name.
Come and follow me,
I will bring you home;
I love you and you are mine.

I am strength for all the despairing,
healing for the ones who dwell in shame.
All the blind will see,
the lame will all run free,
and all will know my name.   *Refrain*

I am the Word that leads all to freedom,
I am the peace the world cannot give.
I will call your name,
embracing all your pain,
stand up, now walk, and live!   *Refrain*
David Haas

77

O Lord, I know you are near,
standing always at my side.
You guard me from the foe
and you lead me in ways everlasting.

Lord, you have searched my heart
and you know when I sit and when I
    stand.
Your hand is upon me, protecting me
    from death,
keeping me from harm.

Where can I run from your love?
If I climb to the heavens, you are there.
If I fly to the sunrise or sail beyond the
    sea
still I'd find you there.

3 You know my heart and its ways,
   you who formed me before I was born,
   in secret of darkness, before I saw the sun,
   in my mother's womb.

4 Marvellous to me are your works;
   how profound are your thoughts my Lord!
   Even if I could count them, they number
       as the stars,
   you would still be there.
       Daniel L. Schutte, from Psalm 139

778

1 You know me, Lord, you search my
       heart,
   my thoughts are open to your gaze.
   Protect me, Lord, from evil ways
   and guide me in the path of life.

2 Before a word is on my tongue
   you know the secrets of my heart.
   Be close to me, surround me, Lord,
   from all my terrors set me free.

3 Where could I go to flee from you?
   How can I shelter from your face?
   If heavenward, I find you there:
   in earth's dark depths you follow me.

4 If I could take the wings of dawn
   and journey to the ends of earth,
   your hands would still be guiding me,
   your right hand still would hold me
       fast.

5 If darkness came to swallow me
   and night surround me in its grasp,
   no darkness would there be for you:
   the light would be as light as day.

6 For it was you who fashioned me;
   knit bone to bone and flesh on flesh.
   I thank you, Lord, Creator God,
   that you should think and breathe on
       me.

7 *Repeat verse 1*
       James Walsh, from Psalm 139

779

1. O God, you search me and you know me.
   All my thoughts lie open to your gaze.
   When I walk or lie down you are
      before me:
   ever the maker and keeper of my days.

2. You know my resting and my rising.
   You discern my purpose from afar.
   And with love everlasting you besiege
      me:
   in ev'ry moment of life or death, you are.

3. Before a word is on my tongue, Lord,
   you have known its meaning through and
      through.
   You are with me, beyond my understanding:
   God of my present, my past and future,
      too.

4. Although your Spirit is upon me,
   still I search for shelter from your light.
   There is nowhere on earth I can escape you:
   even the darkness is radiant in your sight.

5. For you created me and shaped me,
   gave me life within my mother's womb.
   For the wonder of who I am, I praise you:
   safe in your hands, all creation is made new.
   Bernadette Farrell, from Psalm 139

780

1 Be still, my soul; the Lord is on your side;
  bear patiently the cross of grief or pain;
  leave to your God to order and provide;
  in every change he faithful will remain.
  Be still, my soul; your best, your
     heavenly Friend
  through thorny ways leads to a joyful end.

2, Be still, my soul; your God will undertake
  to guide the future as he has the past.
  Your hope, your confidence let nothing
     shake;
  all now mysterious shall be bright at last.
  Be still, my soul; the waves and wind
     still know
  his voice who ruled them while he dwelt
     below.

3 Be still, my soul; when dearest friend
     depart
  and all is darkened in the vale of tear
  then you will better know his love, hi
     heart,
  who comes to soothe your sorrow, ca
     your fears.
  Be still, my soul; for Jesus can repay
  from his own fullness all he takes aw

4 Be still, my soul; the hour is hastening
  when we shall be forever with the Lo
  when disappointment, grief, and fear
     gone,
  sorrow forgotten, love's pure joy
     restored.
  Be still, my soul; when change and te
     are past,
  all safe and blessèd we shall meet at ▮
     Katharina von Schlegel, b.1697,
     tr. Jane L. Borthwick (1813-1897)

781

1 Look and learn from the birds of the ▮
  flying high above worry and fear:
  neither sowing nor harvesting seed,
  yet they're given whatever they need
  If the God of earth and heaven
  cares for birds as much as this,
  won't he care much more for you,
  when you put your trust in him?

2 Look and learn from the flowers of th
     field,
  bringing beauty and colour to life;
  neither sewing nor tailoring cloth,
  yet they're dressed in the finest attire.
  If the God of earth and heaven
  cares for flowers as much as this,
  won't he care much more for you
  when you put your trust in him?

3 What God wants should be our will;
where God calls should be our goal.
When we seek the kingdom first,
all we've lost is ours again.

Let's be done with anxious thoughts,
set aside tomorrow's cares,
live each day that God provides
putting all our trust in him.

Nah Young-Soo, from Matt 6:23-24.
English version by John L. Bell

782 Toi, tu nous aimes/Lord God, you love us

Lord   God, you   love   us,   source   of   com - pas - sion.
Toi,   tu   nous   ai - mes,   sour - ce   de   vie.

Taizé chant by Jacques Berthier (1923-1994)

783

Lord of life, we come to you;
Lord of all, our Saviour be;
come to bless and to heal
with the light of your love.

2 Through the days of doubt and toil,
in our joy and in our pain,
guide our steps in your way,
make us one in your love.

Catherine Walker

784

Praise we our God with joy
and gladness never ending;
angels and saints with us
their grateful voices blending.
He is our Father dear,
o'er filled with parent's love;
mercies unsought, unknown,
he showers from above.

He is our shepherd true;
with watchful care unsleeping,
on us, his erring sheep
an eye of pity keeping;
he with a mighty arm
the bonds of sin doth break,
and to our burden'd hearts
in words of peace doth speak.

Graces in copious stream
from that pure fount are welling,
where, in our heart of hearts,
our God hath set his dwelling.
His word our lantern is;
his peace our comfort still;

his sweetness all our rest;
our law, our life, his will.

Frederick Oakeley (1802–80), and others

785

Though the mountains may fall, and the
*   hills turn to dust,*
yet the love of the Lord will stand
as a shelter for all who will call on his
*   name.*
Sing the praise and the glory of God.

1 Could the Lord ever leave you?
Could the Lord forget his love?
Though the Mother forsake her child,
he will not abandon you.

2 Should you turn and forsake him,
he will gently call your name.
Should you wander away from him,
he will always take you back.

3 Go to him when you're weary;
he will give you eagle's wings.
You will run, never tire,
for your God will be your strength.

4 As he swore to your Fathers,
when the flood destroyed the land.
He will never forsake you;
he will swear to you again.

Daniel L. Schutte,
based on Isaiah 54:6-10; 49:15; 40:31-32

786

Turn to me, O turn, and be saved,
says the Lord, for I am God
there is no other, none beside me.
I call your name.

1 I am God who comforts you;
who are you to be afraid,
of flesh that fades,
is made like the grass of the field
soon to wither.

2 Listen to me, my people;
give ear to me, my nation:
a law will go forth from me,
and my justice for a light to the people.

3 Lift up your eyes to the heavens,
and look at the earth down below.
The heavens will vanish like smoke,
and the earth will wear out like a
garment.

John Foley SJ, based on Isaiah 45, 51

787

Sing it in the valleys,
shout it from the mountain tops;
Jesus came to save us,
and his saving never stops.
He is King of Kings,
and new life he brings,
sing it in the valleys,
shout it from the mountain tops, (Oh!)
shout it from the mountain tops.

1 Jesus, you are by my side,
you take all my fears.
If I only come to you,
you will heal the pain of years.

2 You have not deserted me,
though I go astray.
Jesus take me in your arms,
help me walk with you today.

3 Jesus, you are living now,
Jesus, I believe.
Jesus, take me, heart and soul,
yours alone I want to be.

Mike Anderson

788

1 Praise to the Holiest in the height,
and in the depth be praise,
in all his words most wonderful,
most sure in all his ways.

2 O loving wisdom of our God!
When all was sin and shame,
a second Adam to the fight,
and to the rescue came.

3 O wisest love! That flesh and blood
which did in Adam fail,
should strive afresh against the foe,
should strive and should prevail;

4 And that a higher gift than grace
should flesh and blood refine,
God's presence and his very self,
and Essence all divine.

5 O generous love! That he who smote
in man for man the foe,
the double agony in man
for man should undergo;

6 And in the garden secretly
and on the Cross on high,
should teach his brethren, and inspire
to suffer and to die.

7 Praise to the Holiest in the height,
and in the depth be praise,
in all his words most wonderful,
most sure in all his ways.

John Henry Newman (1801–90)

789

Trust is in the eyes of a tiny babe
leaning on his mother's breast.
In the eager beat of a young bird's wings
on the day it leaves the nest.
It is the living Spirit
filling the earth, bringing to birth
a world of love and laughter,
joy in the light of the Lord.

Hope is in the rain that makes crystal
    streams
tumble down a mountain side,
and in every man who repairs his nets,
waiting for the rising tide.

Love is in the hearts of all those who
    seek
freedom for the human race.
Love is in the touch of the hand that
    heals,
and the smile that lights a face.

Strength is in the wind as it bends the
    trees,
warmth is in the bright red flame,
light is in the sun and the candle–glow,
cleansing are the ocean's waves.
Estelle White (1926-2011)

790

Christ has no hands but ours;
no hands but ours to do his work.
Hands that reach out to touch and heal,
sharing Christ's peace with all we meet,
Christ has no hands but ours.

Christ has no feet but ours;
no feet but ours to walk his path.
Walking with hope beside the lost,
following Christ: the way of life.
Christ has no feet but ours.

Christ has no eyes but ours;
no eyes but ours to see his face.
Looking for Christ in those we meet,
finding in Christ the truth we seek.
Christ has no eyes but ours.

4. Christ has no voice but ours;
no voice but ours to speak his truth,
Joining as one to sing his praise.
Speaking for those who have no voice.
Christ has no voice but ours.

5. Christ lives in us to-day.
We are his body in the world:
Called to be Christ in all we do;
living our faith in joy and hope.
Christ lives in us to-day.
    The last line may be sung twice more.

Martin Foster, based on
St Teresa of Avila (1515–1582)

791

1. All praise to thee, for thou, O King divine,
didst yield the glory that of right was thine,
that in our darkened hearts thy grace
    might shine:
    Alleluia!

2. Thou cam'st to us in lowliness of
    thought,
by thee the outcast and the poor were
    sought,
and by thy death was God's salvation
    wrought:
    Alleluia!

3. Let this mind be in us which was in thee,
who wast a servant that we might be
    free,
humbling thyself to death on Calvary:
    Alleluia!

4. Wherefore, by God's eternal purpose,
    thou
art high exalted o'er all creatures now,
and given the name to which all knees
    shall bow:
    Alleluia!

5. Let every tongue confess with one accord
in heaven and earth that Jesus Christ is
    Lord;
And God the Father be by all adored:
    Alleluia!
    F. Bland Tucker (1895-1984)
    based on Philippians 2:5-11

792

Refrain

Eye has not seen, ear has not heard what God has read-y for those who love him; Spir-it of love, come, give us the mind of Je-sus,____ teach us the wis-dom of God.____

Last time

1 When pain and sorrow weigh us down,
   be near to us, oh Lord,
   forgive the weakness of our faith,
   and bear us up within your peaceful word.

2 Our lives are but a single breath,
   we flower and we fade,
   yet all our days are in your hands,
   so we return in love what love has made.

3 To those who see with eyes of faith,
   the Lord is ever near,
   reflected in the faces
   of all the poor and lowly of the world.

4 We sing a myst'ry from the past,
   in halls where saints have trod,
   yet ever new the music rings,
   to Jesus, living song of God.

Marty Haugen

793

If God is for us, who can be against,
if the Spirit of God has set us free?
If God is for us, who can be against,
if the Spirit of God has set us free?

1 I know that nothing in this world
   can ever take us from his love.

2 Nothing can take us from his love,
   poured out in Jesus, the Lord.

3 And nothing present or to come
   can ever take us from his love.

4 I know that neither death nor life
   can ever take us from his love.

John B. Foley SJ, based on Romans 8

794

1 God is love: his the care,
   tending each, everywhere.
   God is love, all is there!
   Jesus came to show him,
   that we all might know him!

Sing aloud, loud, loud!
Sing aloud, loud, loud!
God is good! God is truth!
God is beauty!
Praise him!

2 None can see God above;
   humankind we can love;
   thus may we Godward move,
   finding God in others,
   sisters all, and brothers:

3 Jesus shared all our pain:
   strove and died, rose again,
   rules our hearts now as then,
   for he came to save us
   by the truth he gave us:

4 To our Lord praise we sing,
   light and life, friend and king,
   coming down love to bring,
   pattern for our duty,
   showing God in beauty:

Percy Dearmer (1867–1936), alt.

795

I heard the voice of Jesus say,
'Come unto me and rest;
lay down, you weary one, lay down
your head upon my breast.'
I came to Jesus as I was,
weary, and worn, and sad;
I found in him a resting-place
and he has made me glad.

I heard the voice of Jesus say,
'Behold, I freely give
the living water, thirsty one;
stoop down, and drink, and live.'
I came to Jesus, and I drank
of that life-giving stream;
my thirst was quenched, my soul
    revived,
and now I live in him.

I heard the voice of Jesus say,
'I am this dark world's Light;
look unto me, your morn shall rise
and all your day be bright.'
I looked to Jesus, and I found
in him my Star, my Sun;
and in that light of life I'll walk
till travelling days are done.
    Horatius Bonar (1808-89)

796

I will never forget you, my people,
I have carved you on the palm of my
    hand.
I will never forget you;
I will not leave you orphaned.
I will never forget my own.

Does a mother forget her baby?
Or a woman the child within her womb?
Yet, even if these forget,
yes, even if these forget,
I will never forget my own.

Repeat Verse 1

    Carey Landry

797

1   Jesu, lover of my soul!
    Let me to thy bosom fly,
    while the nearer waters roll,
    while the tempest still is high;
    hide me, O my Saviour, hide,
    till the storm of life is past;
    safe into the haven guide,
    O receive my soul at last.

2   Other refuge have I none;
    hangs my helpless soul on thee;
    leave, ah! leave me not alone,
    still support and comfort me.
    All my trust on thee is stayed,
    all my help from thee I bring;
    cover my defenceless head
    with the shadow of thy wing.

3   Thou, O Christ, art all I want;
    more than all in thee I find;
    raise the fallen, cheer the faint,
    heal the sick and lead the blind.
    Just and holy is thy name;
    I am all unrighteousness;
    false and full of sin I am,
    thou art full of truth and grace.

4   Plenteous grace with thee is found,
    grace to cover all my sin
    let the healing streams abound;
    make and keep me pure within.
    Thou of life the fountain art,
    freely let me take of thee;
    spring thou up within my heart,
    rise to all eternity.
        Charles Wesley (1707–88)

798

1   Jesu, the very thought of thee
    with sweetness fills my breast;
    but sweeter far thy face to see,
    and in thy presence rest.

2   Nor voice can sing, nor heart can frame,
    nor can the memory find,
    a sweeter sound than thy blest name,
    O Saviour of mankind.

3 O hope of every contrite heart,
   O joy of all the meek,
   to those who fall, how kind thou art,
   how good to those who seek!

4 But what to those who find? Ah, this
   nor tongue nor pen can show;
   the love of Jesus, what it is
   none but his lovers know.

5 Jesu, our only joy be thou,
   as thou our prize wilt be;
   Jesu, be thou our glory now,
   and through eternity.
   11th century,
   tr. Edward Caswall (1814–78)

799

1 O Sacred Heart,
   our home lies deep in thee;
   on earth thou art an exile's rest,
   in heav'n the glory of the blest,
   O Sacred Heart.

2 O Sacred Heart,
   thou fount of contrite tears;
   where'er those living waters flow,
   new life to sinners they bestow,
   O Sacred Heart.

3 O Sacred Heart,
   our trust is all in thee,
   for though earth's night be dark and drear,
   thou breathest rest where thou art near,
   O Sacred Heart.

4 O Sacred Heart,
   when shades of death shall fall,
   receive us 'neath thy gentle care,
   and save us from the tempter's snare,
   O Sacred Heart.

5 O Sacred Heart,
   lead exiled children home,
   where we may ever rest near thee,
   in peace and joy eternally,
   O Sacred Heart.
   Francis Stanfield (1835–1914)

800

1 To Jesus' Heart, all burning
   with fervent love for all,
   my heart with fondest yearning
   shall raise its joyful call.

   While ages course along,
   blest be with loudest song
   the sacred heart of Jesus
   by ev'ry heart and tongue.
   The sacred heart of Jesus
   by ev'ry heart and tongue.

2 O Heart, for me on fire
   with love no–one can speak,
   my yet untold desire
   God gives me for thy sake.

3 Too true, I have forsaken
   thy love for wilful sin;
   yet now let me be taken
   back by thy grace again.

4 As thou art meek and lowly,
   and ever pure of heart,
   so may my heart be wholly
   of thine the counterpart.

5 When life away is flying,
   and earth's false glare is done;
   still, Sacred Heart, in dying
   I'll say I'm all thine own.
   Aloys Schlör (1805–52),
   tr. A.J. Christie (1817–1891)

801

1 Love divine, all loves excelling,
   joy of heav'n, to earth come down,
   fix in us thy humble dwelling,
   all thy faithful mercies crown.

2 Jesus, thou art all compassion,
   pure unbounded love thou art;
   visit us with thy salvation,
   enter every trembling heart.

3 Come, almighty to deliver,
   let us all thy life receive;
   suddenly return, and never,
   never more thy temples leave.

Thee we would be always blessing,
serve thee as thy hosts above;
pray, and praise thee without ceasing,
glory in thy perfect love.

Finish then thy new creation,
pure and sinless let us be;
let us see thy great salvation
perfectly restored in thee.

Changed from glory into glory,
till in heaven we take our place,
till we cast our crowns before thee,
lost in wonder, love, and praise.
Charles Wesley (1707–88)

02

Loving shepherd of thy sheep,
keep me, Lord, in safety keep;
nothing can thy pow'r withstand,
none can pluck me from thy hand.

Loving shepherd, thou didst give
thine own life that I might live;
may I love thee day by day,
gladly thy sweet will obey.

Loving shepherd, ever near,
teach me still thy voice to hear;
suffer not my steps to stray
from the strait and narrow way.

Where thou leadest may I go,
walking in thy steps below;
then before thy Father's throne,
Jesu, claim me for thine own.
Jane E. Leeson (1809–91)

03

Love is his word, love is his way,
feasting with kin, fasting alone,
living and dying, rising again,
love, only love, is his way.
Richer than gold is the love of my Lord:
better than splendour and wealth.

Love is his way, love is his mark,
sharing his last Passover feast,
Christ at the table, host to the Twelve,
love, only love, is his mark.

3 Love is his mark, love is his sign,
bread for our strength, wine for our joy,
'This is my body, this is my blood,'
love, only love, is his sign.

4 Love is his sign, love is his news,
'Do this,' he said, 'lest you forget
all my deep sorrow, all my dear blood,'
love, only love, is his news.

5 Love is his news, love is his name,
we are his own, chosen and called,
family, brethren, cousins and kin.
Love, only love, is his name.

6 Love is his name, love is his law.
Hear his command, all who are his:
'Love one another, I have loved you.'
Love, only love, is his law.

7 Love is his law, love is his word:
love of the Lord, Father and Word,
love of the Spirit, God ever one,
love, only love, is his word.
Luke Connaughton (1919–79)

804

1 The King of love my shepherd is,
whose goodness faileth never;
I nothing lack if I am his
and he is mine for ever.

2 Where streams of living water flow
my ransomed soul he leadeth,
and where the verdant pastures grow
with food celestial feedeth.

3 Perverse and foolish oft I strayed
but yet in love he sought me,
and on his shoulder gently laid,
and home, rejoicing, brought me.

4 In death's dark vale I fear no ill
with thee, dear Lord, beside me;
thy rod and staff my comfort still,
thy cross before to guide me.

5 Thou spread'st a table in my sight,
thy unction grace bestoweth:
and O what transport of delight
from thy pure chalice floweth!

6 And so through all the length of days
  thy goodness faileth never;
  good Shepherd, may I sing thy praise
  within thy house for ever.

  H.W.Baker (1821–77), from Psalm 23

805

1 The living God my shepherd is,
  I know no care or need.
  You guide me where rich pastures grow
  along the verdant mead,
  where ev'ry day by pleasant way
  my hungering soul may feed.

2 You lead me where cool waters flow
  by rippling stream and rill,
  where I may taste the springs of life,
  my thirsting spirit fill;
  you near me bide and homeward guide
  my vagrant heart and will.

3 I nothing fear; for you, O Lord
  are with me night and day,
  intent, with shepherd's staff and rod,
  to guide me when I stray,
  and in the fold you will uphold
  my fainting heart always.

4 And so through all the length of days,
  your mercy waits on me,
  at last within my Father's house
  your glory I shall see;
  you evermore will I adore
  through all eternity.

  John Driscoll SJ (1865-1940), from Psalm 23

806

1 The Lord's my shepherd, I'll not want,
  he makes me down to lie
  in pastures green. He leadeth me
  the quiet waters by.

2 My soul he doth restore again,
  and me to walk doth make
  within the paths of righteousness,
  e'en for his own name's sake.

3 Yea, though I walk in death's dark val
  yet will I fear none ill.
  For thou art with me, and thy rod
  and staff me comfort still.

4 My table thou hast furnishèd
  in presence of my foes,
  my head thou dost with oil anoint,
  and my cup overflows.

5 Goodness and mercy all my life
  shall surely follow me.
  And in God's house for evermore
  my dwelling–place shall be.

  Psalm 23 from the Scottish Psalter, 165(

807

1 Praise, my soul, the king of heaven!
  To his feet thy tribute bring.
  Ransomed, healed, restored, forgiven,
  who like me his praise should sing?
      Praise him! Praise him!
      Praise him! Praise him!
  Praise the everlasting king!

2 Praise him for his grace and favour
  to our fathers in distress;
  praise him still the same for ever,
  slow to chide and swift to bless.
      Praise him! Praise him!
      Praise him! Praise him!
  Glorious in his faithfulness!

3 Father–like he tends and spares us;
  well our feeble frame he knows;
  in his hands he gently bears us,
  rescues us from all our foes.
      Praise him! Praise him!
      Praise him! Praise him!
  Widely as his mercy flows!

4 Angels, help us to adore him;
  ye behold him face to face;
  sun and moon bow down before him,
  dwellers all in time and space.
      Praise him! Praise him!
      Praise him! Praise him!
  Praise with us the God of grace!

  H. F. Lyte (1793–1847) from Psalm 103

808

The love we have for you, O Lord,
is only a shadow of your love for us,
only a shadow of your love for us:
your deep abiding love.

The bread we take and eat, O Lord,
is your body broken and shared with us;
your body broken and shared with us;
the gift of your great love.
Our lives are in your hands;
our lives are in your hands.
Our love for you will grow, O Lord;
your light in us will shine.

Our own belief in you, O Lord,
is only a shadow of your faith in us:
only a shadow of your faith in us:
your deep and lasting faith.

The dreams we share today, O Lord,
are only a shadow of your dreams for us:
only a shadow of your dreams for us:
if we but follow you.
Our lives are in your hands....

The joy we share today, O Lord,
is only a shadow of your joys for us:
only a shadow of your joys for us:
when we meet face to face.
Our lives are in your hands....

Carey Landry

809

There is a green hill far away,
without a city wall,
where the dear Lord was crucified
who died to save us all.

We may not know, we cannot tell,
what pains he had to bear,
but we believe it was for us
he hung and suffered there.

He died that we might be forgiven,
he died to make us good;
that we might go at last to heaven,
saved by his precious blood.

4 There was no other good enough
to pay the price of sin;
he only could unlock the gate
of heaven, and let us in.

5 O, dearly, dearly has he loved,
and we must love him too,
and trust in his redeeming blood,
and try his works to do.
Cecil Frances Alexander (1818–95)

810

1 There's a wideness in God's mercy
like the wideness of the sea;
there's a kindness in God's justice
which is more than liberty.
There is plentiful redemption
in the blood that has been shed;
there is joy for all the members
in the sorrows of the Head.

2 For the love of God is broader
than the measures of our mind,
and the heart of the Eternal
is most wonderfully kind.
If our love were but more simple
we should take him at his word,
and our lives would be thanksgiving
for the goodness of our Lord.

3 Troubled souls, why will you scatter
like a crowd of frightened sheep?
Foolish hearts, why will you wander
from a love so true and deep?
There is welcome for the sinner
and more graces for the good;
there is mercy with the Saviour,
there is healing in his blood.
F. W. Faber (1814-63), alt.

811

1 God is Love: let heav'n adore him;
God is Love: let earth rejoice;
let creation sing before him,
and exalt him with one voice.
God who laid the earth's foundation,
God who spread the heav'ns above,
God who breathes through all creation,
God is Love, eternal Love.

2 God is Love: and he enfoldeth
all the world in one embrace;
with unfailing grasp he holdeth
every child of every race.
And when human hearts are breaking
under sorrow's iron rod,
then they find that selfsame aching
deep within the heart of God.

3 God is Love; and though with blindness
sin afflicts all human life,
God's eternal loving-kindness
guides us through our earthly strife.
Sin and death and hell shall never
o'er us final triumph gain;
God is Love, so Love for ever
o'er the universe must reign.
Timothy Rees (1874-1939)

812

1. Christ be near at either hand,
Christ behind, before me stand,
Christ with me where e'er I go,
Christ around, above, below.

2 Christ be in my head and mind
Christ within my soul enshrined,
Christ control my wayward heart;
Christ abide and ne'er depart.

3 Christ my life and only way.
Christ my lantern night and day;
Christ be my unchanging friend,
Guide and shepherd to the end.

4 Christ be all my strength and might
Christ my captain for the fight;
Christ fulfil my soul's desire;
Christ ennoble and inspire.

5 Christ the King and Lord of all
find me ready at his call;
Christ receive my service whole
hand and body, heart and soul.

6 Christ the King of kings descend
and of tyrants make an end;
Christ on us and all below
concord, love and peace bestow.

7 Thanks to him, who for our food
gives his sacred flesh and blood;
praise to him unceasing rise.
Christ whose glory fills the skies.
John Fennelly (1890-1966)

Bless the Lord *Taizé chant by Jacques Berthier (1923-199...)*

813

Bless the Lord, my soul, and bless God's ho - ly name.

Bless the Lord, my soul, who leads me in - to life.

The Kingdom

314

Blest are they, the poor in spirit,
theirs is the kingdom of God.

Blest are they, full of sorrow,
they shall be consoled.

Re - joice and be glad! Bless-ed are you, ho - ly are you! Re-joice and be glad! Yours is the king-dom of God!

Blest are they, the lowly ones,
they shall inherit the earth.
Blest are they who hunger and thirst;
they shall have their fill.

Blest are they who show mercy,
mercy shall be theirs.
Blest are they, the pure of heart,
they shall see God!

4 Blest are they who seek peace;
they are the children of God.
Blest are they who suffer in faith,
the glory of God is theirs.

5 Blest are you who suffer hate,
all because of me.
Rejoice and be glad, yours is the kingdom;
shine for all to see.

The refrain is sung twice to conclude

315

Blessed are they who fol - low God's law and walk in his way: the Kingdom is theirs.

Cantor/Choir sing verses from Matt. 5:3-10 over refrain.

316

*The Kingdom of Heaven
the Kingdom of Heaven is yours.
A new world in Jesus,
a new world in Jesus is yours.*

Blessed are you in sorrow and grief:
for you shall all be consoled.
Blessed are you the gentle in heart;
you shall inherit the earth.

Blessed are you who hunger for right:
for you shall be satisfied.

Blessed are you the merciful ones:
for you shall be pardoned too.

3 Blessed are you whose hearts are pure:
your eyes shall gaze on the Lord.
Blessed are you who strive after peace:
the Lord will call you his own.

4 Blessed are you who suffer for right:
the Heavenly Kingdom is yours.
Blessed are you who suffer for me:
for you shall reap your reward.

Mike Anderson, from Matt 5:3-10

817

1. Bless - ed are they who are poor in spir - it,
2. Bless - ed are they who are meek and hum - ble,
3. Bless - ed are they who will mourn in sor - row,
4. Bless those who hun - ger and thirst for jus - tice,
5. Bless - ed are they who show oth - ers mer - cy,
6. Bless - ed are hearts that are clean and ho - ly,
7. Bless - ed are they who bring peace a - mong us,
8. Bless those who suf - fer from per - se - cu - tion,

1. Theirs is the king - dom of God. Bless us, O Lord, make us
2. They will in - her - it the earth. Bless us, O Lord, make us
3. They will be com - fort - ed. Bless us, O Lord, when we
4. They will be sat - is - fied. Bless us, O Lord, hear our
5. They will know mer - cy too. Bless us, O Lord, hear our
6. They will be - hold the Lord, Bless us, O Lord, make us
7. They are the chil - dren of God. Bless us, O Lord, may your
8. Theirs is the king - dom of God. Bless us, O Lord, when they

1. poor in spir - it; Bless us, O Lord, our God.
2. meek and hum - ble; Bless us, O Lord, our God.
3. share their sor - row; Bless us, O Lord, our God.
4. cry for jus - tice; Bless us, O Lord, our God.
5. cry for mer - cy; Bless us, O Lord, our God.
6. pure and ho - ly; Bless us, O Lord, our God.
7. peace be with us; Bless us, O Lord, our God.
8. per - se - cute us; Bless us, O Lord, our God.

We are the light of the world, may our light shine be - fore all,

that they may see the good that we do, and give glo - ry to God.

Jean Anthony Greif, from Matt 5:3-10

➤ *See also Russian Beatitudes (615), As a tree (370)*

---

818 .

Rejoice! Rejoice! Christ is in you,
the hope of glory in our hearts.
He lives! He lives!
His breath is in you,
arise, a mighty army, we arise.

1 Now is the time for us
to march upon the land,
into our hands
he will give the ground we claim.
He rides in majesty
to lead us into victory,
the world shall see that Christ is Lord!

God is at work in us
his purpose to perform,
building a kingdom
of power not of words,
where things impossible
by faith shall be made possible;
let's give the glory
to him now.

Though we are weak, his grace
is everything we need;
we're made of clay
but this treasure is within.
He turns our weaknesses
into his opportunities,
so that the glory
goes to him.

Graham Kendrick

19

Make way, make way,
for Christ the King in splendour arrives.
Fling wide the gates
and welcome him into your lives.
Make way! Make way!
for the King of kings.
Make way! Make way!
And let his kingdom in.

He comes the broken hearts to heal
the prisoners to free.
the deaf shall hear, the lame shall dance,
the blind shall see.

And those who mourn with heavy hearts,
who weep and sigh;
with laughter, joy and royal crown
he'll beautify.

We call you now to worship him
as Lord of all.
To have no gods before him
their thrones must fall!

Graham Kendrick

20

Seek ye first the Kingdom of God,
and his righteousness,

and all these things shall be added unto
    you;
allelu, alleluia.
Alleluia, alleluia, alleluia,
allelu, alleluia.

2 Ask and it shall be given unto you,
seek and ye shall find;
knock and it shall be opened unto you;
allelu, alleluia.

3 We do not live by bread alone
but by ev'ry word
that comes forth from the mouth of God:

4 Where two or three are gathered in
    my name,
there am I in your midst;
and whatsoever you ask I will do:

V.1 Karen Lafferty, vv. 2-4 Anon.

821

1 The kingdom of God is justice and joy;
for Jesus restores what sin would destroy.
God's power and glory in Jesus we know;
and here and hereafter the kingdom shall
    grow.

2 The kingdom of God is mercy and grace;
the captives are freed, the sinners find place,
the outcast are welcomed God's banquet
    to share;
and hope is awakened in place of despair.

3 The kingdom of God is challenge and
    choice:
believe the good news, repent and rejoice!
His love for us sinners brought Christ to
    his cross:
our crisis of judgement for gain or for
    loss.

4 God's kingdom is come, the gift and the
    goal;
in Jesus begun, in heaven made whole.
The heirs of the kingdom shall answer
    his call;
and all things cry 'Glory!' to God all
    in all.

Bryn Rees (1911–83)

The Church on earth

822

Alleluia! Alleluia!
Raise the Gospel over the earth,
Alleluia! Alleluia!
Peace and justice bringing to birth!

1. Blessed those whose hearts are gentle.
   Blessed those whose spirits are strong.
   Blessed those who choose to bring forth
   right where there is wrong.

2. Blessed those who work for justice.
   Blessed those who answer the call.
   Blessed those who dare to dream of
   lasting peace for all.

3. Tremble, you who build up riches.
   Tremble, you with opulent lives.
   Tremble, when you meet the poor and
   see Christ in their eyes.

4. Tremble, you who thirst for power.
   Tremble, you who live for acclaim.
   Tremble, when you find no comfort
   in your wealth and fame.

5. Glory like the stars of heaven –
   Glory like the sun in the sky.
   Glory shines upon all people,
   equal in God's eyes.

6. Glory to the Word of Justice.
   Glory to the Spirit of Peace.
   Glory to the God of Love
   whose blessings never cease.
   Owen Alstott,
   vv. 1-4 based on Luke 6:20-25

823

1.Ma - ny are the light-beams from the one light. Our one light is Je - sus.

Ma - ny are the light-beams from the one light; we are one in Christ.

2　Many are the branches
of the one tree.
Our one tree is Jesus.
Many are the branches
of the one tree;
we are one in Christ.

3　Many are the gifts giv'n,
love is all one.
Love's the gift of Jesus.
Many are the gifts giv'n,
love is all one;
we are one in Christ.

4　Many ways to serve God,
the Spirit is one;
servant spirit of Jesus.
Many ways to serve God,
the Spirit is one;
we are one in Christ.

5　Many are the members,
the body is one;
members all of Jesus.
Many are the members,
the body is one;
we are one in Christ.

Cyprian of Carthage (d. A.D. 258), tr. Anders Frostenson. Music by Olle Widestra

824

Awake from your slumber!
Arise from your sleep!
A new day is dawning
for all those who weep.
The people in darkness
have seen a great light.
The Lord of our longing
has conquered the night.
  Let us build the city of God.
  May our tears be turned into dancing!
  For the Lord, our light and our Love,
  has turned the night into day!

We are sons of the morning;
we are daughters of day.
The One who has loved us
has brightened our way.
The Lord of all kindness
has called us to be
a light for his people
to set their hearts free.

God is light; in him there is no darkness.
Let us walk in his light, his children,
  one and all.
O comfort my people;
make gentle your words.
Proclaim to my city
the day of her birth.

O city of gladness, now lift up your voice!
Proclaim the good tidings that all may
  rejoice!
  Daniel L. Schutte

825

Church of God, elect and glorious,
holy nation, chosen race;
called as God's own special people,
royal priests and heirs of grace:
know the purpose of your calling,
show to all his mighty deeds;
tell of love which knows no limits,
grace which meets all human needs.

2 God has called you out of darkness
  into his most marvellous light,
  brought his truth to life within you,
  turned your blindness into sight.
  Let your light so shine around you
  that God's name is glorified;
  and all find fresh hope and purpose
  in Christ Jesus crucified.

3 Once you were an alien people,
  strangers to God's heart of love;
  but he brought you home in mercy,
  citizens of heaven above.
  Let his love flow out to others,
  let them feel a Father's care;
  that they too may know his welcome
  and his countless blessings share.

4 Church of God, elect and holy,
  be the people he intends;
  strong in faith and swift to answer
  each command your master sends:
  royal priests, fulfil your calling
  through your sacrifice and prayer;
  give your lives in joyful service -
  sing his praise, his love declare.
      J. E. Seddon (1915-1983) (from 1 Peter 2)

826

1 Christ's church shall glory in his power
  and grow to his perfection;
  he is our rock, our mighty tower,
  our life, our resurrection.
  So by his skilful hand
  the church of Christ shall stand;
  the master–builder's plan
  he works, as he began,
  and soon will crown with splendour.

2 Christ's people serve his wayward world
  to whom he seems a stranger;
  he knows its welcome from of old,
  he shares our joy, our danger.
  So strong, and yet so weak,
  the church of Christ shall speak;
  his cross our greatest need,
  his word the vital seed
  that brings a fruitful harvest.

3 Christ's living lamp shall brightly burn,
and to our earthly city
forgotten beauty shall return,
and purify and pity.
To give the oppressed their right
the church of Christ shall fight;
and though the years seem long
God is our strength and song,
and God is our salvation.

4 Christ's body triumphs in his name;
one Father, sovereign giver,
one Spirit, with his love aflame,
one Lord, the same for ever.
To you, O God our prize,
the church of Christ shall rise
beyond all measured height
to that eternal light,
where Christ shall reign all–holy.

Christopher Idle

827

1 Glorious things of you are spoken,
Sion, city of our God:
he whose word cannot be broken
formed you for his own abode.
On the Rock of Ages founded,
what can shake your sure repose?
With salvation's walls surrounded,
you may smile at all your foes.

2 See, the streams of living waters,
springing from eternal love,
well supply your sons and daughters
and all fear of want remove:
who can faint, while such a river
ever flows their thirst to assuage –
grace, which like the Lord, the giver,
never fails from age to age?

3 Blest inhabitants of Sion,
washed in their Redeemer's blood:
Jesus, whom their souls rely on,
makes them Kings and priests to God.
'Tis his love his people raises
over self to reign as kings,
and, as priests, his solemn praises
each for a thank–offering brings.

4 Saviour, since of Sion's city
I, through grace, a member am,
let the world deride or pity,
I will glory in your name:
fading is the wordling's pleasure,
all his boasted pomp and show;
solid joys and lasting treasure
none but Sion's children know.

John Newton (1725–1807)

828

1 As a fire is meant for burning
with a bright and warming flame,
so the Church is meant for mission,
giving glory to God's name.
As we witness to the gospel,
we would build a bridge of care,
joining hands across the nations,
finding neighbours ev'rywhere.

2 We are learners; we are teachers;
we are pilgrims on the way.
We are seekers; we are givers;
we are vessels made of clay.
By our gentle, loving actions,
we would show that Christ is light.
In a humble, list'ning Spirit,
we would live to God's delight.

3 As a green bud in the springtime
is a sign of life renewed,
so may we be signs of oneness
'mid earth's peoples, many hued.
As a rainbow lights the heavens
when a storm is past and gone,
may our lives reflect the radiance
of God's new and glorious dawn.

Ruth Duck

829

1 O Christ, the great foundation
on which your people stand
to preach your true salvation
in every age and land:
pour out your Holy Spirit
to make us strong and pure,
to keep the faith unbroken
as long as worlds endure.

Baptized in one confession,
one church in all the earth,
we bear our Lord's impression,
the sign of second birth:
one holy people gathered
in love beyond our own,
by grace we were invited,
by grace we make you known.

Where tyrants' hold is tightened,
where strong devour the weak,
where innocents are frightened
the righteous fear to speak,
there let your church awaking
attack the powers of sin
and, all their ramparts breaking,
with you the victory win.

This is the moment glorious
when he who once was dead
shall lead his church victorious,
their champion and their head.
The Lord of all creation
his heavenly kingdom brings
the final consummation,
the glory of all things.
Timothy T'infang Lew (1891-1947), alt.

30

The Church's one foundation,
is Jesus Christ, her Lord;
she is his new creation,
by water and the Word;
from heav'n he came and sought her
to be his holy bride,
with his own blood he bought her,
and for her life he died.

Elect from every nation,
yet one o'er all the earth,
her charter of salvation
one Lord, one faith, one birth;
one holy name she blesses,
partakes one holy food,
and to one hope she presses,
with every grace endued.

3 'Mid toil, and tribulation,
and tumult of her war,
she waits the consummation
of peace for evermore;
till with the vision glorious
her longing eyes are blest,
and the great Church victorious
shall be the Church at rest.

4 Yet she on earth hath union
with God the Three in One,
and mystic sweet communion
with those whose rest is won:
O happy ones and holy!
Lord, give us grace that we
like them, the meek and lowly
on high may dwell with thee.
S. J. Stone (1830–1900)

831

1 In Christ there is no east or west,
in him no south or north,
but one great fellowship of love
throughout the whole wide earth.

2 In him shall true hearts ev'rywhere
their high communion find.
His service is the golden cord
close-binding humankind.

3 Join hands, disciples in the faith
whate'er your race may be.
Who serve each other in Christ's love
are surely kin to me.

4 In Christ now meet both east and west,
in him meet south and north.
All Christly souls are one in him
throughout the whole wide earth.
John Oxenham (1852–1941)

832

One bread, one body, one Lord of all,
one cup of blessing which we bless.
And we, though many, throughout the earth,
we are one body in this one Lord.

1 Gentile or Jew, servant or free,
woman or man, no more.

2 Many the gifts, many the works,
  one in the Lord of all.

3 Grain for the fields, scattered and grown,
  gathered to one, for all.
  John B. Foley SJ

833

1 O thou, who at thy Eucharist didst pray
  that all thy Church might be for ever one,
  grant us at every Eucharist to say,
  with longing heart and soul, 'Thy will be
      done'.
  O may we all one bread, one body be,
  one through this sacrament of unity.

2 For all thy Church O Lord, we intercede;
  make thou our sad divisions soon to cease;
  draw us the nearer each to each, we plead,
  by drawing all to thee, O Prince of peace;
  thus may we all one bread, one body be,
  one through this sacrament of unity.

3 We pray thee too for wanderers from thy
      fold,
  O bring them back, good shepherd of the
      sheep,
  back to the faith which saints believed of
      old,
  back to the Church which still that faith
      doth keep;
  soon may we all one bread, one body be,
  one through this sacrament of unity.

4 So, Lord, at length when sacraments shall
      cease,
  may we be one with all thy Church above,
  one with thy saints in one unbroken peace,
  one with thy saints in one unbounded love:
  more blessed still, in peace and love
      to be
  one with the Trinity in unity.
  W.H. Turton (1856–1938)

834

Father God, bless this family;
Brother Christ, remain with us;
Holy Love, Spirit of unity,
make us one family,
God's Holy Family.

1 For the Word of God proclaimed,
  for the signs we celebrate,
  Word and sacrament giving life:
  This is our family, God's holy family,
  God's holy family.

2 For the help to those in need,
  for the healing of our pain,
  loving service we give to all:
  This is our family...

3 For the welcome that we feel,
  for the friends who share our days,
  watching, waiting in hope and joy:

4 For the blessings of the past,
  for the hope of days to come,
  young and old joining hands and heart
  John Schiavo

835

Out of darkness God has called us,
claimed by Christ as God's own peopl
Holy nation, royal priesthood,
walking in God's marvellous light.

1 Let us take the words you give,
  strong and faithful words to live.
  Words that in our hearts are sown;
  words that bind us as your own.

2 Let us take the Christ you give.
  Broken Body, Christ we live.
  Christ the risen from the tomb;
  Christ who calls us as your own.

3 Let us take the love you give,
  that the way of love we live.
  Love to bring your people home;
  love to make us all your own.

Verses for Easter
1 Sing a joyful Alleluia,
  sing to Christ the Risen Saviour,
  'He is not among the dead!
  He is risen, as he said.'

2 We have died to sin with Christ.
  We will rise with him at last.
  Now the second Adam lives.
  Now eternal life he gives!

Let your sadness be no more,
Christ has opened heaven's door.
Death has no more power to slay.
This is Resurrection Day!
Christopher Walker

5 Draw together at one table
   all the human family;
   shape a circle ever wider
   and a people ever free.
   Delores Dufner OSB

36

Summoned by the God who made us
rich in our diversity,
gathered in the name of Jesus,
richer still in unity:
Let us bring the gifts that differ
and, in splendid, varied ways,
sing a new church into being
one in faith and love and praise.

Radiant risen from the water,
robed in holiness and light,
male and female in God's image,
male and female, God's delight:

Trust the goodness of creation;
trust the Spirit strong within.
Dare to dream the vision promised
sprung from seed of what has been.

Bring the hopes of ev'ry nation;
bring the art of ev'ry race.
Weave a song of peace and justice;
let it sound through time and space.

837

1 Faith of our fathers! Living still
   in spite of dungeon, fire and sword;
   oh, how our hearts beat high with joy
   whene'er we hear that glorious word!
   Faith of our fathers! Holy Faith!
   We will be true to thee till death,
   we will be true to thee till death.

2 Our fathers, chained in prisons dark,
   were still in heart and conscience free;
   how sweet would be their children's fate,
   if they, like them, could die for thee!

3 Faith of our fathers, Mary's prayers
   shall win our country back to thee.
   And through the truth that comes from God
   our land shall then indeed be free.

4 Faith of our fathers, we will love
   both friend and foe in all our strife,
   and preach thee too, as love knows how,
   by kindly words and virtuous life.
   F.W. Faber (1814–63)

Forgiveness, Penance & Reconciliation

38

O Lord, be not mind-ful of our guilt and our sins;
O Lord, do not judge us for our faults and of-fen-ces. May your
mer-ci-ful love be___ u-pon___ us.

Help your people, Lord, O God our Saviour,
deliver us for the glory of your name!

Pardon us, O Lord, all our sins, ...

3 Praise to you, O Lord,
   through all the ages without end...

Lucien Deiss CSSp (1921-2007)

Ostende nobis (Canon)

Taizé chant by Jacques Berthi

839

O-sten-de no-bis, Do-mi - ne, mi-se-ri-cor-di-am tu -

am. A-men! A-men!— Ma-ra-na-tha! Ma-ra-na-tha!

Show us, O Lord, your mercy (Ps 84(85):8

840

1 God of mercy and compassion,
Lord of life and blinding light,
truth whom creatures would refashion,
place on us the gift of sight.
   Truth insistent and demanding
   Love resented and ignored,
   Life beyond all understanding,
   give us peace and pardon, Lord.

2 God most holy and forgiving,
penetrate our pride and sloth;
on a people partly living,
place the gift of life and growth.

3 Lord, who out of love consented
to the worst that we could do;
Lord, abandoned and tormented,
let us love and suffer too.
   Michael Hodgetts, alt.

841

1 Diverse in culture, nation, race,
we come together by your grace.
God, let us be a meeting ground
where hope and healing love are found.

2 God, let us be a bridge of care
connecting people everywhere.
Help us confront all fear and hate
and lust for power that separate.

3 When chasms widen, storms arise,
O Holy Spirit, make us wise.
Let us resolve, like steel, be strong
to stand with those who suffer wrong.

4 God, let us be a table spread
with gifts of love and broken bread,

where all find welcome, grace attends
and enemies arise as friends.
   Ruth Duck

842

1 Come back to me with all your heart.
Don't let fear keep us apart.
Trees do bend, though straight and tal
so must we to others' call.
   Long have I waited
   for your coming home to me
   and living deeply our new life.

2 The wilderness will lead you
to your heart, where I will speak.
Integrity and justice
with tenderness you shall know.

3 You shall sleep secure with peace;
faithfulness will be your joy.

4 Come back to me with all your heart.
Don't let fear keep us apart.
Trees do bend, though straight and ta
so must we to others' call.
   Gregory Norbet, based on Hosea

843

Remember, remember your mercy, Lor
Remember, remember your mercy, Lor
Hear your people's prayer as they
   call to you,
Remember, remember your mercy, Lor

1 Lord, make me know your ways.
Lord, teach me your paths.
Make me walk in your truth, and teach m
for you are God my Saviour.

Remember your mercy, Lord,
and the love you have shown
   from of old.
Do not remember the sins of my youth.
In your love, remember me,
in your love remember me,
because of your goodness, O Lord.

The Lord is good and upright.
He shows the path to all who stray,
he guides the humble in the right path;
he teaches his way to the poor.
Response: Paul Inwood,
Verses: Psalm 25:4-9 Grail version

44
How can we sing with joy to God,
how can we pray to him,
when we are far away from God
in selfishness and sin?

2 How can we claim to do God's will
   when we have turned away
   from things of God to things of earth,
   and willed to disobey?

3 How can we praise the love of God
   which all his works make known,
   when all our works turn from his love
   to choices of our own?

4 God knows the sinful things we do,
   the godless life we live,
   yet in his love he calls to us
   so ready to forgive.

5 So we will turn again to God -
   his ways will be our ways,
   his will our will, his love our love,
   and he himself our praise!
   Brian Foley (1919-2000)

Melody by
Stephen Dean

1. How can we sing with joy to God, how can we pray to him,
when we are far a - way from God in sel - fish - ness and sin?

45
'Forgive our sins as we forgive,'
you taught us, Lord, to pray,
but you alone can grant us grace
to live the words we say.

How can your pardon reach and bless
the unforgiving heart
that broods on wrongs and will not let
old bitterness depart?

In blazing light your Cross reveals
the truth we dimly knew:
what trivial debts are owed to us,
how great our debt to you!

Lord, cleanse the depths within our souls
and bid resentment cease.
Then, bound to all in bonds of love,
our lives will spread your peace.
Rosamond Herklots

846
1 Amazing grace! How sweet the sound
   that saved a wretch like me.
   I once was lost but now I'm found,
   was blind, but now I see.

2 'Twas grace that taught my heart to fear,
   and grace my fears relieved.
   How precious did that grace appear
   the hour I first believed.

3 Through many dangers, toils and snares
   I have already come.
   'Tis grace hath brought me safe thus far,
   and grace will lead me home.

4 The Lord has promised good to me;
   his word my hope secures.
   He will my shield and portion be
   as long as life endures.
   John Newton (1725–1807)

847

1 Oh Lord, all the world belongs to you,
  and you are always making all things new.
    What is wrong you forgive,
    and the new life you give
  is what's turning the world upside down.

2 The world's only loving to its friends,
  but you have brought us love that never
    ends;
    loving enemies too,
    and this loving with you
  is what's turning the world upside down.

3 This world lives divided and apart.
  You draw us together and we start
    in your body to see
    that in fellowship we
  can be turning the world upside down.

4 The world wants the wealth to live in state,
  but you show us a new way to be great;
    like a servant you came,
    and if we do the same,
  we'll be turning the world upside down.

5 Oh Lord, all the world belongs to you,
  and you are always making all things new.
    Send your Spirit on all
  in your Church whom you call
  to be turning the world upside down.
          Patrick Appleford

848

1 The Master came to bring good news,
  the news of love and freedom,
  to heal the sick and seek the poor,
  to build the peaceful kingdom.
  Father, forgive us! Through Jesus hear us!
  As we forgive one another!

2 The Law's fulfilled through Jesus Christ,
  the man who lived for others,
  the law of Christ is: Serve in love
  our sisters and our brothers.

3 To seek the sinners Jesus came,
  to live among the friendless,
  to show them love that they might share
  the kingdom that is endless.

4 Forgive us, Lord, as we forgive
  and seek to help each other.
  Forgive us, Lord, and we shall live
  to pray and work together.
          Ralph Finn

849

1 God forgave my sin in Jesus' name;
  I've been born again in Jesus' name;
  and in Jesus' name I come to you
  to share his love as he told me to.
  He said: 'Freely, freely, you have received
  freely, freely give.
  Go, in my name, and because you believe
  others will know that I live.'

2 All pow'r is giv'n in Jesus' name,
  in earth and heav'n in Jesus' name;
  and in Jesus' name I come to you
  to share his pow'r as he told me to.

3 God gives us life in Jesus' name,
  he lives in us in Jesus' name;
  and in Jesus' name I come to you
  to share his peace as he told me to.
          Carol Owens

850

1 Take this moment, sign and space;
  take my friends around;
  here among us make the place
  where your love is found.

2 Take the time to call my name,
  take the time to mend
  who I am and what I've been,
  all I've failed to tend.

3 Take the tiredness of my days,
  take my past regret,
  letting your forgiveness touch
  all I can't forget.

4 Take the little child in me,
  scared of growing old;
  help him/her here to find his/her worth
  made in Christ's own mould.

5 Take my talents, take my skills,
  take what's yet to be;

let my life be yours, and yet,
let it still be me.
John L. Bell and Graham Maule

51

Awake, awake: fling off the night!
For God has sent his glorious light;
and we who live in Christ's new day
must works of darkness put away.

Awake and rise, in Christ renewed,
and with the Spirit's power endued,
the light of life in us will glow,
and fruits of truth and goodness show.

3 Let in the light; all sin expose
to Christ, whose life no darkness knows.
Before his cross for guidance kneel;
his light will judge and, judging, heal.

4 Awake, and rise up from the dead,
and Christ his light on you will shed.
Its power will wrong desires destroy,
and your whole nature fill with joy.

5 Then sing for joy, and use each day;
give thanks for everything alway.
Lift up your hearts; with one accord
praise God through Jesus Christ our Lord.
J.R. Peacey (1896–1971), from Eph. 5:6-20

Commitment, Discipleship, Mission

52

We have a gospel to proclaim,
good news for all throughout the earth;
the gospel of a saviour's name:
we sing his glory, tell his worth.

Tell of his birth at Bethlehem,
not in a royal house or hall
but in a stable dark and dim:
the Word made flesh, a light for all.

Tell of his death at Calvary,
hated by those he came to save;
in lonely suffering on the cross
for all he loved, his life he gave.

Tell of that glorious Easter morn:
empty the tomb, for he was free;
he broke the power of death and hell
that we might share his victory.

Tell of his reign at God's right hand,
by all creation glorified;
he sends his Spirit on his church
to live for him, the lamb who died.

Now we rejoice to name him king;
Jesus is Lord of all the earth;
the gospel–message we proclaim:
we sing his glory, tell his worth.
Edward J. Burns

853

1 Forth in the peace of Christ we go;
Christ to the world with joy we bring;
Christ in our minds, Christ on our lips,
Christ in our hearts, the world's true King.

2 King of our hearts, Christ makes us kings;
kingship with him his servants gain;
with Christ, the Servant–Lord of all,
Christ's world we serve to share Christ's
reign.

3 Priests of the world, Christ sends us forth
the world of time to consecrate,
the world of sin by grace to heal,
Christ's world in Christ to recreate.

4 Prophets of Christ, we hear his word:
he claims our minds, to search his ways,
he claims our lips, to speak his truth,
he claims our hearts, to sing his praise.

5 We are the Church; he makes us one:
here is one hearth for all to find,
here is one flock, one Shepherd–King,
here is one faith, one heart, one mind.
James Quinn SJ (1919-2010)

854

1 You are salt for the earth, O people:
   salt for the Kingdom of God!
   Share the flavour of life, O people:
   life in the Kingdom of God!

   Bring forth the Kingdom of mercy,
   bring forth the Kingdom of peace;
   bring forth the Kingdom of justice,
   bring forth the City of God!

2 You are a light on the hill, O people:
   light for the city of God!
   Shine so holy and bright, O people:
   shine for the Kingdom of God!

3 You are a seed of the Word, O people:
   bring forth the Kingdom of God!
   Seeds of mercy and seeds of justice,
   grow in the Kingdom of God!

4 We are a blest and a pilgrim people:
   bound for the Kingdom of God!
   Love our journey and love our homeland:
   love is the Kingdom of God!

                              Marty Haugen

855

Sent by the Lord am I;
my hands are ready now
to make the earth the place
in which the kingdom comes.
Sent by the Lord am I;
my hands are ready now
to make the earth the place
in which the kingdom comes.

The angels cannot change
a world of hurt and pain
into a world of love,
of justice and of peace.
The task is mine to do,
to set it really free.
Oh, help me to obey;
help me to do your will

                    Nicaraguan traditional,
                      tr. Jorge Maldonado

856

1 Take the Word of God with you as you
   Take the seeds of God's Word and
      make them grow.
   Go in peace to serve the world,
   in peace to serve the world.
   Take the love of God, the love of God
   with you as you go.

2 Take the peace of God with you as you
   Take the seeds of God's peace and
      make them grow.

3 Take the joy of God with you as you g
   Take the seeds of God's joy and
      make them grow.

4 Take the love* of God with you as yo
      go.
   Take the seeds of God's love and
      make them grow.

* Add other words if needed, such as 'faith', 'hc
                              James Harr

857

1 Sing to the world of Christ our Sovere
      Lord;
   tell of his birth which brought new lif
      all.
   Speak of his life, his love, his holy w
   let every nation hear and know his call.
   Sing to the world of Christ our Sovere
      Lord.

2 Sing to the world of Christ the Prince
      peace,
   showing to us the Father's loving car
   pleading that love should reign and w
      might cease,
   teaching we need the love of God to sha
   Sing to the world of Christ the Prince
      peace.

3 Sing to the world of Christ our steadf
      friend,
   off'ring himself to live the constant si
   food for our souls until we meet life's er

gives us his flesh for bread, his blood for
    wine.
Sing to the world of Christ our steadfast
    friend.

Sing to the world of Christ our Saviour
    King,
born that his death the world's release
    should win;
hung from a cross, forgiveness he could
    bring;
buried, he rose to conquer death and sin.
Sing to the world of Christ our Saviour
    King.

Sing to the world of Christ at God's right
    hand,
praise to the Spirit both have sent from
    heav'n;
living in us till earth shall reach its span,
time be no more, and Christ shall come
    again.
Sing to the world of Christ at God's right
    hand.
    Patrick Lee (1930-2004)

58

God has chosen me, God has chosen me
to bring good news to the poor.
God has chosen me, God has chosen me
to bring new sight to those searching for
    light:
God has chosen me, chosen me:
And to tell the world that God's kingdom
    is near,
to remove oppression and break down
    fear,
yes, God's time is near, God's time is near,
God's time is near, God's time is near.

God has chosen me, God has chosen me
to set alight a new fire.
God has chosen me, God has chosen me
to bring to birth a new kingdom on earth:
God has chosen me, chosen me:

3 God is calling me,
  in all whose cry is unheard.
  God is calling me, God is calling me,
  to raise up the voice with no power or
    choice:
  God is calling me, calling me.
    Bernadette Farrell

859

We have been told, we've seen his face,
and heard his voice alive in our hearts;
'Live in my love with all your heart,
as the Father has loved me,
so I have loved you.'

1 'I am the vine, you are the branches,
  and all who live in me will bear great
    fruit.'

2 'You are my friends, if you keep my
    commands,
  no longer slaves, I call you friends.'

3 'No greater love is there than this:
  to lay down one's life for a friend.'
    David Haas

860

1 Fight the good fight with all thy might,
  Christ is thy strength, and Christ thy
    right;
  lay hold on life and it shall be
  thy joy and crown eternally.

2 Run the straight race through God's good
    grace,
  lift up thine eyes and seek his face;
  life with its way before us lies,
  Christ is the path, and Christ the prize.

3 Cast care aside, lean on thy Guide
  his boundless mercy will provide;
  trust, and the trusting soul shall prove
  Christ is its life, and Christ its love.

4 Faint not nor fear, his arms are near,
  he changeth not, and thou art dear;
  only believe, and thou shalt see
  that Christ is all in all to thee.
    J. S. B. Monsell (1811–75)

861

1 Forth in thy name, O Lord, I go,
   my daily labour to pursue;
   thee, only thee, resolved to know,
   in all I think or speak or do.

2 The task thy wisdom hath assigned
   O let me cheerfully fulfil;
   in all my works thy presence find,
   and prove thy good and perfect will.

3 Thee may I set at my right hand,
   whose eyes my inmost substance see,
   and labour on at thy command,
   and offer all my works to thee.

4 Give me to bear thy easy yoke,
   and every moment watch and pray,
   and still to things eternal look,
   and hasten to thy glorious day;

5 For thee delightfully employ
   whate'er thy bounteous grace hath given,
   and run my course with even joy,
   and closely walk with thee to heaven.
   Charles Wesley (1707–88)

862

1 He who would valiant be
   'gainst all disaster,
   let him in constancy
   follow the Master
   There's no discouragement
   shall make him once relent
   his first avowed intent
   to be a pilgrim.

2 Who so beset him round
   with dismal stories,
   do but themselves confound:
   his strength the more is.
   No foes shall stay his might
   though he with giants fight;
   he will make good his right
   to be a pilgrim.

3 Since, Lord, thou dost defend
   us with thy Spirit,
   we know we at the end
   shall life inherit.

Then fancies flee away!
I'll fear not what they say,
I'll labour night and day
to be a pilgrim.
   Percy Dearmer (1867–1936),
   after John Bunyan (1628–88)

863

Follow me, follow me,
leave your home and family,
leave your fishing nets and boats upo
   the shore.
Leave the seed that you have sown,
leave the crops that you've grown,
leave the people you have known and
   follow me.

1 The foxes have their holes
   and the swallows have their nests,
   but the Son of man has no place to la
      down.
   I do not offer comfort, I do not offer
      wealth,
   but in me will all happiness be found

2 If you would follow me,
   you must leave old ways behind.
   You must take my cross and follow o
      my path.
   You may be far from loved ones,
   you may be far from home
   but my Father will welcome you at la

3 Although I go away
   you will never be alone,
   for the Spirit will be there to comfort yo
   Though all of you may scatter,
   each follow his own path,
   still the Spirit of love will lead you hom
   Michael Cockett

864

1 God's Spirit is in my heart,
   who has called me and set me apart.
   This is what I have to do,
   what I have to do.
   He sent me to give the Good News to
      the poor,

tell prisoners that they are prisoners
no more,
tell blind people that they can see,
and set the downtrodden free,
and go tell ev'ryone
the news that the Kingdom of God has
come,
and go tell ev'ryone
the news that God's kingdom has come.

Just as the Father sent me,
so I'm sending you out to be
my witnesses throughout the world,
the whole of the world.

Don't carry a load in your pack,
you don't need two shirts on your back.
A workman can earn his own keep,
can earn his own keep.

Don't worry what you have to say,
don't worry because on that day
God's spirit will speak in your heart,
will speak in your heart.
Alan Dale (1902-79)
and Hubert Richards (1921-2010)

65

I, the Lord of sea and sky,
I have heard my people cry.
All who dwell in dark and sin
my hand will save.
I who made the stars of night,
I will make their darkness bright.
Who will bear my light to them?
Whom shall I send?
Here I am, Lord. Is it I, Lord?
I have heard you calling in the night.
I will go, Lord, if you lead me.
I will hold your people in my heart.

I, the Lord of snow and rain,
I have borne my people's pain.
I have wept for love of them.
They turn away.
I will break their hearts of stone,
give them hearts for love alone.
I will speak my word to them.
Whom shall I send?

3 I, the Lord of wind and flame,
I will tend the poor and lame.
I will set a feast for them.
My hand will save.
Finest bread I will provide
till their hearts be satisfied.
I will give my life to them.
Whom shall I send?
Daniel L. Schutte

866

I will be with you wherever you go.
Go now throughout the world!
I will be with you in all that you say.
Go now and spread my word!

1 Come, walk with me on stormy waters.
Why fear? Reach out, and I'll be there.

2 And you, my friend, will you now leave me,
or do you know me as your Lord?

3 Your life will be transformed with power
by living truly in my name.

4 And if you say: 'Yes, Lord I love you,'
then feed my lambs and feed my sheep.
Gerald Markland

867

Leave your country and your people,
leave your fam'ly and your friends.
Travel to the land I'll show you;
God will bless the ones he sends.

1 Go like Abraham before you,
when he heard the Father's call,
walking forth in faith and trusting;
God is master of us all.

2 Sometimes God's Word is demanding,
leave security you know,
breaking ties and bonds that hold you,
when the voice of God says: 'Go'.

3 Take the path into the desert,
barren seems the rock and sand.
God will lead you through the desert
when you follow his command.

4 Go with courage up the mountain,
  climb the narrow, rocky ledge,
  leave behind all things that hinder,
  go with only God as pledge.
  Willard F. Jabusch

868

1 'Moses I know you're the man,'
    the Lord said.
  'You're going to work out my plan,'
    the Lord said.
  'Lead all the Israelites out of slavery.
  And I shall make them a wandering race
  called the people of God.'
  So ev'ry day we're on our way,
  for we're a travelling, wandering race
  called the people of God.

2 'Don't get too set in your ways,'
    the Lord said.
  'Each step is only a phase,' the Lord said.
  'I'll go before you and I shall be a sign
  to guide my travelling, wandering race.
  You're the people of God.'

3 'No matter what you may do,'
    the Lord said,
  'I shall be faithful and true,' the Lord said.
  'My love will strengthen you as you go
    along,
  for you're my travelling, wandering race.
  You're the people of God.'

4 'Look at the birds in the air,'
    the Lord said,
  'They fly unhampered by care,'
    the Lord said.
  'You will move easier if you're travelling
    light,
  for you're a wandering vagabond race.
  You're the people of God.'

5 'Foxes have places to go,' the Lord said.
  'But I've no home here below,'
    the Lord said.
  'So if you want to be with me all your days,
  keep up the moving and travelling on.
  You're the people of God.'
  Estelle White (1926-2011)

869

1 Lord of Creation, to you be all praise!
  Most mighty your working, most
    wondrous your ways.
  Your glory and might are beyond us t
    tell,
  and yet in the heart of the humble you
    dwell.

2 Lord of all power, I give you my will,
  in joyful obedience your tasks to fulfi
  Your bondage is freedom, your servic
    is song,
  and, held in your keeping, my weakne
    is strong.

3 Lord of all wisdom, I give you my mi
  rich truth that surpasses our knowled
    to find.
  What eye has not seen and what ear h
    not heard
  is taught by your Spirit and shines fro
    your Word.

4 Lord of all bounty, I give you my hea
  I praise and adore you for all you impa
  your love to inspire me, your counsel
    guide,
  your presence to cheer me, whatever
    betide.

5 Lord of all being, I give you my all;
  if e'er I disown you I stumble and fall
  but, sworn in glad service your word
    obey,
  I walk in your freedom to the end of t
    way.
  Jack C. Winslow (1882-1974)

870

1 Lord, you give the great commission:
  'Heal the sick and preach the word.'
  Lest the Church neglect its mission,
  and the Gospel go unheard,
  help us witness to your purpose
  with renewed integrity;

  With the Spirit's gifts empower us
  for the work of ministry.

Lord, you call us to your service:
'In my name baptise and teach.'
That the world may trust your promise,
life abundant meant for each,
give us all new fervour, draw us
closer in community;

Lord, you make the common holy:
'This my body, this my blood.'
Let us all, for earth's true glory,
daily lift life heavenward,
asking that the world around us
share your children's liberty;

Lord, you show us love's true measure;
'Father, what they do, forgive.'
Yet we hoard as private treasure
all that you so freely give.
May your care and mercy lead us
to a just society;

Lord, you bless with words assuring:
'I am with you to the end.'
Faith and hope and love restoring,
may we serve as you intend,
and, amid the cares that claim us,
hold in mind eternity;

Jeffrey Rowthorn

71

Lord, you have come to the seashore,
neither searching for the rich nor the
   wise,
desiring only that I should follow.
O Lord, with your eyes set upon me,
gently smiling, you have spoken my name,
all I longed for I have found by the
   water,
at your side, I will seek other shores.

Lord, see my goods, my possessions;
in my boat you find no power, no
   wealth.
Will you accept then, my nets and
   labour?

Lord, take my hands and direct them,
help me spend myself in seeking the lost.
Returning love for the love you gave me.

4 Lord, as I drift on the waters,
be the resting place of my restless heart.
My life's companion, my friend
   and refuge.
Cesareo Gabarain (1936-91), tr. Robert Trupia

872

1 My God, accept my heart this day,
and make it wholly thine,
that I from thee no more may stray,
no more from thee decline.

2 Before the cross of him who died,
behold, I prostrate fall;
let every sin be crucified,
and Christ be all in all.

3 Anoint me with thy heavenly grace,
and seal me for thine own,
that I may see thy glorious face,
and worship at thy throne.

4 Let every thought, and work and word
to thee be ever given,
then life shall be thy service, Lord,
and Death the gate of heaven.

5 All glory to the Father be,
all glory to the Son,
all glory, Holy Ghost, to thee,
while endless ages run.
Matthew Bridges (1800-94)

873

1 Come, Lord Jesus, come.
Come, take my hands, take them for
   your work.
Take them for your service, Lord.
Take them for your glory, Lord,
Come, Lord Jesus, come.
Come, Lord Jesus, take my hands.

2 Come, Lord Jesus, come.
Come, take my eyes, may they shine
   with joy.
Take them for your service, Lord.
Take them for your glory, Lord.
Come, Lord Jesus, come.
Come, Lord Jesus, take my eyes.

3 Come, Lord Jesus, come.
  Come, take my lips, may they speak
    your truth.
  Take them for your service, Lord.
  Take them for your glory, Lord.
  Come, Lord Jesus, come.
  Come, Lord Jesus, take my lips.

4 Come, Lord Jesus, come.
  Come take my feet, may they walk
    your path.
  Take them for your service, Lord.
  Take them for your glory, Lord.
  Come, Lord Jesus, come.
  Come, Lord Jesus, take my feet.

5 Come, Lord Jesus, come.
  Come, take my heart, fill it with
    your love.
  Take it for your service, Lord.
  Take it for your glory, Lord.
  Come, Lord Jesus, come.
  Come, Lord Jesus, take my heart.

6 Come, Lord Jesus, come.
  Come, take my life, take it for your own.
  Take it for your service, Lord.
  Take it for your glory, Lord.
  Come, Lord Jesus, come.
  Come, Lord Jesus, take my life.
      Kevin Mayhew

874

1 Take my life, and let it be
  consecrated, Lord, to thee;
  take my moments and my days,
  let them flow in ceaseless praise.

2 Take my hands, and let them move
  at the impulse of thy love.
  Take my feet, and let them be
  swift and purposeful for thee.

3 Take my voice, and let me sing
  always, only, for my King.
  Take my intellect, and use
  every power as thou shalt choose.

4 Take my will, and make it thine:
  it shall be no longer mine.
  Take my heart; it is thine own:
  it shall be thy royal throne.

5 Take my love; my Lord, I pour
  at thy feet its treasure–store.
  Take myself, and I will be
  ever, only, all for thee.
      Frances R. Havergal (1836–

875

1 O Jesus, I have promised
  to serve thee to the end;
  be thou for ever near me,
  my Master and my Friend;
  I shall not fear the battle
  if thou art by my side,
  nor wander from the pathway
  if thou wilt be my guide.

2 O let me feel thee near me:
  the world is ever near;
  I see the sights that dazzle,
  the tempting sounds I hear;
  my foes are ever near me,
  around me and within;
  but, Jesus, draw thou nearer,
  and shield my soul from sin.

3 O let me hear thee speaking
  in accents clear and still,
  above the storms of passion,
  the murmurs of self-will;
  O speak to reassure me,
  to hasten or control;
  O speak, and make me listen,
  thou guardian of my soul.

4 O Jesus, thou hast promised
  to all who follow thee,
  that where thou art in glory
  there shall thy servant be;
  and, Jesus, I have promised
  to serve thee to the end:
  O give me grace to follow,
  my Master and my Friend.

O let me see thy foot–marks,
and in them plant mine own;
my hope to follow duly
is in thy strength alone:
O guide me, call me, draw me,
uphold me to the end;
and then in heaven receive me,
my Saviour and my Friend.

J.E. Bode (1816-1874)

76

Thy hand, O God, has guided
thy flock from age to age;
the wondrous tale is written,
full clear, on ev'ry page;
our fathers owned thy goodness,
and we their deeds record;
and both of this bear witness:
one Church, one Faith, one Lord.

Thy heralds brought glad tidings
to greatest, as to least;
they bade them rise, and hasten
to share the great king's feast;
and this was all their teaching,
in every deed and word,
to all alike proclaiming
one Church, one Faith, one Lord.

When shadows thick were falling,
and all seemed sunk in night,
thou, Lord, didst send thy servants,
thy chosen ones of light.
On them and on thy people
thy plenteous grace was poured,
and this was still their message:
one Church, one Faith, one Lord.

Through many a day of darkness,
through many a scene of strife,
the faithful few fought bravely,
to guard the nation's life.
Their gospel of redemption,
sin pardoned, hope restored,
was all in this enfolded:
one Church, one Faith, one Lord.

5 And we, shall we be faithless?
Shall hearts fail, hands hang down?
Shall we evade the conflict,
and cast away our crown?
Not so: in God's deep counsels
some better thing is stored;
we will maintain, unflinching,
one Church, one Faith, one Lord.

6 Thy mercy will not fail us,
nor leave thy work undone;
with thy right hand to help us
the vict'ry shall be won;
and then, by earth and heaven
thy name shall be adored.
And this shall be their anthem:
one Church, one Faith, one Lord.

E.H. Plumptre (1821–91)

877

1 Will you come and follow me
if I but call your name?
Will you go where you don't know
and never be the same?
Will you let my love be shown,
will you let my name be known,
will you let my life be grown
in you and you in me?

2 Will you leave yourself behind
if I but call your name?
Will you care for cruel and kind
and never be the same?
Will you risk the hostile stare
should your life attract or scare?
Will you let me answer prayer
in you and you in me?

3 Will you let the blinded see
if I but call your name?
Will you set the prisoners free
and never be the same?
Will you kiss the leper clean,
and do such as this unseen,
and admit to what I mean
in you and you in me?

4 Will you love the 'you' you hide
  if I but call your name?
  Will you quell the fear inside
  and never be the same?
  Will you use the faith you've found
  to reshape the world around,
  through my sight and touch and sound
  in you and you in me?

5 Lord, your summons echoes true
  when you but call my name.
  Let me turn and follow you
  and never be the same.
  In your company I'll go
  where your love and footsteps show.
  Thus I'll move and live and grow
  in you and you in me.
John L. Bell & Graham Maule

878

1 You shall go out with joy
  and be led forth with peace.
  The mountains and the hills will
  break forth before you;
  there'll be shouts of joy,
  and all the trees of the field
  will clap, will clap their hands.

2 And all the trees of the field
  will clap their hands,
  the trees of the field
  will clap their hands.
  The trees of the field
  will clap their hands
  while you go out with joy.

Repeat You shall go out …
Stuart Dauermann

Justice & Peace

880

1 Tell out, my soul, the greatness of the Lord!
  Unnumbered blessings, give my spirit
    voice;
  tender to me the promise of his word;
  in God my Saviour shall my heart rejoice.

879

Take Christ to the world,
celebrate our faith,
manifest his love to all;
Take Christ to the world,
show that we are his in the way we li

1 We are the body of Christ made incarna
  in this time and place.
  Let us open ourselves to be truly
  pathways of his grace.

2 When we gather together to pray
  in his holy name,
  he is our strength and the song on our li
  he is present in our midst.

3 We are called to be hearers and beare
  of the word of Christ;
  may it flourish and grow in our hearts
  bringing others to his light.

4 When we offer ourselves to join
  more completely in his life,
  we are the altar, we are the meal,
  we become his sacrifice.

5 Going forth, we can be for the world
  living witnesses of love
  in our service to all those we meet
  as we journey on in faith.

Refrain (above) then:
Take Christ to the world,
celebrate our faith,
dedicate our lives to him;
Take Christ to the world,
show that we are his in the way we li
Paul Inwood

➤ See also: Blessing and dismissal (652-54)

2 Tell out, my soul, the greatness of his na
  Make known his might, the deeds his
    has done;
  his mercy sure, from age to age the sa
  his holy name – the Lord, the Mighty O

Tell out, my soul, the greatness of his
  might!
Powers and dominions lay their glory by.
Proud hearts and stubborn wills are put
  to flight,
the hungry fed, the humble lifted high.

Tell out, my soul, the glories of his word!
Firm is his promise, and his mercy sure.
Tell out, my soul, the greatness of the Lord
to children's children and for evermore!

Timothy Dudley–Smith
(from the Magnificat, Luke 1:46-55)

81

God of day and God of darkness,
now we stand before the night;
as the shadows stretch and deepen,
come and make our darkness bright.
All creation still is groaning
for the dawning of your might,
when the Sun of peace and justice
fills the earth with a radiant light.

Still the nations curse the darkness,
still the rich oppress the poor;
still the earth is bruised and broken
by the ones who still want more.
Come and wake us from our sleeping,
so our hearts cannot ignore,
all your people lost and broken,
all your children at our door.

Show us Christ in one another,
make us servants strong and true;
give us all your love of justice,
so we do what you would do.
Let us call all people holy,
let us pledge our lives anew,
make us one with all the lowly,
let us all be one in you.

You shall be the path that guides us,
you the light that in us burns;
shining deep within all people,
yours the love that we must learn

for our hearts shall wander restless
'til they safe to you return;
finding you in one another,
we shall all your face discern.

5 Praise to you in day and darkness,
you our source and you our end:
praise to you who love and nurture us,
like a father, mother, friend.
Grant us all a peaceful resting,
let each mind and body mend,
so we rise refreshed tomorrow,
hearts renewed to kingdom tend.

Marty Haugen

882

1 Christ's is the world in which we move,
Christ's are the folk we're summoned to
    love,
Christ's is the voice which calls us to
    care,
and Christ is the one who meets us here.

To the lost Christ shows his face;
to the unloved he gives his embrace;
to those who cry in pain or disgrace,
Christ makes, with his friends,
    a touching place.

2 Feel for the people we most avoid,
strange or bereaved or never employed;
feel for the women, and feel for the men
who fear that their living is all in vain.

3 Feel for the parents who've lost their child,
feel for the women whom men have
    defiled,
feel for the baby for whom there's no
    breast,
and feel for the weary who find no rest.

4 Feel for the lives by life confused,
riddled with doubt, in loving abused;
feel for the lonely heart, conscious of sin,
which longs to be pure but fears to
    begin.

John L. Bell

883

1 Longing for light, we wait in darkness.
Longing for truth, we turn to you.
Make us your own, your holy people,
light for the world to see.
Christ be our light!
Shine in our hearts,
shine through the darkness.
Christ, be our light!
Shine in your church gathered today.

2 Longing for peace, our world is troubled.
Longing for hope, many despair.
Your word alone has power to save us,
Make us your living voice.

3 Longing for food, many are hungry,
Longing for water, many still thirst.
Make us your bread, broken for others,
shared until all are fed.

4 Longing for shelter, many are homeless.
Longing for warmth, many are cold.
Make us your building, sheltering others,
walls made of living stones.

5 Many the gifts, many the people,
many the hearts that yearn to belong.
Let us be servants to one another,
Making your kingdom come.
Bernadette Farrell

883a Easter Vigil words

1 This is the night of new beginnings.
This is the night when heaven meets earth.
This is the night filled with God's glory,
promise of our new birth!
Christ be our light!
Shine in our hearts,
shine through the darkness.
Christ, be our light!
Shine in your church gathered today.

2 This is the night Christ our redeemer
rose from the grave triumphant and free,
leaving the tomb of evil and darkness,
empty for all to see.

3 Now will the fire kindled in darkness
burn to dispel the shadows of night.
Star of the morning, Jesus our Saviou
you are the world's true light!

4 Sing of the hope deeper than dying.
Sing of the power stronger than deatl
Sing of the love endless as heaven,
dawning throughout the earth.

5 Into this world morning is breaking,
All of God's people, lift up your voic
Cry out with joy, tell out the story,
all of the earth rejoice.
Bernadette Farrell

884

1 God, whose purpose is to kindle:
now ignite us with your fire;
while the earth awaits your burning,
with your passion us inspire.
Overcome our sinful calmness,
stir in us your saving name;
baptise with your fiery Spirit,
crown our lives with tongues of flam

2 God, who in your holy gospel
wills that all should truly live,
make us sense our share of failure,
our tranquillity forgive.
Teach us courage as we struggle
in all liberating strife;
lift the smallness of our vision
by your own abundant life.

3 God, who still a sword delivers
rather than a placid peace,
with your sharpened word disturb us,
from complacency release!
Save us now from satisfaction,
when we privately are free,
yet are undisturbed in spirit
by our neighbour's misery.
David E. Trueblood (1900-1994)

885

Lord, whose love in humble service
bore the weight of human need,
who upon the Cross forsaken,
offered mercy's perfect deed;
we, your servants, bring the worship
not of voice alone, but heart:
consecrating to your purpose
ev'ry gift which you impart.

Still your children wander homeless;
still the hungry cry for bread;
still the captives long for freedom;
still in grief we mourn our dead.
As, O Lord, your deep compassion
healed the sick and freed the soul,
use the love your Spirit kindles
still to save and make us whole.

As we worship, grant us vision,
till your love's revealing light,
till the height and depth and greatness
dawns upon our human sight:
making known the needs and burdens
your compassion bids us bear,
stirring us to tireless striving,
your abundant life to share.

Called from worship into service
forth in your great name we go,
to the child, the youth, the aged,
love in living deeds to show;
hope and health, goodwill and comfort,
counsel, aid, and peace we give
that your children, Lord, in freedom,
may your mercy know and live.
Albert F. Bayly (1901-84)

886

For the healing of the nations,
Lord, we pray with one accord,
for a just and equal sharing
of the things that earth affords.
To a life of love in action
help us rise and pledge our word.

2 Lead us forward into freedom,
from despair your world release,
that, redeemed from war and hatred,
all may come and go in peace.
Show us how through care and goodness
fear will die and hope increase.

3 All that kills abundant living,
let it from the earth be banned;
pride of status, race or schooling,
dogmas that obscure your plan.
In our common quest for justice
may we hallow life's brief span.

4 You, creator–God, have written
your great name on humankind;
for our growing in your likeness
bring the life of Christ to mind;
that by our response and service
earth its destiny may find.
Fred Kaan (1929-2009)

887

1 God, whose almighty Word
chaos and darkness heard,
and took their flight;
hear us, we humbly pray,
and where the Gospel–day
sheds not its glorious ray
let there be light!

2 Saviour, who came to bring
on your redeeming wing
healing and sight,
health to the sick in mind,
sight to the inly blind,
ah! Now to all mankind
let there be light.

3 Spirit of truth and love,
life–giving, holy dove,
speed forth your flight!
Move on the water's face,
bearing the lamp of grace,
and in earth's darkest place
let there be light!

4 Blessed and holy Three,
  glorious Trinity,
  wisdom, love, might;
  boundless as ocean tide
  rolling in fullest pride,
  through the world far and wide
  let there be light!
    J. Marriott (1780–1825)

888

1 When I needed a neighbour
  were you there, were you there?
  When I needed a neighbour
  were you there?
  And the creed and the colour
  and the name won't matter,
  were you there?

2 I was hungry and thirsty, …

3 I was cold, I was naked, …

4 When I needed a shelter, …

5 When I needed a healer, …

6 Wherever you travel, I'll be there,
  I'll be there.
  Wherever you travel, I'll be there.
  And the creed and the colour
  and the name won't matter, I'll be there.
    Sydney Carter (1915-2004)

889

1 Jesus Christ is waiting, waiting in the
    streets;
  no-one is his neighbour, all alone he eats.
  Listen, Lord Jesus, I am lonely too.
  Make me, friend or stranger, fit to wait
    on you.

2 Jesus Christ is raging, raging in the
    streets,
  where injustice spirals and real hope
    retreats.
  Listen, Lord Jesus, I am angry too.
  In the Kingdom's causes let me rage with
    you.

3 Jesus Christ is healing, healing in the
    streets;

curing those who suffer, touching tho
    he greets.
  Listen, Lord Jesus, I have pity too.
  Let my care be active, healing just like ye

4 Jesus Christ is dancing, dancing in the
    streets,
  where each sign of hatred he, with lov
    defeats.
  Listen, Lord Jesus, I should triumph to
  On suspicion's graveyard let me danc
    with you.

5 Jesus Christ is calling, calling in the
    streets,
  'Who will join my journey? I will gui
    their feet.'
  Listen, Lord Jesus, let my fears be fev
  Walk one step before me; I will follow you
    John L. Bell and Graham Maule

890

1. The God of liberation
  has challenged us to fight
  injustice, exploitation
  and sins against the light
  by state or corporation
  or any seeking gain
  from human degradation
  or profit wrought from pain.

2 The God of recreation
  has called us to proclaim
  the work of reparation,
  of rescue from our shame;
  the city's restoration,
  repair for homes and ways,
  a time for jubilation,
  fresh hope, new faith and praise.

3 The God of our salvation
  has sent us Christ to be
  our source of inspiration,
  the truth which sets us free;
  a reconciliation,
  the pathway to release,
  and healing for the nation,
  where justice leads to peace.
    Patrick Lee (1930-2004)

91

1. Poor folk won't al-ways be for-got-ten, nor will the hope-less hope in

vain. Rise, God, re-strain the cruel ex-ploi-ters, strike them with fear.

God has prepared a throne for judgement;
nations will know who reigns supreme.
God will judge all the earth with justice
and equity.

May God indeed empower the weary,
and for the troubled be their tower.
Lord, do not turn from those who seek you,
trusting your name.

4 Sing, sing to God among the nations,
proclaim our great avenger's name.
God keeps in mind all the afflicted;
God hears their cry.

5 So, with a full heart, Lord, I praise you,
grateful for all you are and do.
I shall sing out for you, the highest;
I shall rejoice.

John L. Bell

92

The Lord hears the cry of the poor,
blessed be the Lord.

I will bless the Lord at all times,
with praise ever in my mouth.
Let my soul glory in the Lord,
who will hear the cry of the poor.

Let the lowly hear and be glad:
the Lord listens to their pleas;
and to hearts broken God is near,
who will hear the cry of the poor.

Ev'ry spirit crushed God will save;
will be ransom for their lives;
will be safe shelter for their fears,
and will hear the cry of the poor.

We proclaim your greatness, O God,
your praise ever in our mouth;
ev'ry face brightened in your light,
for you hear the cry of the poor.

John B. Foley SJ, based on Psalm 34

93

What does the Lord require
for praise and offering?
What sacrifice, desire
or tribute bid you bring?
Do justly; love mercy;
walk humbly with your God.

2 Rulers of earth, give ear!
should you not justice know?
Will God your pleading hear,
while crime and cruelty grow?
Do justly; love mercy;
walk humbly with your God.

3 All who gain wealth by trade,
for whom the worker toils,
think not to win God's aid
if greed your commerce soils.
Do justly; love mercy;
walk humbly with your God.

4 Still down the ages ring
the prophet's stern commands:
to merchant, worker, king,
he brings God's high demands:
Do justly; love mercy;
walk humbly with your God.

5 How shall our life fulfil
God's law so hard and high?
Let Christ endue our will
with grace to fortify.
Then justly, in mercy;
we'll humbly walk with God.

Albert F. Bayly (1901–84)

894

1. The gift of the Holy Spirit
   is the gift of God's great love.
   To us comes the touch of healing
   from the God of heaven above;
   joy and strength for our daily living,
   trust and love for the work of giving,
   and the spirit of true forgiving each one.

2 Anointed, we are Christ's witness
   in the walk of life each day,
   a comfort and light to others
   whom we meet along the way.
   We will cherish your life within us,
   show the mercy you show to sinners,
   by your suffering, you chose to win us
   from death.

3 Thanksgiving we bring, and honour,
   to the Father and the Son
   and, with them, the Holy Spirit,
   God for ever, Three in One.
   Praise and glory we give and blessing,
   one faith, one in truth confessing,
   one in love in your all–embracing design.
   Sr. Katherine Boschetti, M.S.C.

895

1. Community of Christ, who make the
   Cross your own,
   live out your creed and risk your life
   for God alone:
   the God who wears your face, to whom
   all worlds belong,
   whose children are of every race and
   every song.

2. Community of Christ, look past the
   Church's door
   and see the refugee, the hungry,
   and the poor.
   Take hands with the oppressed, the
   jobless in your street,
   take towel and water, that you wash
   your neighbour's feet.

3. Community of Christ, through whom
   the word must sound -
   cry out for justice and for peace the
   whole world round:
   disarm the powers that war and all th[ey]
   can destroy,
   turn bombs to bread, and tears of
   anguish into joy.

4. When menace melts away, so shall
   God's will be done,
   the climate of the world be peace an[d]
   Christ its Sun;
   our currency be love and kindliness
   our law,
   our food and faith be shared as one
   for evermore.
   Shirley Erena Murray

896

1 The Church of Christ, in every age
   beset by change but Spirit-led,
   must claim and test its heritage
   and keep on rising from the dead.

2 Across the world, across the street,
   the victims of injustice cry
   for shelter and for bread to eat,
   and never live until they die.

3 Then let the servant Church arise,
   a caring Church that longs to be
   a partner in Christ's sacrifice,
   and clothed in Christ's humanity.

4 For he alone, whose blood was shed
   can cure the fever in our blood,
   and teach us how to share our bread
   and feed the starving multitude.

5 We have no mission but to serve
   in full obedience to our Lord:
   to care for all, without reserve,
   and spread his liberating Word.
   F. Pratt Green (1903-2000)

97

1. Like a migh-ty ri-ver flo-wing, like a flower in beau-ty gro-wing, far be-yond all hu-man kno-wing is the per-fect peace of God.

Like the hills serene and even,
like the coursing clouds of heaven,
like the heart that's been forgiven
is the perfect peace of God.

Like the summer breezes playing,
like the tall trees softly swaying,
like the lips of silent praying
is the perfect peace of God.

4 Like the morning sun ascended,
like the scents of evening blended,
like a friendship never ended
is the perfect peace of God.

5 Like the azure ocean swelling,
like the jewel all-excelling,
far beyond our human telling
is the perfect peace of God.
Michael Perry (1942-96)

98

Make me a channel of your peace.
Where there is hatred, let me bring your
　love.
Where there is injury your pardon, Lord.
And where there's doubt true faith in you.

Make me a channel of your peace.
Where there's despair in life, let me
　bring hope.
Where there is darkness only light,
and where there's sadness ever joy.

Oh, Master, grant that I may never seek
so much to be consoled as to console,
to be understood as to understand,
to be loved, as to love with all my soul.

Make me a channel of your peace.
It is in pardoning that we are pardoned,
in giving of ourselves that we receive,
and in dying that we're born to
　eternal life.
　Sebastian Temple (1928-97)
　from the 'Prayer of St Francis'

99

Lord, make me a means of your peace.
Where there's hatred grown, let me sow
　your love.

Where there's injury, Lord, let forgive–
　ness be my sword.
Lord, make me a means of your peace.

2 Lord, make me a means of your peace.
Where there's doubt and fear, let me
　sow your faith.
In this world's despair, give me hope in
　you to share.

3 Lord, make me a means of your peace.
Where there's sadness here, let me sow
　your joy.
When the darkness nears, may your
　light dispel our fears.

4 Lord, grant me to seek and to share:
less to be consoled than to help console,
less be understood than to understand
　your good.

5 Lord, grant me to seek and to share:
to receive love less than to give love free,
just to give in thee, just receiving from
　your tree.

6 Lord, grant me to seek and to share:
to forgive in thee, you've forgiven me:
for to die in thee is eternal life to me.
John Foley SJ. from the 'Prayer of St Francis'

900

1 O day of peace that dimly shines
through all our hopes and prayers and
   dreams,
guide us to justice, truth and love,
delivered from our selfish schemes.
May swords of hate fall from our hands,
our hearts from envy find release,
till by God's grace our warring world
shall see Christ's promised reign of peace.

2 Then shall the wolf dwell with the lamb
nor shall the fierce devour the small;
as beasts and cattle calmly graze,
a little child shall lead them all.
Then enemies shall learn to love,
all creatures find their true accord;
the hope of peace shall be fulfilled,
for all the earth shall know the Lord.

Carl P. Daw, Jr.

901

The peace of the earth be with you,
the peace of the heavens too;
the peace of the rivers be with you,
the peace of the oceans too.
Deep peace falling over you;
God's peace growing in you.

Guatemalan, tr. Christine Carson

902

1 Peace is flowing like a river,
flowing out through you and me,
spreading out into the desert,
setting all the captives free.

2 Love is flowing like a river …

3 Joy is flowing like a river …

4 Hope is flowing like a river …

Carey Landry

903

1. People of Jesus, trusted to be
bearers of peace from God's living tr
peace that the world itself cannot kno
the peace that is given to plant and to g

2. Feel for the ones who have no more
   bread,
feel for the ones with children unfed,
longing for food, they find in our han
a mountain of weapons more sacred
   than land.

3. Feel for the ones whose homes are
   destroyed,
feel for the lives now shattered and vo
Waiting for loved ones nobody saw:
the innocent people who suffer in wa

4. Stand with the ones who see a new w
people of faith who struggle and pray
given the call to shape and rebuild
our actions, our consciences, our
   broken world.

5. Pray for the day our children will see
war strange and distant as slavery.
Work for a world where new ways
   abound
to meet and to dialogue till peace is fou

6. Why spend your tears on what canno
   heal?
Why spend your rage on what you
   conceal?
God's living Word cries out to reveal
a love that will satisfy, hope that is re

7. Children of peace, go forth through t
   earth,
healing our world and bringing to bir
vision to build and fashion a way:
the fulness of life for God's people tod

Bernadette Farrell

904

Do - na no - bis pa - cem cor - di - um.

*Give us peac
heart.*

Taizé chant
Jacques Ber
(1923-94)

05

All that I counted as gain
now I consider as loss,
empty and worthless to me
in the light of the love of the Lord.

2 Riches and honours will fade,
earthly delights disappear,
fade like the grass of the field
in the light of the love of the Lord.

Refrain *after vv 2, 4*

What more could bring us hope than to know the power of his life?__ What

more could bring us peace than to share in his suff-'ring and death?__ What

more could be our fi - nal wish than to live in the love of the Lord?__

Silver and gold have I none,
no land to count as my home, yet
wealth beyond measure I own
in the light of the love of the Lord.

4 Faith is the wealth I possess
finding its source in my God:
faith in the promise of Christ
is my life and my love of the Lord.

Phil. 3:7-11, adapted by Michael Joncas

06

If we are living
we are in the Lord,
and if we die
we are in the Lord,
for if we live
or if we die
we belong to God,
we belong to God.

3 When there is sadness,
when there is pain
in Christ the Lord,
we have love to gain.
Whether we suffer
or we rejoice,
we belong to God,
we belong to God.

Throughout our lives
we have fruit to bear.
All of our good works
are for us to share.
Whether we give,
or we receive
we belong to God,
we belong to God.

4 And in this world
we will always find
those who are weeping,
sick in heart and mind.
They need our help,
they need our care.
we belong to God,
we belong to God.

v.1: Romans 14:8; vv2-4: traditional
Spanish. tr. Deborah L. Schmitz

907

1 Abide with me, fast falls the eventide;
the darkness deepens, Lord, with me abide!
When other helpers fail, and comforts flee,
help of the helpless, O abide with me.

2 Swift to its close ebbs out life's little day;
earth's joys grow dim, its glories pass away;
change and decay in all around I see;
O thou who changest not, abide with me.

3 I need thy presence every passing hour;
what but thy grace can foil the tempter's
power?
Who like thyself my guide and stay can be?
Through cloud and sunshine, O abide
with me.

4 I fear no foe with thee at hand to bless;
ills have no weight and tears no bitterness.
Where is death's sting? Where, grave,
thy victory?
I triumph still, if thou abide with me.

5 Hold thou thy Cross before my closing
eyes;
shine through the gloom, and point me
to the skies;
heaven's morning breaks, and earth's
vain shadows flee:
in life, in death, O Lord, abide with me!
H. F. Lyte (1793–1847)

908

1 Blest are the pure in heart,
for they shall see our God;
the secret of the Lord is theirs,
their soul is Christ's abode.

2 The Lord who left the heavens
our life and peace to bring,
to dwell in lowliness with us,
our pattern and our king.

3 Still to the lowly soul
he doth himself impart
and for his dwelling and his throne
chooseth the pure in heart.

4 Lord, we thy presence seek;
may ours this blessing be:

give us a pure and lowly heart,
a temple meet for thee.
Vv 1, 3: John Keble (1792–1866), vv 2, 4
from W. J. Hall's Psalms and Hymns (183

909

1 Be still and know that I am God,
be still and know that I am God,
be still and know that I am God.

2 I am the Lord that healeth thee...

3 In thee, O Lord, I put my trust...
Anonymous

910

1 Christ be beside me, Christ be before m
Christ be behind me, King of my hea
Christ be within me, Christ be below n
Christ be above me, never to part.

2 Christ on my right hand, Christ on my
left hand,
Christ all around me, shield in the stri
Christ in my sleeping, Christ in my sitti
Christ in my rising, light of my life.

3 Christ be in all hearts thinking about n
Christ be in all tongues telling of me.
Christ be the vision in eyes that see n
in ears that hear me, Christ ever be.
Adapted from 'St Patrick's Breastpla
by James Quinn SJ (1919-2010)

911

1 Come, my Way, my Truth, my Life:
such a Way, as gives us breath;
such a Truth, as ends all strife;
such a Life, as killeth death.

2 Come, my Light, my Feast, my Streng
such a Light, as shows a feast;
such a Feast, as mends in length;
such a Strength, as makes his guest.

3 Come, my Joy, my Love, my Heart:
such a Joy, as none can move;
such a Love, as none can part;
such a Heart, as joys in love.
George Herbert (1593-1633)

12

God is my great desire,
his face I seek the first;
to him my heart and soul aspire,
for him I thirst.
As one in desert lands,
whose very flesh is flame,
in burning love I lift my hands
and bless his name.

God is my true delight,
my richest feast his praise,
through silent watches of the night,
through all my days.
To him my spirit clings,
on him my soul is cast;
beneath the shadow of his wings
he holds me fast.

God is my strong defence
in ev'ry evil hour;
in him I face with confidence
the tempter's power.
I trust his mercy sure,
with truth and triumph crowned:
my hope and joy for evermore
in him are found.

Timothy Dudley–Smith

13

Jesus, my Lord, my God, my all,
how can I love thee as I ought?
And how revere this wondrous gift
so far surpassing hope or thought?
Sweet Sacrament, we thee adore;
Oh, make us love thee more and more.

Had I but Mary's sinless heart
to love thee with, my dearest King,
O, with what bursts of fervent praise
thy goodness, Jesus, would I sing!

Ah, see! Within a creature's hand
the vast Creator deigns to be,
reposing, infant–like, as though
on Joseph's arm, or Mary's knee.

4 Thy body, soul, and Godhead, all;
O mystery of love divine!
I cannot compass all I have,
for all thou hast and art are mine;

5 Come now ye angels to our aid,
sound, sound God's praises higher still;
'tis God, whose power created us,
and in whose praise creation thrills.
F.W. Faber (1814–63), alt.

914

1 God be in my head, and in my
understanding;
God be in mine eyes, and in my looking;
God be in my mouth, and in my
speaking;
God be in my heart, and in my thinking;
God be at mine end, and at my departing.
Anon. from a Book of Hours of the
Blessed Virgin Mary (1514)

915

We hold a treasure, not made of gold,
in earthen vessels, wealth untold;
one treasure only: the Lord, the Christ,
in earthen vessels.

1 Light has shone in our darkness;
God has shone in our heart,
with the light of the glory of Jesus,
the Lord.

2 He has chosen the lowly,
who are small in this world;
in this weakness is glory, in Jesus, the Lord.
John B. Foley SJ (2 Cor 4:6-7; 1 Cor 1:27-29)

916

1 Lord, it belongs not to my care
whether I die or live;
to love and serve thee is my share,
and this thy grace must give.

2 If life be long, I will be glad
that I may long obey;
if short, yet why should I be sad
to end my little day?

3 Christ leads me through no darker rooms
   than he went through before;
   he that into God's kingdom comes
   must enter by this door.

4 Come, Lord, when grace hath made
   me meet
   thy blessèd face to see:
   for if thy work on earth be sweet,
   what will thy glory be!

5 My knowledge of that life is small,
   the eye of faith is dim;
   but 'tis enough that Christ knows all,
   and I shall be with him
      Richard Baxter (1615-91), alt.

917   Jésus le Christ/Lord Jesus Christ

Lord Jesus Christ, your light shines within us. Let not my doubts and my darkness speak to me. Lord Jesus Christ, your light shines in us. Let my heart always welcome your love.

Taizé chant by Jacques Berthier (1923-19

Love for one another
918

Where there is love, there is God.
The love of God has gathered us
together. Alleluia.

1 Love is patient, love is kind,
   never jealous, never proud,
   never seeking for one's self,
   Love never leads to anger.

2 Love is gracious and forgiving,
   taking no delight in wrong;
   love rejoices in the truth;
   love will endure.

3 Many things will pass away,
   there are but three things that last;
   Faith, Hope and Love;
   the greatest of these is Love.
      David Haas, from 1 Jn 4:16;
      1 Cor 13:4-7.10.13

19

Not for tongues of heaven's angels,
not for wisdom to discern,
not for faith that masters mountains,
for this better gift we yearn:
  May love be ours, O Lord,
  may love be ours.

Love is humble, love is gentle,
love is tender, true and kind;
love is gracious, ever patient,
generous of heart and mind.

Never jealous, never selfish,
love will not rejoice in wrong;
never boastful nor resentful,
love believes and suffers long.

In the day this world is fading,
faith and hope will play their part:
but when Christ is seen in glory,
love shall reign in every heart.
  Timothy Dudley-Smith, from 1 Cor 13

20

A new Commandment I give unto you,
that you love one another as I have loved
  you,
that you love one another as I have loved
  you.
By this shall all mankind know you are
  my disciples,
if you have love one for another.
By this shall all mankind know you are
  my disciples,
if you have love one for another.
  Anonymous, based on John 13:34–35

21

This is my will, my one command,
that love should dwell among you all.
This is my will, that you should love
as I have shown that I love you.

No greater love can be than this:
to choose to die to save one's friends.
You are my friends if you obey
what I command that you should do.

3 I call you now no longer slaves;
no slave knows all his master does.
I call you friends, for all I hear
my Father say you hear from me.

4 You chose not me, but I chose you,
that you should go and bear much fruit.
I chose you out that you in me
should bear much fruit that will abide.

5 All that you ask my Father dear
for my name's sake you shall receive.
This is my will, my one command,
that love should dwell in each, in all.
  James Quinn SJ (1919-2010),
  from John 15:12-17

922

Bind us together, Lord,
bind us together with cords
that cannot be broken.
Bind us together, Lord,
bind us together, Lord.
Bind us together with love.

1 There is only one God.
there is only one King.
there is only one Body.
that is why we sing:

2 Made for the glory of God,
purchased by his precious Son,
born with the right to be free,
Jesus the victory has won.

3 We are the family of God,
we are the promise divine,
we are God's chosen desire,
we are the glorious new wine.
  Bob Gillman

923

Our Father, by whose name
all parenthood is known,
in love divine you claim
each fam'ly as you own.
Bless mothers, fathers, guarding well,
with constant love as sentinel,
the homes in which your people dwell.

2 O Christ, yourself a child
within an earthly home,
with heart still undefiled,
to full adulthood come;
our children bless in every place
that they may all behold your face
and knowing you may grow in grace.

3 O Holy Spirit, bind
our hearts in unity
and teach us how to find
the love from self set free,
in all our hearts such love increase
that every home, by this release,
may be the dwelling-place of peace.
F. Bland Tucker (1895-1984)

924

1 Brother, sister, let me serve you,
let me be as Christ to you;
pray that I may have the grace to
let you be my servant too.

2 We are pilgrims on a journey,
we are trav'llers on the road;
we are here to help each other
walk the mile and bear the load.

3 I will hold the Christ–light for you
in the night–time of your fear;
I will hold my hand out to you,
speak the peace you long to hear.

4 I will weep when you are weeping;
when you laugh I'll laugh with you.
I will share your joy and sorrow
till we've seen this journey through.

5 When we sing to God in heaven
we shall find such harmony,
born of all we've known together
of Christ's love and agony.

6 Brother, sister, let me serve you,
let me be as Christ to you;
pray that I may have the grace to
let you be my servant too.
Richard Gillard

925

Shalom, my friend,
shalom my friend, shalom, shalom
May peace and joy be with you today
shalom, shalom.
Traditional Israeli song

926

*Whatsoever you do
to the least of my people,
that you do unto me.*

1 When I was hungry you gave me to e
When I was thirsty you gave me to
drink.
Now enter into the home of my Fathe

2 When I was homeless you opened
door.
When I was naked you gave me your
Now enter into the home of my Fathe

3 When I was weary you helped me fin
rest.
When I was anxious you calmed all n
fears.
Now enter into the home of my Fathe

4 When in a prison you came to my cel
When on a sick bed you cared for my n
Now enter into the home of my Fathe

5 When I was aged you bothered to sm
When I was restless you listened and
cared.
Now enter into the home of my Fathe

6 When I was laughed at you stood by
side.
When I was happy you shared in my
Now enter into the home of my Fathe
W. F. Jabusch

927

1 Where charity and love prevail
there God is ever found;
brought here together by Christ's love
by love are we thus bound.

With grateful joy and holy fear
his charity we learn;
let us with heart and mind and soul
now love him in return.

Forgive we now each other's faults
as we our faults confess;
and let us love each other well
in Christian holiness.

4 Let strife among us be unknown,
let all contention cease;
be his the glory that we seek,
be ours his holy peace.

5 Let us recall that in our midst
dwells God's begotten Son;
as members of his body joined
we are in him made one.

6 No race nor creed can love exclude
if honoured be God's name;
our common life embraces all
whose Father is the same.

Omer Westendorf (1916-97)

etition

➤ *See also nos 9, 26-29, 547-52, 740, 988*

28

Lord, to whom shall we go? Yours are the words of e-ter-nal life.

John L. Bell & Graham Maule

29 **O Lord, hear my prayer**   *Taizé chant. Music by Jacques Berthier (1923-1994)*

O Lord. hear my prayer, O Lord, hear my prayer. When I call   an-swer me.
The Lord is my song, the Lord is my praise: all my hope comes from God.

O Lord. hear my prayer, O Lord, hear my prayer. Come and lis-ten to me. O
The Lord is my song, the Lord is my praise: God, the well-spring of life. The

930

Lis - ten, Lord, Lis - ten, Lord, not to our words but to our prayer. You a - lone, you a - lone un - der - stand and care.

1. Where the voice that once was welcome
   sounds no more,
   send your love to homes turned silent,
   hearts turned sore.

2. Where the faith that once was firm
   is bruised and torn,
   place a manger where heaven's stranger
   may be born.

3. Where the wisdom meant to heal is
   spent to harm,
   rouse the smothered conscience,
   sounding heaven's alarm.

4. Where the withered hands and hopes
   stretch out in vain,
   burst the storehouse of your grace
   and of our grain.

5. Turn the world and spurn the spite of
   human greed,
   train our adult eyes on where a child
   may lead.

John L. Bell

931

O living water, refresh my soul.
O living water, refresh my soul.
Spirit of joy, Lord of creation.
Spirit of hope, Spirit of peace.

1. Spirit of God. Spirit of God.

2. O set us free. O set us free.

3. Come, pray in us. Come, pray in us.
   Sr Virginia Vissing, SSMN

932

Abba, Abba, Father, you are the potter,
we are the clay, the work of your hands.

1. Mould us, mould us and fashion us
   into the image
   of Jesus, your Son,
   of Jesus, your Son.

2. Father, may we be one in you
   ⌐s he is in you,
       ⌐ou are in him,
       ⌐are in him.

3. Glory, glory and praise to you,
   glory and praise to you
   for ever. Amen.
   For ever. Amen.
   Carey Landry

933

1. Father, hear the prayer we offer:
   not for ease that prayer shall be,
   but for strength that we may ever
   live our lives courageously.

2. Not for ever in green pastures
   do we ask our way to be;
   but the steep and rugged pathway
   may we tread rejoicingly.

3. Not for ever by still waters
   would we idly rest and stay;
   but would smite the living fountains
   from the rocks along the way.

4. Be our strength in hours of weakness,
   in our wanderings be our guide;
   through endeavour, failure, danger,
   Father, be there at our side.
   Love Maria Willis (1824–1908), and othe

34

Dear Lord and Father of mankind,
forgive our foolish ways!
Re–clothe us in our rightful mind,
in purer lives thy service find,
    in deeper reverence praise. *(repeat)*

In simple trust like theirs who heard,
beside the Syrian sea,
the gracious calling of the Lord,
let us, like them, without a word,
    rise up and follow thee.

O Sabbath rest by Galilee!
O calm of hills above,
where Jesus knelt to share with thee
the silence of eternity,
    interpreted by love!

Drop thy still dews of quietness,
till all our strivings cease;
take from our souls the strain and stress,
and let our ordered lives confess
    the beauty of thy peace.

Breathe through the heats of our desire
thy coolness and thy balm;
let sense be dumb, let flesh retire;
speak through the earthquake, wind
    and fire,
    O still small voice of calm!
               J.G Whittier (1807–92)

35

O God of earth and altar,
bow down and hear our cry,
our earthly rulers falter,
our people drift and die;
the walls of gold entomb us,
the swords of scorn divide,
take not thy thunder from us,
but take away our pride.

From all that terror teaches,
from lies of tongue and pen,
from all the easy speeches
that comfort cruel men,
from sale and profanation
of honour and the sword,
from sleep and from damnation,
deliver us, good Lord!

3   Tie in a living tether
the prince and priest and thrall,
bind all our lives together,
smite us and save us all;
in ire and exultation
aflame with faith, and free,
lift up a living nation,
a single sword to thee.
           G. K. Chesterton (1874–1936)

936

1   'Look around you, can you see?
Times are troubled, people grieve.
See the violence, feel the hardness;
all my people, weep with me.'
     Kyrie eleison, Christe eleison,
     Kyrie eleison.

2   'Walk among them, I'll go with you.
Reach out to them with my hands.
Suffer with me, and together
we will serve them, help them stand.'

3   Forgive us, Father; hear our prayer.
We would walk with you anywhere,
through your suff'ring, with forgiveness;
take your life into the world.
        Jodi Page Clark

937

1   Lord Jesus, we must know you
if we would make you known;
for how can we proclaim you
but by your grace alone?
We long to know your fullness,
your life of risen power,
for you alone can answer
the challenge of this hour.

2   Our broken world is seeking
what only you can give;
our words may go unheeded,
but not the way we live.
O Saviour, live within us
your life so strong, so true,
that others, touched with wonder,
may seek and worship you!

3 Lord Jesus, by your Spirit
  renew your Church, we pray,
  till what we are makes valid
  the truth of what we say.
  So truly may we know you,
  so make your life our own,
  that we become so like you
  our lives must make you known.
  Margaret Clarkson

938

1 Soul of my Saviour, sanctify my breast;
  Body of Christ, be thou my saving guest;
  Blood of my Saviour, bathe me in thy
      tide,
  wash me with water flowing from thy side.

2 Strength and protection may thy Passion be;
  O Blessed Jesus, hear and answer me;
  deep in thy wounds, Lord, hide and
      shelter me;
  so shall I never, never part from thee.

3 Guard and defend me from the foe malign;
  in death's dread moments make me only
      thine;
  call me, and bid me come to thee on high,
  when I may praise thee with thy saints
      for aye.
  Ascribed to John XXII (1249–1334), tr. anon.

939

1 Spirit of truth and grace,
  come to us in this place
  as now in Jesus's name God's people
      gather.
  Open our eyes to see
  truths that will ever be,
  and in communion draw us close
      together.

2 Spirit of joy and peace
  make all anxieties cease
  with knowledge of the Father's perfect
      caring.

Then may God's children know
love that won't let us go
and joy that fills each day, beyond
    comparing.

3 Spirit of life and power,
  revive us in this hour
  and stir our hearts to praise with true
      devotion.
  Fill us with heavenly fire,
  and every heart inspire,
  that we may serve the world with your
      compassion.
  Iain D. Cunningham

940

1 Lord, for tomorrow and its needs
  I do not pray;
  keep me, my God, from stain of sin,
  just for today.

2 Let me both diligently work
  and duly pray;
  let me be kind in word and deed,
  just for today.

3 Let me be slow to do my will,
  prompt to obey;
  help me to mortify my flesh,
  just for today.

4 Let me no wrong or idle word
  unthinking say;
  set thou a seal upon my lips,
  just for today.

5 And if today my tide of life
  should ebb away,
  give me thy sacraments divine,
  sweet Lord, today.

6 So, for tomorrow and its needs
  I do not pray;
  but keep me, guide me, love me, Lord
  just for today.
  Sister M. Xavier SND
  (Sybil Farish Partridge, 1856-1917)

941
There is a long-ing in our hearts, O Lord, for

you to re-veal your-self to us.___ There is a long-ing in our
hearts for love we on-ly find in you, our God.

For justice, for freedom, for mercy:
hear our prayer.
In sorrow, in grief:
be near, hear our prayer, O God.

For wisdom, for courage, for comfort:
hear our prayer.
In weakness, in fear:
be near, hear our prayer, O God.

3 For healing, for wholeness, for new life:
hear our prayer.
In sickness, in death:
be near, hear our prayer, O God.

4 Lord save us, take pity,
light in our darkness.
We call you, we wait:
be near, hear our prayer, O God.

Anne Quigley

ᴛhanksgiving

942

Lord, for the years your love has kept
and guided,
urged and inspired us, cheered us
on our way,
sought us and saved us, pardoned and
provided:
Lord of the years, we bring our thanks
today.

Lord, for that word, the word of life
that fires us,
speaks to our hearts and sets our souls ablaze,
teaches and trains, rebukes us and
inspires us:
Lord of the word, receive your people's
praise.

Lord, for our land in this our generation,
spirits oppressed by pleasure, wealth
and care:
for young and old, for commonwealth
and nation,
Lord of our land, be pleased to hear our
prayer.

Lord, for our world: when we disown and
doubt him,
loveless in strength, and comfortless in pain,
hungry and helpless, lost indeed without him:
Lord of the world, we pray that Christ
may reign.

5 Lord, for ourselves; in living power
remake us -
self on the cross and Christ upon the throne,
Past put behind us, for the future take us,
Lord of our lives, to live for Christ alone.
Timothy Dudley-Smith

943

1 Give thanks to the Lord who does
wondrous deeds,
who masters the winds and the raging seas,
whose love is for ever,
whose love is for ever,
whose love is for evermore!

2 Give thanks to the Lord who has
blessed our land,
who guards every step with a mighty hand,
whose love is for ever...

3 O bless the Lord for every gift
that comes to grace our way,
and praise the God of faithfulness
who comes to light our day.

4 Give thanks to the God of the summer
rains,
who spreads out the hills and the golden
plains,
whose love is for ever...

5 Give thanks to the Lord who is merciful,
   whose kindness is wide, and love bountiful,
   whose love is for ever...

6 O bless the Lord with music,
   every creature great and small,
   and sing through all the ages
   of God's favour to us all.

7 Give thanks to the Lord for the blazing sun,
   for great, rolling waves where the
      dolphins run:
   whose love is for ever...

8 Give thanks to the Lord for the crimson
   skies,

for wild windy heights where the eagle fli
whose love is for ever...

9 O bless the Lord all people
   for the music of the skies,
   and tell the wondrous story
   of a love that never dies.

10 Give thanks to the Lord who has set us
      free,
   who raised us to life on a blessed tree.
   whose love is for ever,
   whose love is for ever,
   whose love is for evermore!
      Daniel L. Schutte

944 In the Lord

Taizé chant by Jacques Berthie

In the Lord I'll be ev-er thank-ful, in the Lord I will re-joice! Look to God, do not be a

fraid; lift up your voi-ces, the Lord is near; lift up your voi-ces, the Lord is near.

945

1 Now thank we all our God,
   with heart and hands and voices,
   who wondrous things hath done,
   in whom his world rejoices;
   who from our mother's arms
   hath blessed us on our way
   with countless gifts of love,
   and still is ours today.

2 O may this bounteous God
   through all our life be near us,
   with ever joyful hearts
   and blessed peace to cheer us;

and keep us in his grace,
and guide us when perplexed,
and free us from all ills
in this world and the next.

3 All praise and thanks to God
   the Father now be given,
   the Son, and him who reigns
   with them in highest heaven,
   the one Eternal God,
   whom earth and heaven adore;
   for thus it was, is now,
   and shall be evermore.
      Martin Rinkart (1586–1649),
      tr. Catherine Winkworth (1827-78)

46

Thanks be to God whose love has
gathered us today.
Thanks be to God who helps and guides
us on our way;
thanks be to God who gives us voice,
that we may thank him:
Deo gratias, Deo gratias,
Thanks be to God most high.

Thanks be to God for all the gifts of life
and light;
thanks be to God whose care protects us,
day and night;
thanks be to God who keeps in mind us
who forget him:

Thanks be to God who knows our secret
joys and fears;

thanks be to God who when we call him,
always hears;
thanks be to God our rock and strength,
ever sustaining:

4 Thanks be to God who never turns his
face away;
thanks be to God who heals and pardons
all who stray;
thanks be to God who welcomes us into
the Kingdom:

5 Thanks be to God who made our world
and all we see;
thanks be to God who gave his Son to
set us free;
thanks be to God whose Spirit brings
warmth and rejoicing:
Deo gratias, Deo gratias,
Thanks be to God most high.

Stephen Dean

Trust, Hope Guidance

Nada te turbe/Nothing can trouble

St Teresa of Avila.
Music: Taizé chant by Jacques Berthier

Na-da te tur-be, na-da te es-pan-te, Quien a Dios tie - ne
No-thing can trou-ble, no-thing can frigh-ten. Those who seek God shall

na-da le fal - ta. Na-da te tur - be, na-da te es-pan-te, so-lo Dios bas-ta.
ne-ver go wan-ting. Nothing can trou-ble, no-thing can frigh-ten. God al-one fills us.

48

Because the Lord is my shepherd,
I have ev'rything I need.
He lets me rest in the meadow
and leads me to the quiet streams.
He restores my soul and he leads me
in the paths that are right:

Lord, you are my shepherd,
you are my friend.
I want to follow you always,
just to follow my friend.

2 And when the road leads to darkness,
I shall walk there unafraid.
Even when death is close
I have courage for your help is there.
You are close beside me with comfort,
you are guiding my way:

3 In love you make me a banquet
for my enemies to see.
You make me welcome, pouring down
honour from your mighty hand;
and this joy fills me with gladness,
it is too much to bear:

4 Your goodness always is with me
and your mercy I know.
Your loving kindness strengthens me
always as I go through life.
I shall dwell in your presence forever,
giving praise to your name:

Christopher Walker, from Psalm 23

949

Where your treasure is,
there your heart shall be.
All that you possess
will never set you free.
Seek the things that last,
come and learn from me.
Where your treasure is,
your heart shall be.

1. What do you gain from all your worry,
what you should eat or what to wear?
There is no peace in stress and hurry,
do you not know that you are held
within God's care?

2. Look at the ravens high above you,
they do not work their whole life through,
and yet God feeds them and protects
them,
so how much more will God protect
and care for you?

3. Behold the lilies in their splendour,
in grace and beauty are they dressed,
And yet so soon their bloom is faded.
So how much more will those who look
to God be blessed?

4. Do not fear, little flock,
for God delights to give you
the blessed reign of God.
Give your possessions to the needy;
gain a treasure that will not fade.

Marty Haugen (from Luke 12:29-32)

950

My soul is longing for your peace,
near to you, my God.

1 Lord, you know that my heart is not pr
and my eyes are not lifted from the eart

2 Lofty thoughts have never filled my m
far beyond my sight all ambitious deed

3 In your peace I have maintained my sc
I have kept my heart in your quiet pea

4 As a child rests on a mother's knee,
so I place my soul in your loving car

5 Israel, put all your hope in God,
place your trust in God, now and
evermore.

Lucien Deiss CSSp (1921-2007) from Ps.130 (

➤ *See also: Like a child rests (*

951

Shepherd me, O God,
beyond my wants, beyond my fears,
from death into life.

1 God is my shepherd, so nothing shall
want,
I rest in the meadows of faithfulness
and love,
I walk by the quiet waters of peace.

2 Gently you raise me and heal my wea
soul,
you lead me by pathways of righteou
ness and truth,
my spirit shall sing the music of your
name.

3 Though I should wander the valley of d
I fear no evil, for you are at my side,
your rod and your staff, my comfort a
my hope.

You have set me a banquet of love
in the face of hatred,
crowning me with love beyond my
    pow'r to hold.

Surely your kindness and mercy follow me
all the days of my life;
I will dwell in the house of my God for
    evermore.
      Psalm 23, Marty Haugen

52

You who dwell in the shelter of the Lord,
who abide in his shadow for life,
say to the Lord:'My refuge,
my Rock in whom I trust!'
And he will raise you up on eagle's wings,
bear you on the breath of dawn,
make you to shine like the sun,
and hold you in the palm of his hand.

The snare of the fowler will never
    capture you,
and famine will bring you no fear:
under his wings your refuge
his faithfulness your shield.

You need not fear the terror of the night,
nor the arrow that flies by day;
though thousands fall about you,
near you it shall not come.

For to his angels he's given a command
to guard you in all of your ways;
upon their hands they will bear you up,
lest you dash your foot against a stone.
And he will raise you up on eagle's wings,
bear you on the breath of dawn,
make you to shine like the sun,
and hold you in the palm of his hand;
and hold you, hold you in the palm of
    his hand.
    Michael Joncas, from Psalm 91

53

Safe in the shadow of the Lord,
beneath his hand and power,
I trust in him, I trust in him,
my fortress and my tower.

2 My hope is set on God alone
    though Satan spreads his snare;
    I trust in him, I trust in him
    to keep me in his care.

3 From fears and phantoms of the night,
    from foes about my way,
    I trust in him, I trust in him
    by darkness as by day.

4 His holy angels keep my feet
    secure from every stone;
    I trust in him, I trust in him
    and unafraid go on.

5 Strong in the everlasting name,
    and in my Father's care,
    I trust in him, I trust in him
    who hears and answers prayer.

6 Safe in the shadow of the Lord,
    possessed by love divine,
    I trust in him, I trust in him
    and meet his love with mine.
    Timothy Dudley–Smith, from Psalm 91

954

Blest be the Lord; blest be the Lord,
the God of mercy, the God who saves.
I shall not fear the dark of night,
nor the arrow that flies by day.

1 He will release me from the nets
    of all my foes.
  He will protect me from their
    wicked hands.
  Beneath the shadow of His wings
    I will rejoice
  to find a dwelling place secure.

2 I need not shrink before the terrors
    of the night,
  nor stand alone before the light of day.
  No harm shall come to me,
    no arrow strike me down,
  no evil settle in my soul.

3 Although a thousand strong have
    fallen at my side,
  I'll not be shaken with the Lord at hand.

His faithful love is all the armour
that I need
to wage my battle with the foe.
Daniel L. Schutte, from Psalm 91

955

1 O God, our help in ages past,
our hope for years to come,
our shelter from the stormy blast,
and our eternal home;

2 Beneath the shadow of thy throne,
thy saints have dwelt secure;
sufficient is thine arm alone,
and our defence is sure.

3 Before the hills in order stood,
or earth received her frame,
from everlasting thou art God,
to endless years the same.

4 A thousand ages in thy sight,
are like an evening gone;
short as the watch that ends the night
before the rising sun.

5 Time, like an ever–rolling stream,
bears all its sons away;
they fly forgotten, as a dream
dies at the opening day.

6 O God, our help in ages past,
our hope for years to come,
be thou our guard while troubles last,
and our eternal home.
Isaac Watts (1674–1748) from Psalm 90

956

1 I watch the sunrise lighting the sky,
casting its shadows near.
And on this morning
bright though it be,
I feel those shadows near me.
But you are always close to me
following all my ways.
May I be always close to you
following all your ways, Lord.

2 I watch the sunlight shine through the
clouds,
warming the earth below.
And at the mid–day life seems to say:

'I feel your brightness near me.'
For you are always ...

3 I watch the sunset fading away,
lighting the clouds with sleep.
And as the evening closes its eyes
I feel your presence near me.
For you are always ...

4 I watch the moonlight guarding the nig
waiting till morning comes.
The air is silent, earth is at rest -
only your peace is near me.
Yes, you are always ...
John Glynn

957

1 As if you were not there,
the skies ignite and thunder,
rivers tear their banks asunder,
thieves and nature storm and plunder:
all beware,
as if you were not there.

2 As if you were not there,
famine and flood together
usher death, disease and terror;
stricken mothers wonder whether
God heeds prayer,
as if you were not there.

3 As if you were not there,
we televise the dying,
watch the helpless victims crying,
salve our consciences by sighing
'Life's unfair!'
as if you were not there.

4 As if you were not there,
your Son, when they defied him,
faced a crowd which crucified him,
leaving friends who had denied him
in despair,
as if you were not there.

5 Because he rose again
and showed God's love is vaster
than the ultimate disaster,
we entreat you now to master
strife and pain,
because he rose again.
John L. Bell

58

God is our fortress and our rock,
our mighty help in danger;
he shields us from the battle's shock
and thwarts the devil's anger:
for still the prince of night
prolongs his evil fight;
he uses every skill
to work his wicked will –
no earthly force is like him.

Our hope is fixed on Christ alone,
the Man, of God's own choosing;
without him nothing can be won
and fighting must be losing:
so let the powers accursed
come on and do their worst,
the Son of God shall ride
to battle at our side,
and he shall have the victory.

The word of God will not be slow
while demon hordes surround us,
though evil strike its cruellest blow
and death and hell confound us:
for even if distress
should take all we possess,
and those who mean us ill
should ravage, wreck, or kill,
God's kingdom is immortal!
after M. Luther (1483-1546) by
Michael Perry (1942-96)

59

All my hope on God is founded;
he doth still my trust renew.
Me through change and chance he
guideth,
only good and only true.
God unknown, he alone
calls my heart to be his own.

Human pride and earthly glory,
sword and crown betray God's trust;
what with lavish care man buildeth,
tower and temple, fall to dust.
But God's power, hour by hour,
is my temple and my tower.

3 God's great goodness ay endureth,
deep his wisdom, passing thought:
splendour, light and life attend him,
beauty springeth out of nought.
Evermore, from his store
new–born worlds rise and adore.

4 Daily doth the almighty giver
bounteous gifts on us bestow;
his desire our soul delighteth
pleasure leads us where we go.
Love doth stand at his hand,
joy doth wait at his command.

5 Still from earth to God eternal
sacrifice of praise be done,
high above all praises praising
for the gift of Christ his Son.
Christ doth call one and all;
ye who follow shall not fall.
Robert S. Bridges (1844–1930)
based on a hymn by J. Neander (1650–80)

960

1 Guide me, O thou great Redeemer,
pilgrim through this barren land;
I am weak, but thou art mighty,
hold me with thy pow'rful hand:
bread of heaven,
feed me till I want no more.

2 Open now the crystal fountain,
whence the healing stream doth flow;
let the fire and cloudy pillar
lead me all my journey through;
strong Deliverer,
be thou still my strength and shield.

3 When I tread the verge of Jordan,
bid my anxious fears subside,
death of death, and hell's destruction,
land me safe on Canaan's side;
songs of praises
I will ever give to thee.
W. Williams (1717–91),
tr. P. and W. Williams

Welsh version overleaf

960a ORIGINAL VERSION

1 Arglwydd, arwain drwy'r anialwch
fi, bererin gwael ei wedd,
nad oes ynof nerth na bywyd,
fel yn gorwedd yn y bedd:
    hollalluog,
ydyw'r un a'm cwyd i'r lan.

2 Colofn dân rho'r nos i'm harwain,
a rho golofn niwl y dydd;
dal fi pan fwy'n teithio'r mannau
geirwon yn fy ffordd y sydd;
    rho i mi fanna,
fel na bwyf yn llwfwrhau.

3 Agor y ffynhonnau melys
sydd yn tarddu o'r graig i maes;
r hyd yr anial mawr canlyned
afon iachawdwriaeth gras:
    rho i mi hynny;
dim i mi ond dy fwynhau.
            William Williams (1717-91)

961

1 Lead, kindly light amid th' encircling
    gloom,
lead thou me on;
the night is dark, and I am far from home,
lead thou me on.
Keep thou my feet; I do not ask to see
the distant scene; one step enough for me.

2 I was not ever thus, nor prayed that thou
    shouldst lead me on;
I loved to choose and see my path; but now
lead thou me on.
I loved the garish day, and, spite of fears,
pride ruled my will; remember not past
    years.

3 So long thy power hath blest me, sure it
    still
will lead me on
o'er moor and fen, o'er crag and torrent, till
the night is gone,
and with the morn those angel faces smile
which I have loved long since, and lost
    awhile.
            J.H. Newman (1801–90)

962

1 Firmly I believe and truly
God is three, and God is one,
and I next acknowledge duly
manhood taken by the Son.

2 And I trust and hope most fully
in that manhood crucified;
and each thought and deed unruly
do to death, as he has died.

3 Simply to his grace and wholly
light and life and strength belong;
and I love supremely, solely,
him the holy, him the strong.

4 And I hold in veneration,
for the love of him alone,
Holy Church, as his creation,
and her teachings, as his own.

5 Adoration aye be given,
with and through th' angelic host,
to the God of earth and heaven,
Father, Son and Holy Ghost.
            J.H. Newman (1801–90)

963

1 Eternal Father, strong to save,
whose arm doth bind the restless wav
who bidd'st the mighty ocean deep,
its own appointed limits keep:
O hear us when we cry to thee
for those in peril on the sea.

2 O Saviour, whose almighty word
the winds and waves submissive hea
who walkedst on the foaming deep
and calm amid its rage didst sleep:
O hear us when we cry to thee
for those in peril on the sea.

3 O sacred Spirit, who didst brood
upon the waters dark and rude,
and bid their angry tumult cease,
and give, for wild confusion, peace:
O hear us when we cry to thee
for those in peril on the sea.

O Trinity of love and power,
our brethren shield in danger's hour.
From rock and tempest, fire and foe,
protect them whereso'er they go,
and ever let there rise to thee
glad hymns of praise from land and sea.
W. Whiting (1825–78)

64

You shall cross the barren desert,
but you shall not die of thirst.
You shall wander far in safety
though you do not know the way.
You shall speak your words in foreign lands
and they will understand.
You shall see the face of God and live.
Be not afraid, I go before you always.
Come, follow me, and I will give you rest.

If you pass through raging waters in the
   sea,
you shall not drown.
If you walk amid the burning flames,
you shall not be harmed.
If you stand before the pow'r of hell
and death is at your side,
know that I am with you through it all.

Blessed are your poor,
for the kingdom shall be theirs.
Blest are you that weep and mourn,
for one day you shall laugh.
And if wicked tongues insult and hate you
all because of me,
blessed, blessed are you!
Robert J. Dufford, S.J.

55

As the deer pants for the water,
so my soul longs after you.
You alone are my heart's desire
and I long to worship you.
You alone are my strength, my shield,
to you alone may my spirit yield.
You alone are my heart's desire
and I long to worship you.

2 I want you more than gold or silver,
only you can satisfy.
You alone are the real joy–giver
and the apple of my eye.

3 You're my Friend and you're my Brother,
even though you are a king.
I love you more than any other,
so much more than anything.
Martin Nystrom

966

Walk with me, oh my Lord,
through the darkest night and brightest day.
Be at my side, oh Lord,
hold my hand and guide me on my way.

1 Sometimes the road seems long,
my energy is spent.
Then, Lord, I think of you
and I am given strength.

2 Stones often bar my path
and there are times I fall,
but you are always there
to help me when I call.

3 Just as you calmed the wind
and walked upon the sea,
conquer, my living Lord,
the storms that threaten me.

4 Help me to pierce the mists
that cloud my heart and mind
so that I shall not fear
the steepest mountain–side.

5 As once you helped the lame
and gave sight to the blind,
help me when I'm downcast
to hold my head up high.
Estelle White

967

1 O, the love of my Lord is the essence
of all that I love here on earth.
All the beauty I see
he has given to me
and his giving is gentle as silence.

2 Every day, every hour, every moment
  have been blessed by the strength of his
    love.
  At the turn of each tide
  he is there at my side,
  and his touch is as gentle as silence.

3 There've been times when I've turned
  from his presence,
  and I've walked other paths, other ways.
  But I've called on his name
  in the dark of my shame,
  and his mercy was gentle as silence.
Estelle White

968

1 Be still, and know I am with you,
  be still, I am the Lord.
  I will not leave you orphans.
  I leave with you my world. Be one.

2 You fear the light may be fading,
  you fear to lose your way.
  Be still, and know I am near you.
  I'll lead you to the day and the sun.

3 Be glad the day you have sorrow,
  be glad, for then you live.
  The stars shine only in darkness,
  and in your need I give my peace.
Anne Conway

969

1 Lord of all hopefulness, Lord of all joy,
  whose trust, ever child–like, no cares
    could destroy,
  be there at our waking, and give us, we
    pray,
  your bliss in our hearts, Lord, at the
    break of the day.

2 Lord of all eagerness, Lord of all faith,
  whose strong hands were skilled
    at the plane and the lathe,
  be there at our labours and give us, we
    pray,
  your strength in our hearts, Lord, at the
    noon of the day.

3 Lord of all kindliness, Lord of all grace,
  your hands swift to welcome, your
    arms to embrace,
  be there at our homing and give us, w
    pray,
  your love in our hearts, Lord, at the
    eve of the day.

4 Lord of all gentleness, Lord of all cal
  whose voice is contentment, whose
    presence is balm,
  be there at our sleeping and give us, v
    pray,
  your peace in our hearts, Lord, at the
    end of the day.
Jan Struther (1901–53)

970

1 Be thou my vision, O Lord of my hea
  naught be all else to me save that thou a
  thou my best thought in the day and t
    night,
  waking or sleeping, thy presence my lig

2 Be thou my wisdom, be thou my true
    Word;
  I ever with thee, and thou with me, Lor
  thou my great Father, and I thy true so
  thou in me dwelling, and I with thee on

3 Be thou my breast–plate, my sword
    the fight;
  be thou my armour, and be thou my mig
  thou my soul's shelter, and thou my hi
    tower,
  raise thou me heavenward, O Power
    my power.

4 Riches I heed not, nor man's empty
    praise,
  thou mine inheritance through all my
    days;
  thou, and thou only, the first in my hea
  high King of heaven, my treasure thou a

High King of heaven, when battle is done,
grant heaven's joy to me, O bright
   heaven's sun;
Christ of my own heart, whatever befall,
still be my vision, O Ruler of all.
   Irish, c. 8th C, tr. Mary Byrne (1881–1931),
    versified by Eleanor Hull (1860–1935)

71

Father, I place into your hands
the things I cannot do.
Father, I place into your hands
the things that I've been through.
Father, I place into your hands
the way that I should go,
for I know I always can trust you.

Father, I place into your hands
my friends and family.
Father, I place into your hands
the things that trouble me.
Father, I place into your hands
the person I would be,
for I know I always can trust you.

Father, we love to see your face,
we love to hear your voice.
Father, we love to sing your praise
and in your name rejoice.
Father, we love to walk with you
and in your presence rest,
for we know we always can trust you.

Father, I want to be with you
and do the things you do.
Father, I want to speak the words
that you are speaking too.
Father, I want to love the ones
that you will draw to you,
for I know that I am one with you.
    Jenny Hewer

972

Do not be afraid,
for I have redeemed you.
I have called you by your name;
you are mine.

1 When you walk through the waters I'll
    be with you.
    You will never sink beneath the waves.

2 When the fire is burning all around you,
    you will never be consumed by the flames.

3 When the fear of loneliness is looming,
    then remember I am at your side.

4 When you dwell in the exile of the
    stranger,
    remember you are precious in my eyes.

5 You are mine, O my child, I am your
    Father,
    and I love you with a perfect love.
    Gerald Markland

973

1 He's got the whole world in his hand,
    he's got the whole world in his hand,
    he's got the whole world in his hand,
    he's got the whole world in his hand.

2 He's got you and me, brother, in his hand...
    he's got the whole world in his hand.

3 He's got you and me, sister, in his hand...
    he's got the whole world in his hand.

4 He's got everybody here in his hand...
    he's got the whole world in his hand.

5 He's got the little tiny baby in his hand...
    he's got the whole world in his hand.

repeat verse 1
    Traditional

974

1 Colours of day dawn into the mind,
the sun has come up, the night is behind.
Go down to the city, into the street,
and let's give the message to the people
  we meet.
So light up the fire and let the flame burn,
open the door, let Jesus return.
Take seeds of his Spirit, let the fruit grow,
tell the people of Jesus, let his love show.

2 Go through the park, on into the town
the sun still shines on, it never goes dow
The light of the world is risen again;
the people of darkness are needing ou
  friend.

3 Open your eyes, look into the sky,
the darkness has come, the sun came to d
The evening draws on the sun disappea
but Jesus is living, and his Spirit is nea
Sue McClellan, John Paculabo
& Keith Rycroft

The Word of God

975

In the land,__ in the land__ is a hun - ger, in the la
__ is a hun - ger__ for more than bread.__ In our hearts, in our hear
__ is a hun - ger, in our hearts__ is a hun - ger for the Word of God.__

1 Listen, all who fear, listen all who search,
to the voice that speaks of peace:
one who knows your name, one who calls
  you home,
one who waits to hear your cry.

2 Listen, all who mourn, listen, all who
  weep,
to the hope you fear is gone:

One who shared our fate, one who d
  our death,
one who lives to set us free.

3 Listen, all who hope, listen all who dr
to the promise we have heard:
One who routs the proud, sets the
  captive free,
one whose world is upside down.
Bernadette Farrell

976

In the land there is a hunger,
in the land there is a need
not for the taste of water,
not for the taste of bread.
In the land there is a hunger,
in the land there is a need
for the sound of the word of God
upon every word we feed.

1 Hear, O Lord my cry, day and night I
My soul is thirsting for you, my God.

2 Your word, O Lord is spirit and life
You have the words, Lord, of
  everlasting life.

3 Only in God is my soul at rest.
He is my rock and my salvation.
Mike Lynch

977

Lord, thy word abideth,
and our footsteps guideth;
who its truth believeth
light and joy receiveth.

When our foes are near us,
then thy word doth cheer us,
word of consolation,
message of salvation.

When the storms are o'er us,
and dark clouds before us,
then its light directeth,
and our way protecteth.

Who can tell the pleasure,
who recount the treasure,
by thy word imparted
to the simple-hearted?

Word of mercy, giving
courage to the living;
word of life, supplying
comfort to the dying.

O that we discerning
its most holy learning,
Lord, may love and fear thee,
evermore be near thee!
H.W. Baker (1821-1877)

978

Lord, your word shall guide us,
and with truth provide us:
teach us to receive it
and with joy believe it.

When our foes are near us,
then your word shall cheer us,
word of consolation,
message of salvation.

When the storms distress us,
and dark clouds oppress us,
then your word protects us,
and its light directs us.

4 Who can tell the pleasure,
who recount the treasure,
by your word imparted
to the simple-hearted?

5 Word of mercy, giving
courage to the living;
word of life, supplying
comfort to the dying.

6 O that we discerning
its most holy learning,
Lord, may love and fear you,
evermore be near you!
H.W. Baker (1821-1877)
altered by Michael Perry (1944-97)

979

*Oh the word of my Lord, deep within my
  being,
oh the word of my Lord, you have filled
  my mind.*

1 Before I formed you in the womb
I knew you through and through,
I chose you to be mine.
Before you left your mother's side
I called to you, my child, to be my sign.

2 I know that you are very young,
but I will make you strong –
I'll fill you with my word;
and you will travel through the land,
fulfilling my command which you have
  heard.

3 And ev'rywhere you are to go
my hand will follow you;
you will not be alone.
In all the danger that you fear
you'll find me very near, your words my
  own.

4 With all my strength you will be filled:
you will destroy and build,
for that is my design.
You will create and overthrow,
reap harvests I will sow – your word is
  mine.
Damian Lundy (1942-97)

980

Your words are spirit and life, O Lord
richer than gold, stronger than death.
Your words are spirit and life, O Lord;
life everlasting.

1 God's Law is perfect, refreshing the soul,
   reviving the weary spirit.
   God's rule can be trusted: bringing us
      wisdom,
   bringing God's wisdom to birth.

2 God's precepts keep us, their purpose is
      right,
   They gladden the hearts of people.
   God's command is so clear, it brings us
      new vision;
   bringing God's light to our eyes.

3. Living by God's truth is holy and sure;
   God's presence is everlasting.
   God's truth is eternal, bringing us justice;
   bringing God's justice to earth.

4. God's word is precious, desired more
      than gold;
   worth more than we dare imagine
   and, sweeter than honey, this word will
      feed us,
   bringing fulfilment and joy.
   Bernadette Farrell, from Ps 18(19):8-11

981

1 *To everything there is a season;*
   a time to be born and a time to die.
   A time to plant, and a time for harvest;
   a time to meet and a time to part.
   A sower went out to sow the seed.
   Some of it fell upon the path,
   some fell on shallow, rocky soil;
   and some among choking thorns.

2 *To everything there is a season;*
   a time to be born and a time to die.
   A time to speak, and a time for silence;
   a time to wound and a time to heal.
   Nothing can grow in barren soil;
   briars and ravens take their toil;
   still there is grain a hundredfold,
   from seed that took root and grew.

3 *To everything there is a season;*
   a time to be born and a time to die.
   A time to speak, and a time for silenc
   a time to wound and a time to heal.
   God's word is like the farmer's seed,
   rooted in joyful, loving hearts,
   growing like grain in fertile groumd,
   a harvest that overflows.

4 *To everything there is a season;*
   a time to be born and a time to die.
   A time to plant, and a time for harves
   a time to meet and a time to part.
   M.D.Ridge, based on Eccl 3:1-9;
   Mt 13:4-8.

The Lord's Coming

982

1 O Jesus Christ, remember,
   when thou shalt come again,
   upon the clouds of heaven,
   with all thy shining train;
   when every eye shall see thee
   in deity revealed,
   who now upon this altar
   in silence art concealed.

2 Remember then, O Saviour,
   I supplicate of thee,
   that here I bowed before thee
   upon my bended knee;
   that here I owned thy presence,
   and did not thee deny,
   and glorified thy greatness
   though hid from human eye.

3 Accept, divine Redeemer,
   the homage of my praise;
   be thou the light and honour
   and glory of my days.
   Be thou my consolation
   when death is drawing nigh:
   be thou my only treasure
   through all eternity.
   Edward Caswall (1814–78)

983

Hills of the north, rejoice;
river and mountain–spring,
hark to the advent voice;
valley and lowland, sing:
though absent long, your Lord is nigh;
he judgement brings and victory.

Isles of the southern seas,
deep in your coral caves
pent be each warring breeze,
lulled be your restless waves:
he comes to reign with boundless sway,
and makes your wastes his great highway.

Lands of the east, awake,
soon shall your sons be free;
the sleep of ages break, and rise to liberty.
On your far hills, long cold and grey,
has dawned the everlasting day.

Shores of the utmost west,
ye that have waited long, unvisited, unblest,
break forth to swelling song;
high raise the note, that Jesus died,
yet lives and reigns, the Crucified.

Shout, while ye journey home;
songs be in every mouth;
lo, from the north we come,
from east and west and south.
City of God, the bonds are free,
we come to live and reign in thee!
C.E. Oakley (1832–65)

984

All over the world the Spirit is moving,
all over the world
as the prophets said it would be.
All over the world there's a mighty
    revelation
of the glory of the Lord
as the waters cover the sea.

All over this land...

All over the church...

All over us all...

Deep down in my heart...
Roy Turner

985

1 In God's good time our eyes will open,
    we'll see great signs and marvels,
      and know the day has come:
  Yes, in God's good time we will hear
    glad music,
  and angels and archangels will call us
    home.
  *Who can tell when these wonders will
    happen?*
  *We know not the second, the minute,
    the hour*
  *but the day will come when our chains
    will break*
  and our tears will dry away
    in God's good time.

2 In God's good time, the poor will prosper,
    the hungry will be sated, the sick will
      be made whole,
  yes, in God's good time things we
    dare not dream of
  will fill our deepest longings of heart
    and soul.
  *None can tell when such marvels will
    happen;*
  it may be tomorrow, it may be today
  *but the day will come when the clouds
    will burst*
  and the night will turn to day
    in God's good time.

3 In God's good time all war will vanish
    old hates will be forgotten, old enemies
      forgive:
  and all hearts will stir, and all swords
    will shatter,
  what's hidden will be open, what's dead
    will live.
  Come, Lord Jesus, and change us for ever,
  we're getting impatient, so hasten the day
  *when the world will sing and a great
    hosanna*
  will arise from earth to heaven
    in God's good time.

Stephen Dean

986

*In the day of the Lord, the sun will shine
like the dawn of eternal day.
All creation will rise to dance and sing
the glory of the Lord!*

1 And on that day will justice triumph,
on that day will all be free:
free from want, free from fear, free to
live!

2 Then shall the nations throng together
to the mountain of the Lord:
they shall walk in the light of the Lord!

3 And they shall beat their swords to
ploughshares;
there will be an end to war:
one in peace, one in love, one in God!

4 For Israel shall be delivered,
and the desert lands will bloom.
Say to all, 'Do not fear. Here is your God!'

5 And on that day of Christ in glory,
God will wipe away our tears,
and the dead shall rise up from their
graves!

6 O, give us eyes to see your glory,
give us hearts to understand.
Let our ears hear your voice till you
come!
M. D. Ridge

987

1 Mine eyes have seen the glory of the
coming of the Lord.
He is trampling out the vintage
where the grapes of wrath are store
He has loosed the fateful lightning of
terrible swift sword.
His truth is marching on.
Glory, glory hallelujah!
Glory, glory hallelujah!
Glory, glory hallelujah!
His truth is marching on.

2 I have seen him in the watchfires of a
hundred circling camps.
They have gilded him an altar in the
evening dews and damps.
I can read his righteous sentence by th
dim and flaring lamps.
His day is marching on.

3 He has sounded forth the trumpet that
shall never sound retreat.
He is sifting out the hearts of all befor
his judgement seat.
O, be swift my soul to answer him, be
jubilant my feet!
Our God is marching on.

4 In the beauty of the lilies Christ was
born across the sea
with a glory in his bosom that
transfigures you and me.
As he died to make us holy, let us ma
all people free,
whilst God is marching on.
Julia Ward Howe (1819–1910)

988

Sha-rers in the pro-mise, hea-rers of the Word, may we work for one same King-dom, may we serve one Lord.

Stephen Dea

89

Word made flesh, Son of God.
Come, Lord Jesus, come again;
Come, Lord Jesus, come again;

Lord and Saviour, Son of God:

3   Prince of Peace, Son of God:
4   Alleluia, Son of God:
5   Bread of life, Son of God:
6   Light of the World, Son of God:
7   Jesus Christ, Son of God;
    Sister Virginia Vissing, SS.M.N.

ße Heavenly City

90

One thing I ask of the Lord, for this I long, to
live in the house of the Lord, all the days of my life.

The Lord is my light and my help.
Whom shall I fear?
The Lord is the stronghold of my life,
before whom shall I shrink?

Though armies do battle against me
my heart will not fear.
Though war and destruction break forth,
even then would I trust.

For there in his house I am safe
in evil's dark hour.
He hides me and shelters my soul,
my defender, my rock.

4   There is one thing I ask of the Lord,
    for this I long:
    to live in the house of the Lord
    all the days of my life,
    to savour the sweetness of the Lord,
    to behold his temple.

5   I know I shall see the Lord's goodness
    in his promised land.
    Take heart and stand firm, O my soul,
    put your hope in the Lord!
    Verses from Ps 26 (27). Music by Stephen Dean

91

Jerusalem the golden,
with milk and honey blest,
beneath thy contemplation
sink heart and voice oppressed.
I know not, ah, I know not
what joys await us there,
what radiancy of glory,
what bliss beyond compare.

They stand, those halls of Sion,
all jubilant with song,
and bright with many an angel,
and all the martyr throng;
the Prince is ever with them,
the daylight is serene;
the pastures of the blessed
are decked in glorious sheen.

3   There is the throne of David;
    and there, from care released,
    the shout of them that triumph,
    the song of them that feast;
    and they, who with their leader
    have conquered in the fight,
    for ever and for ever
    are clad in robes of white.

4   O sweet and blessed country,
    the home of God's elect!
    O sweet and blessed country
    that eager hearts expect!
    Jesus, in mercy bring us
    to that dear land of rest;
    who art, with God the Father
    and Spirit, ever blest.
    from De Contemptu Mundi (c.1140), Bernard
    of Cluny, tr. J. M. Neale (1818–66)

992

1 I rejoiced when I heard them say:
'Let us go to the house of God.'
And now our feet are standing
in your gates, O Jerusalem!
Shalom, shalom,
the peace of God be here.
Shalom, shalom,
God's justice be ever near.

2 Like a temple of unity
is the city, Jerusalem.
It is there all tribes will gather,
all the tribes of the house of God.
Chorus

3 It is faithful to Israel's law,
there to praise the name of God.
All the judgement seats of David
were set down in Jerusalem.

4 For the peace of all nations, pray:
for God's peace within your homes.
May God's lasting peace surround us;
may it dwell in Jerusalem.

5 For the love of my friends and kin
I will bless you with signs of peace.
For the love of God's own people
I will labour and pray for you.
Bernadette Farrell, from Psalm

993

Ho-ly Ci-ty, new Je-ru-sa-lem, heaven's bright-ness to us bring
By the shi-ning of his glo - ry, light the com - ing of our King!

1 Surely sheltering God's people,
Mother Church, you watch and pray,
feeding us with heaven's graces:
now look up to see God's day.

2 And I saw a new creation
(for the first had passed from sight)
and the sea of tears and mourning
driven back before God's might.

3 And I heard a Voice declaring,
'Soon I come to be with you:
soon to dwell with all my people,
I, the Lord, make all things new!'

4 Bride in beauty for your Husband,
waiting long till he appear:
ready coming with your children,
run to greet the Voice you hear!
Mark Woodruff

I am with you always

994

May you walk with Christ be-side you, Saints and an - gels share you
way. May the Ho-ly Spi-rit guide you to the dawn of end-less day.

1 Peace in hearth and home,
peace surround you,
peace of Christ our God
in hearts of those around you.
Chorus

2 Light to bless your eyes,
light to lead you,
light of Christ to shine
and on your journey speed you.

Christ to hold and heal,
Christ to welcome,
Christ to bring the wanderer
home to fold and shelter.

4 Three to guard and shield,
   Three unsleeping
   Father, Son and Spirit,
   rest you in their keeping.

Stephen Dean

95

Repeat ad libitum

Sing in four part canon.   *Julie McCann*

There is a time for pray-ing,—— and a place in our hearts for ev'ry-one.

96

Stand,—— O— stand firm; stand,— O—stand firm;— stand,—O—

stand firm and see what the Lord can do.   *O my sis-ters, stand ve-ry firm!*

my brothers, stand very firm...   All you elders, stand very firm...
ll you children, stand very firm...   Let God's people stand very firm...

From Cameroon

97

Cantor   (1. My sis-ters,)   (my sis-ters,)   (my sisters,)

Joyfully   Bless   the Lord,   bless   the Lord,

(2. My bro-thers),

bless the Lord: there is no o - ther God.

You children . . .
You elders . . .
All people . . .
Together . . .
          etc,
From Kenya

998 Glory to God: hymn of praise

George Salazar, arr. Paul Inwo

Refrain

¡Glo - ria! ¡Glo - ria! ¡Glo - ria al Se - ñor.
Glo - ry! Glo - ry! Glo - ry to God!
Ca - nwn ni o - go - niant i Dduw,

¡Glo - ria! ¡Glo - ria! ¡Glo - ria a mi Dios.
Glo - ry! Glo - ry! Glo - ry to God!
Ca - nwn ni o - go - niant i Dduw.

Verses

1. Glo - ry to God in the heights of the hea - vens.
2. Son of the Fa - ther, all glo - ry and wor - ship;
3. You take a - way the sin of the world;
4. Sea - ted in pow'r at the right of the Fa - ther,
5. And with the Spi - rit of love e - ver - las - ting,

Peace to God's peo - ple, all peo - ple on earth.
praise and thanks - gi - ving to you, Lamb of God.
have mer - cy on us, re - ceive our prayer.
Je - sus a - lone is the Lord, the Most High.
reig - ning in glo - ry for e - ver. A - men.

999 Glory to God (ICEL version)

Jacques Berth

Refrain

Glo - ry to God in the high - est, and on earth peace,

Glo - ry to God in the high - est, peace to peo - ple of good will.

Verse 1

We praise you, we bless you, we a - dore you, w

glo - ri - fy you, we give you thanks for your great glo - ry.

Lord God, hea-ven-ly King, O God, al-migh-ty Fa-ther.

Lord_____ Je-sus Christ, On-ly Be-got-ten Son._____

Verse 2

Lord God, Lamb of God, Son of the Fa-ther, you take a-way the

sins of the world, have mer-cy on us; you take a-way the

sins of the world, re-ceive our prayer; you are sea-ted at the

to Refrain

right hand of the Fa-ther, have mer-cy on us.

Verse 3

For you a-lone are the Ho-ly One, you a-lone are the Lord,

you a-lone are the Most_____ High, Je-sus Christ,_____

with the_____ Ho-ly Spi-rit, in the glo-ry of God the Fa-ther.

to Refrain

A-men. A-men, in the glo-ry of God the Fa-ther.

000

Suzanne Toolan, RSM

Je-sus Christ, Je-sus Christ, yes-ter-day,_____ to-day and for-e-ver.

Supplementary Mass Settings

The Belmont Mass   *Christopher Walker*

Kyrie

1001

Cantor/Choir, All repeat

Ky - ri - e, e - le - i - son.
Lord,— have— mer - cy.

Chris - te, e - le - i - son.
Christ,— have mer - cy.

Ky - ri - e, e - le - i - son.
Lord,— have— mer - cy.

The priest sings the absolution, which ends: **All**

...and bring us to e - ver - las - ting life.   A - men.

1002
Gloria

Glory to God in the highest, and on earth peace to peo - ple of good will

We praise you, we bless you, we a - dore you, we glorify you, we give you thanks

for your great glory, Lord God, hea - ven - ly King, O God, al - migh - ty Father.

Lord Jesus Christ, Only Be - got - ten Son, Lord God, Lamb of God, Son of the Father,

you take away the sins of the world, have mer - cy on us;

you take away the sins of the world, re - ceive our prayer;

you are seated at the right hand of the Father, have mer - cy on us.

For you a-lone are the Holy One, you a-lone are the Lord,

you alone are the Most High, Je-sus Christ, with the Ho-ly Spirit,

in the glory of God the Father. A-men, a - men.

spel Acclamation

003 Al-le-lu - ia, al-le-lu - ia, al-le-lu - ia.

t Gospel Acclamation

004 Praise— and hon-our to you, Lord— Je - sus Christ!

ly, Holy, Holy

005 Ho - ly, Ho - ly, Ho - ly Lord God of hosts.

Hea-ven and earth are full of your glory. Ho-san-na in the high-est.

Bles - sed is he who comes in the name of the Lord.

Ho-san-na in the high-est, Ho-san-na in the high - est.

emorial Acclamation 1

006 We pro - claim your Death, O Lord,

and pro-fess your Re - sur-rec-tion un - til you come a - gain.

Memorial Acclamation 2

1007

When we eat this Bread and drink this Cup,

we pro - claim your Death, O Lord, un - til you come a - gain.

Memorial Acclamation 3

1008

All:

Save— us, Sa-viour of the world, for by yo

Cross and Re - sur - rec - tion you have set us free.

Amen

1009

Priest:

all glo ry and ho - nour is yours,

All:

for ev - er and ev - er. A - men, a - men.

Our Father

1010

Our Father, who art in heaven, hallowed be thy name,

thy kingdom come, thy will be done on earth as it is in heaven.

Give us this day our dai - ly bread, and forgive us our trespasses,

as we for - give those who trespass a - gainst us;

and lead us not in - to temp - tation, but de - liver us from evil.

est: Deliver us, O Lord, we pray...
.... and the coming of our Saviour, Jesus Christ.

For the kingdom, the power and the glory are yours now and for ever.

mb of God

011

Cantor or All   (All)

Lamb—— of God, you take a-way the sins of the world,

Cantor or All   (All)

have mer - cy on us.— Lamb— of God, you take a-way the sins

of the world, grant— us peace,— grant— us peace.

ss of Christ our Saviour   *Dan Schutte*

012 Kyrie

Cantor   All repeat

Lord,———— have mer - cy.
Ky - ri - e,   e - lei - son.

Christ,———— have mer - cy.
Chris - te,   e - lei - son.

Lord,— have mer - cy, have mer - cy.
Ky - ri - e, e - lei - son, e - le - i - son.

1013 Gloria

Memorial Acclamation 1

1015

We pro - claim your Death, O Lord, and profess your Re - sur - rec - tion un - til you come a - gain.

Memorial Acclamation 2

1016

When we eat this___ Bread and___ drink this___ Cup,___ we pro-claim your Death, O Lord,___ un - til you come a - gain.

Memorial Acclamation 3

1017

Save___ us, save___ us, Sa - viour of the world, for by your Cross and Re - sur - rec tion you have set us___ free.

1018 Amen

A - men, a - men, a - men.

1019 Lamb of God

Cantor *All*

Lamb___ of God, you take a - way the sins of the

Repeat as needed *Final*

world, have mer - cy on us. world, grant___ us___ peace.

)20   **Kyrie**

fine

Ar - glwydd, tru-gar-ha   wrth - ym,   Ar - glwydd, tru-gar-ha_ wrth-ym.

Crist,   tru-gar - ha   wrth - ym,   Crist,   tru-gar - ha   wrth - ym.

Repeat 'Arglwdd trugarha wrthym'

)21   **Cytgan**   *First time only: repeat*

oria

Go - go - niant i Dduw,   go - go - niant i Dduw,   go -

go - niant i Dduw yn   y   gor - u   -   chaf.

Penill   **Cytgan**

Ac ar y ddae - ar tang - ne-fedd i ddyn-ion o e-wyll ys   da.

Penill

Mo - lian-nwn di, ben - dith-iwn di,   add - ol - wn di, go-go-

Cytgan

ne-ddwn di, di - olch - wn i ti   am dy   fawr o - go - niant.

Penill   **Cytgan**

Ar - glwydd Dduw,   fre - nin ne - fol,   Duw Dad Ho-lla - llu - og,

Penill

Ar - glwydd Ie - su   Grist;   yr   un - nig - a - ne - dig

Fab, Ar-glwydd Dduw, Oen Duw, Fab y Tad.

Penill

Ty - di sy'n dwyn y-maith be - chod-au'r byd, tru-gar-ha_ wrth-ym._

_ Ty - di sy'n dwyn y-maith be-chod-au'r byd, der - byn ein gwe -

ddi. Ty - di sy'n eis-tedd ar dde - heu-law'r Tad, tru-gar-ha_ wrth - ym.

Penill

O - ble - gid ti yn un - ig sy'n sanc-taidd, ti yn un - ig yw

Ar - glwydd, ti yn un - ig Ie - su Grist sy'n or - u-chaf, gy-da'

Ys-bryd Glan yng ngo - go - niant Duw Dad, A - men.___

1022   **Sanctus**

Sanc - taidd,_ Sanc-taidd, Sanc-taidd, Ar - glwydd Dduw'r llu-oedd, ma

nef a_ dae - ar yn llawn o'th o - gon - iant. Ho - san - na, h

san - na, ho - san - n yn y gor - u - chaf.

Ben - di - ge - dig yw'r hwn sy'n dy - fod yn en - w'r Ar - glwydd. Ho -

san - na, ho - san - na, ho - san - na yn y gor - u - chaf.

023

Acclamation 1

Cy - hoedd - wn dy far - wo - laeth Ar - glwydd, a -

dde - fwn dy at - gy - fod - iad nes i ti ddod.

024

Acclamation 2

Bob tro y bwy - tawn y ba - ra hyn ac y - fed y cw - pan, cy -

hoedd - wn dy far - wo - laeth, Ar - glwydd, nes i ti ddod.

025

Acclamation 3

Iach - aw - dwr y byd, ia - châ ni; trwy dy

groes a'th at - gy - fo - diad, yr wyt we - di ein rhydd - hau.

026

Amen

A - men, a - men, a - men.

Agnus Dei

1027

Oen— Duw, sy'n dwyn— y-maith be-cho-dau'r byd,
tru-gar-ha— wrth - ym. Oen— Duw, sy'n dwyn— y-maith
cho - dau'r— byd, tru-gar-ha wrth - ym. Oen— Duw, sy'n
dwyn— y-maith be - cho-dau'r byd, dy-ro i ni dang - ne-fedd.

1028

1 Nid wy'n gofyn bywyd moethus,
aur y byd na'i berlau mân:
gofyn 'rwyf am galon hapus,
calon onest, calon lân.

Calon lân yn llawn daioni,
tecach yw na'r lili dlos:
dim ond calon lân all ganu
canu'r dydd a chanu'r nos.

2 Pe dymunwn olud bydol,
chwin adenydd iddo sydd;
golud calon lân, rinweddol,
yn dwyn bythol elw fydd.

3 Hwyr a bore fy nymuniad
gwyd i'r nef ar adain cân
ar i Dduw, er mwyn fy Ngheidwad,
roddi i mi galon lân.

Daniel James (1848-1920)

Original version - hymn 636

636a

I received the living God,
and my heart is full of joy.
I received the living God,
and my heart is full of joy.

1 He has said: I am the Bread
kneaded long to give you life;
you who will partake of me
need not ever fear to die.

2 He has said: I am the Way,
and my Father longs for you;
so I come to bring you home
to be one with him anew.

3 Jesus said: I am the Truth;
if you follow close to me,
you will know me in your heart,
and my word shall make you free.

4 Jesus said: I am the Life
far from whom no thing can grow,
but receive this living bread,
and my Spirit you shall know.

Go out to the whole world; pro-claim the Good News!—
(Al - le - lu - ia, al - le - lu - ia.)—

Choosing Hymns for the Liturgical Year

LAUDATE is arranged in liturgical order. However, the categories cannot reflect all the possible ways the hymns can be used. These pages offer some help in finding hymns for the seasons of the year, using the whole book.

Advent 64-117

Sunday 1: Day of the Lord: esp. 81-92, 109. ➤ *Also* The Lord's coming (982-989); I rejoiced (992)
Sunday 2: John the Baptist cries in the desert. See especially 83, 92, 94, 96, 97, 108
Sunday 3: John the Baptist foretells Jesus. See especially 96-108. 'Gaudete' Sunday: 851
Sunday 4: 'O' antiphons (111-112); hymns 113-117; ➤ *Also* Our Lady (Annunciation, 330-334; The Magnificat: 23-25, 335-340, 880)

Christmas: seasonal music 118-123   Christmas hymns   124-164

➤ Word of God (Christmas Day, 2nd Sunday): 85, 158, 160, 161, 738-742
➤ The Holy Family: 131, 143. 144, 147-149; Into one we all are gathered (243), Sing of Mary (341), God's Holy Family (834); Like a child rests (453); Sections: Love of God in us (906-927, esp. 923) Psalm: 58, 409

New Year, Epiphany 165-170; Baptism of the Lord 171-173   ➤ *See also Advent section*
Candlemas 174-178

Ordinary Time before Lent

➤ Sunday 2 always uses the Gospel of John. Yrs A, B: Behold the Lamb of God (98, 598). Year C tells of the marriage feast of Cana: use songs about the Banquet (613-635).

From then on the Calling of the Disciples (Sundays 3A, 3B) and Jesus's first preaching of the Kingdom are the subject of the Gospels. See sections: Jesus ministering (738-47); Kingdom (814-821); Justice and Peace (887-904); Sending out/Discipleship.Commitment (852-875, esp. 871).

In *Year A,* the Year of Matthew, the Sermon on the Mount dominates the season (Sundays 4-7). Settings of the Beatitudes (read on Sunday 4) are: 370, 814-816, 615 (for Communion)
In *Year B* Sundays 4-6 Jesus's miracles are proclaimed; see the section on Healing (427-437)
In *Year C* Sunday 3: Jesus Word of God, Ps 18 (19); Sunday 5: 'Holy, Holy'; Sunday 6: the Beatitudes (822); Sunday 7: see sections: Love of God in us (906-927), God's love and mercy (774-813)

Lent 179-226

➤ *See also* Forgiveness/Penance/Reconciliation (838-851); God's love and mercy (774-813); Petition (928-941); Trust etc (947-74) For the RCIA: nos 391-395. For each Sunday there is a Gospel Response (188-190) which could be sung straight after the gospel or at the Prep. of Gifts. Consult the Psalms index (p.409) to see if the Lectionary psalm for the day is there. A second setting of the day's psalm could be sung, for instance, at Communion.
➤ Ash Wednesday: Psalm 50(51), no 48 (also for Sunday 1A.) For the Ashes rite: Come back to the Lord (193), Turn to me (786). ➤ *See also* God's love and mercy (774-813), Forgiveness, penance, reconciliation (838-851)
➤ Sunday 1: Psalm for year A 50(51)no 48; year B 24(25) no 43; Year C 90 (91) no 51. In choosing hymns, look for those referring to Christ's temptation, or the desert (e.g. 201, 315, 964).
➤ Sunday 2: Transfiguration (208-209, 215); Christ is the world's Light (744); Be thou my vision (969)
➤ Year A, Sunday 3: Thirst (203, settings of Ps 41/42: 213-5, 219, 450). Covenant: 664
Sunday 4: He healed the darkness (435). Psalm 22 (23) as Communion Song: 42, 757
Sunday 5: Out of the depths (see Psalm Index, p.409). Deep within (218); Grant to us (220).
➤ Year B, Sunday 3: Psalm 18(19); Not on bread alone (191).
Sunday 4: The waters of Babylon (216); Awake, awake (851). See also Jesus suffering (748-57)
Sunday 5: Unless a grain (748); Deep within (218); Grant to us (220); Jesus suffering (748-57)
➤ Year C, Sunday 3: Ps 102(103) - see Psalm index (p.409); also God's love and mercy (774-813)
Sunday 4: The Prodigal Son. Our Father we have wandered (211); Praise we our God with joy (784); God forgave my sin (849). Communion song: Taste and see (617-8).

Sunday 5: See section Forgiveness/Penance (838-851).

Palm Sunday: ➤ See Lent section (nos. 227-237); Jesus Suffering (748-757).

The Paschal Triduum   227-253

LAUDATE contains a basic repertoire of music for the Three Days (Maundy Thursday evening to Easter evening).the centre of the Church's year, when all Christians relive their own symbolic dying and rising in baptism.

Maundy Thursday ➤ See nos. 238-249. No 238 is an entry hymn for the whole Triduum. For the Washing of Feet and the Procession of Gifts, see also: Love of others (906-927), esp. 920, 921, 927. Psalm: 55a, Eucharist: Communion songs (613-651) esp. 613, 616, 628, 638; also no. 833.

Good Friday See nos 250-253. Also: When I survey (756), Praise to the holiest (788).

Easter Vigil *Psalms for Liturgy of the Word:* 1st: nos. 299 or 45. 2nd: no.40. 3rd: no.254. 5th: no 692. 7th: no 48 or a version of Ps 41(42): nos. 47, 213-4, 219.

Baptismal liturgy: see nos 396-408; also 369 (Litany), 517-519; Out of darkness (835).

Easter Day: the following are particularly suitable: 255-257; 260, 267, 265-66, 269.

Eastertide   254-288

➤ *See also* Jesus in glory (758-773); Christ the King (319-327)

➤ Sunday 2, ABC: Ps 117(118). The doubting Thomas story: We walk by faith (284); O sons and daughters (264, 28(

➤ Sunday 3, Year A: The Emmaus Road. Nos 263, 288; also Communion Processional songs, especially 624, 63(

Year B: the end of the Emmaus story; meeting Jesus in the breaking of bread.

Year C: Meeting Jesus in a meal: see Communion sections. The Gospel also emphasises Jesus's command 'F my sheep', see Sending Out section (852-879), esp. 852, 871, 878-9

➤ Sunday 4, 'Good Shepherd' Sunday. Year A: see versions of Ps 22(23) p.409. Look in sections God's love and mercy (774-813); Trust/Hope Guidance (947-973)

Year B: Psalm 117(118) esp. no 258, and as last year • Year C: Psalm 99(100) esp. no 53, and as other years

➤ Sunday 5, Year A: Way Truth and Life. Jesus you are Lord (766), and section Trust/Hope/Guidance (947-973) especially Nada te turbe (947).

Year B: The Vine. Shepherd of souls (665); Unless a grain (748)

Year C: Love of others. See section Love of God in us (906-917) esp. 920

➤ Sunday 6, Year A: Love of God (906-917); God's love and mercy (774-813)

Year B: as above, and also: Unless a grain (748); This is my will (921)

Year C: as above, A & B. See also This is my body (627).

Ascension   289-294

➤ *see also* Jesus in Glory (758-73); Christ the King; and pre-Pentecost, 304, 627, 644; Psalm 26(27), see Psalm Index (p.420), would make a communion song.

Pentecost   295-311

The day of Pentecost is the end of the Fifty Days of Eastertide. No.299 is today's Psalm, and 294 may be used as the Gospel acclamation. The sequence (300-1, 304) is sung. A communion song: Come and eat this bread (496)

Trinity Sunday   312-317

➤ Many hymns are Trinitarian in structure (e.g. 887, 315). God beyond all names (686) is an expression of the mystery of God and the limitations of all words and titles applied to God.

Corpus Christi   318

➤ *see also* Maundy Thursday (239, 246-80), Preparation of Gifts (599-612), Communion sections (613-651), a 769, 773, 774, 803.

Other feasts which can be celebrated on Sunday: St John the Baptist (June 24), The Transfiguration (Aug. 6); Assumption (Aug. 15); Triumph of the Cross (Sept. 14), St John Lateran (9 Nov.) All Saints (1 Nov.) See Full Music

Year A	Year B	Year C
A house built on rock.	*Master of the Sabbath.*	*Faith of a foreigner* Ps 116 (117)
Love Divine; Trust/hope /guidance	Gathering, Praise. 464, 765, 992	Praise. 698, 700, 852
Not the virtuous, but sinners	*The end of Satan.* Psalm 129(130)	*The widow's daughter raised to life*
Sending out; Forgiveness	Forgiveness etc. Kingdom. 201, 834	Jesus ministering; Healing
We belong to him. Psalm 99(100)	*The Kingdom is like a seed.*	*Your sins are forgiven*
Sending out. 743, 825, 852	God the creator. Kingsom. 2r: 906	Forgiveness etc. Petition 221, 632, 844
Be not afraid.	*Calming the Sea.* Love of God in us;	*You are the Christ.* Ps 62(63)
Sending out. 794, 883, 894	Trust/Hope. 745, 934/58/63/66	Trust/hope; Jesus suffering. 679, 962
Welcoming the Lord's disciples.	*Restored to life.* Jesus' ministry; Healing;	*Following Christ.* Ps 15(16)
Sending out. 743; 400 (2nd R.)	Praise. 427, 431, 433	Sending out. Kingdom. 824, 877
Gentle and humble of heart.	*Our eyes are on the Lord.* Praise;	*Rejoice in the Lord.* As last week;
Love divine; Sending out; Trust etc.	Trust/Hope; Love divine 854, 969	also Justice/Peace. 828, 856 2R:756
Word, seed, harvest.	*Go; prophesy.* Psalm 84(85)	*Who is my neighbour?* Ps 18(19)
Harvest. 637, 737, 748, 887.1R: 203/612	Sending out. 851, 858, 870,871	Love of God in us/Love of others 609, 831
Slow to Anger. Psalm 102(103)	*Sheep without a shepherd.* Ps 22(23)	*God among us* Trust/Hope;
Forgiveness. Harvest. Kingdom. 821/54	Love divine. Word of God. 975,976	Love of God in us; Petition 650, 912, 941
The real treasure.	17-21. JOHN 6: the eucharistic Gospel.	*Ask and you shall receive* Ps 137(138)
Trust/hope/guidance. 821/48, 969/78	Ps 144(5). Gathering; Love Div.; Comm.	Petition; Trust/hope/guidance 61, 313
A God who feeds us. 1R: 203/612	*I am the bread of life.*	*Look for the things of heaven Ps 94(95)*
Communion sections. 477, 684, 692	Trust/hope/guidance. 203, 629/40, 960	Trust/hope etc; Love of God in us 737,811
Calming the sea. 745, 934, 963/6	*Taste and see.* Ps 33(34)	*Stay awake.* Ps 32(33) Gosp: 949
Love of God in us/Trust. hope etc.	Communion 473, 615, 636, 748	Sending out; Church; Gathering 469,855
God loves all peoples.	*My flesh is real food.*	*Fire on the earth* Kingdom;
Praise; Gathering; Sending out. 857	Versions of Ps 115(116) 664,748	Church; Sending out 828, 884, 972
On this rock... 284, 958	*Lord, to whom shall we go?*	*Gathering the people* Ps 116(117)
Kingdom; Trust/hope; Love divine	Hope/trust/guidance 41, 928	Kingdom; Church; Gathering 458,775,831
If you would follow me... Ps 62(63)	*God's word in your heart.* 195, 370	*The banquet*
Jesus suffering; Love of God 222,727	Word of God in Scripture. Just/Peace.	Communion; Gathering 623, 632
Helping, forgiving each other Ps 94(95)	*The deaf hear, the dumb speak.* 471,	*God's mysterious ways*
Jus/Peace; Forgiveness; Love of God 827	Healing; Jesus' ministry; Kingdom 821	Sending out; Hope/trust 743,877,916,955
Slow to anger, rich in mercy. Ps 102(3)	*You are the Christ.* Ps115(116)	*The Prodigal Son.*
Jus/Peace; Love of God in us; 621, 810	Trust/hope. Jesus suffering. 679, 962	cf Lent 4C. Forgiveness. 211, 646, 672
God's Ways. Ps 144(145)	*Be the servant of all.*	*You cannot serve two masters*
Harvest, Praise, Thanksgiving. 203, 612	Love of God in us/L. of others 743, 924	Justice & Peace. 625; 883,891/2/4
The path to those who stray. Ps 24(25)	*For Jesus or against him?* Ps18(19)	*The Lord loves the just*
Forgiveness etc. 843, 124. 2nd R: 754/5/791	Sending out. Forgiveness. 41, 926	Justice & Peace. 688, 882, 883, 890
The Vineyard of the Lord.	*God's holy family.* Ps127(128)	*Increase our faith.* Ps 94(95)
Jesus Suffering/risen. 22, 222, 734, 852	Marriage; love of God in us 834, 923	Petition; Trust/Hope 284, 708
The Wedding Feast. Ps 22(23)	*Wisdom to know what is God's*	*The Ten Lepers.* Healing;
Gathering.Communion. 475, 623, 830	Gathering, Kingdom, Healing 435, 955	Thanksgiving; Praise 713, 745, 945
No other God beside me.	*The Son of God came to give his life.*	*Never lose heart.*
Praise. 857; 882	Ps 32(33). Jesus suffering; Lent; Praise	Trust; Petition. 892, 930, 995
The greatest commandment. 811, 882	*Your faith has healed you.* Ps125(126)	*The Pharisee and the Publican.*
Love divine; Love of God in us; Just/P	Healing; Jesus' ministry. 475	Petition; Forgiveness. 882,892
Being a servant. Ps 130(131)	*Love of God, our strength.*	*Zacchaeus.* Ps 144(145)
Love of God in us. 908, 924	Trust/hope/guidance; Love of God in us	Forgiveness; Love of God; Sending out
Watch and Wait. Ps 62(63)	*The welcoming community.*	*The Resurrection* Jesus in glory;
Advent; Coming of the Lord. 88, 839	Gathering. Justice and peace. 625	Heaven; Easter 748, 761,990
Well done, faithful servant Ps 127(128)	*The day of the Lord.*	*The Lord comes to rule*
Coming of the Lord. 600, 896	Advent. The Lord's coming. 985, 990	Thse Lord's coming; Advent. 475,985, 90
Jesus's paschal mystery; Justice & Peace;	*The King of All*	*A Suffering King.*
Praise	89, 327, 857, 942, 998	Jesus suffering. Jesus in glory. 253

Settings (complete or partial) of the psalm text in the Grail version have no extra indication. The other settings listed are categorised th■
PsS indicates a verse/response song. H is a hymn (metrical) version.   A: contains a slight allusion (e.g. one verse)

Acknowledgements

© James Quinn SJ, administered by OCP Publications
Verses © The Grail; Music & refrain text: © 1998 S. Dean
Text and music © The Grail (England)
© James Quinn SJ, administered by OCP Publications
Text: © The Grail. Music: © 1998 Stephen Dean
© 1992 G.I.A. Publications Inc.
© 1998 Stephen Dean
Music: © 1988 Worth Abbey Music, Crawley, RH10 4SB
   Text: Bishops' Conference of England & Wales (BCEW);
Music: © 1998 Stephen Dean
Text © 1987 Patrick Lee; Music: © 1988 Worth Abbey Music
© The Church Pension Fund. All rights reserved. Used by per-
mission of Church Publishing Incorporated, 445 Fifth Avenue,
New York, NY 10016, USA
© 1983 Paul Inwood, published by OCP Publications
Text: © The Grail. Music: © 1994 Stephen Dean
© 1997 G.I.A. Publications, Inc.
Text: © The Grail. Music: © 1989 Stephen Dean
Music: © Margaret Daly-Denton
Text © 1989, National Council of Churches of Christ. Response
music: © Martin Foster. Vv: © Ampleforth Abbey Trustees
Text as no 21. Music: © Stephen Dean
Text & Music: © The Grail (England)
The Grail (England); Music: © Ampleforth Abbey Trustees
Text © 2005 Martin Foster
© 1986 Paul Inwood, published by OCP Publications
© 1989 Stephen Dean
© 1990 Stephen Dean
© 1991 Stephen Dean
see 11
Music: © Philip Duffy
© 1995 Saint Mary's Abbey, West Malling, Kent, ME19 6JX
   Words: © The Grail (England); Music: © M. Daly-Denton
Words: © The Grail (England); Music: © Stephen Dean
Words: © BCEW. Music: © 1988 Stephen Dean
Words: © The Grail (England); Music: © 1988 Stephen Dean
© The Grail (England)
Words: © The Grail (England); Music © 1985, 1992 P. Inwood
Words: © The Grail (England); Music: © 1985 P. Inwood
Words: © The Grail (England); Music: © 1987 Stephen Dean
© The Grail (England)
Text: The © Grail (England); R. 1: © Stephen Dean. Psalmtone:
© Ampleforth Abbey Trustees. Second setting: © 1996 P.Jones
Text: The Grail (England); Music: © 1987 S.Dean
Text: The Grail (England). Music: Resp. 1: © Anne Ward.
Psalmtone: © Stephen Dean. Second setting: © 1984, 1992 Paul
Inwood, published by OCP Publications
Words: © The Grail (England). Music: Response: © estate of the
late Mgr Francis Duffy. Psalmtone: © Stephen Dean.
Words, R. 2 & Psalmtone 2: © The Grail. R1 & Psalmtone: ©
1982 Irish Church Music Association (ICMA).
Words & Psalmtone: © The Grail (England). Responses 1 &
2: © Stephen Dean
© 1987 G.I.A. Publications, Inc.
Words: The Grail (England); Music: © 1987 Alan Smith
Words: The Grail (England); Music: Resp. 1 & Psalmtone: ©
1972 Bill Tamblyn. Alt Psalmtone: © Stephen Dean. Response
2 and Psalmtone: Notre Dame
Words and Psalmtone 2: © The Grail (England); Music: Resp. 1 &
Psalmtone: © ICMA. Response 2: © Stephen Dean.
Words: © The Grail (England); Music: © 1993 Stephen Dean.
Words: © The Grail (England); Music: © ICMA
Words: © The Grail; Music: © Stephen Dean.
© 1988 Bob Hurd, published by OCP Publications
Words: © The Grail (England); Music: © ICMA
Words: © The Grail (England); Music: © Stephen Dean

58   Words: © The Grail (England); Music: © 1981 P. Inwood
59   Words: © The Grail (England); Music: © ICMA
60   Words and music © 1959 The Grail (England)
61   Words and music © 1959 The Grail (England)
62   Words and music © 1989 G.I.A. Publications, Inc.
63   Words: © The Grail (England). R. 1 & Psalm: © McCrimmon
     Publishing Co. Ltd. R. 2 & Psalm: © Stephen Dean
64   © 1987 B. Farrell, published by OCP Publications
65   © 1988 John Schiavone, published by OCP Publications
66   © 1991 G.I.A. Publications Inc.
67   © 1994 Stephen Dean
68   © 1994 Ken Simmons, published by OCP Publications
69   © 1988 G.I.A. Publications, Inc.
70   Music © 1973 G.I.A. Publications, Inc.
71   © 1978 Christopher Walker
72   © 1988, 1989, 1990 C. Walker, published by OCP Publications
73   © 1996 C. Walker, published by OCP Publications
74   Music © 1996, 2011 Stephen Dean
75a-c Text © 2010 ICEL. Music © 2011 Stephen Dean
76, 77 Music © 2011 Stephen Dean
78   © 1982 B. Farrell, published by OCP Publications
79   © 1995 Stephen Dean
80   © 1986 G.I.A. Publications, Inc
81   © 1982 B. Farrell, published by OCP Publications
82   © 1990, 1991 Peter McGrail
83   © 1993 Owen Alstott, published by OCP Publications
84   © 1976 Kevin Mayhew Ltd, from Hymns Old & New
85   © Revd. Herbert O'Driscoll,1000 Jasmine Avenue, Victoria, BC
     Canada V82 2P4
87   © 1959 The Order of St Benedict, Inc. Collegeville, MN 56321
88   © 1984 Ateliers et Presses de Taizé
89   © Willard F. Jabusch, exclusive agent OCP Publications
90   © Christopher Idle/Jubilate Hymns
93   © 1992 Wild Goose Resource Group
95   translation: © McCrimmon Publishing Co Ltd
96   © 1981, 1982 Jan Michael Joncas Trust. Pub. by OCP
97   © Panel on Worship of the Church of Scotland
98   © 1984 Stephen Dean, published by OCP Publications
99   © Chrysogonus Waddell OCSO, Gethsemani Abbey, Trappist,
     Kentucky 40073
101 © Willard F. Jabusch, exclusive agent OCP Publications.
103 © Roger Ruston
104 Words: © Mrs B. Perry/Jubilate Hymns. Music: © Hymns
     Ancient & Modern Ltd
107 Words © Willard F. Jabusch, exclusive agent OCP Pubs.
108 Words © McCrimmon Publishing Co Ltd
111 © 1982 G.I.A. Publications, Inc
114 Words © Mrs B. Perry/Jubilate Hymns
116 Words © 1971 Stainer & Bell Ltd.
118 Verse text © 1996 Bob Hurd, published by OCP Pubs.
119 © Paul Inwood
120 Text © 2010 ICEL, music © 1996,2011 Bob Hurd. Pub. by OCP
121 © 1983 G.I.A. Publications, Inc
122 © 1980 S.Dean, published by OCP Publications
123 © 1982 Bernadette Farrell, published by OCP Pubs.
124 © 1989 Wild Goose Resource Group
125 © 1980 ICEL. From A Resource Collection of Hymns and
     Music for the Liturgy
126 © Faber Music Ltd, from the New Catholic Hymnal
132 © 1927 Frederick Harris Music Co. Ltd.Unit 1, 5865 McLaughlin
     Road, Chris Luce, Mississauga, Ontario, Canada L5R 1B8
134 © Oxford University Press
142 © Mrs B. Perry/Jubilate Hymns
143 © 1987 Wild Goose Resource Group
146 © James Quinn SJ, administered by OCP Publications
147 © 1994 Stephen Dean, published by OCP Publications

ACKNOWLEDGEMENTS

148 © 1987 G.I.A. Publications, Inc.
149 Words © 1984, 1993 C. Walker, published by OCP Publications
157 © 1983 G.I.A Publications, Inc.
158 © 1967 Gooi en Sticht, bv. Exclusive agent for English language countries: OCP Publications
161 © 1976 Joint Board of Christian Education and Youth, 2nd floor, 10 Queen St, Melbourne, Victoria 3000, Australia
162 © copyright control
163 © 2002 Stephen Dean. Published by OCP Publications
165 © 1989 Wild Goose Resource Group
171 © Stanbrook Abbey, Wass, York YO61 4AY
173 © 1979, 1982 Timothy Dudley-Smith. Administered by O.U.P.
176 Text: A Liturgical Psalter: A text for study and comment © 1994 ICEL. Music © 1995 P. McGrail
177 Words © 1992 G.I.A. Publications Inc
179 © 1994 G.I.A. Publications, Inc.
180 © 1996 Bob Hurd, published by OCP Publications
181 © 1996 Bob Hurd, published by OCP Publications
182 © World Library Publications, Inc.
183 © 1993 G.I.A. Publications, Inc
184 Music © James Walsh
185 Music © Martin Foster
186 © Chris O'Hara & McCrimmon Publishing Co Ltd
187 © Stephen Dean. Published by Decani Music
188-90 © 1982, 1983, 1993 The Sisters of St Benedict, S Joseph, MN. Published by OCP Publications
191 © 1996 Stephen Dean. Published by Decani Music
192 © 1986 G.I.A. Publications, Inc
193 © 1990, 1991 G.I.A. Publications, Inc
194 © 1986 Stephen Dean, administered by OCP
195 © 1988, 1989 Christopher Walker, published by OCP Pubs.
196 ©1980 ICEL. From A Resource Collection of hymns and music for the Liturgy
197 © 1973 Peter McGrail. Published by Decani Music
198 © 1994 OCP Publications
199 © Peter J.Scagnelli
200 © 1986 B. Farrell, published by OCP Publications
201 © 1996 Wild Goose Resource Group
202 © 1980 ICEL, From A Resource Collection.. (as 196)
203 © 1984 Kevin Mayhew Ltd, from Hymns Old & New.
207 © 1993 Wild Goose Resource Group
208 © 1989 G.I.A. Publications, Inc
210 © 1976 OCP Publications
211 © 1980 ICEL. From A Resource Collection.. (see 196)
213 © 1982 G.I.A. Publications Inc
214 © 1988 Bob Hurd, published by OCP Publications
215 © 2002 Bob Hurd. Published by OCP Publications.
217 © 1980 Robert C. Trupia. Published by OCP Pubs.
218 © 1987 G.I.A. Publications Inc.
219 Refrain: © Charles Watson, O.S.B./Abbey of Tamie Verses:The Grail Music: Abbey of Tamié, by permission of SEFIM
220 © 1965, 1966, 1968, 1973 World Library Publications
221 © 2007 Ateliers et Presses de Taizé
222 © 1991 Ateliers et Presses de Taizé
224 © 1995 Suzanne Toolan, R.S.M. published by OCP Pubs.
227 © Ateliers et Presses de Taizé
228 © 1988 Christopher Walker, published by OCP Pubs.
231 © 1992 Stephen Dean
233 © 1984 Ateliers et Presses de Taizé
234 © 1993 S. Dean, published by OCP Publications
235 © 1994 P. Jones, administered by OCP Publications
236 © Faber Music Ltd
237 © OCP Publications
238 © 1992 John Ainslie
240 © 1989 John Schiavone, published by OCP Publications
241 © 1982 Hope Publishing Co.
242 © James Quinn SJ , administered by OCP Publications
243 © McCrimmon Publishing Co. Ltd
244b © 1979 Ateliers et Presses de Taizé

245 © 2000, 2007 Stephen Dean. Published by OCP
248 © 1974 Stainer & Bell Ltd.
249 © Ateliers et Presses de Taizé
251 © 1992 P. Jones, published by OCP Publications
253 © Ateliers et Presses de Taizé
254 Music © 1989 Stephen Dean. Published by Decani Music
255 © Oxford University Press, taken from The English Hymnal
256 © 1992 S.Dean, administered by OCP Publications
257 © 1981, 1982 Jan Michael Joncas Trust. Pub. by OCP Pubs.
258 Verses: © The Grail (England). Refrain text and music © 1 Bernadette Farrell, published by OCP Publications
259 © James Quinn SJ, administered by OCP Publications
260 English text © Peter J. Scagnelli
262 © 1988, 1990 Bernadette Farrell, published by OCP Pubs
263 © 1989 S.Dean, published by OCP Publications
265 © Ateliers et Presses de Taizé
266 © 1984 Ateliers et Presses de Taizé
268 © 1973 The Word of God. Admin. by Song Solutions Copy
270 © 1978 Pamela Stotter
271 © OCP Publications
272 © 1969, 1995 Stainer & Bell Ltd.
274 © 1988 Wild Goose Resource Group
276 © Willard F. Jabusch, published by OCP Pubs.
277 © James Quinn SJ, administered by OCP Publications
278 © Oxford University Press, from The Oxford Book of Caro
281 © 1986 G.I.A. Publications, Inc.
282 © 1975 Robert J. Dufford SJ and OCP Publications
284 Melody © 1984 G.I.A. Publications, Inc
285 © 1989 G.I.A. Publications, Inc.
288 Words © 1995 G.I.A.Publications, Inc.
289 © James Quinn SJ, administered by OCP Publications
292 © OCP Publications
293 © 1974, 1993 Sisters of St Mary of Namur
294 © 1982 James Walsh. Published by OCP Publications
295 Words © 1977, 1978 Michael Shaw & Paul Inwood. Mus 1977 Paul Inwood. Published by OCP Publications
298 © Ateliers et Presses de Taizé
299 Melody: © 1984, 1985 C. Walker, pub. by OCP Pubs.
304 © 2001 Stephen Dean, published by OCP Publications.
305 © 1988 Wild Goose Resource Group
306 © 1935 Birdwing Music/EMI Christian Music/Small Stone. Adm Song Solutions Daybreak
307 © 1982 Christopher Walker, published by OCP Publilcation
308 Words © 1967 Gooi en Sticht, bv. Exclusive agent for Eng language countries: OCP Publications
309 © Bernadette Farrell, published by OCP Publications
310 Words: © 1968 Timothy Dudley-Smith, Administered by O Melody: © 1985, 1988 G.I.A. Publications, Inc
311 © Faber Music Ltd. From The New Catholic Hymnal
313 © Christian Conference of Asia
314 © James Quinn SJ, administered by OCP Publications
317 Chevalier Press, P.O. Box 13, Kensington, New South Wa 2033, Australia
317 © Oxford University Press
318 © James Quinn SJ, administered by OCP Publications
319 © OCP Publications
320 © OCP Publications
324 © 1982 Authentic Publishing, Admin.by Song Solutions Copy
325 © McCrimmon Publishing Co. Ltd
328 Copyright control
329 © Kevin Mayhew Ltd, from Hymns Old & New
330 © 1994 C. Walker, published by OCP Publications
331 © Mary J. Hancock
332 Text © Pamela Stotter. Music © SEFIM, 13 avenue Savorn 94240 L'Hay des Roses, France
333 Words and music © 2005 Stephen Dean
335 © 1979 Ateliers et Presses de Taizé
336 © 1984, 1991 OCP Publications
337 © 1993 Peter Jones, published by OCP Publications

420

Text © 1983 Owen Alstott. Music © 1983 Bernadette Farrell
© Religious of the Sacred Heart, 4389 West Pine Blvd, St Louis, Missouri 63108
© The Estate of the late Roland F. Palmer
© 1993 Anne Ward, published by OCP Publications
© McCrimmon Publishing Co. Ltd
© 1975 Oxford University Press
Translation and Music: © 1988 Christopher Willcock SJ, published by OCP Publications
Words: © Patrick Lee, music: © Stephen Dean, admin. by OCP
© Kevin Mayhew Ltd, from Hymns Old & New
© James Quinn SJ, administered by OCP Publications
Words © 1987 The Sisters of St Benedict, St Joseph, MN 54674-0277. Published by OCP Publications
© James Quinn SJ, administered by OCP Publications
© 1978 Kevin Mayhew Ltd, from Hymns Old & New
© 1971 Faber Music Ltd, from the New Catholic Hymnal
Music: © Mgr Francis Duffy, c/o Calamus
©J.P. Lécot, English language rights admin. by K Mayhew Ltd
a, 368a © James Quinn SJ, administered by OCP Publications
© 1982 James Walsh, published by OCP Publications
© 1984 G.I.A. Publications Inc
© The Church Pension Fund
© 1979 Hymn Society of America, admin. by SongSolutions CopyCare
© 1974 Stanbrook Abbey.
© 1998 Patrick Lee
© Bishop Donal Murray
© 1989 Wild Goose Resource Group
Words © Hymns Ancient & Modern; In this version words © Jubilate Hymns
© 1995 ICEL. © 1995 G.I.A. Publications Inc
© 1995 G.I.A. Publications, Inc
© 1998 Stephen Dean. Published by Decani Music
© 1988, 1989, 1990 C. Walker, published by OCP Pubs.
Music © 1999 Stephen Dean. Published by Decani Music
© 1997 395a © 1998 Wild Goose Resource Group
© 1998 G.I.A. Publications Inc.
© 1990 Bob Hurd. Published by OCP Publications
© 2001 G.I.A. Publications Inc.
© 1996 Bob Hurd. Published by OCP Publications.
Refrain text © 1969 ICEL. Music and Verse text © 1983 Stephen Dean, published by OCP Publications.
© Archdiocese of Durban, 408 Innes Road, Durban 4001 SA
© 1985, 1992 Sisters of St Benedict, St Joseph, MN. Pub. by OCP
© 1986, 1987 Stephen Dean, pub.by OCP Publications
© 1989 Wild Goose Resource Group
© 1993 Stephen Dean, published by OCP Publications
© 1981 Michael Saward/Jubilate Hymns
© 1978 John B. Foley SJ and OCP Publications
© 1987, 1993 G.I.A. Publications Inc.
Words: © 1973 The Central Board of Finance of the Church of England, Church House, Great Smith Street, London SW1P 3NZ. Music © 1990, 1993 Paul Inwood, published by OCP
© 1989 G.I.A. Publications Inc.
Words: © Josephine O'Carroll. Music: © Fintan O'Carroll
© The Rev. Basil E. Bridge
© 1989 Wild Goose Resource Group
© 1983 Stainer & Bell Ltd.
© 1982 McCrimmon Publishing Co. Lrd
Words © Oxford University Press
© 1989 Ernest Sands, published by OCP Publications
Vv 1-2 © 1978 Lutheran Book of Worship, by permission of Augsburg Fortress, 426 S. Fifth Street, Box 1209, Minneapolis MN 55540
© Anthony Sharpe
Refrain text & Melody: © 1985 Paul Inwood. Verses: © 1963 The Grail. Published by OCP Publications
Words © 1963 The Grail (England). Music © 1995 Stephen

Dean, published by OCP Publications
425 © 1992 G.I.A. Publications, Inc
426 © 1991 G.I.A. Publications, Inc.
427 © 1987 G.I.A. Publications, Inc.
428 © Stainer & Bell
429 © 1980 I.C.E.L. Inc. From A Resource Collection
430 © 1969 Stainer & Bell Ltd
431 Words © 1986 G.I.A. Publications, Inc.
432 © 1977 OCP Publications
433 © 1989 Wild Goose Resource Group
434 © Mrs B. Perry/Jubilate Hymns
435 Words: © 1982 Stainer & Bell Ltd. Music: © 1988 G.I.A.
436 © 1988 G.I.A. Publications, Inc.
437 © 1987 Wild Goose Resource Group
439 © 1983, 1987 OCP Publications, Inc
441 © 1989, 1990. S. Dean. Published by OCP Publications
442 Translation © 1983 OCP Publications
443 © 1990 Ernest Sands & OCP Publications
444 © 1996 Wild Goose Resource Group
445 © James Quinn SJ, administered by OCP Publications
447 © James Quinn SJ, administered by OCP Publications
448 © 1996 Wild Goose Resource Group
449 © 1996 Wild Goose Resource Group
452 © 1989 Scott Soper, published by OCP Publications
453 © 1988 Christopher Walker & OCP Publications
454 Text: © The Grail (England). Music: © 1994 S. Dean
455 © 1989 G.I.A. Publications, Inc.
457 © 1982 OCP Publications
458 © 1994 G.I.A. Publications, Inc.
459 © 1987 C. Walker, published by OCP Publications
460 © 1965 World Library Publications, Inc.
461 © Mrs Josephine O'Carroll
462 © 1991 Bob Hurd, published by OCP Publications
463 © 1977 James Walsh, published by OCP Publications
465 © 1967, 1980 Scripture in Song. Administered in Europe by SongSolutions.
467 © James Quinn SJ, administered by OCP Publications
469 Words © 1987, 1993 The Sisters of St Benedict, St Joseph, MN. Published by OCP Publications
470 © 1996 Bob Hurd. Published by OCP Publications
471 © 1977, 1980 Kingsway's Thankyou Music
472 © Willard F. Jabusch, published by OCP Publications
473 © 1989 G.I.A. Publications, Inc.
474 © 1996 Daniel L. Schutte & OCP Publications
475 © 1982 G.I.A. Publications, Inc.
476 © 1995 Bernadette Farrell. Published by OCP Publications
477 Words © 1991 G.I.A. Publications, Inc.
478 © Ateliers et Presses de Taizé
479 From The Roman Missal © 2010 ICEL
480, 480a Text © 2010 ICEL. Music © 2011 Peter Jones
481 Text © 2010 ICEL. Music © 2011 Peter Jones.
482 Music © 2011 Peter Jones
483, 484 Text © 2010 ICEL. Music © 2011 Peter Jones.
484 Text © 2010 ICEL. Music © 2011 Peter Jones.
485 © 2010 ICEL. Music © 2011 Peter Jones.
486, 487 Music © 2011 Peter Jones
488, 489 Text © 2010 ICEL. Music © 2009 G.I.A. Publications Inc.
490 Music © 2009 G.I.A. Publications, Inc.
491-4 Text © 2010 ICEL. Music © 2009 G.I.A. Publications, Inc.
495 © 1984, 2010 G.I.A. Publications, Inc.
511 © 1995 G.I.A. Publications, Inc.
512 © 1982 Stephen Dean, published by OCP Publications
513 © 1985 Chris O'Hara & McCrimmons Publishing Co Ltd
514 © 1980, 1981 Bernadette Farrell. Published by OCP
516-7 © Ateliers et Presses de Taizé
518 Absolution Text © 2010 ICEL. Music © 2010 C. Walker
520 Absolution Text © 2010 ICEL. Music © 1988 Paul Inwood
521 Absolution Text © 2010 ICEL. Music © 1991 S. Dean
522 Absolution Text © 2010 ICEL. Music © 2010 GIA Pubs, Inc.

ACKNOWLEDGEMENTS

523 Music © 2009 Alan Smith
524 Text © 2010 ICEL. Music © 2009 Alan Smith
525 Text © 2010 ICEL. Music © 2011 Anne Ward
526 Text © 2010 ICEL. Music © 1982, 2011 Peter Jones
527 Text © 2010 ICEL. Music © the estate of the late Mgr F. Duffy
528 Text © 2010 ICEL. Music © 2008 Stephen Dean
529 Text © 2010 ICEL. Music © 2010 Christopher Walker
530 Text © 2010 ICEL. Music © 1982, 2001 2010 C.Walker
531 Text © 2010 ICEL. Music © 1991, 2009 Stephen Dean
532 Text © 2010 ICEL. Music © 2010 GIA Publications, Inc.
533 Text © 2010 ICEL. Music © 2005, 2009 Paul Inwood
534 © 1986 Christopher Walker. Published by OCP Publications
535 © 1980 ICEL. From *A Resource Collection*... (see 126)
536 © Ampleforth Trustees
537 © Stephen Dean
538 © 1980 ICEL *A Resource Collection*... (see 126)
539-540 © Ateliers et Presses de Taizé
541 © 1994 James Walsh. Published by OCP Publications
542 © Mick Truman
543 © 2005, 2011 Stephen Dean
545 Text © 2010 ICEL. Music © 2011 Stephen Dean
546 © 2010 Stephen Dean
548 © 1997 Paul Inwood
549, 550 © 1998 Stephen Dean
551 © 1990 GIA Publications, Inc.
552 © 1997 Wild Goose Resource Group
553 Music © 2010 Christopher Walker
554a-c Text © 2010 ICEL. Music © 2010 Christopher Walker
555 © 2010 ICEL. Music © 2010 Christopher Walker
556 Music © 1981, 2011 Seóirse Bodley
557a-c Text © 2010 ICEL. Music © 1981, 2011 Seóirse Bodley
558 Text © 2010 ICEL. Music © 1981, 2011 Seóirse Bodley
559 Music © 1985, 2010 Bernadette Farrell. Pub. by OCP
560 Text © 2010 ICEL. Music © 2010 Bernadette Farrell. Pub. by OCP
561a, b Text © 2010 ICEL. Music © 2010 Bernadette Farrell. Published by OCP Publications
562 Text © 2010 ICEL. Music © 1985, 2010 Bernadette Farrell. Published by OCP Publications
563 Music © 1971, 1977, 2010 GIA Publications, Inc.
564a-cText © 2010 ICEL. Music © 1971, 1977, 2010 GIA
564d Music © 1971, 1977, 2010 GIA Publications, Inc.
565 Music © 1984, 2010 Stephen Dean
566-8Text © 2010 ICEL. Music © 2010 Stephen Dean.
569 Text © 2010 ICEL. Music © 1997, 2010 Stephen Dean.
570 Music © 2010 Paul Inwood.
571a-cText © 2010 ICEL. Music © 2010 Paul Inwood.
572 Text © 2010 ICEL. Music © 2010 Paul Inwood
573 Music © 1982, 2010 Paul Inwood
574a-cText © 2010 ICEL. Music © 1982, 2010 Paul Inwood
575 Music © 1982 Paul Inwood
576 Music © 1984, 2010 G.I.A. Publications, Inc
577a-c Text © 2010 ICEL. Music © 1984, 2010 G.I.A . Pubs. Inc
578 Music © 1984 G.I.A. Publications, Inc.
579 Music © 2008 Alan Smith
580a-cText © 2010 ICEL. Music © 2008 Alan Smith
581 Text © 2010 ICEL. Music © 2008 Alan Smith.
582 Music © 1982, 2011 John Lillis
583a-c Text © 2010 ICEL. Music © 1982, 2011 John Lillis
583d Music © 2011 John Lillis
584 Music © 2009 GIA Publications, Inc.
585a-c Text © 2010 ICEL. Music © 2009 G.I.A. Publilcations, Inc.
586 Text © 2010 ICEL. Music © 2009 G.I.A. Publications, Inc.
588 Embolism text © 2010 ICEL. Music © 1997, 2011 Christopher Walker. Published by OCP Publications
589 Music © 2008 Alan Smith.
590 Music © 2009 GIA Publications, Inc.
591 Music © 2010 Christopher Walker.
592 Music © 1991, 2011 Stephen Dean
593 Music © 2011 Christopher Walker

595 Music © 2011 Martin Foster
596 © 1998 John Schiavone, published by OCP Publications
597 © 1993 G.I.A. Publications, Inc.
598 © OCP Publications
599 © Abbaye de Sylvanès
600 © OCP Publications
603 © 1984 Kevin Mayhew Ltd, from Hymns Old & New
605 © 1966 Joe Wise, administeterd by G.I.A. Publications
606 © copyright control
608 © 1967 OCP Publications
609 © 1976 Kevin Mayhew Ltd, from Hymns Old & New
610 © 1995 Wild Goose Resource Group.
611a © 1982 Paul Inwood
611b © 1982 Paul Inwood
612 © 1991 Bernadette Farrell. Published by OCP
613 © 1994 Stephen Dean. Published by OCP Publications
614 © 1985 David Haas. Published by OCP Publications
615 Refrain arr. © Stephen Dean
616 Melody © James Walsh
617 © 1982 S.Dean. Published by OCP Publications
618 © 1983 G.I.A. Publications, Inc.
619 © 1987 S.Dean. Published by OCP Publications
620 © 1994 John Glynn
621 © 1983 G.I.A. Publications, Inc
622 © 1992 G.I.A. Publications, Inc.
623 © 1986 G.I.A. Publications, Inc.
624 Music and text © 1984 Bob Hurd, revised text © 1987 Bob & Michael Downey, published by OCP Publications.
625 © 1990 B. Farrell, published by OCP Publications
626 © 1994 S. Dean, published by OCP Publications
627 © Bud John Songs Ltd/EMI Chrstian Publishing, administer Kevin Mayhew Ltd
629 © 1966, 1970, 1986, 1993 G.I.A. Publications, Inc.
630 © 1984 Timothy Dudley-Smith. Administered by O.U.P. Music © 1993 James Walsh, pub. by OCP Publications.
631 © 1995 CJM Music Ltd.
632 © 1992 Daniel L. Schutte. Published by OCP Publications
633 © 1984 Ateliers et Presses de Taizé
634 © 1984, 1997 G.I.A. Publications, Inc.
635 © 1988 Paul Inwood
636 © G.I.A. Publications, Inc.
637 © 1987 Ekklesia Music, admin. by OCP Publications
638 © 1988 Wild Goose Resource Group
639 © 1993 S. Dean, published by OCP Publications
640 © 1995 G.I.A. Publications, Inc.
641 © 1998 G.I.A. Publications, Inc.
642 © C.J. Marivoet
643 © 1978 Kevin Mayhew Ltd, from Hymns Old & New
645 © Church Publishing, Inc.
646 © 1972 Dawn Treader Music, admin. by SongSolutions CopyCa
647 © 1968 Stainer & Bell Ltd.
648 © OCP Publications.
651 © 1996 Bob Hurd. Published by OCP Publications
652 © McCrimmon Publishing Co Ltd.
653 © 1988 Christopher Walker, pub. by OCP Publications
654 © The Trustees for Roman Catholic Purposes Registered, Mount Street, London W1Y 6AH.
655a © James Quinn SJ, administered by OCP Publications
657 © James Quinn SJ, administered by OCP Publications
658 © Burns & Oates Ltd
665 © 1964 World Library Publications, Inc.
667 © Ateliers et Presses de Taizé
668 Words: © 1987 Timothy Dudley-Smith. Administered by O. Music: © 1993 James Walsh, published by OCP
669 Words: © 1984 Timothy Dudley-Smith. Administered by O. Music: © 1993 Stephen Dean, published by OCP
671 Words © Eleanor Farjeon, by permission of David Highams A sociates Ltd., 7th Floor, Waverley House, 7–12 Noel Street London W1F 8GQ • http://www.davidhigham.co.uk/contact

© 1971 Faber Music Ltd., from The New Catholic Hymnal Words: © James Quinn SJ, administered by OCP Publications. Music: © 1993 G.I.A. Publications, Inc.

© Tony Barr, published by OCP Publications Words: © 1974 Stainer & Bell Ltd. Music: © 1985 GIA Pubs Inc.

© 1995 Stephen Dean

© James Quinn SJ, administered byocp Publications

© 1993 P.Mcgrail, published by OCP Publications

© 1990 B.Farrell, published by OCP Publications Words © 1973 Stainer & Bell Ltd. Music: © 1979 Stainer & Bell Ltd. and the Trustees for Methodist Church Purposes. Used by permission of Stainer & Bell Ltd.

Text © 1992, Music © 1994 G.I.A. Publications, Inc.

© Ateliers et Presses de Taizé

© Pablo D. Sosa. Administered by OCP Publications

© Ateliers et Presses de Taizé

© 1988 Paul Inwood, published by OCP Publications

© 1980 G.I.A. Publications, Inc.

© 1976 Daniel L. Schutte and OCP Publications

© 1995 G.I.A. Publications, Inc.

© 1972 Daniel L. Schutte. Admin. by OCP Publications

© 1980 Ateliers et Presses de Taizé

© 1984 Paul Inwood, published by OCP Publications

© James Quinn SJ, administered by OCP Publications-

© 1982 Ateliers et Presses de Taizé

© 1970 Timothy Dudley-Smith. Administered by O.U.P.

© Mrs B. Perry/Jubilate Hymns

© 1993 Peter Jones, published by OCP Publications

© 1985 Fintan O'Carroll. Verses © 1985 C Walker, pub. by OCP

© 1998 Christopher Walker, published by OCP Publications

© 1981 Ernest Sands, published by OCP Publications

© 1974, 1975 The Community of Celebration PO Box 309, 809 Franklin Avenue, Aliquippa PA 1500

© 1986 Kingsway's Thankyou Music

© 1953 Stuart K. Hine. Admin by Kingsway's Thankyou Music Music arrangement © 1993 Geoff Weaver/Jubilate Hymns

© Mrs B. Perry/Jubilate Hymns Words: © 1972 Stainer & Bell Ltd.

© 1997 C.Walker, published by OCP Publications

© 1970 Stainer & Bell Ltd.

© James Quinn SJ, administered by OCP Publications Words © Mrs B.P. Arlott

© McCrimmon Publishing Co. Ltd Translation: © James Quinn SJ, admin. by OCP Publications

739 © 1987 Wild Goose Resource Group

© 1995 Wild Goose Resource Group

© James Quinn SJ, administered by OCP Publications

© Oxford University Press

© 1986, 1988 B. Farrell, published by OCP Publications

© 1969 Stainer & Bell Ltd.

© 1981 Timothy Dudley-Smith. Administered by O.U.P.

© Dermott Monahan/Copyright control

© 1974 The Word of God, admin. by Song Solutions CopyCare

© 1983 B. Farrell, published by OCP Publications

© 1983 Kingsway's Thankyou Music

© 1986 Kingsway's Thankyou Music

© Brian Black and Word & Music/Jubilate Hymns

© 1994 Stephen Dean

© Ateliers et Presses de Taizé Words © Stainer & Bell Ltd. Music © O.U.P.

© 1991 Daniel L. Schutte. Published by OCP Publilcations.

© 1987 Kingsway's Thankyou music

© Michael Saward/Jubilate Hymns

© 2003 Christopher Walker & Paule Freeburg DC. Pub. by OCP

© 1963 Stainer & Bell Ltd.

© 1978 Kevin Mayhew Ltd, from Hymns Old & New

© 1976 Rocksmith Music. Administered by MCS Music Ltd., 10 Heathfield Terrace, London W4 4JE

© 1974 Kingsway's Thankyou Music,

770 © 1987 Make Way Music,,Caladine, Chantry House, 22 Upperton Road, Eastbourne BN21 1BF . All rights reserved.

771 © Kevin Mayhew Ltd

772 © 1960 Josef Weinberger Ltd 12-14 Mortimer Street London W1T 3JJ www.josef-weinberger.com

773 © 1965 World Library Publications

774 © 1989 Stephen Dean, published by OCP Publications

775 © 1979 OCP Publications

776 © 1991 G.I.A. Publications, Inc.

777 © 1971, 1974 Daniel L.Schutte. Admin. by OCP Pubs.

778 © 1989 J. Walsh, published by OCP Publications

779 © 1992 B. Farrell, published by OCP Publications

780 © 1997 Wild Goose Resource Group

781 © Nah Young-Soo. Tr. & arr. © Wild Goose Resource Group

782 © Ateliers et Presses de Taizé

783 © St Mungo Music, St Leo's, 5 Beech Avenue, Dumbreck, Glasgow G41 5BY

785 © 1975 Daniel L. Schutte and OCP Publications

786 © 1975 John B. Foley SJ and OCP Publications

787 © 1998 Kevin Mayhew Ltd

789 © McCrimmon Publishing Co. Ltd

790 © 2006 Martin Foster

791 From The Hymnal 1982 © 1985 the Church Pension Fund. All rights reserved. By permission of Church Publishing Incorpo-rated, New York, NY.

792 © 1982 G.I.A. Publications, Inc.

793 © 1975 John B. Foley SJ and OCP Publications

796 © 1975 Carey Landry & and OCP Publications

803 © McCrimmon Publishing Co. Ltd

805 © Peter Janson-Smith/copyright control

808 © 1971 Carey Landry & NALR

812 © OCP Publications

813 © Ateliers et Presses de Taizé

814 © 1985 G.I.A. Publications, Inc.

815 © 1983, 1991 Stephen Dean, published by OCP Publications

816 © 1998 Kevin Mayhew Ltd.

817 © 1968 Vernacular Hymns Publishing Co.

818 © 1983 Kingsway's Thankyou Music

819 © 1986 Kingsway's Thankyou Music

820 © 1972 Maranatha! Music. Administered by CopyCare

821 © Olwen Scott

822 Text © 2002 Owen Alstott. Music © 2001, 2002 B. Farrell. Publshed by OCP Publications

823 © Verbum Forlong AB, Box 15169, S-104 Stockholm

824 © 1981 Daniel L.Schutte & OCP Publications

825 James Seddon © Mrs M. Seddon/Jubilate Hymns

826 © Christopher Idle/Jubilate Hymns

828 © 1992 G.I.A. Publications, Inc.

829 © Christian Conference of Asia

832 © 1978 John B. Foley SJ and OCP Publications

834 © 1988 OCP Publications

835 © 1989 C.Walker, published by OCP Publications

836 Words © 1991 The Sisters of St Benedict, St Joseph, MN. Published by OCP Publications

838 © 1965 World Library Publications

839 © Ateliers et Presses de Taizé

840 © Michael Hodgetts

841 © 1992 G.I.A. Publications, Inc.

842 © The Benedictine Foundation of the State of Vermont, Inc.

843 Refrain & Music © 1981 Paul Inwood, published by OCP Publica-tions. Verses: © The Grail.

844 Words: © 1971 Faber Music Ltd. from the New Catholic Hym-nal. Music: © 1998 S. Dean

845 © Oxford University Press

847 © 1960 Josef Weinberger Ltd. (see 772)

848 © 1965 G.I.A. Publications, Inc.

849 © 1972 Bud John Songs, administered by SongSolutions Day-break

850 © 1989 Wild Goose Resource Group

Acknowledgements

851 © Mary J. Hancock
852 © The Rev. Canon Edward J. Burns
853 © James Quinn SJ, administered by OCP Publications
854 © 1986 G.I.A. Publications, Inc.
855 © Dr Jorge Maldonado, Centro Hispano de Estudios Teologicos, 6133 Clara Street, Bell Gardens, California 90201
856 Words: © 1991 James Harrison, published by OCP Publications
857 © 1978 Patrick Lee, published by OCP Publications
858 © 1990 B. Farrell, published by OCP Publications
859 © 1983 G.I.A. Publications, Inc.
863 © 1974, 1976 Kevin Mayhew Ltd, from Hymns Old & New
864 © 1982 Kevin Mayhew Ltd, from Hymns Old & New.
865 © 1981 Daniel L. Schutte & OCP Publications
866 © 1978 Kevin Mayhew Ltd, from Hymns Old & New.
867 © Willard F. Jabusch, published by OCP Publications.
868 © 1969 McCrimmon Publishing Co. Ltd
869 © Mrs J. Tyrrell
870 © Hope Publishing Co., Carol Stream, Ilinois
871 Melody & text © 1979 Cesareo Gabarain. Tr © 1987 OCP
873 © 1974, 1976 Kevin Mayhew Ltd, from Hymns Old & New
877 © 1987 Wild Goose Resource Group
878 © 1975 Lillenas Publishing Co., admin. by Song Solutions CopyCare
879 © 1990 Paul Inwood, published by OCP Publications
880 © 1961 Timothy Dudley-Smith. Administered by O.U.P.
881 © 1985, 1994 G.I.A. Publications, Inc.
882 © 1989 Wild Goose Resource Group
883 © 1994 Bernadette Farrell, published by OCP Publications
884 © 1967 David Elton Trueblood
885 © Albert F. Bayly, by permission of Oxford University Press
886 © 1968 Stainer & Bell Ltd
888 © 1965 Stainer & Bell Ltd
889 © 1988 Wild Goose Resource Group
890 Words: © 1993 Patrick Lee. Music: © 1994 Stephen Dean
891 © 1997 Wild Goose Resource Group
892 © 1978, 1991 John B. Foley, SJ & OCP Publications
893 © Albert F. Bayly, by permission of Oxford University Press
894 © Sr Kathleen Boschetti, Suite 412, 343 Little Collins Street, Melbourne, Victoria 3000, Australia
895 Text © 1992 Hope Publishing Company, Carol Stream, IL 60188. Used with permission. Music © 2002 Bernadette Farrell, published by OCP
896 © 1971 Stainer & Bell Ltd.
897 Words: © Mrs B. Perry/Jubilate Hymns. Music: © Noel Tredinnick/Jubilate Hymns
898 © 1967, 1975, 1980 OCP Publications
899 © 1976 John B. Foley, SJ and OCP Publications
900 © 1982 Carl P. Daw, Jr
901 © 1998 Christine Carson & Wild Goose Resource Group
902 © 1975, 1979 Carey Landry & New Dawn Music
903 © 1999 Bernadette Farrell. Published by OCP Publications
904 © Ateliers et Presses de Taizé
905 © 1988 G.I.A. Publications, Inc.
906 Translation © 1994 G.I.A. Publications, Inc.
910 © James Quinn SJ, administered by OCP Publications
912 © 1982 Timothy Dudley-Smith. Administered by O.U.P.
915 © 1975 John B. Foley, SJ and OCP Publications
917 © Ateliers et Presses de Taizé
918 © 1985 David Haas, published by OCP Publications
919 © 1984 Timothy Dudley-Smith. Administered by O.U.P. Music © 1999 Stephen Dean, pub. by OCP Publications
921 © James Quinn SJ, administered by OCP Publications
922 © 1977 Kingsway's Thankyou Music
923 © 1941 The Church Pension Fund
924 © 1977 Scripture in Song/Maranatha! Music, administered by Song Solutions CopyCare
926 © Willard F. Jabusch, published by OCP Pubs
927 Text & music © 1961, 1962 World Library Publications
928 © 1995 Wild Goose Resource Group
929 © 1982 Ateliers et Presses de Taizé

930 © 1995 Wild Goose Resource Group
931 © 1974, 1993 Sisters of St Mary of Namur
932 © 1977 Carey Landry & NALR
934 Administered by SongSolutions CopyCare
936 © The Community of Celebration PO Box 309, 809 Frankli Avenue, Aliquippa PA 15001
937 © 1987 Hope Publishing Co.
939 Words: © The Rev. Iain D. Cunningham
941 © 1992 Anne Quigley, published by OCP Publications
942 Words: © 1967 Timothy Dudley-Smith. Admin.by O.U.P.
943 © 1992 Daniel L. Schutte. Published by OCP Publications.
944 © 1986, 1991 Ateliers et Presses de Taizé
946 © 1994 Stephen Dean, published by OCP Publications
947 © 1986, 1991 Ateliers et Presses de Taizé
948 © 1985 Christopher Walker, published by OCP Publication
949 © 2000 GIA Publications, Inc.
950 © 1965 World Library Publications, Inc.
951 © 1986 G.I.A. Publications Inc.
952 © 1979, 2003 OCP Publications
953 © 1970 Timothy Dudley-Smith. Administered by O.U.P.
954 © 1976 Daniel L. Schutte and OCP Publications
956 © John Glynn
957 © 1989 Wild Goose Resource Group
958 © Mrs B. Perry/Jubilate Hyms
964 © 1975 Robert J.Dufford, S.J. & OCP Publications
965 © 1983 Restoration Music Ltd., adminstered by Sovereign M UK, PO Box 356, Leighton Buzzard, Beds LU7 8WP
966 © McCrimmon Publishing Co. Ltd.
967 © McCrimmon Publishing Co. Ltd.
968 © 1984 Anne Scott, 1 Sunset Crescent, Kalamunda, W. Australia
969 © Oxford University Press, from Enlarged Songs of Praise
971 © 1975 Kingsway's Thankyou Music
972 © 1978 Kevin Mayhew Ltd, from Hymns Old & New.
974 © 1974 Kingsway's Thankyou Music
975 © 1990 B.Farrell, published by OCP Publications
976 © 1981, 1986 C & M Productions. Published by OCP Pubs
978 © Mrs B. Perry/Jubilate Hymns
979 © 1978 Kevin Mayhew Ltd, from Hymns Old & New.
980 © 1993 Bernadette Farrell. Published by OCP Publications
981 © 1987 OCP Publications
984 © 1984 Kingsway's Thankyou Music
985 © 1998 Stephen Dean
986 © 1992, M.D.Ridge, published by OCP Publications
988 © 1994 Stephen Dean
989 © 1974, 1993 Sisters of St Mary of Namur
990 Words: © The Grail. Music: © 1984 S Dean, published by C
992 © 1992 Bernadette Farrell, published by OCP Publications
993 © 1993 Mark Woodruff
994 © 1995 Stephen Dean, published by OCP Publications
995 © 1998 Julie McCann
996 arr. © 1990 Wild Goose Resource Group
997 coypright control
998 © 1984 George Salazar, arr © 1992 Paul Inwood, pub. by C
999 © Studio SM, 54 Rue Michel Ange, F 75015 Paris
1000 © 1988 G.I.A. Publications, Inc.
1001 © 2011 Christopher Walker, published by OCP Publication
1002 Text © 2010 ICEL. Music © 2011 C. Walker, pub. by OCP
1003-5 Music © 2011 C. Walker, pub. by OCP
1006-9 Text © 2010 ICEL. Music © 2011 C. Walker, pub. by OCP
1010-11 Music © 2011 C. Walker, pub. by OCP
1012 Music © 2007, 2009 D.Schutte, pub. by OCP
1013 Text © 2010 ICEL. Music © 2007, 2009 D.Schutte, pub.OCP
1014 Music © 2007, 2009 D.Schutte, pub. by OCP
1015-17 Text © 2010 ICEL. Music © 2007, 2009 D.Schutte, pub.OCP
1018-19 Music © 2007, 2009 D.Schutte, pub. by OCP
1020-27 Text © 198 Y Cylch Catholig, c/o Ty'r Esgob,Ffordd Son Wrecsam LL13 7EW, curia@wrexhamdiocese.org.uk. Music © Belmont Abbey. Hereford, HR2 9RZ
Go out to the whole world © 1972 Bill Tamblyn

Index of First Lines